ALCOHOLISM AND ADDICTION

Dr. Richard P. Swinson
Toronto General Hospital
and
Dr. Derek Eaves,
Western Regional Medical Centre, British Columbia

MACDONALD AND EVANS

MACDONALD & EVANS LTD.
Estover, Plymouth PL6 7PZ

First published 1978

ISBN: 0 7121 0161 6

Text set in 11/12 pt Photon Times, printed by photolithography, and bound in Great Britain at The Pitman Press, Bath

Contents

Editor's Foreword

If we think about the subject at all, we may well carry in our minds a stereotyped picture of the "typical alcoholic" and the "typical drug addict". The former is probably a dishevelled, tramp-like figure, lying on a heap of garbage in a back alley and recovering from a monumental binge in which, at least part of the time, he drank methylated spirits. The latter is a wild-eyed young junkie, murdering innocent bystanders to get enough money for his next "fix" and leading a life of total parasitism on the community.

It has been estimated that there are perhaps half a million people in Great Britain who abuse alcohol sufficiently to be regarded as alcoholics. There certainly isn't that number of skid-row alcoholics lying around back alleys and in fact the number of down-and-out meths drinkers probably runs into only a few thousands in all. Many alcoholics are well-fed, well-clothed individuals who still remain pillars of the community, at least until the time when their addiction's effects catch up on them and their physical and mental health deteriorates—their family life begins to suffer and they are unable to function effectively at work any longer. As for drug addiction, many addicts are perfectly respectable middle-aged and elderly ladies who have been unable to sleep these past ten or twenty years unless they take a sleeping tablet or two before going to bed. Although they would be horrified at any thought that they were habituated to their sedative, many of them would suffer quite severe physical withdrawal symptoms if they had to stop it suddenly—one criterion of addiction.

The abuse of drugs, including alcohol, is a subject that always arouses great emotion and it is only very recently that people have begun to look at it at all objectively. The more we look, the wider are its ramifications: we begin to discover the appalling statistics about road accidents and deaths due to drunken driving, the enormous losses to industry due to alcoholism, the epidemic of drug overdoses among young people and so on. But these figures only tell us the extent of the problems: they tell us little or nothing about the mass of human misery that leads people to abuse alcohol or drugs in the first place, thereafter increasing almost geometrically as the situation becomes ever more out of hand.

Alcohol exists, as does a variety of official drugs, as does cannabis and heroin: we cannot deny them out of existence. We cannot simply ban their use: prohibition does not work. Some of these substances are very useful and, for example, the newer psychotropic drugs used in psychiatry are leading us into entirely novel and effective fields of therapy. Alcohol has many social uses and, if used moderately, can be highly beneficial to the smoother running of society. Some people, especially in the younger age-groups, would say that marijuana is a safer and pleasanter alternative to alcohol and should be legalised by society. Heroin, cocaine, LSD and amphetamines have occasional medical value but their abuse leads only to sickness and misery and it is impossible to justify their unofficial use.

The above paragraph contains a large number of value judgments and possibly prejudices. These inevitably appear when we begin to discuss drug abuse. Then our stereotyped images and attitudes come out and we begin to produce our individual master plans to deal with the problem. We rarely stop to ask for information on which to base our opinions, but if we are to tackle the situation in any rational way we need accurate facts. In order to get these we need to begin to agree on our terms of reference and our definitions, and we must have a great deal of high-quality research.

A great many people talk and write about alcoholism and addiction but not so many take the trouble to carry out the rigorous investigations which are necessary before we can begin to make generalisations about causes and effects, and about the usefulness of the various preventative and therapeutic approaches we employ. Drs. Swinson and Eaves have both been involved in research, both have been active in the therapy of alcoholism and various forms of drug abuse, and both are active in teaching their expertise to members of the helping professions and to lay people. They are therefore particularly well-qualified to write a book like this one, in which knowledge replaces prejudice and data are included only if its pedigree is respectable.

There is much dispute in this field and the authors honestly acknowledge this. They make no attempt to draw unjustifiable conclusions, but they present their material in such a way that any intelligent individual will be bound to emerge at the end of the book very much better informed than he or she was before and, it is to be hoped, with a far greater appreciation of the enormity of the problems of alcohol and drug abuse and the urgency of the need to cope with them. I assume that many readers will have been motivated to buy the book because of a prior interest in its subject matter but even the casual reader could not fail to have his interest—and I hope also his compassion—stimulated.

The book is aimed towards members of all the helping professions, including doctors, who need to know how to recognise and deal with alcoholism and drug dependence. It will also prove of interest to many members of the general public who come in contact, for one reason or another, with these grave disorders and it should provide valuable reading for senior-school pupils who need to be informed of the facts. Finally, for those people who suspect that they themselves are developing a problem with drink or drugs, reading this book could well act as a stimulus to encourage them to seek help before it is too late. I am grateful to Drs. Swinson and Eaves for taking on the task of writing this volume (and it was no easy task). I think they have made an important contribution to the literature by so doing.

Alistair Munro
Toronto, 1977

Preface

Until recently the problems of alcoholism and drug dependence have been regarded as presenting fairly infrequent difficulties and as having a virtually negligible impact upon the average person.

With the activities of Alcoholics Anonymous and the occasional confession by a well-known person of his or her own alcohol problems, alcoholism has gradually come to be more generally recognised as a disorder of middle-aged people. Yet it is still usually viewed as a condition that affects other people, like syphilis and bankruptcy, rather than being something one can talk about or—even worse—admit to.

Alcoholism is a subject that the majority of people seem to be most comfortable with at arm's length. By way of contrast, drug-related problems burst upon the public awareness in a very dramatic fashion in the late 1960s in the U.K. following a remarkable and frightening increase in the number of cases of narcotic addiction occurring in young people. At that time, newspapers, magazines, radio and television devoted a great deal of time and space to accounts of what seemed to be an absolute epidemic of drug abuse. Far from being a distant experience, the effects of drug dependence, or at least opiate dependence in young people, were brought close to most people. For many, this was an alarming experience and the thought that one's children might be caught up in an uncontrollable upsurge of addiction was extremely frightening.

A combination of this highly emotionally-charged event and a distinct shortage of hard evidence, produced many opinions about the causes and control of drug abuse. Unfortunately, some people, who came to be regarded as experts, expressed opinions based upon their own personal biases rather than upon known fact. Examples of issues upon which people have taken sides rather arbitrarily are the questions of the escalation of drug use, from cannabis to heroin; the safety of the continued use of cannabis or LSD; and whether or not alcoholics can ever return to social drinking.

Together with a number of other workers, we have been involved in the organisation of several conferences on the topics of alcoholism and drug dependence. It was interesting to note, each time, that the people who attended these conferences were extremely concerned with certain circumscribed subjects and tended to have very strong views about their own areas of interest. In general, the participants were interested either in alcoholism *or* drug dependence, but not so often in both and, overwhelmingly, in how to help people with one or other of the problems.

A further striking observation at the conferences we have attended has been the wide range of professional backgrounds from which the participants have come. The largest single group at the 1972 Liverpool Conference consisted of probation officers, with other law-enforcement agencies providing a further large proportion of the total attendance. It was with this in mind, together with the regrettable lack of knowledge of addiction problems on the part of the average medical practitioner, that we chose to write this book. It presents an overview that we trust will be comprehensible to people with or without a medical background, especially perhaps to those who have no specialised knowledge of any of the health professions but who do have a concern about alcoholism and addiction. We hope that in this book we can explore some of those areas in which we do have solid data, and that we can set forth some more cogent arguments from various theoretical and practical points of view on subjects where, until now, dogmatism has served to obscure the lack of actual knowledge. We also hope that in presenting a resumé of what is known about alcoholism and drug dependence together in one volume, we will have made apparent some of the many similarities between the two states, while at the same time stressing the obvious differences between them.

No doubt we will give evidence of our own biases by the references we select for mention and those we fail to acknowledge. We have taken a fairly narrow view of "addictions" and have not spent a lot of time in considering those involving tobacco or food, nor have we considered other repeated behaviours of an habitual nature that some might consider analogous to addictions. It is clearly not possible to give references to all the investigations on any single topic, let alone to all which exist in two such enormous fields of study. However, we have tried to cover the field as fairly as possible and the interested reader is encouraged to follow up the references given at the end of each chapter, and particularly to refer to the appropriate specialised journals such as the *International Journal of Addictions* and the *Quarterly Journal of Studies on Alcohol.* Because of the wide variety in the professional backgrounds of people writing on alcoholism and drug dependence, articles tend to be found scattered throughout the medical, psychiatric, psychological, sociological, theological and other literatures and even in the popular magazines. Sex is probably the only other subject with so diffuse a literature!

The comparison with sex can be taken further. It is only in the recent past that there has been a general acceptance that there is a wide range of normal sexual behaviour and that the appearance of a problem, for example impotence, on a single occasion does not necessarily have any long-range implications. Similarly, an incidence of a memory blank after drinking, or the smoking of a marijuana cigarette, does not allow any judgments to be made regarding potential mental illness or likely future drug-taking habits.

People are now much freer than they previously were to choose whether or not they will use alcohol or other drugs and if they do so, the extent to which they indulge is also largely a matter of choice. There *are* familial, social, religious and legal controls on much of our behaviour, but most of us will never experience the restrictions brought about by being truly addicted to some substance, with the need to obtain it at almost any cost. We hope that we can demonstrate how an unfortunate minority of the population does come to find itself in the position of having to respond to chemically-induced demands, rather than the ordinary external and internal cues to which the non-addict continually responds.

The extreme emotional reactions of the public to the spread of drug abuse have died down considerably and the problem has been put more into perspective in the recent past. But it would be unfortunate if, in breathing a sigh of relief regarding the failure of the threatened heroin-dependence explosion to materialise, we were now to neglect the problems that many other different substances may engender. Drug dependence and alcoholism are not new phenomena. There have been well-documented waves of widespread dependence on depressants and stimulants dating back at least two hundred years, and in places as far apart as Britain, America, Sweden, Japan and China.

We should be able to extract information from these phenomena so that eventually we may predict and react rationally and helpfully, and, let us hope, control further threatened epidemics of a similar nature. Obviously, the factors determining such events take place at many different levels, from the global/political to the intracellular/molecular. An ideal system of legislation, therapy and prevention would take heed of all these factors, once they have been elucidated and evaluated. We are a long way from that desirable situation at present, but there is a large body of knowledge already in existence to help us make at least reasonable interim decisions when these are required. We hope that the contents of this book may set forth the present state of that knowledge in a comprehensive form.

We wish to express our gratitude to some of the many people who have helped us prior to and during the preparation of this book. Three such people who were instrumental in teaching us a great deal of what we have learnt are the late Professor F. J. Fish, Professor of Psychiatry, University of Liverpool, Dr. J. S. Madden, Consultant Psychiatrist, Addiction Unit, Moston Hospital Chester and W. H. Kenyon, Executive Director, Merseyside and Lancashire Council on Alcoholism. Without their initial support and encouragement we would not have started our studies in this area.

Professor Alistair Munro as general editor of this series was gently insistent about the rate of production of the manuscript and also very supportive as our departmental head during the writing of the initial drafts.

Our publishers, in the figures of Mr. D. A. F. Sutherland and Mr.

Peter Drew have exhibited extraordinary patience and have been ever helpful in turning our scribblings into a final manuscript.

Lastly our wives and families are now free to claim the time we owe to them and our secretaries can relax a little. To them all we wish to express our sincere thanks.

R. P. Swinson
Derek Eaves
November, 1977

1 Normal drinking and drug-taking

"Normal" drug-taking and "normal" drinking are behaviours which remain within certain legal, moral and cultural restraints, do not unduly interfere with the person's psychological or social integrity, and which do not cause him any physical harm. Normality applied to such complex behaviours is a relative concept, and the application of objective, quantifiable parameters may add little to the meaning, but may have real practical value. If we take a simple example from a different field, say obesity, defined as an excessive accumulation of fat in the body, we run into difficulties. Weight, a quantifiable measure, is no guide by itself to obesity until qualified by relation to age, sex and size of body frame. The use of weight tables for "average" figures would also give no guide if the number of obese people in the population were to increase. Many physicians would argue that obesity is a subjective matter, and almost all would agree that "normal" drinking, infinitely more complex, must be arbitrarily defined. "Normal" can be used to mean normal in a statistical sense, an ideal sense; a qualitative or quantitative, continuous or discontinuous variation from "abnormal".

NORMAL DRINKING

The figures

Recently the average British household spent £1·46 each week on all kinds of alcoholic beverages (Department of Employment,

Family Expenditure Survey, 1971). Consumer expenditure has risen in recent years, in "real" as well as in actual amount, so that in 1971 the proportion of income spent on alcohol was 4·7 per cent, compared with 3·39 per cent for the period 1963–5. Households may actually underestimate the amount spent on drink, and the combined amount spent on alcohol and tobacco exceeds the amount spent on clothing. Table I gives details of the amount spent on alcohol in relation to income, and includes the amounts spent on tobacco and medicines to give overall figures for money spent on licit "drugs".

TABLE I

Money spent in 1971 on licit drugs (per household, per week) in the U.K.

Amount spent on	*Income* £10–15	£20–25	£30–35	£40–45	£50–60	£80+	*All households*	%
Alcohol	0·28	0·84	1·30	1·64	2·28	4·16	1·46	4·7
Tobacco	0·57	1·09	1·47	1·58	1·78	1·87	1·30	4·1
Medicines	0·13	0·19	0·15	0·17	0·19	0·25	0·16	0·5
Total	0·98	2·12	2·92	3·39	4·25	6·28	2·92	9·3

National drinking habits

The Ansvar Insurance Company has carried out a survey of drinking habits on a nationally representative sample of 3,201 adults, using a random location technique, a method evolved to eliminate the unsatisfactory features of quota sampling (Lindgren and Williams, 1973). They found that only 7 per cent of the population had never consumed alcohol. Not surprisingly, they found that beer was the commonest drink for men, particularly for frequent drinkers, while wine was the commonest drink of women and those who only drink occasionally. A recent survey of a London borough covering all social classes found that 11 per cent of men drank every day, and a further 11 per cent drank very regularly, while the Ansvar study put the figure of "frequent" drinking at 18 per cent. Only 11 per cent of females described themselves as frequent drinkers, but 45 per cent drank at least once a week, compared with nearly two-thirds of the men. There were no marked regional variations other than the fact that beer appeared to be most popular in Yorkshire and least popular in Scotland, and wine and spirit drinking markedly less in rural areas. Wallace (1970) found that spirit drinking occurs to a greater extent in Scotland, so that overall alcohol consumption is no less there than anywhere else in the country, although Scottish women tend to be extremely

TABLE II
Regional household expenditure (1970–1) on alcohol, tobacco and medicines in the U.K.

	North	*North West*	*W. Midlands*	*London*	*Wales*	*Scotland*	*N. Ireland*
Alcohol (£s per week)	1·64	1·57	1·55	1·45	1·18	1·49	1·01
Tobacco (£s per week)	1·47	1·49	1·38	1·46	1·33	1·54	1·38
Medicines (£s per week)	0·13	0·14	0·14	0·17	0·15	0·13	0·12
Total	3·24	3·20	3·07	3·08	2·66	3·16	2·51

light drinkers. Table II gives details of regional household expenditure, 1970–1, on alcohol, and again includes details of tobacco and proprietary medicines for comparison. It will be seen that expenditure on alcohol is generally higher in those regions where tobacco expenditure is high.

Drinking behaviours are known to vary with age, marital status, and class differences. The number of frequent drinkers is higher in young, single men, and decreases with social class. The Ansvar study showed that 23 per cent of upper- and middle-class males, 20 per cent of lower middle-class men, 18 per cent of skilled working-class and 15 per cent of working-class males could be described as frequent drinkers. Frequency of drinking is important, but frequency patterns can conceal the total amount drunk. Working-class males are more likely to be heavy weekend drinkers, whereas upper-class males drink more frequently but less heavily, and are more likely to consume alcohol in their own homes than in a pub. If income levels are kept steady, manual workers spend more on alcohol and tobacco than professional and clerical workers. Table III shows this in two income groups.

TABLE III

Household weekly expenditure on alcohol and tobacco by occupation (in £s)

	Income group					
	Professional		*Clerical*		*Manual*	
	£30–40	*£40–50*	*£30–40*	*£40–50*	*£30–40*	*£40–50*
Alcohol	1·22	1·32	1·06	1·32	1·39	1·77
Tobacco	1·11	0·99	1·10	1·14	1·60	1·76
Total	2·33	2·31	2·16	2·46	3·99	3·53

Developmental aspects of normal drinking

There is a considerable body of knowledge regarding the life history of adult alcoholics, rather less about the drinking habits of adolescents and young adults, and there has, until recently, been very little interest in the way children learn about attitudes and concepts relating to alcohol. Jahoda and Cramond (1972) felt the reason was the widespread belief that children are innocents with regard to alcohol, but they have produced authoritative evidence to the effect that this is not so. Alcohol consumption is an important facet of life, and most children encounter it from a very early age. Retrospective reports in the past have suggested that, for the majority, drinking begins in adolescence, but there is no doubt now that the majority of children experience drinking personally in the early years of primary school. Children below the age of six cannot conceptualise alcoholic drinks as different from non-alcoholic drinks, but they can by the age of eight. At the age of six most of the Glasgow children who were asked said confidently that they intended to drink when older, but by the age of eight many were beginning to doubt the wisdom of such a course, and by the age of ten negative attitudes to later drinking became pronounced. Jahoda and Cramond felt that emergent, negative attitudes could simply reflect the children's maturing perception in making socially-appropriate responses, but they could also be much deeper than this, and be internalised attitudes arising from adverse experiences of alcohol. An interesting statistical analysis they performed was a multiple-regression analysis for predicting the intention to drink, although of course they did not provide any information about actual future drinking. Important factors were as follows:

1. If a child perceives his father and other adult males to enjoy drinking, the more likely he is to intend to drink.
2. If he can recognise alcohol by smell, or has tasted it, the more likely he is to intend to drink.
3. If he perceives his mother enjoying alcohol, the more likely he is to intend to drink.
4. If he has experienced his father's drunkenness the *less* likely he is to intend to drink.

This last factor was not very important, nor was the parents' actual drinking behaviour, which is perhaps surprising.

For several reasons, Jahoda and Cramond do not believe that the negative attitude change that occurs from the age of six to ten is merely overt verbal compliance, and therefore they present a paradox in which the children's declared intention to drink declines just before the likelihood that they will begin drinking alcohol in the ten to fourteen age-group increases. Gossett and colleagues (1971) found that one-third of American school children had taken drinks by the age of twelve, Davies and Stacey (1972) found that 92 per cent of Glasgow boys had taken drinks by the age of fourteen (with nearly as many girls). Obviously very important events occur in this critical period that sway the children back to a more favourable attitude. Parental influences may be important because most boys and girls report that their parents were the first to introduce them to alcohol in the home situation. Two-thirds of the children of heavy drinkers say they will drink when older, whilst two-thirds of the children of abstainers say they will abstain. Bacon and Jones (1968) felt that adolescent drinking patterns reflected those of their parents, whilst Strauss and Bacon (1953) felt that the onset of college drinking depended on parental example. The matter is complex, however, because both teenage heavy drinkers and abstainers tend to have parents who are restrictive about, and disapproving of, teenage drinking. The general rule (Stacey and Davies, 1970) is that restrictive environments lead to the less widespread use of alcohol but a greater number of heavy drinkers, whereas permissive environments lead to the more widespread use of alcohol but in a more controlled way.

At the age of ten to fourteen, children begin to question the values of their parents. The dominant influence can cease to be either parent, but can pass to the peer group. The child may be caught in an approach-avoidance conflict. If he moves in a group which regards smoking and drinking as more adult and desirable behaviours, "good" behaviour will be rewarded by the peer group at the risk of parental censure. The threat of ostracism from the group, or criticism, is greater than parental approval for not indulging in these activities.

Between the ages of fourteen and seventeen more boys than girls drink but the proportion of girls increases each year until at the age of seventeen, 98 per cent of boys and 96 per cent of girls report tasting alcohol (Davies and Stacey, 1972). At the age of fourteen, consumption occurs at weddings, birthdays, Christmas, and other special occasions, mostly in the parental home. Preferred drinks are beer and lager for the boys, and shandy and cider for the girls. When young people drink in the homes of friends this tends not to be under the control of adults. In situations outside the home, popular drinks are (for boys) still beer and lager, followed by shandy, cider and whisky, and similar drinks for girls, albeit with a wider spectrum of spirits. Drinking at the age of fourteen is confined to open-air situations such as parks, but there is a transition towards drinking in public houses at the age of seventeen, so that by seventeen or eighteen many have already developed regular drinking habits.

Young people as they grow older have more money to spend on alcohol. The people who have most money to spend are those who leave school early and are, as a rule, the children of parents in lower-class occupations. There is a clear association between heavy drinking amongst youths and low occupational status of parents. Those who have more money to spend on alcohol also have more to spend on cigarettes. Both behaviours are seen by young people as tough, and drinking as an attractive and social pastime. Many are perhaps motivated to drink, not for any positive benefits, but in order to avoid the stigma of weakness and lack of sociability associated with not drinking. Heavy drinking is seen as an index of toughness and rebellion, but not as sociable or attractive, and this may be a deterrent from heavy consumption for some. However, heavy drinkers fail to see themselves in this light, even if they perceive other heavy drinkers as falling into the unsociable/unattractive stereotype. Since drinking is more common than abstention in adolescents, heavy drinking is more favoured than abstention, which is highly unlikely to receive any peer group standing or favour at all.

Church attendance is a characteristic of abstainers and lower-drinking groups, but the reverse does not hold true. A standpoint of many religious groups is prohibition on drinking, or declaration of it as a vice, so that it is not surprising that Mormons, Baptists and other more esoteric religious sects have greater numbers of abstainers in their midst. Davies and Stacey (1972) found no evidence that the extent of drinking is related to religious affiliation, in that there were no differences between the Roman Catholics and Protestants in their samples. Involvement in social groups, other than religious ones, tends to promote drinking, but to decrease the extent of problem drinking. Drinking is a group activity, and drinkers give their main reason for drinking as the intention to be friendly and sociable. Abstainers tend to be on the periphery of social groups, whilst heavy drinking amongst adolescents takes place for the most part in more closely integrated groups, where it is condoned or often positively reinforced, even for its irresponsibility.

"NORMAL" DRUG-TAKING

If youthful drinking mirrors parental drinking, then it is reasonable to postulate that illicit drug-taking in adolescents reflects the drug-taking habits of parents. This has been shown to be true, as a correlation exists not between parents' illicit drug-taking, but between legal consumption, e.g., of aspirins, and children taking illicit drugs.

The maintenance of good health is, rightly, a major preoccupation of our society, although one could argue cynically that there is a considerable investment and morbid interest in bad health. Surveys have shown that only one-third of people consider their health to be perfect, and another third consider their health poor or only fair. With greater probing, it emerges that 95 per cent of people interviewed about their health report health complaints of some kind over the previous fortnight, and a substantial proportion of these will have specific mental symptoms. Of all those interviewed and reporting symptoms, only a third will attend their doctor, and even fewer of those with "nervous" symptoms attend. Of the patients who actually present to their doctor, about half will not have an organic illness but will have numerous social or psychological reasons for their presence. Unfortunately, of patients not reporting their sickness, many had swollen joints, chest pains, painful limbs, ear diseases or anaemia—a whole host of conditions that really require expert attention.

Patients treat themselves for many trivial illnesses—tummy troubles, nervousness, backache, constipation and eye strain, but also for ailments which might well be symptoms of serious disease processes. A survey in Hertfordshire (Jefferys *et al.*, 1960) found that two out of three people had taken proprietary drugs in a period of one month, and four out of ten adults had taken non-prescribed pain relievers. A general rule is that for every medicine prescribed by a doctor, two others are purchased without prescription. Annual expenditure on proprietary medicines is rising, and although it is in total an enormous amount, it represents well under one per cent of household expenditure. The advent of the National Health Service in the U.K. has had, surprisingly, very little effect on the level of proprietary medicine sales.

People who self-medicate tend to be the same people who attend the doctor frequently. They take proprietary and prescribed medications concurrently and, therefore, self-treatment by itself does not lead to undue delays in presenting for medical treatment of the more serious conditions. Self-treatment is an important aspect of medical care, and is unlikely to decline. Most of the medicines are taken in unsystematic ways that can have unfortunate effects on individuals and society alike. A great number of people are now known to abuse aspirins, which is one of the major causes of iron-deficiency anaemia, and there have actually been well-documented case studies of people dependent on aspirins. Laxatives taken in excess, as they so often are, can deplete the body of essential salts, particularly potassium, and cause serious complications in certain individuals.

The broader issue of the effect of drug-taking on society concerns the widely-discussed aspect of the stress of modern living, and our increasing intolerance of suffering from such stress. Indices of social stability have been derived from criminal statistics, divorce rates, attempted suicide and the like, and similarly the number of proprietary medicines and prescribed medicines can be seen as an index of the physical and mental health of a community. A quarter of all preparations prescribed under the National Health Service in England and Wales are for drugs acting on the central nervous system as can be seen in Table IV.

TABLE IV

National Health Service Prescriptions, 1964/65 and 1970/71, England and Wales (in millions)

	1964	*1965*	*1970*	*1971*
Barbiturates	16·1	17·2	12·2	10·9
Other hypnotics	2·6	2·7	6·6	7·1
Tranquillisers	9·0	10·9	16·0	17·1
Anti-depressants	2·8	3·5	6·0	6·6
Stimulants (appetite depressants)	5·1	5·3	3·1	2·7
Total (CNS drugs)	55·7	64·3	68·3	67·9
Total (all drugs)	209·4	244·3	247·7	247·5

These figures refer only to general practitioner prescribing and not to hospital figures. The cost of all drugs in 1971 in the U.K. was £136·6 million, of which £31·8 million was on drugs acting on the central nervous system, and £10·2 million on tranquillisers (Annual Report of the D.H.S.S., 1971). Barbiturates reached a peak in 1965, but have subsequently declined. Almost all the other groups, with the exception of stimulants, have shown spectacular increases, and are probably still rising.

A fascinating account of the prescribing habits of general practitioners is given by Balint and his colleagues, who formed a seminar study group at University College Hospital, London (Balint *et al.*, 1970). Records from nine general practices were examined for the proportion of people on their lists who were reliant on psychotropic substances on two dates, one in 1957 and one ten years later. "Reliance" meant the continuous daily consumption of drugs for at least one year. They found that 1·4 per cent of chronic consumers in 1957 had risen to 3·9 per cent by

1967, and the average time since continuous consumption began, in a large group of patients, was 5·2 years. Since many patients had taken intermittent courses of drugs before taking them continuously, and most of the patients were over the age of forty, a great number of people were leading long stretches of their lives completely or almost completely under the influence of psychotropic drugs. It has been estimated that enough tranquillisers are prescribed in the U.K. to give every third person one month's course of treatment every year. Once they embark on daily psychotropic drugs it is very difficult to wean patients from them, so that only a quarter of patients who began taking continuous medication in 1957 had ceased taking them by 1967.

Balint's training groups have always attracted doctors with psychodynamic leanings, who frown on narrow "organic" approaches to their patients' problems. It is very revealing to learn that this group prescribed more drugs acting on the central nervous system than other N.H.S. practitioners and, specifically, more barbiturates, hypnotics and tranquillisers (54 per cent of centrally-acting drugs versus 43 per cent for other doctors). Drugs with central activity were twice as likely to be prescribed for periods of six months or longer than for just a single administration, and half of these were likely to be for over four years. They only considered four out of 145 patients to be addicted or habituated, a surprisingly low figure considering that habituation is partly defined by chronicity, and addiction by the inability to stop taking medication!

A general conclusion they reached was that repeat-prescriptions of six months or less differ in character from long regimes. They felt that short repeats of all categories of drugs fitted comfortably into the framework of "scientific" medicine. Long-term, repeat prescriptions appeared to be functions not so much of the patients' illnesses as of the doctor's attitudes to his patients. General practitioners who were inclined to recognise psychological factors were said to resort less often to long-repeat regimes, and those who had somewhat hostile relations with their patients likewise had fewer long-repeat patients. From the incredible number of tranquillisers prescribed, perhaps we should assume that doctors as a whole are a passive group, are not inclined to recognise psychological factors, and give repeat prescriptions of psychotropic agents to many who do not have psychological components to their illnesses.

The pressures on doctors to prescribe psychotropic medicines are difficult to resist. A general practitioner sees patients for only five to ten minutes and cannot in this time explore fully a patient's symptomatology. A hospital psychiatrist in Britain spends even less time on average with each of his patients, no more than five minutes on average each week for all patients, and no more than thirty minutes with the most demanding neurotic patients. Time factors alone make short-cuts inevitable, and may determine prescribing habits more than the individual formulation of a patient's true needs. A local joke concerns the psychiatrist who treats his patients, regardless of diagnosis, first with a barbiturate-induced abreaction, secondly with electro-shock therapy if they fail to respond, and as a last resort he takes a history! We would not like to suggest that the great majority of doctors have an empirical, drug-orientated approach to their patient's problems, but few patients leave surgeries or clinics without a prescription of some kind. It has been suggested that there are half a million patients (Joyce, 1969) who are dependent on the symbolic rather than the actual functions of medication, and a large proportion of doctor-time is spent on prescribing worthless drugs. At least a fifth of all prescriptions have no more than placebo value.

Doctors vary greatly in the kinds and quantities of drugs they prescribe. A survey of ninety-three randomly-selected doctors in industrial towns (Joyce *et al.*, 1968) revealed some of the personal factors which determined prescribing habits. A multivariate analysis yielded factors termed "quality of practice", "whole-person orientation", and "education". Those doctors who showed a rounded approach, who were more psycho-socially aware, better trained and with positive attitudes to change, prescribed fewer drugs of all kinds. Whilst they showed great variations in what kind of drugs and how much they prescribed, their individual habits remained stable over time.

Many doctors in the study were very critical of their training in, and knowledge of, therapeutics; yet it is those who are least well-trained who are least critical and more prone to prescribing in cavalier fashion as unrestrained therapeutic enthusiasm overcomes judgment. The number of doctors who are totally irresponsible is, of course, very low indeed, but without any doubt this factor has gravely altered the drug addiction problem, as testified by the

Wootton Committee reports. The recent increase in heroin addiction in the U.K. was initiated almost entirely by the activities of only six London doctors.

In any large professional group there will be a minority who act in illegal or unethical ways, but a more serious matter than irresponsible prescribing by a handful of doctors is the torpid response of the medical profession as a whole to new situations and new information. The incredible delays in the recognition of the dangers of amphetamines are worthy of mention. Connell had published his monograph on amphetamine psychosis as early as 1958, and the United Nations warned doctors and pharmaceutical companies of the dangers shortly afterwards. The dangers were so apparent that, by 1964, "Drinamyl", an amphetamine-barbiturate mixture, had been withdrawn from the market. In spite of these events, the period 1963–6 saw a three-fold increase in amphetamine prescribing by doctors (Wade and Hood, 1972*b*). Even in 1971 in Northern Ireland, 59 per cent of practices were still prescribing amphetamines, although only in a few practices was prescribing maintained at high levels. One suspects that many doctors were unaware until a late date (and possibly some still are) of the adverse reactions to amphetamines, and that many doctors fail to keep abreast of new developments in medicine.

In the past decade, dozens of new psychotropic substances have appeared on the market, all of them purporting to be major advances on previous drugs. Many are of real merit, but others are of dubious value, introduced for even more dubious reasons. Wade and Hood (1972*a*) have described Mandrax-prescribing in Northern Ireland in 1966–70, and in so doing have described the typical "life-cycle" of a new drug. From small beginnings in 1966, by 1969 Mandrax accounted for 25 per cent of all hypnotic prescribing. There were great variations in the individual prescribing habits of doctors, some prescribing none at all, and some prescribing over 4,000 tablets each month for each thousand patients on their practice lists. Doctors who became frequent prescribers persisted in being frequent prescribers, but by 1969 it was being widely acknowledged that Mandrax had certain disadvantages, and prescribing decreased thereafter. Perhaps after the lessons learned from amphetamines, doctors had become more discriminating about new drugs.

The "life cycles" of so many of the new drugs run such identical courses that we can talk of the five-year "half-life" of new psychotropic agents. The initial rise in prescribing may be due to the dissatisfaction of doctors and patients with drugs already on the market. The desire to prescribe something new would account for both the initial rise and subsequent fall, particularly if the expectancy of effectiveness is not fulfilled. Each new drug arrives with a splendid accompaniment of glossy advertisements, pressure from sales representatives, and informative films and discussions followed by delicious dinners, which inevitably make an impact. It is well known that some doctors are prone to incorporate new drugs very early into their therapeutic armamentarium, and drug companies are adept at exploiting doctors' weaknesses. It became known at a recent symposium that dossiers were kept on doctors, indicating the sales approaches which might have the most beneficial results from the drug companies' viewpoint.

The Monopolies Commission (1973) has reported on what were, in their opinion, excessive profits made by the Roche Group from the sale of two minor tranquillisers, diazepam and chlordiazepoxide. The matter of the profits is not our concern, but it emerged that in 1970 Roche spent £1·5 million promoting their products, no less than 11 per cent of the price of the drugs. Much of this amount was spent on sales promotion of only two drugs, Librium (chlordiazepoxide) and Valium (diazepam). It is uncertain how much such advertising helps doctors to prescribe more effectively.

There are so many psycho-active drugs available, and so much research literature, it is impossible to keep abreast of it all. One monograph on Tofranil (Angst and Theobald, 1970), an antidepressant drug, quoted nearly four-and-a-half thousand references, and four hundred more are added every year. Imipramine ("Tofranil") was introduced in 1957, and is probably still the most reliable drug for the treatment of depression, in spite of the dozens of newer drugs on the market. Chlorpromazine was the first major tranquilliser, and subsequent therapeutic innovations have proved modestly more successful. Whilst it is possible that major break-throughs will be made, many distinguished people advocate a moratorium on the marketing of new products until the bewildering number available has been thoroughly evaluated. Certainly, new drugs should replace older ones only if they are genuinely better, not because the patent has run out on the older proprietary product. Many drugs heralded as harmless have been found to be habit-forming, or dangerous in a hundred different ways, yet the horror story of Thalidomide has not restrained the enthusiasm of many who ought to know better.

REFERENCES

Angst, J. and Theobald, W., *Tofranil*, Verlag Stampfli and Cie AG, Berne, 1970.

Bacon, M. and Jones, M. B., *Teenage Drinking*, Crowell, New York, 1968.

Balint, M. *et al.*, *Treatment or Diagnosis: A Study of Repeat Prescriptions in General Practice*, Tavistock Publications, London, 1970.

Connell, P. H., "Amphetamine Psychosis", *Maudsley Monograph No. 5*, Oxford University Press, 1958.

Davies, J. and Stacey, B., *Teenagers and Drinking, A Developmental Study in Glasgow*, H.M.S.O., London, 1972.

Department of Employment, *Family Expenditure Survey 1971*, H.M.S.O., London, 1971.

Department of Health and Social Security, *Annual Report 1971*, H.M.S.O., London, 1971.

Gossett, J. T., Lewis, J. M. and Phillips, U. A., "Extent and Prevalence of Illicit Drug Use as Reported by 56,745 Students", *Journal of the American Medical Association*, 216: 1464–70, 1971.

Jahoda, E. and Cramond, J., *Children and Alcohol*, Vol. 1, H.M.S.O., London, 1972.

Jefferys, M., Brotherson, H. J. F. and Cartwright, A., "Consumption of Medicines on a Working-Class Housing Estate", *British Journal of Preventive and Social Medicine*, 14: 64–76, 1960.

Joyce, C. R. B., "Quantitative Estimates of Dependence on the Symbolic Function of Drugs", in Steinberg, H. (ed.), op. cit.

Joyce, C. R. B., Last, J. M. and Weatherall, M., "Personal factors as a Cause of Differences in Prescribing by General Practitioners", *Br. J. Prev. Soc. Med.*, 22: 170–7, 1968.

Lindgren, A. and Williams, G., "British Drinking Habits and Some International Comparisons", a Paper presented to the Second International Conference on Alcoholism and Drug Dependence, Liverpool, April, 1973.

Monopolies Commission, *A Report on the Supply of Chlordiazepoxide and Diazepam*, H.M.S.O., London, 1973.

Stacey, B. and Davies, J., "Drinking Behaviour in Childhood and Adolescence—An Evaluative Review", *British Journal of Addiction*, 65: 203–12, 1970.

Steinberg, H. (ed.), *Scientific Basis of Drug Dependence*, Churchill, London, 1969.

Strauss, R. and Bacon, S., *Drinking in College,* Yale University Press, New Haven, Connecticut, 1953.

Wade, O. L. and Hood, H., "An Analysis of Prescribing of an Hypnotic in the Community", *Br. J. Prev. Soc. Med.*, 26: 121–8, 1972*a*.

Wade, O. L. and Hood, H., "Prescribing of Drugs Reported to Cause Adverse Reactions", *Br. J. Prev. Soc. Med.*, 26: 205–11, 1972*b*.

Wallace, J., "Who Drinks What in Britain", a Paper presented to the Third International Conference on Alcohol and the Addictions, Cardiff, 1970.

Wootton report: *Report by the Advisory Committee on Drug Dependence: Cannabis*, H.M.S.O., London, 1968.

Wootton report: *Report by the Advisory Committee on Drug Dependence: the Amphetamines and LSD*, H.M.S.O., London, 1970.

The tables presented in this chapter have been extracted from the Family Expenditure Survey of the Department of Employment and the Annual Reports of the Department of Health and Social Security.

2 The problem of alcoholism and drug dependence

EXTENT OF THE PROBLEM

Stereotypes of the "typical alcoholic" and the "typical drug addict" exist and vary from one person to the next. Depending on the stereotype held, so the estimate of how many alcoholics or drug-dependent people there are in the community will vary. To an ardent abstainer in a temperance movement, there will appear to be far more "alcoholics" around than there will be to the labouring man who habitually consumes in excess of a gallon (five litres) of beer daily.

Alcoholism

The findings of how many alcoholics and how many drug-dependent people there are also varies in the scientific literature, according to the standpoint taken and the definition applied by each investigator.

Using the common stereotype of an alcoholic as a skid-row man drinking methylated spirits, an examination of the population would probably produce a figure for the whole of the U.K. of a few hundred or, at the most, a few thousand people. The comparable stereotype of a young, homeless hippy who injects himself with heroin or habitually takes LSD would also produce a total U.K. figure of, at most, a few thousand people.

In other words there are as many or as few drug-dependent people, including alcoholics, as there are arbitrarily defined to be. In recent years, with the growing concern about the consumption of all psycho-active substances, there has been an increasing recognition of the widespread dependence on drugs. Alcoholism and drug dependence occur in both sexes, in all age groups, in all walks of life and thoughout the length and breadth of the U.K. Nevertheless, it is still true that certain age groups, occupations and other factors are found to be in special association with both alcoholism and drug dependence, and these bias the population findings.

The questions remain: how many people are there who are drug dependent? Who are they? It is not merely academic curiosity that motivates these questions. It is essential to have an accurate estimate of the total numbers involved in order to plan the services needed logically to deal with the problem and also assess what proportion of the people needing the services are receiving them. A knowledge of the total number of drug dependents at varying times would also be of value in assessing the efficacy of methods of prevention or treatment.

Although the central theme of this book is that alcoholism and drug abuse can be considered as parts of a single phenomenon, the details of the extent of alcohol and drug use will have to be considered separately, since that is the way the data have been collected. There is, however, an overlap between the two groups of abusers. Alcoholics frequently abuse tobacco, tranquillisers and barbiturates and many drug-dependent people also abuse alcohol, which tends to be included as one drug in multiple drug abuse.

To use direct questions regarding alcohol and drug abuse (such as: "Are you an alcoholic?") would, in all likelihood, produce few truthful replies. An interesting thought is that the highest prevalence of alcoholics found by this method would probably occur in a non-drinking group; that is, in those people who have been successful in carrying out the Alcoholics Anonymous programme. Immediately, an area of difficulty is obvious in enumerating the alcoholics in a population. Can someone who has abstained from drinking still be called an alcoholic? For many reasons the term "recovered alcoholic" is used to describe such people and there are good reasons to include them in a head count. In the methods detailed below, such cases would sometimes be included and in others the experimental methodology would rule them out.

In quoting any numbers or percentages of alcoholics or drug abusers, it is essential to know the precise method of detection used, the reliability of that method, the population under study and a comparison of the study population with the general population.

The figures of 350,000 to 500,000 alcoholics in England and Wales and 6,000,000 in the U.S.A. are often quoted and may be accurate. We shall examine the methods by which these figures have been produced and, in doing so, will consider alcoholism first.

ESTIMATES OF THE PREVALENCE OF ALCOHOLISM FROM CIRRHOSIS OF THE LIVER

Jellinek (1960) used the number of deaths reported to be due to cirrhosis of the liver as the basis for calculating the number of alcoholics in the general population.

The formula used is

$$A = \left(\frac{D \times P}{K}\right)R$$

where:

A = the number of alcoholics in any year in the population;
D = the number of deaths due to cirrhosis of the liver in that year;
P = the percentage of such deaths due to alcoholism;
K = the percentage of all alcoholics with complications who die of cirrhosis;
R = the ratio of all alcoholics to alcoholics with complications.

The appropriate figures for 1948 for England and Wales produce an estimate of 1,100 alcoholics per 100,000 of the population (1·1 per cent). For France, the data for 1951 produce an estimate of 5·2 per cent of the total population. The accuracy of such findings is open to question from various aspects. D relies on all cirrhosis deaths being correctly identified and then reported, but there is pressure on doctors not to report deaths from alcoholism due to the stigma for the relatives; no doubt many a blind eye is turned in this respect. The reliability of *P* is therefore also in doubt, since it relies on a recognition of "alcoholism" and this is bound to be interpreted individually and arbitrarily.

Popham (1970) has reviewed the indirect methods for estimating the prevalence of alcoholism and has criticised the use of the Jellinek formula. The estimates of liver cirrhosis vary from time to time in the same population and therefore *D* will vary. Strong objections have been raised against the use of the values for *P*, *K* and *R* that Jellinek originally calculated. The interested reader is advised to consult Popham's original article for the detailed objections, but the overall effect is that the values of *K* and *R* in use would probably lead to an under-estimation of the prevalence of alcoholism.

Despite the criticisms of the Jellinek formula, Popham reaches the conclusion that the results obtained by its use compare reasonably well with the results from independent estimations. For this reason, the formula is sufficient to provide an estimate of the total number of alcoholics in a population at any one time, provided the population investigated is larger than 300,000 people. It is not acceptable, however, to use this method to estimate differences in prevalence over time, or between places.

A comparison of the figures produced by the Jellinek formula and an independent method of assessment from the Addiction Research Foundation in Toronto showed that the independent method reduced the estimated prevalence rates in England and Wales from 1·1 per cent to 0·86 per cent, but in Switzerland it increased from 2·1 per cent to 2·7 per cent and in France the increase was from 5·2 per cent to 7·3 per cent. It was further estimated that approximately 20 per cent of the adult population in France suffers from alcoholism at some time in their lives.

SURVEYS OF ALCOHOLISM

Parr (1957) carried out a survey of general practitioners in an attempt to assess the incidence of alcoholism in the population. A questionnaire was sent to 480 general practitioners and of those replying, 20 per cent had had no contact with anyone with a drinking problem in the previous year and also said they had no alcoholics amongst their patients. The overall estimate of alcoholics on the general practitioners' lists of 0·11 per cent of the population at that particular time was only one-tenth as great as that produced by the Jellinek formula.

The findings are open to criticism on many grounds (Glatt, 1957) and in all likelihood the patients identified as alcoholic represent only the most obvious cases of alcoholism. Apart from the failure of doctors to identify most of the alcoholics in their practices, there are many wandering alcoholics with no regular general practitioner who rely on hospital emergency services and are not available for identification in such a study.

The Jellinek formula for England and Wales estimates that there are about 86,000 alcoholics with complications, in the total population. By using a survey of health visitors and probation officers, as well as general practitioners, Prys-Williams (1965) arrived at a total figure of 70,000 alcoholics with complications and a total population figure of 280,000.

The most complete survey carried out so far in the U.K. is that of Moss and Beresford Davies (1968) in Cambridgeshire. This study set out to define the number of persons over the age of fifteen suffering from alcoholism at some time during a three-year period, the way these people were distributed in the population, and the adverse effects of alcoholism on them.

The diagnosis of alcoholism was made on the basis of evidence from a reliable source of regular, or periodic, heavy drinking known to have occurred between 1961 and 1964. In addition, it had to be evident that ill-effects occurred because of the drinking in that period. Examples of the ill-effects indicating alcoholism included: two or more prosecutions for drunkenness; evidence of drinking surgical spirits; losing a job through drinking; and the wife or husband threatening to leave the home because of their partner's drinking.

A direct study of the population was not attempted, due to the difficulty of interviewing many thousands of people. The method chosen was to interview sources in contact with the alcoholic and his family. These sources comprised hospital out-patient and in-patient records, general practitioners, consultant psychiatrists, local authority officers, the police and probation services, Alcoholics Anonymous and other social and welfare organisations.

Following a pilot survey in nearby counties, the actual study was performed with great care and admirable attention to detail. Although the survey uncovered more than five hundred cases of alcoholism, the sources of information co-operated to such an extent that in only nineteen patients was the full amount of information required not forthcoming. The main defect of the study, admitted by the investigators, was that the information from general practitioners was derived from their memories and not cross-checked with their records.

The total number of alcoholics found was 527, of whom 423 were males and 104 were females. These figures give an incidence of 6·2 per 1,000 of the male population of fifteen years and over and 1·4 per 1,000 of the female population. In Parr's study, regional differences in the incidence rates were found. Using the Cambridgeshire figures and Parr's regional variations, the total figure for alcoholics in England and Wales is approximately 220,000. Thus it can be seen that varied methods of estimating the total number of alcoholics produce figures of between 200,000 and 400,000. If the assumption is made that these are minimal rather than maximal estimates, then the original figures of 350,000 to 500,000 appear fairly reasonable.

Thus far we have been concerned with England and Wales. Scotland and Ireland are accepted in lay opinion as notable sources of alcoholics and surveys have also been carried out in these areas.

A review of alcoholism in Scotland has been published by Warder and Ross (1971). It appears that the prevalence of alcoholism in Scotland is higher than in England and Wales and this is shown by the fact that hospital admissions for persons diagnosed as alcoholic in Scotland for the first time show rates seven times as high for men and five times as high for women as they do in England and Wales. The admissions to psychiatric hospitals also reveal that the diagnosis of alcoholic psychosis is much commoner in Scotland than England and Wales. In Scotland, the diagnosis constitutes 31 per cent of total psychiatric admissions, whereas in England and Wales the comparable figure is 7 per cent.

Alcoholics are not evenly distributed throughout Scotland. In the Northern Region the incidence of alcoholism is 76 per 100,000 and in the rest of Scotland 18 per 100,000. (These are incidence, or new case, figures. The earlier, apparently higher, figures for England and Wales are prevalence, or total existing case, figures.)

Ireland also has a major problem with alcoholism. In 1964 the rates of first admission to psychiatric hospitals for alcoholism and alcoholic psychoses were approximately ten times as high as in England and Wales. Walsh (1969) reported the Irish rate of first admissions for alcoholism to be 24·5 per 100,000 of the total population, which is surpassed only by France. The Irish who leave Ireland also commonly suffer from alcoholism. In a study of chronic-drunkenness offenders in London, the Irish-born were found to be represented ten times more frequently than would have been expected from the proportion of Irish-born in the general population (Gath, 1969).

In a study of male alcoholics carried out in Chester, one-third of the patients were of Irish or Scottish origin and many of these had no roots or connection with the Merseyside area.

In Manhattan a survey of over 4,387 families was carried out by Margaret Bailey and her colleagues. The families were selected on a random basis from an urban area and one member of each family was interviewed about the drinking habits of the family. Questions were also asked about the effects that excessive drinking might have on the family members. By this method the rate of alcoholism in Washington Heights was found to be 19 per 1,000.

ESTIMATES OF ALCOHOLISM FROM ALCOHOL CONSUMPTION

A totally different approach to the above survey method of identifying alcoholic individuals within a group of largely normal people has been used by a number of investigators (de Lint and Schmidt, 1971). There is a close connection between the level of consumption of alcohol *per capita* and the prevalence of cirrhosis of the liver in any population. It is the basis of the Jellinek formula that the prevalence of alcoholism is related to the prevalence of liver cirrhosis and, therefore, a relationship can be expected between the rates of alcoholism and the *per capita* alcohol consumption.

De Lint and Schmidt have shown that it is possible to draw a graph of consumption *per capita* against the number of people consuming any particular amount of alcohol and that, for varying average amounts of alcohol consumed in a population, the graph is a constant shape. The curve produced is termed a logarithmic normal curve. The shape of the curve shows that most people drink a little alcohol and a few people drink a great deal. It is likely that those who drink a great deal are the alcoholics in the population.

As the authors of this book point out, there is no sharp dividing-line between alcoholics and heavy drinkers, in terms of the amount of alcohol consumed, and any definition of alcoholism on consumption grounds is therefore arbitrary. A level of consumption equal to 150 ml (approximately 5 fl. oz.) of *absolute* alcohol per day was arbitrarily chosen as the cut-off point between excessive and alcoholic drinkers. A recent paper (1972) on the diagnosis of alcoholism by the National Council on Alcoholism of America defined the drinking of more than one-fifth of a (U.S.) gallon (760 ml) of whisky (or equivalent) in one day, for more than one day, by an 82 kg (180 lb.) man as being indicative of alcoholism. This amount approximates to 300 ml (10 fl. oz.) of absolute alcohol.

A comparison of the total annual amount of alcohol consumed per drinker, the number of drinkers taking in excess of a daily average of 150 ml of absolute alcohol, and the rates of death from cirrhosis of the liver show positive correlations between the factors involved. For example, France has an annual average consumption of 25·9 litres (911·5 fl. oz.) of absolute alcohol, 9,405 drinkers per 100,000 in excess of 150 cc of alcohol and a rate of death from cirrhosis of the liver of 45·3 per 100,000. The comparable figures for the U.S.A. are 12·0 litres (422·3 fl. oz.), 2,198 per 100,000 and 18·4 per 100,000 and for England and Wales 10·9 litres (383·6 fl. oz.), 1,946 per 100,000 and 3·7 per 100,000. Because of the constancy of these findings, it has been suggested that the one way to influence rates of alcoholism is to limit the production and availability of alcohol. One way of limiting its availability is to make alcoholic beverages expensive in comparison to available income. Incidentally, it is necessary to apply the increased cost to all forms of alcoholic drink; if spirits, for example, are comparatively more heavily taxed than other beverages then the consumption of beer and wine increases to make up for the reduction in spirit consumption.

It is frequently said that the prevalence of alcoholism is increasing in England and Wales. This is extremely difficult to determine with accuracy. It may well be that the condition is diagnosed more commonly than in earlier years, or that the consequences of alcoholism are now properly attributed to their cause. If there is an increased recognition of any condition, then its prevalence can apparently increase. A real increase or decrease could only be demonstrated by two studies separated in time that used exactly the same diagnostic criteria on the same population.

Assuming that the relationship between the prevalence of alcoholism and general overall consumption is a real one, then a look at the overall consumption rates of alcoholic beverages may well give an indirect clue to changes in the prevalence of alcoholism. Using the consumption figures for alcoholic drinks in the U.K. for the years 1951/52 and 1971/72 the following changes occurred:

Beer consumption increased from 25·6 to 35·8 million bulk barrels (3,624–5,068 million litres).
Wine consumption increased from 14·50 to 53·9 million gallons (65·98–245·26 million litres).
Spirits consumption increased from 9·67 to 21·3 million proof gallons (25·05–55·17 million litres).

It can be seen that overall the consumption of alcoholic drinks has increased over the past twenty years by a staggering amount. Although the population of the U.K. has gone up over the same twenty-year period, it has certainly not increased at a comparable rate. The consumption average has therefore grown over this time and, by the same token, the prevalence of alcoholism has also probably shown a genuine increase.

As every person who drinks alcoholic beverages is aware, the cost of his drinks has also increased steadily, at times dramatically, over this period. Large increases in price have merely slowed down the rate of increase in consumption until the money available for the purchase of alcohol catches up again.

Over the centuries, the rates of public drunkenness and alcoholism have varied widely in the British Isles due to a series of measures introduced to control the production and consumption of alcoholic drinks. Controls introduced in the fourteenth and fifteenth centuries appear to have had little effect on slowing production. Prior to the end of the seventeenth century, ale and, latterly, beer were the commonest alcoholic drinks. From 1688, the distillation of spirits increased because it was made legal for anyone to produce distilled spirits on paying a small tax fee. In the forty years following 1688, the annual production of spirits increased by 700 per cent. The dreadful consequences of this phenomenal growth in spirit consumption have been well illustrated by William Hogarth, and a number of Acts were introduced to control the manufacture and sale of spirits. At the same time, people such as John Wesley preached about the evils of strong alcoholic drinks.

The improvement brought about by these measures lasted for approximately a century when the excessive consumption of beer and gin finally brought about the introduction of the 1872 Licensing Acts. The Temperance movement, which appeared and became powerful throughout the same period, influenced many thousands of people to become total abstainers and to press for the total suppression of alcohol production and sale. The development of the Temperance movements has been described by Harrison (1971).

Although improvements were brought about by these means, excessive drinking remained a serious problem until the First World War, when the hours available for selling alcoholic drinks were sharply curtailed. Following a reduction in the number of arrests for drunkenness in the early twentieth century, there has been a steady increase in such arrests since the end of the Second World War. There has not been a return to common public drunkenness but presumably, after a period of lessening prevalence of alcoholism, we are now in a phase in which the prevalence is on the increase again. Visitors from abroad and many native Britons complain about the restricted hours available for drinking and there are suggestions that the laws might be relaxed in this regard. In view of the results of lax licensing laws in the past it might be expected that liberalising the laws from their present state will be followed by even more public drunkenness, drunken driving offences and alcoholism.

Drug dependence

Although there has long been a general acceptance that alcoholism and its consequences constitute something of a social and medical problem, the acceptance of drug dependence as a similar problem occurred rapidly and dramatically only in the middle and late 1960s in Britain. This was due to the sudden increase in dependence on heroin and cocaine by people in their teens. It was the spread in heroin dependence particularly that caused a great deal of alarm in Britain and this drug will be discussed first.

HEROIN DEPENDENCE

In 1961 the first report of the Brain committee (the Interdepartmental Committee on Drug Addiction) reported that there appeared to be very little abuse of opiate drugs and that there was no evidence of any real increase in abuse over recent years. No change was recommended in the law at that time, particularly since illicit use was regarded as being extremely minor in amount. In 1965 the second report of the Interdepartmental Committee on Drug Addiction described a situation very different from that of only four years earlier. During that time the number of opiate-dependent people had increased from 470 to 927. At the same time the proportion of new cases reported was increasing with each year. A particularly disturbing feature was the increase in people below the age of thirty-five, from 96 to 492.

It was considered that the origin of the heroin being used illicitly was the prescription of excessive amounts to addicts by a very small number of doctors. The heroin on the British market was therefore predominantly pure heroin manufactured to the highest standards. Heroin is banned in the U.S.A. and therefore street heroin in the U.S.A. is either illegally imported or prepared illicitly within the country. By whatever way it arrives on the street, the heroin in the U.S.A. is far from pure and is usually adulterated with other substances, varying from talc to quinine. This accounts, at least in part, for the differences in the effects of the injection of "heroin" in the two countries.

The origins of the increase in the illicit use of heroin in Britain have been traced by Spear (1969) to a robbery from a hospital pharmacy in 1951. As already mentioned, it was not until more than ten years later that the problem of increasing opiate dependence became obvious. The arrival in the U.K. of a number of Canadian heroin addicts, who took advantage of the British system of heroin supply, also increased the number of cases throughout the middle 1960s.

Although it has been obligatory to record the prescription of all opiates since the introduction of the Dangerous Drugs Acts 1920, there was no statutory notification of opiate users until 1968. In February of that year the Dangerous Drugs (Notification of Addicts) Regulations came into force.

Prior to 1968 the members of the medical profession were free to prescribe heroin or morphine to addicts undergoing withdrawal treatment and to those addicts in whom withdrawal treatment had not succeeded. This system, which had existed from 1926, was reviewed in 1961 by the Brain committee who left it unchanged.

The intervening change in the prevalence of opiate dependence occurring between 1961 and 1965 led to a radical change in the British system of opiate control. The Dangerous Drugs Act 1967 removed the right of most doctors to prescribe heroin and cocaine to addicts. Only doctors on the staff of specialised treatment centres set up for the treatment of addiction were empowered to prescribe to addicts. Another major change was the introduction of the statutory notification of addicts. Any medical practitioner coming into contact with an addict in a professional relationship has a statutory obligation to notify the Home Office. The notification form is a fairly lengthy document which not only records the patient's name (or names), address and basic demographic characteristics, but also includes a detailed description of the patient, so that checks can be kept to guard against any addict receiving supplies from two clinics at the same time.

The majority of British heroin addicts have always been in and around London. In the provinces, there was some evidence that the doctors empowered to prescribe heroin took what might be described as a hard line in their management of the problem. Although the prescription of heroin to outpatients was allowed, this was interpreted by some as being somewhat equivalent to maintaining alcoholics on a free supply of alcohol. The successful treatment of both groups was seen as being total abstinence from the drug of dependence. Therefore, it followed that the treatment for heroin dependence should be a period of in-patient stay during the withdrawal period, and perhaps replacement of the heroin with methadone. A number of heroin addicts were unwilling to accept this regime and this probably induced them to leave the provinces for London, where their chances of continued outpatient maintenance on heroin was higher.

Before the growth of the problem of heroin dependence amongst the young it had been restricted to three main groups. People of Chinese origin in the areas of seaports have used opium for many years and only rarely do cases of abuse come to the notice of the medical profession. In Liverpool, for instance, only one case of opiate abuse in a Chinese man came to the attention of the Regional Addiction Unit in the first eight years of its operation. The two other groups who comprised the majority of the 400 or so cases reported each year were, firstly, professionals in medicine and nursing or pharmacists to whom opiates were freely available, and secondly therapeutic addicts who had become addicted during the medical treatment of some painful condition.

By and large, these people were middle-aged and the therapeutic addicts were mostly female and addicted to morphine. It was this population that the Rolleston report of 1926 and the first Brain committee of 1961 saw as constituting the then small problem of opiate dependence in Britain.

Table V illustrates the growth in heroin dependence from 1955 onwards.

TABLE V

Heroin addicts in Britain known annually from 1955 to 1968 (*after* Pierce James, 1971)

	Total	*Therapeutic*	*Non-therapeutic*	*New Cases*
1955	54	18	36	10
1956	53	17	36	10
1957	66	21	45	7
1958	62	19	43	11
1959	68	21	47	11
1960	94	22	72	24
1961	132	20	112	56
1962	175	18	157	72
1963	237	18	222	90
1964	342	13	329	162
1965	521	12	509	259
1966	899	13	885	522
1967	1,299	9	1,290	745
1968	2,240	8	2,232	1,306

The age distribution showed a profound change over the same period as can be seen from Table VI.

TABLE VI
Age distribution of opiate addicts, 1959–68

	1959	*'60*	*'61*	*'62*	*'63*	*'64*	*'65*	*'66*	*'67*	*'68*
Under 20 years										
All Drugs	—	1	2	3	17	40	145	329	395	764
Heroin	—	1	2	3	17	40	145	317	381	709
20–34 years										
All Drugs	50	52	94	132	184	257	347	558	906	1,530
Heroin	35	52	87	126	162	219	319	479	827	1,390
35–49 years										
All Drugs	92	91	95	107	128	138	134	162	142	146
Heroin	7	14	19	24	38	61	62	83	66	78
Over 50 years										
All Drugs	278	267	272	274	298	311	291	285	279	260
Heroin	26	27	24	22	20	22	16	20	24	20

The notification of heroin addicts changed following the introduction of the Dangerous Drugs (Notification of Addicts) Regulations in 1968. During the year of 1968, 1,782 new addicts came to notice but by the end of the year only, 1,817 in total were receiving opiates, as at 31st December 1969. Of these 1,466, most were not receiving heroin but were being prescribed methadone.

Table VII (*see* over) illustrates the changes in the numbers of notified addicts from 1969 to 1972.

After the decrease in the number of cases reported from 1969 to 1970, there has been an increase, which has made up for and exceeded the previous fall in terms of active addicts known at the year end. The numbers on heroin continue to fall and the increase in opiate users lies mainly with the methadone users. A statistic which gives rise to concern is the origin of addiction. The number of non-therapeutic addicts has risen considerably over the period

TABLE VII

Numbers of notified heroin addicts, 1969–72

	1969		*1970*		*1971*		1972	
	Year total	*As at 31.12.69*	*Year total*	*As at 31.12.70*	*Year total*	*As at 31.12.71*	*Year total*	*As at 31.12.72*
Total no.	2,881	1,446	2,661	1,430	2,769	1,555	2,944	1,619
No. on heroin	1,417	499	914	437	959	385	868	339
No. on methadone	1,687	1,011	1,820	992	1,927	1,160	2,171	1,280
Non-therapeutic origin	2,533	1,196	2,321	1,177	2,457	1,313	2,659	1,413

covered. It can be assumed that, because the number of addicts of non-therapeutic origin is increasing, there is a pool of people in the population who are taking heroin that they are obtaining from friends or dealers and who are not known to the authorities. The figures in Table VII thus represent a minimum estimate of opiate takers in the U.K. at the present time.

The number of opiate addicts below the age of twenty has fallen steadily over the period 1969–72 and this may be an indication that fewer young people are becoming opiate users. The number aged twenty to twenty-four continues to increase, probably as a result of some teenage addicts continuing their drug-taking as they move to the next age grouping. As the age groups of the opiate addicts notified increases, the proportion of heroin and/or methadone decreases and there is a higher proportion taking morphine and pethidine, indicating that a large proportion of the older opiate addictions are of therapeutic origin and that the addicts are members of professional groups with access to various opiates.

The treatment of alcoholism and drug dependence will be discussed more fully in Chapters 8 and 9. Briefly, however, the British system for the treatment of heroin dependence has centred round attempts to withdraw the addict from heroin, usually in hospital, and if total withdrawal has failed then methadone has been substituted. One important aspect of the system in Britain has been that heroin or a substitute is in fact available to any addict, merely by his going to a designated centre. This differs from the situation in America where all heroin addicts are maintained on illicit street-drugs and, consequently, they are involved in a great deal of crime to obtain the money to support their addiction.

In 1914, in America, the Harrison Act restricted the supply of opiates to doctors; prior to that date opiates had been available directly from pharmacists and also from mail-order houses. The law was apparently not intended to be used restrictively but was in effect extremely restrictive. This came about because, although physicians could supply opiates to addicts in the course of their professional duties, addiction had not been defined as an illness and therefore the prescription of opiates to an addict could not be interpreted as being a professional act. The interpretation of the Act in this way meant that doctors were unwilling to risk dealing with addicts and thus the addicts had to look for alternative sources of supply.

TABLE VIII

Ages and sex distribution of notified opiate addicts, 1969–72

	1969		*1970*		*1971*		*1972*	
	Year total	*As at 31.12.69*	*Year total*	*As at 31.12.70*	*Year total*	*As at 31.12.71*	*Year total*	*As at 31.12.72*
Under 20 years	637	224	405	142	338	118	279	96
Under 20 years on heroin	598	221	365	136	304	111	260	95
20–34 years	1,789	897	1,813	959	2,010	1,123	2,262	1,221
20–34 years on heroin	1,709	872	1,705	921	1,912	1,088	2,178	1,195
35–49 years	174	116	158	112	156	112	178	120
35–49 years on heroin	101	69	95	69	94	73	126	87
Over 50 years	241	204	253	195	226	179	204	165
Over 50 years on heroin	46	40	50	39	47	35	42	36
Unknown age	40	25	32	22	39	23	21	17
Unknown age on heroin	26	13	18	10	19	9	7	5
Male addicts	2,295	1,067	2,071	1,053	2,134	1,135	2,272	1,197
Female addicts	586	399	590	377	635	420	672	422

Heroin = heroin and/or methadone.

By 1918, it was estimated that the illegal trade in narcotics in America was equal in volume to the legitimate medical prescribing. At the same time it was reported that a nationwide organisation of drug pedlars had formed and that overall narcotic dependence was on the increase in the large American cities.

In 1924 the import of heroin into the U.S.A. was totally banned. The ban included the medical use of the drug as an analgesic. Despite this ban, heroin dependence increased in the U.S.A. and the Harrison Act came in for a great deal of criticism from the late 1920s onwards. Because of the total ban on obtaining heroin from legitimate sources, the addict had to turn to illegal supplies. The illicit drugs were naturally expensive and because of this the association between opiate dependence and other crime became established. There is a marked difference in the law-breaking activity of heroin addicts in North America and those in Britain, where a legal supply is available.

Not only did the Harrison Act fail to control the spread of heroin dependence but further, stricter, laws also failed. The problem of opiate dependence in America is still very large and it was estimated that in 1971 there were between 250,000 and 300,000 opiate addicts in the U.S.A.

As methadone has been used to replace heroin in treatment centres, so the percentage of methadone users amongst opiate addicts has increased. Of 107 heroin addicts seen in London treatment centres, 91 had had methadone prescribed and 95 had used methadone at some time. The United States Food and Drug Administration (1973) has announced that, due to growing abuse in the use of methadone, the drug will be supplied only to hospital pharmacies, approved maintenance programmes and certain drug stores.

CANNABIS

Cannabis, in its various forms, holds at present a position intermediate between alcohol and the opiates. Alcohol is generally accepted and widely used and some people are known to suffer ill-effects from it. Opiates, or more precisely heroin, are not generally accepted and are seen as being almost invariably harmful to the users. Cannabis on the other hand has changed in Britain from a drug with few users and low acceptance to a situation where it is commonly used and is accepted by some groups in society. There is a great deal of confusion and ignorance about the distinction between its actual and its alleged effects. The confusion and ignorance occur in both cannabis-using and non-using groups.

The determination of the epidemiology of cannabis use presents formidable problems. None of the methods used in studying alcohol or the opiates is available for use with cannabis. There are no records of consistent cannabis side-effects that can be used in the way cirrhosis of the liver is, nor do cannabis users have to be notified to any central agency. That cannabis use has grown throughout the 1960s and '70s is not in question. Reference to any popular publication aimed at a teenage market will bear witness to the way people in this age group view cannabis use.

Two methods have been used to assess cannabis use. It is illegal in the U.K. to possess or to deal in it. Records of convictions related to cannabis possession will therefore give some indirect assessment of the direction in which cannabis use is going. An important variable in these figures is the zeal of the police in making arrests under the appropriate law. The total convictions for offences involving cannabis have increased steadily from 663 recorded in 1963. By 1969 the annual figure had reached 4,683. In 1970 this rose to 7,520 and in 1971 to 9,219 cases. A similar situation obtains in America. In California there were 1,156 arrests involving marijuana in 1954. In 1968 this had increased to 50,327 and accounted for almost 60 per cent of all drug arrests in that state.

The second method of assessing the extent of cannabis use is the questionnaire approach in selected populations. The Wootton report (1968) estimated that there were between 30,000 and 300,000 people in Britain who had used cannabis at some time. Practically everybody who has any contact with the drug scene feels that this is an under-estimate. Young (1971) makes the straightforward statement that the most popular drug, amongst all the hippie groups in the world, is marijuana.

Hindmarch (1972) estimated that approximately 2,000,000 people in Britain had tried cannabis and he found that 34 per cent of students in a northern university used cannabis on at least a casual basis. In a review of drug use in Britain, Pierce James (1971) estimated that about 30 per 100,000 of the total population were regular users and that 10 per cent of the student population were users.

In Canada, where the population is approximately 22,000,000, the Le Dain Commission (1972) produced estimates of the total number of people who had ever used cannabis. The sources of the data were school children aged twelve to nineteen, college and university students and a sample of householders. The results of the investigation showed a marked increase in cannabis use from 1966 onwards. In 1966 a total of 79,000 were estimated to have used cannabis at some time. This figure increased to 758,000 by 1970. In 1966–67 the percentage of university and college students who had ever used the drug was 3·9 per cent and this figure also showed a startling increase to 29·0 per cent by 1970.

Recently, there has been some evidence that the rate of increase in Canada has at least slowed and that the peak use may have been reached. The Royal Canadian Mounted Police officer in charge of drug enforcement reported in the *Addiction Research Foundation Journal* in October 1972 that cannabis arrests for the first half of 1972 showed a decrease of 5·7 per cent compared with the 1971 figure. This is the first time in over ten years that a decrease has been recorded.

A series of studies by Smart, Fejer and White (1973) confirmed the slowing down in the rate of increase in marijuana use. In 1968, 6·7 per cent of school children aged twelve to nineteen reported using marijuana and this increased to 18·3 per cent in 1970 and to 20·9 per cent in 1972. Over the same period there has been an increase in the use of alcohol in the group studied, from 46·3 per cent in 1968 to 70·6 per cent in 1972.

An interesting study was carried out by Lipp and Benson (1972) who investigated the use of marijuana, alcohol and tobacco in a group of 1,314 physicians in America. As they say, doctors are supposed to be experts in the effects of drug abuse and many people do turn to them for advice in this area. Of the doctors replying to a questionnaire approach, 37 per cent said they had been exposed to marijuana and 25 per cent said they had tried it on at least one occasion; 7 per cent described themselves as current users of the drug. Conversely, only 8 per cent were total abstainers from alcohol.

LSD AND PSYCHEDELICS

The psychedelic agent most commonly used in Britain would seem to be lysergic acid (LSD) but the data on the amount of use are very deficient and are based even more on guesswork than the preceding drug-use estimates have been.

Hindmarch (1972) quoted Bewley's 1969 estimates of between one and five people per 100,000 as users of LSD. In his own surveys of English students and school children, Hindmarch reported that 10 per cent of drug-taking children aged sixteen to eighteen took LSD and one in three of drug-taking university students had also taken LSD. The exposure to LSD was usually brief and consisted of a few isolated experiences with the drug.

In Dublin, the situation with regard to LSD use was reported by Carney and his colleagues (1972) to be different from that in Britain. They studied 50 drug-dependent people between the ages of fifteen and twenty-four, of whom 42 were male. Every one of the 50 had tried cannabis and LSD at some time. These two drugs were also the commonest with regard to current use: 38 per cent of the subjects were using cannabis and 28 per cent LSD.

There have been waves of drug abuse in various centres at various times. Carney and his co-workers suggested that the spread of LSD in Dublin recently was the equivalent phenomenon to the spread of amphetamine and preludin abuse in Sweden. LSD use does appear to be correlated with the illicit use of other drugs: 74 per cent of heroin users had tried LSD, although only 9 per cent had used it lately (Stinson and Ogborn, 1970).

In North America the situation with regard to LSD use has fluctuated over the years. In 1963 there was reported to be little use of hallucinogens but by 1965 and 1966 the amount of use had grown tremendously and it continued to grow until 1968, when it appeared to taper off again. One explanation given for the decrease is that during the expansion in LSD use, impurities were introduced and many takers suffered "bad trip" experiences. In the late 1960s evidence that LSD might cause genetic damage was published. Although there is little evidence to support the idea that the warning of users about harmful drug effects influences the habit, such warning may conceivably have prevented some people starting to take the drug and thereby contributed to the lessening in the proportion of drug-takers choosing LSD.

LSD-taking is still common amongst certain groups of people in the U.S.A. A study of 15- to 25-year-olds attending a psychiatric emergency service in Massachusetts revealed that over half of the 100 subjects studied had used marijuana and 35 had used LSD or amphetamines. In the study quoted above of professional students and graduates, 4 per cent admitted to LSD use.

A disturbing finding was reported in San Mateo County in California. In 1969, 23 per cent of boys in school admitted to having used LSD, though this figure decreased slightly in 1970 (Richards and Carroll, 1970). In Canadian cities Smart (1971) found that between one and three per cent of school children aged twelve to nineteen had tried LSD on at least one occasion. A repeat survey in 1972 revealed little change in this figure.

AMPHETAMINES

Amphetamines have been in medical use for over thirty years for many conditions. Latterly the main indications have been depression and obesity. Partly due to the introduction of much more effective treatments for depression, the use of amphetamines has decreased over the last few years. In 1961 six million prescriptions were issued in England and Wales for amphetamines and appetite suppressants. This had fallen to 3·9 million by 1968.

The use of amphetamines in Britain parallels in many ways the use of opiates although this is not meant to convey that there is an association between the use of the two groups of drugs. Initially, opiates and amphetamines were largely prescribed for patients by medical practitioners and a proportion of the patients became dependent on the drug prescribed. The addicted patients were then maintained by the doctor who had originally supplied the preparation. In some cases illicit supplies would be obtained by such patients but the problem of abuse of amphetamines and opiates remained fairly minimal until the 1960s. After a period of rapid growth of abuse, both groups of drugs are now subject to very stringent legal control, which is aimed at reducing the total number recipients and abusers.

The problem of amphetamine abuse seems only to have been evident since the 1960s but in fact restrictions were originally introduced in 1939 and increased in 1956. This latter legislation consisted of controlling amphetamines under Section 4 of the Poisons Rule. This move was in response to the increasing use of amphetamine in nasal inhalers. Whereas most users of the inhalers used them in the way designed, a small proportion of users would break open the container and dissolve the amphetamine base from the contents and then drink the resulting solution.

Stimulants were widely used in Japan during the Second World War and after the war they were freely available without prescription. By 1954 it was estimated that 2 per cent of the total population was addicted to amphetamines. Legal controls accompanied by the spread of information regarding the possible ill-effects resulted in the problem coming under control within three years.

At the time the Japanese problem was coming under control, Connell (1958) in England reported cases of psychosis occurring as a result of the excessive intake of amphetamine preparations. The general population levels of amphetamine abuse are again not precisely determined but a study in Newcastle upon Tyne (Kiloh and Brandon, 1962) showed that 1 per cent of the population was receiving amphetamines. The worrying feature of this finding was that one in five of those receiving amphetamines showed signs of being dependent on them.

Amphetamines were commonly mixed with barbiturates in a single tablet as in Drinamyl ("purple hearts"). This mixture was found to be worse than straightforward amphetamine in a study of patients in general practice. In this situation 58 per cent of those receiving the mixture were noted to be dependent on it.

At this time, the problem of amphetamine abuse was restricted to the middle-aged, most of whom were females receiving the drug for depression or obesity. Although these patients were abusing amphetamines they used the oral preparation. The oral route continued to be used initially by the increasing number of young people who were found to be taking amphetamines.

In selected populations the percentage of users has been found to be very high. A study of boys in London remand homes in 1965 (Scott and Wilcox, 1965) showed that 18 per cent of the boys had taken amphetamines shortly before their detention in the home. Two patterns of drug use were identified amongst these boys. The "benign" users took amphetamines at the weekends and kept to a particular dose. The "malignant" users tended to take amphetamines throughout the week and also to increase the dose with time. The malignant users were found to come from severely disturbed or unfavourable backgrounds and to show signs of personality disturbance which were not shown by the "benign" users. Although further studies have confirmed that comparable subjects do still take amphetamines, the proportions discovered have tended to be lower than the 1965 survey and have been in the 7–8 per cent range.

The drug problems in Britain appear to echo those in the U.S.A. and to occur about five years after their appearance on the west coast of America. In 1962, American manufacturers of injectable amphetamine became aware of an illicit trade in their product and the supply to general pharmacists was cut off. As has happened with other drugs, once the legal supply is totally removed the illicit trade changes from one simply of dealing in the drug to one of manufacturing and dealing. No doubt the profits are greater this way.

In 1967, reports on the effects of intravenous amphetamine began to appear. The amphetamine used was usually methylamphetamine which acquired the synonym of "speed". Speed replaced LSD as the drug of choice in the Haight-Ashbury district of San Francisco in the late 1960s.

In Britain, the problem of amphetamine injection appeared in 1968, at a time when methylamphetamine could be prescribed by any physician. In contrast to the illicit manufacture occurring in the USA., methylamphetamine appears to have been supplied in Britain, mainly in London, by private medical practitioners. The population taking amphetamine in this way were young, single men from disturbed backgrounds, who had also abused other drugs.

In retrospect, it now seems that it took the law a long time to change in response to the spread of heroin dependence. In contrast, there was a very rapid change in the situation with respect to methylamphetamine, which was restricted to hospital pharmacists in late 1968. This change was voluntarily brought about by the manufacturers. A further voluntary change came about through the co-operation of general practitioners in a plan initiated in Ipswich by Dr. Wells.

Through this plan, it is unnecessary for general chemists to stock amphetamines. These stocks are targets for robbery designed to supply the illicit trade. By agreeing to monitor their own prescribing of amphetamines and, in cases where the drug is necessary, accepting a two-day delay in the supply of the tablet from the manufacturers, general practitioners contributed to the decrease in the legal and illegal supply of amphetamines.

In Canada, the prescription of amphetamines has come under strict control with effect from 1st January 1973 (*Canadian Gazette*, 29th December 1972). Amphetamines were only allowed in cases of narcolepsy, over-activity in children, Parkinson's disease, epilepsy, minimal brain dysfunction and in special situations in anaesthesia. Upon prescribing an amphetamine preparation, a physician in Canada must notify the Bureau of Dangerous Drugs in Ottawa, and to continue the drug for more than 30 days the opinion of an independent physician must be obtained. Due to objections raised by the medical profession, however, these controls were later reduced in their effectiveness.

Under the heading of amphetamines, mention must be made of an outbreak of dependence on phenmetrazine (Preludin) that occurred in Sweden in the 1960s. Sweden had the greatest problem in the world with stimulant abuse, following the legalising of the prescription of stimulants in 1965. In 1967 the law was reversed, but stimulant abuse continued to increase. At the present time, such preparations are forbidden in Sweden apart from their use in certain specific medical conditions.

BARBITURATES AND HYPNOTICS

Barbiturates have now been in use for seventy years and it still amazes the writers how few prescribers and users of these compounds are aware of the dangers associated with their use. The barbiturates are extremely commonly prescribed. Approximately 15 million prescriptions per annum were issued every year from 1961 to 1968 in the U.K. Combined with non-barbiturate hypnotics they accounted for 9 per cent of all prescriptions issued in England and Wales in 1961 and 7·9 per cent in 1968 (Zacune and Hensman, 1971).

Dunlop (1970) estimated that every tenth night's sleep in the U.K. could have been induced by the amount of hypnotics prescribed. A feature of barbiturate and amphetamine prescribing which causes concern was published by Balint, as has been discussed in Chapter 1. He found that 40 per cent of patients in a general practice setting are given repeat prescriptions of psychotropic medication. Of those receiving barbiturates or amphetamines on at least one occasion, 50 per cent were still receiving the same medication four years later. This decreased to 25 per cent at eight years but after sixteen years 9 per cent were still receiving the medication. It is highly unlikely that the original indications for the prescription were still evident by then.

In 1968 Dunlop (1970) reported that 16 per cent of the total prescriptions in the U.K. were for medications designed to affect the emotions, behaviour or sleep. Of these psychotropic agents, the most commonly prescribed were the barbiturates, with almost 25 million prescriptions. The number of tablets in a single prescription varies but at twenty-five tablets per prescription the total number of tablets dispensed is enormous. Some of the barbiturates prescribed were long-acting ones such as phenobarbitone, used in the treatment of epilepsy. The short- and medium-acting barbiturates amounted to 16·5 million prescriptions. In addition, 5·5 million prescriptions were issued for non-barbiturate hypnotics of which over 40 per cent were for Mandrax at that time (Mandrax being a methaqualone and diphenhydramine combination).

With so many barbiturate tablets being freely available in people's homes, the problem of barbiturate dependence might well be expected to be considerable. Bewley (1966) estimated the total number of barbiturate dependents in the U.K. to be in the region of 100,000, with 500,000 others being regular users without showing dependence.

As with amphetamines, there appear to be two groups affected by barbiturate dependence and the groups are very similar to those described under amphetamine dependence. The larger group dependent on barbiturates are middle-aged and mainly female. The smaller group consists of young people who take barbiturates orally, but amongst whom there was a short-lasting and exceedingly dangerous vogue for intravenous administration.

In subjects who are dependent on other drugs, illicit barbiturate use has been found to be common. Mitcheson *et al.* (1970) documented the increase in the abuse of barbiturates amongst heroin addicts and described their findings in a series of sixty-five such cases. Although the criterion for inclusion in the study was that the subjects had taken heroin daily, all of them had also taken other drugs. In fact all but one had taken amphetamines. It was found that 95 per cent of the subjects had used barbiturates and 75 per cent of them had used them daily at some time; 80 per cent of them had also injected barbiturates.

In contrast only 6 per cent of the drug-dependent subjects interviewed by Carney in Dublin had taken barbiturates. A survey of school children in Wolverhampton (Wright, 1970) revealed that only 1 per cent of the children asked about drugs they knew to be taken by addicts mentioned barbiturates, as against 98 per cent mentioning cannabis and 91 per cent heroin. In the San Mateo County study (U.S.A.) it was found that marijuana was taken more commonly than amphetamines and that tranquillisers and barbiturates were the next most common.

Surveys of drug dependence in psychiatric patients have produced quite widely-varying figures. A study by Bellinger (1972) of 378 patients showed that 104 (27·5 per cent) were drug-dependent. Of those receiving barbiturates for the four weeks prior to admission 91 per cent were considered to be dependent on this group of drugs, methaqualone-produced dependency occurred in 80 per cent and nitrazepam (Mogadon) dependency in 71 per cent. Amongst the group studied, dependence on prescribed drugs increased with the age of the patient up to the 60–69-year-old group in which 46 per cent were dependent on some drug. Among patients below the age of thirty only 5 per cent were drug-dependent.

There is a close connection between the abuse of alcohol and that of other drugs. In a group of 893 alcoholics admitted to an alcoholic ward in Toronto, 129 (15 per cent) were found to be abusing another drug (Deveny and Wilson, 1971), the commonest drugs being barbiturates which were abused by 70 per cent of those individuals. This figure was equivalent to 10 per cent of all the alcoholics admitted. The barbiturate abusers tended to be younger than the non-barbiturate users and the proportion of women was increased in the drug-abusing group.

A feature of barbiturate-taking in the U.K. over the last ten years has been that barbiturate overdose deaths have doubled in this period, though overall the suicide rate has declined gradually. In the alcoholic group discussed above, 38 per cent of those taking barbiturates had taken an overdose and about half of these admitted to suicidal intent.

GLUE AND SOLVENT-SNIFFING

The inhalation of the fumes from glue or from other sources has always appeared to be a minor part of drug abuse in Britain. A very specialised group, anaesthetists, has been known to include a few members who would habitually join their patients in inhaling the gases used in anaesthesia, but such practices are liable to be noticed by colleagues and are rare.

Hindmarch (1972) described glue and solvent-sniffing as occurring in 14- and 15-year-olds and being an almost purely adolescent phenomenon. In Canada there was a considerable problem with glue-sniffing in 1968. At that time, 5·7 per cent of 12- to 19-year-olds reported having experienced intoxication in this way. The proportion of school children reporting such abuse has fallen steadily since that time and in 1972 was down to 2·9 per cent. Another study in Eastern Canada (Whitehead, Smart and Laforest, 1972) has found that amongst marijuana-using school children, almost one in five had also sniffed glue whereas amongst the non-marijuana-using subjects only 3 per cent had tried glue. Isolated cases of death due to glue-sniffing have been reported.

MULTIPLE DRUG-ABUSE

One of the points made repeatedly in this chapter has been that, if you want to find a user of a particular drug, first find a group of abusers of another drug.

Abusers of drugs, particularly young ones, are nowadays highly likely to use more than one drug. This is true for drug-users in Britain and North America. The findings of Mitcheson and his colleagues on sedative abuse in heroin addicts have already been discussed, as have the findings of Stinson and Ogborne in England and Carney and his colleagues in Dublin. The Grosse Point study in Michigan (Levengood, Lowinger and Schooff, 1973) identified 300 children as heroin users. Sixty of them were interviewed and it was found that heroin use was preceded by the use of marijuana for approximately two years. Marijuana was followed by the use of barbiturates, LSD and amphetamines before heroin was used.

A study indicating that multiple drug-abuse was a problem amongst school children was reported by Wiener (1970). A pilot study in an area in London had revealed that 10 per cent of the subjects admitted to taking illicit drugs. It was therefore decided to conduct a survey of areas considered to have high, medium or low concentrations of drug abuse. A research design allowing for sampling across various types of schools in the appropriate areas was produced but unfortunately had to be greatly modified, due to the lack of participation on the part of a number of the schools. As a result of this, the final sample was biased toward selecting grammar-school children, and boys rather than girls.

A total of 1,093 pupils ranging from fourteen to nineteen answered a questionnaire and after the answers were closely checked, 59 (5·39 per cent) of the sample were identified as drug-takers though only 15 were regular drug-users. Of the 59, most (35) had used only one drug, with pep pills or hashish being the usual drug. However, 15 used two drugs, 8 used three drugs and one claimed to use four drugs. Although these figures represent small percentages of the total sample they are probably a minimum estimate of the problem and a further note of caution against complacency is that the study was carried out in 1968, before many reports of multiple drug-abuse had been published.

Excluding alcohol from the consideration of drug-abuse, a study amongst juveniles referred to a drug advisory service near Washington D.C. found that of 35 adolescents, only 3 were taking just one drug; 8 were taking three drugs, 10 were taking four drugs and 9 subjects were taking five.

There has been a great deal of controversy about the possibility of taking one drug increasing the likelihood of taking another. The main concern has been that the taking of a "safe" drug, such as marijuana, might lead to taking an "unsafe" drug such as heroin. The escalation from one drug to another has been a mainstay of the arguments of the group against legalising the use of marijuana.

There is no doubt that amongst drug addicts, drugs such as cannabis and amphetamines are frequently the first to be taken. At the time that cannabis use was apparently uncommon and heroin use was growing at a very rapid pace, the possibility of a connection in the use of the two drugs appeared feasible. Cannabis use has continued to grow over the last few years and, as we have seen, heroin use appears to be fairly well controlled in Britain. Certainly, there is no evidence that the majority of cannabis users progress to other, more serious, drug use. The question of escalation has been considered by Edwards (1968) who found little evidence on which to base a hypothesis that escalation occurs.

There is a lot of evidence that heroin addicts use and have used other drugs of which cannabis is a common one. A retrospective study of drug-taking adolescent boys was undertaken by Noble (1970). Two groups of boys, all known to have taken drugs, who were referred to a remand home between 1965 and 1967 were defined in terms of whether or not they admitted to narcotic use. A follow-up in 1969 comprising an examination of Home Office records showed that almost one in five of the non-narcotic takers had been recorded in the subsequent years as having become narcotic users. It was found that those who had progressed to "hard" drug use came from families having a high incidence of psychiatric illness and they also showed a marked degree of personality deviation.

Whitehead and his co-workers (1972) examined the difference in drug-taking habits between users and non-users of marijuana. The subjects were approximately 12,000 school children in Toronto, Montreal and Halifax (Nova Scotia). Respectively 6·8, 8·5 and 6·5 per cent of the subjects admitted to using marijuana in the last six months. The use of marijuana was closely correlated with the use of a large range of other drugs. Over 80 per cent of users had also taken alcohol and tobacco compared with approximately 40 per cent of non-users. Greater contrasts were evident in the use of other non-legal drugs. Barbiturates, tranquillisers, LSD, stimulants, hallucinogens and opiates were used by 20–35 per cent of marijuana users and by 0·6–0·7 per cent of non-users. The greatest differences occurred with respect to LSD, other hallucinogens and the opiates, in which the likelihood of a marijuana user taking another drug was increased by 25 to 60 times.

It has been suggested that one of the reasons for marijuana takers using other drugs is that the addict becomes involved in a vicious circle of mood "ups" and "downs" and may also need a chemical means of terminating a bad trip. There is no doubt that a proportion of middle-aged barbiturate addicts use amphetamines to "get going" in the mornings and then need the barbiturates to sleep at night. Despite the psycho-pharmacological effects of poly-drug abuse, it is probable that the main causes of multiple drug use are socio-legal. There are many aspects to the social influences on drug abuse and these will be considered in a later chapter (*see* p. 74).

Who are the alcoholics and drug addicts? Epidemiological and demographic characteristics

So far we have been concerned mainly with answering one of the two questions posed at the beginning of the chapter. It is possible to draw up a league table of drug-abuse, based on the totals estimated under each separate drug heading, but in view of the rapid change over the last few years and the multiple use of drugs just described, this may not be very useful.

More important than this is a delineation of just who the people are who make up the 500,000 alcoholics or 2,000 heroin addicts in Britain. Some of the data have already been given above.

AGE FACTORS

Alcoholics who present for treatment are, in the main, middle-aged. In the Cambridgeshire study, the mean age was approximately forty-five years and the ages were distributed statistically "normally" about this point. Similar findings have been reported by Glatt (1970) and many others. In a study of 222 alcoholics in Chester, we found the average age of the males to be forty-four years and the females to be forty-five years.

One of the interesting points about the ages of alcoholics presenting for treatment is that it appears that more young people are nowadays coming with the diagnosis of alcoholism. As already pointed out, many of these young people may also be abusing other drugs in addition to alcohol. In the series in Chester, 25 per cent of the patients were under the age of thirty-five and in a study in Edinburgh, 15 per cent of the patients were aged less than thirty (Ritson and Hassall, 1970). In the Cambridgeshire survey, 26 per cent of the male alcoholics and 20 per cent of the female alcoholics were aged less than thirty-five years.

Evidence of an increase in alcoholism among young people was produced by Glatt (1970) who found that alcoholics aged thirty and under increased to a statistically significant degree from the mid-1950s to the mid-1960s. If the study in Toronto, showing that alcohol is the favourite drug for 13- to 19-year-olds, has any bearing on events in the rest of the world, then a further increase in the number of young alcoholics could well occur.

One apparent source of increase in the number of young alcoholics is the fact that they have become more readily recognised in the last few years. It might be hoped that, by reaching them early, they could be helped all the more easily. Unfortunately, the people who become young alcoholics are usually found to be more disturbed than the average alcoholic and so they pose an even greater problem in terms of management.

A lot of details have been given about the age of diagnosis of drug abuse. In summary, hypnotics and stimulants are mostly abused by middle-aged and elderly people who take them orally. Abuse of these drugs by injection and of other drugs in the same manner is largely confined to teenagers and the twenty-year-olds. Glue-sniffing has a very small age-range and appears to be largely restricted to young adolescents. The use of cannabis on the other hand is becoming more widespread. It is frequently the first drug other than alcohol and tobacco to be experienced and is therefore used by young people. Its use is common in universities and colleges and is spreading to people in their thirties and forties and even older.

SEX DISTRIBUTION

In most surveys, alcoholic men are found to outnumber alcoholic women by 4 or 5 to 1. There are a number of possible explanations for this finding. Men usually drink more than women, they drink more frequently and a greater proportion of the total male population drinks than the female (Edwards, Chandler and Hensman, 1971). In a study of drinking habits in a London suburb, it was found that 22 per cent of the men, but only 8 per cent of the women, said that they drank on most days or every day; 89 per cent of the women said they took four drinks or less on a usual drinking occasion, whereas 51 per cent of the men claimed to drink that amount and 14 per cent said they drank in excess of eleven drinks on a usual drinking occasion.

Drunkenness in women is viewed with a great deal of disfavour and this may protect them from becoming alcoholic as often as men. The chauvinism of the "men only" bar can be interpreted as showing proper concern for the well-being of the females in the community! A further possibility is the unwillingness of doctors and others to recognise alcoholism in women. It will be interesting to see whether legislation towards sex-equality has any effects on these factors.

With regard to other drugs, male addicts outnumber female addicts except for the use of barbiturates and amphetamines by the middle-aged. In the past, the typical opiate addict was also female. In 1957 more than half were women but by 1967 almost 75 per cent were young men.

SOCIAL-CLASS FACTORS

A number of reports concerning social class amongst alcoholics have shown an over-representation of patients of social classes I and II (that is, the upper and upper-middle classes). Moss and Beresford Davies (1968) found that 26·4 per cent of the male alcoholics and 54·4 per cent of the female alcoholics were of social classes I and II. Although the data for the general population was not available it was assumed, quite reasonably, that the female alcoholics would be over-represented in classes I and II. Amongst the male alcoholics, the rates per 10,000 varied between the social classes, being highest in the unskilled at 90 per 10,000, and decreasing slightly through semi-skilled, managerial and professional groups, and being much lower in the non-manual and skilled manual groups (37/10,000).

Alcoholics attending particular treatment facilities may show a different social-class distribution from alcoholics in general, due to varying degrees of knowledge about the facilities available, and the trend for the better-educated to make proportionately greater use of those that existed than those less well-educated. In the clinic in the Edinburgh Royal Infirmary (Ritson and Hassall, 1970) there was found to be a preponderance of social class I and II patients. Middle-class patients were also found to be in excess of the proportion expected in a survey of Alcoholics Anonymous (Edwards *et al.*, 1966). Conversely, the alcoholics in Bailey's study were over-represented amongst those of lower socio-economic status.

In a study of 222 alcoholics in the Addiction Unit in Chester, one of us (Swinson, 1970) found that for the males, the highest proportion of cases came from the skilled (III) and unskilled (V) classes, whereas the females came largely from class III and IV backgrounds. Overall, only 5 per cent of the patients in the study were from social class I.

Particular occupations are at risk from alcoholism and they may well be over-represented in surveys of the clients of treatment agencies. Thus, people whose work brings frequent contact with alcohol tend to develop alcoholism more commonly than people whose work is totally divorced from alcohol. People working in the beer and liquor trade are constantly in contact with alcohol. In the Cambridgeshire study, 25 per cent of the social class II male alcoholics were publicans. Of course, in some cases, it may be that people whose drinking is becoming out of hand seek positions where they can spend a lot of time drinking without drawing attention to themselves and then manage to remain in the job until they develop full-blown alcoholism.

There has been less attention given to the study of socio-economic status in drug dependency. A great many reports have stressed the young addict's instability in employment, but due to the youth of the addicts, any study of social class is likely to be unreliable. The majority of heroin addicts are unemployed and in the study by Stinson and Ogborne (1970) only 26 per cent were wholly supporting themselves financially. The backgrounds of the heroin addicts in this study were found to show an excess of parents in the professional and managerial groups. Marijuana use initially was centred on the middle-class and young people in college and university. However, there are indications that the use of marijuana is spreading to young people of working-class status.

MARITAL STATUS

A consistent finding in studies of alcoholic populations has been the over-representation of people with no marital partner—the single, the widowed and the divorced. The divorced were in great excess in the Cambridgeshire study in both sexes, but in the female alcoholics an excess was also found among married women. In Chester, amongst in-patients it was found that there were very few single men in the sample, but over 30 per cent of the male patients were divorced. The females on the other hand matched the Cambridgeshire findings very closely, although again there were more divorced patients than expected.

It is to be expected that hospital and general population groups will differ, if only in the seriousness of the condition, and part of the change in the proportions of the various marital groups may be due to this variable.

The marital status of drug addicts has not been a subject of much research. Many of the addicts are young and would not be expected to have married. A proportion of them probably reject the idea of formalised relationships and this might bias the findings in comparison with the general population of the same age group.

REFERENCES

Bailey, M., Haberman, P. W. and Alksne, H., "The Epidemiology of Alcoholism in an Urban Residential Area", *Quarterly Journal of Studies on Alcohol*, 26: 19, 1965.

Bellinger, B. R., "Drug dependence in Psychiatric Admissions", *British Journal of Addiction*, 67: 215, 1972.

Bewley, T. H., "Recent Changes in the Pattern of Drug Abuse in the United Kingdom", *Bulletin on Narcotics*, 18 (4): 1, 1966.

Brain committee: Interdepartmental Committee on Drug Addiction, *Drug Addiction*, H.M.S.O., London, 1961.

Carney, P. A., Timms, M. W. H. and Stevenson, R. D., "The Social and Psychological Background of Young Drug Abusers in Dublin", *Br. J. Addict.*, 67: 199, 1972.

Connell, P. H., "Amphetamine Psychosis", *Maudsley Monograph No. 5*, Oxford University Press, London, 1958.

de Lint, J. and Schmidt, W., "Consumption Averages and Alcoholism Prevalence; A Brief Review of Epidemiological Investigations", *Br. J. Addict.*, 66 (2): 97, 1971.

Deveny, P. and Wilson, M., "Abuse of Barbiturates in an Alcoholic

Population", *Canadian Medical Association Journal*, 104: 219, 1971.

Dunlop, D., "The Use and Abuse of Psychotropic Drugs", *Proceedings of the Royal Society of Medicine*, 63: 1,279, 1970.

Edwards, G., "The Problem of Cannabis Dependence", *Practitioner*, 200: 226, 1968.

Edwards, G., Chandler, J. and Hensman, Celia, "Drinking in a London Suburb", *Quart. J. Stud. Alcohol*, Suppl. No. 6, *Surveys of Drinking and Abstaining, Urban, Suburban and National Studies*, 1971.

Edwards, G., Hensman, Celia, Hawker, A. and Williamson, V., "Who goes to Alcoholics Anonymous?", *Lancet*, ii: 382, 1966.

Gath, D., "The Male Drunk in Court", in Gath, D., Cook, T. and Hensman, Celia (eds.), op. cit.

Gath, D., Cook, T. and Hensman, Celia (eds.), *The Chronic Drunkenness Offence*, Pergamon, Oxford, 1969.

Glatt, M. M., *The Alcoholic and the Help he Needs*, Priory Press, Royston, U.K., 1970.

Glatt, M. M., "Alcoholism in General Practice", *Br. J. Addict.*, 54 (1): 47, 1957.

Harrison, B., *Drink and the Victorians*, Faber and Faber, London, 1971.

Hindmarch, I., "Drugs and Their Abuse: Age groups particularly at risk", *Br. J. Addict.*, 67: 209, 1972.

Jellinek, E. M., *The Disease Concept of Alcoholism*, Hillhouse Press, New Haven, Connecticut, 1960.

Kiloh, L. G. and Brandon, S., "Habituation and Addiction to Amphetamines", *British Medical Journal*, ii: 40, 1962.

Le Dain Commission, *Cannabis: A Report of the Commission of Inquiry into the Non-medical Use of drugs*, Information Canada, Ottawa, 1972.

Levengood, R., Lowinger, P. and Schooff, K., "Heroin Addiction in the suburbs: An Epidemiologic Study", *American Journal of Public Health*, 63: 209, 1973.

Lipp, M. A. and Benson, S. G., "Physician Use of Marijuana, Alcohol and Tobacco", *American Journal of Psychiatry*, 129 (5): 612, 1972.

Mitcheson, M., Hawks, D., Davison, J., Hitchens, L. and Malone, S., "Sedative Abuse by Heroin Addicts", *Lancet*, i: 606, 1970.

Moss, M. C. and Beresford Davis, E., *A Survey of Alcoholism in an English County*, Geigy, London, 1968.

National Council on Alcoholism Inc., New York, "Criteria for the Diagnosis of Alcoholism", *Annals of Internal Medicine*, 77: 249–58, 1972.

Noble, P. J. "Drug Taking in Delinquent Boys", *Br. Med. J.*, i: 102, 1970.

Parr, D., "Alcoholism in General Practice", *Br. J. Addict.*, 54: 25, 1957.

Pierce James, I., "The Changing Pattern of Narcotic Addiction in Britain, 1959–1969", *International Journal of Addictions*, 6 (1): 119, 1971.

Popham, R. E., "Indirect Methods of Alcoholism Prevalence Estimation: A Critical Evaluation", in Popham, R. E. (ed.), op. cit.

Popham, R. E. (ed.), *Alcohol and Alcoholism*, University of Toronto, 1970.

Prys-Williams, G., *Chronic Alcoholics*, Rowntree Social Science Trust, London, 1965.

Richards, L. G. and Carroll, E. E., "Illicit Drug Use and Addiction in the United States", *Public Health Reports*, 85 (12): 1,035, 1970.

Ritson, E. B. and Hassall, C., *The Management of Alcoholism*, Livingstone, Edinburgh, 1970.

Scott, P. D. and Wilcox, D. R. C., "Delinquency and the Amphetamines", *British Journal of Psychiatry*, III: 865, 1965.

Smart, R. G., "Illicit Drug Use in Canada: A Review of Recent Epidemiology with clues for Prevention", *Int. J. Addict.*, 6 (3): 383–405, 1971.

Smart, R. G., Fejer, D. and White, J., "Drug Use Trends in Metropolitan Toronto: A Study of Changes from 1968 to 1972", *Journal of the Addiction Research Foundation*, Toronto, 1st Feb. 1973.

Spear, H. B., "The Growth of Heroin Addiction in the United Kingdom", *Br. J. Addict.*, 66 (2): 97, 1969.

Stinson, G. V. and Ogborne, A., "A Survey of a Representative Sample of Addicts Prescribed Heroin at London Clinics", *Bull. Narcotics*, 22 (4): 13, 1970.

Swinson, R. P., *A Study of Genetic Polymorphism in an Alcoholic Population*, M.D. thesis, Liverpool University, unpublished.

Walsh, D., "Alcoholism in the Republic of Ireland", *Br. J. Psychiatry*, 115: 1,021, 1969.

Warder, J. and Ross, C., "Alcoholism and Its Treatment in Scotland; A Critical Review", *Br. J. Addict.*, 66 (2): 110, 1971.

Whitehead, P. C., Smart, R. G. and Laforest, L., "Multiple Drug Use among Marijuana Smokers in Eastern Canada", *Int. J. Addict.*, 7 (1): 179, 1972.

Wiener, R. S. P., *Drugs and Schoolchildren*, Longman, London, 1970.

Wootton Report: *Report by the Advisory Committee on Drug Dependence: Cannabis*, H.M.S.O., London, 1968.

Wright, J. D., "Problems of Drug Addiction", *Proc. R. Soc. Med.*, 63: 725, 1970.

Young, J., *The Drug Takers*, Granada Publishing, London, 1971.

Zacune, J. and Hensman, Celia, *Drugs, Alcohol and Tobacco in Britain*, Heinemann, London, 1971.

3 Drugs and their effects

Most psycho-active drugs have now been studied extensively in animals and man under carefully controlled conditions, and those studies have contributed to an understanding of how human behaviour can be influenced by chemical substances. What is true, however, of a drug used in animals in a laboratory is certainly not necessarily true of drugs affecting human beings in the outside world, and there is any number of reasons why this should be so. Some of the major pharmacological and psychological factors will be discussed in this chapter.

Under certain circumstances, profound behavioural changes can occur in the absence of an active substance being taken. This so-called placebo response is a very important one, illustrated dramatically in the following anecdote:

> In an experiment we were conducting on a group of students, half the subjects were given a large amount of alcohol and half were given water, the smell and taste being carefully camouflaged so that they seemed to be identical. Various responses were seen, but one young man became extremely unsteady on his feet and very confused—the typical picture of a drunkard. So severely was he affected that he was unable to complete the requested tasks, and was taken home by car. When he got out of the car he staggered, fell on the pavement, and crawled off babbling incoherently. Two days later he bravely completed the second part of the experiment

without difficulty and behaved perfectly normally. When the drug-code was broken it was found that he had had water only in the first part, and an amount of alcohol equivalent to six brandies (drunk in five minutes) in the second part of the experiment. There was no possibility of a mistake having been made!

It is a common experience that sometimes we become intoxicated on a small amount of an alcoholic drink, and sometimes we remain sober, and at the same time we can experience quite different moods, sometimes jolly, sometimes miserable. Drugs tend not to have specific actions, but to alter in a general way the emotional arousal of the body. Changes in arousal may or may not be appreciated by an individual and the degree of arousal can be constant for a variety of emotional feelings. A key factor in inducing internal changes, and evoked responses, is the environmental situation at a given time. If, after having had a drink or two alone, we go to a noisy and happy party, the external cues have a feed-back effect on our altered physiological state; we then label that state one of "happiness" and our behaviour alters appropriately. However, if the solitary drinking is due to feelings of sadness, and that feeling is intense, a move to a cheerful environment may not induce mood-elevation, and in fact may result in just the opposite.

The effects of drugs can, therefore, vary with the mood of an individual, his recent and past experiences and the perceptions available to him. The sum of all our past experiences interact with genetic contributions to form personality, and various personality factors are known to affect response to drugs.

Other factors are the expectancy of a drug's effects, motivation, group influences on behaviour, fatigue, and previous drug experiences. An individual who smokes cannabis for the first time may get no pleasurable effects from it and, indeed, the first experience may be unpleasant. Pre-existing anxiety may be one contributory factor, but the whole stimulus situation is important in altering his mental "set". With continued use, given the appropriate external cues, an alteration occurs in the interpretation of the internal state, which comes to be viewed more and more as pleasurable. Obviously, the external cues that determine these experiences include not only the immediate ones, but the whole culture and sub-culture in which the drug user lives, as well as his own personality, attitudes, and value system.

Added to these complex and intricately-related variables are a host of pharmacological factors. Drugs vary in the rate at which they are absorbed; drugs taken intramuscularly or intravenously usually have a much quicker onset of action than drugs taken orally, although inhalation of volatile substances may produce very rapid effects. Absorption of oral drugs can depend on the preparation of the drug, physiological changes in the stomach and intestine, and the intake of food. When drugs are ingested they have to be distributed to the sites of action, and may be bound to proteins in the blood, decreasing the amount of active substance at any one time. Many drugs are not active unless they undergo metabolic changes in the body, and many active drugs are broken down at different rates by bodily enzymes, or are excreted unchanged.

Added to this is an acquired resistance to the effects of a drug given repeatedly, a phenomenon known as tolerance. This can be due to cellular changes affecting the body's sensitivity, or it can be due to induced changes in the enzymes which break down the drug. The dose of a drug has an obvious effect on an organism's functioning, but the effect is not necessarily on a simple proportional basis. Drugs in the nervous system often exert their effect by altering the balance between different functions. The balance may be shifted in one direction by a given range of concentration of a drug, but if the concentration is altered up or down, a quite different effect may ensue. Also, many drugs accumulate in the body and the cumulative effect can be quite different from the acute effect. In addition to this, prolonged use may begin to produce actual physical changes: for example, an individual may smoke cigarettes for many years with little apparent ill-effect. Then at some stage bronchitis begins to develop and thereafter, in an unfortunate minority, lung cancer.

If tolerance develops to one drug, it may also develop towards other drugs similar in structure or action. Such a condition is known as cross-tolerance, well-known examples of which occur between morphine and heroin, and between alcohol and barbiturates.

ADDICTION, HABITUATION AND DEPENDENCY

There is frequently confusion about the way these terms are used. Drug *addiction* is defined as a state of periodic or chronic intoxication, produced by the repeated consumption of a drug. Its characteristics include the following:

1. An overpowering desire or need to continue taking the drug and to obtain it by any means.
2. A tendency to increase the dose, though some patients may stay indefinitely on a stationary dose.
3. A psychological and physical dependence on the effects of the drug.
4. The appearance of a characteristic abstinence syndrome in a subject from whom the drug is withdrawn.
5. An effect detrimental to the individual and to society.

Drug *habituation* is a condition resulting from the continued consumption of a drug. Its characteristics include the following:

1. A desire to continue taking the drug for the sense of improved well being which it engenders.
2. Little or no tendency to increase the dose.
3. Some degree of psychological dependence on the effect of the drug: but absence of physical dependence and hence of an abstinence syndrome.
4. Detrimental effects, if any, primarily on the individual himself.

These are the standard definitions of the World Health Organisation Expert Committee (1964). Tolerance is associated with increasing dependence, and is a feature of addiction. Addiction is therefore largely physical, and habituation totally psychological, but the distinction is not a sharp one. At what stage does a desire become an overpowering desire? It is no longer held that physical and psychological "addictions" are separate, or that one may exist in the absence of the other. Without doubt psychological addiction has a bodily component in which physiological changes occur in the hypothalamic region of the brain, the centre responsible for motivation and drive. Similarly, physical addiction is not a single entity either and withdrawal features can be "learned" by conditioning processes.

There have been many debates about suitable terminology and

these still continue. It is important to use terms in a consistent way, but definitions can become so strict and rigid that they prove an embarrassment. The W.H.O. Expert Committee considered the often confusing ways in which the term "addiction" has been used, and in 1969 decided to introduce the new term "dependence".

Dependence on drugs is "a state, psychic and sometimes physical, resulting from the interaction between a living organism and a drug, characterized by behavioural and other responses that always include a compulsion to take the drug on a continuous or periodic basis in order to experience its psychic effects and sometimes to avoid the discomfort of its absence". Dependence therefore applies to single drugs, although there is a recognition that people can abuse and be dependent on several drugs. The committee defined dependence as applying to morphine, barbiturates, cocaine, cannabis, amphetamines and hallucinogens, but of course there are as many kinds of dependence as there are drugs. "Dependence" does not imply any socially undesirable effects resulting from the continued use of drugs, whereas "addiction" does imply a social and public health risk as well as danger to the individual. It is because of this that we think "addiction" still merits a place as a valuable descriptive term, and indeed it continues to be freely employed and liberally interpreted. It is most commonly used as a synonym for "heroin addiction" and would never be used in connection with cannabis or LSD. The term "drug abuse" is more appropriate in these cases, referring to persistent, sporadic, excessive, often illegal, drug use which occurs in a way unacceptable to normal medical practice.

Patients and drug-abusers commonly take more than one drug at a time and this, too, can cause complications. Sometimes two drugs may act in a simple additive way, but often a potentiating effect occurs when the action of two drugs given together has a greater effect than the sum of the two given separately. Examples will be given of drugs working in opposite or antagonistic ways, whilst with some combinations, totally unpredictable results may be seen.

CLASSIFICATION

Classification is an important aspect of psychopharmacology, which is the study of the action of drugs on the brain and, consequently, on the behaviour of human beings. Difficulties arise, as there are no universally accepted criteria as to whether or not a substance should be called a drug. A discussion on this point would not help a great deal as drugs have, for practical reasons, to be defined in different ways.

Psycho-active drugs can be classed according to their structure, their effect on specific behaviours or their effects on "target" behaviours in patients, but are more usually classified by their non-specific effects in causing excitation, depression, or a more disturbing action on the central nervous system. Most classifications assume that only three kinds of general action can occur, although an incredible number of technical terms tend to obscure this. The World Health Organisation has described five categories, but these still fit into only three global groups, suggesting elevation, reduction, and distortion of mental activity.

Neuroleptics	e.g. phenothiazines, butyrophenones (often known as major tranquillisers).
Anxiolytic sedatives	e.g. benzodiazepines (minor tranquillisers), barbiturates (sedative-hypnotics), alcohol.
Anti-depressants	e.g. mono-amine oxidase inhibitors, tricyclic antidepressants.
Psycho-stimulants	e.g. amphetamines, cocaine.
Psychodysleptics	e.g. LSD, mescaline, cannabis.

Obviously such a classification covers all drugs that have a therapeutic effect on mental disorders, and is therefore clinico-pathologically orientated. Some of the group, e.g. the anti-depressants, are very rarely abused, and are therefore largely outside the scope of this book. The classification excludes the opiate group of analgesic drugs and the anaesthetic solvents, both of which are important in the context of drug abuse.

Let us now consider in a little more detail the more important of the above substances involved in abuse or habituation.

Barbiturates

Barbiturates were introduced into medical practice early this century, and they have been widely used in a variety of conditions.

They are sedative, hypnotic and anti-convulsant, and have been used in anxiety and depressive states, insomnia, physical and psychosomatic disorders and epilepsy, and in general anaesthesia and continuous narcosis. They can be administered orally, intramuscularly or intravenously, the speed of onset of effects varying with the method, dose and the particular form given. Many hundreds of barbiturate drugs have been described, usually under the headings of "long-", "medium-" and "short-acting", although this distinction is not very meaningful.

In low doses they act as cerebral stimulants, and this is reflected in a change of brain-wave pattern as measured by the electroencephalograph (E.E.G.). However, the likeliest effect of a single effective dosage is cerebral depression, which can range from mild sedation to deep sleep. Reaction times are slowed down, co-ordination is impaired, and motor tasks such as simulated driving tests can be seriously affected. Subtle effects can be measured up to twenty-two hours after a single dose. It is inadvisable to drive whilst on daytime medication, and it is highly likely that barbiturates have contributed to many road traffic accidents, and also accidents in the home, especially in older people, who can be very sensitive to their effects.

The sleep that barbiturates induce is not normal sleep. The part of sleep associated with rapid eye movements (R.E.M. sleep) is decreased though there is a rebound increase when the drug is discontinued. Tolerance to a hypnotic dose develops extremely rapidly, so that a vicious-circle effect ensues whereby barbiturates need to be continued to prevent the withdrawal effects consisting of nightmares, a feeling of having slept badly or, often, of actual severe insomnia. Drug-induced sleep is often followed by a "hangover" during which complaints are made of headaches, a general muzziness and an inability to concentrate until the effects have worn off.

The effects of barbiturates are very similar to alcohol and are equally unpredictable. Single doses can produce excitation or disinhibition, euphoria or contentment, sedation or depression and irritability. Tolerance builds up over a period of a few weeks, leading to an increase in dosage and the total amount taken. Unfortunately, tolerance to the adverse effects does not build up to the same degree, so that toxic features appear. Emotional instability and loss of control, mood changes, poor judgment amounting often to confusion, and other personality changes can occur. A characteristic syndrome of general apathy, narrowing of interest, increased suspiciousness, irritability and deterioration in personal standards, is often observed. Epileptics of long-standing treated by barbiturates often show these features, which may well be due to the drugs rather than to personality changes resulting from the epilepsy itself.

Barbiturates probably have multiple sites of action in the central nervous system (C.N.S.), but an important one is thought to be the reticular formation. The reticular formation is a part of the grey matter of the central nervous system, situated in the middle of the spinal cord and extending upwards into the lower parts of the brain. It carries important data from the sensory systems, filters much of this information, and is responsible for alerting the organism in a general way. Barbiturates depress its action directly and therefore alter the sensory filtering mechanism of the brain stem.

Barbiturates may be excreted unchanged in the urine, but for the most part are broken down by enzymes in the liver. In common with many other drugs, they have the effect of stimulating most liver enzymes, including the ones responsible for their own breakdown. This is probably an important factor in the development of tolerance and physical addiction. Such an effect is known as "enzyme induction" and can have very important and wide-reaching consequences. Many drugs are metabolised by the liver and the concomitant administration of barbiturates can greatly alter the action of these other drugs. It is well known that barbiturates interact with many drugs and can act in either an additive or a potentiating way. The best-known example is with alcohol. Such interactions can sometimes be used beneficially; for example, tablets of barbiturate-amphetamine mixtures were once employed extensively in the treatment of depression and this had some value, before true anti-depressants became available. However, they have now been discontinued because their therapeutic effect is unpredictable and there is a real danger of habituation.

Medical opinion about the usage of barbiturates varies a great deal. Many authorities still believe that they are valuable, but an increasing number are concerned about the very serious adverse effects that can occur. Prescriptions, although still numbered in millions each year, are beginning to drop in number. We ourselves feel that there are numerous more suitable alternative drugs now available which will make barbiturates obsolete in the near future.

Alcoholic beverages

Alcoholic beverages contain amounts of ethyl alcohol as follows

Beer	3–8 per cent
Wines	8–14 per cent
Sherry	15–20 per cent
Spirits	40–50 per cent

Although ethyl alcohol is the main active constituent of all of them, they each contain a variety of other substances, termed congeners. Vodka is the purest of the spirits and contains few congeners, but whisky contains small amounts of organic acids, esters, aldehydes and methyl alcohol, as well as substances absorbed from the wooden casks in which it is stored. Wines contain greater amounts of similar congeners, but beer contains large quantities of carbohydrate together with proteins, minerals, carbon dioxide and vitamins.

Congeners on the whole are of very little practical significance, but industrial spirit, which contains 96 per cent ethyl alcohol, also contains methyl alcohol which has a severe toxic effect on the nervous system.

Alcohol is freely water-soluble, and is easily absorbed by simple diffusion through the intestine, more so in the small intestine than from the stomach. The ingestion of food slows down absorption. There is a relationship between concentration and absorption, 30 per cent solutions being most readily absorbed. Alcohol rapidly reaches the tissues and passes freely across blood, brain and placental barriers. There is a great individual variation in the rate of elimination from the body, but the liver is the main centre of metabolism; 90–95 per cent of all ingested alcohol is metabolised, and 75 per cent of this is by the liver. A small proportion, 1–3 per cent, is excreted by the lungs and the remainder is lost in the urine. Alcohol is broken down by an enzyme, alcohol dehydrogenase, to acetaldehyde, and ultimately is oxidised to carbon dioxide and water.

The physiological effects of alcohol are numerous and of great interest. Large doses can initially increase the level of blood sugar, but can later cause it to fall, sometimes to disastrously low levels. It reduces the formation of glucose in the liver, and accelerates the deposition of fat in the liver cells. The heart rate rises with moderate doses of alcohol, but the mechanical efficiency of the heart as a pump is reduced. Alcohol does *not* increase the amount of blood supplied to the heart, and is therefore not helpful in angina. Indeed, it is positively harmful, as it increases blood flow in other areas, thereby reducing blood flow through the coronary vessels themselves. Blood flow to the brain is increased, as is peripheral circulation to the arms and legs.

When the kidneys excrete alcohol, the output of urine is greatly increased so that there is an overall depletion of body fluids. If the dehydration is severe after a heavy drinking bout, the result is a "hangover", as the brain tissues are deprived of fluid. (The second simplest way to prevent a hangover is to drink a pint or two of water or milk after a drinking spell. The simplest is not to drink too much alcohol.)

Surprisingly, the effects of alcohol on human sexual function have been very little studied, but it is known that there is depression of erectile ability in the male and interference with ejaculation. In both sexes, moderate amounts of alcohol often reduce social inhibitions and sexual drive may increase in these circumstances. This is fine for the woman, unless of course she becomes so uninhibited as to behave unwisely, but a man may find that his performance does not measure up to the strength of his urges. A little alcohol may prevent anxiety that is interfering with sexual intercourse, but a lot may well cause the man to be temporarily impotent. Prolonged abuse of alcohol can sometimes lead to permanent impotence.

Alcohol in high concentration increases acid production in the stomach, and has a direct irritant action on the gastric lining.

In low dosages, alcohol increases the sensitivity of the nervous system, but in higher dosages acts as a depressant. Moderate doses excite the brain centres by a direct action and by weakening the inhibitory action of the reticular formation. Temporary arousal by stimulation of the reticular formation gives way to depression at all levels of the brain. Co-ordination is impaired by an effect on the cerebellum, and the motor and sensory systems become less efficient. Memory for words deteriorates and performance on the verbal and non-verbal components of standard intelligence tests declines. Moderate dosages impair accuracy more than speed in arithmetic tests, though low doses can actually improve performance in difficult or unfamiliar intellectual exercises.

Alcohol in many circumstances impairs learning, but the basis of the impairment is not well understood. Animals that are trained and tested whilst drugged may show impairment, not because learning is disrupted but because the drug affects the performance of learned responses. In addition, animals tested in undrugged states, after learning in drugged states, may perform badly because they are unable to "recall" information learned under the drug's influence. Such a situation is called "state-dependent" learning and occurs when a response learned in a given internal state shows a disproportionate decrement when the internal state of the learner is changed. Experiments carried out in animals are now being repeated in humans to see whether this very important phenomenon can be demonstrated. It has been found in both alcoholics and normals that disproportionate decrements do occur after learning tasks with and without alcohol. In some experiments we carried out in volunteers, we found that with a variety of simple and complex learning tasks, we were able to demonstrate some state-dependent learning effects with alcohol but even more with barbiturates (Ley *et al.*, 1972). The existence of such an effect has many wide implications theoretically and practically in alcoholism and many fields of general psychiatry.

The clinical state of drunkenness is so familiar that there is no need to dwell on the overt signs. Drunkenness is a state of disinhibition, in which control of instinctual urges is relaxed, and behaviour may cross over the bounds dictated by prudence and common sense. A conventional medical explanation is that the phylogenetically younger elements of the nervous system, notably the cerebral cortex, are more sensitive than the older parts of the brain and suppression of them leads to the disinhibition. In a drunken state there is clear evidence of sensorimotor incapacity, common to all drunkards to some degree, but drunken behaviour may be minimal or maximal, ranging from tactlessness and silliness to extremes of depravity. It has been argued by some that an organic explanation for drunken comportment is quite untenable, and an alternative social explanation has been expounded by MacAndrew and Edgerton (1970). They give apparently clear evidence that the presence of alcohol in the body does not even conduce to disinhibition, much less inevitably produce a drunken state, but that drunkenness is the result of "social programming". People learn about drunkenness from their culture, and accept and act upon the misunderstandings imparted to them in the course of socialisation. The authors contrast the Abipone Indians of Uruguay, whose behaviour under alcohol turns from taciturn civility to outright savagery, whilst another South American tribe, the Yaruma, become totally withdrawn, and show no evidence at all of disinhibition. They demonstrate convincingly that many cultures become withdrawn and that the Yaruma are by no means unique, and they claim that genetic differences would not explain the variation.

These workers also examine in some detail the extraordinary susceptibility of the North American Indian to alcohol. They feel that the Indians learned by a modelling process the inebriated behaviour of white traders and trappers and incorporated alcohol in their culture, literally and figuratively, as the embodiment of evil. The equating of drunkenness with being possessed by evil spirits absolved them from personal responsibility for the behavioural excesses committed whilst intoxicated. The drunkenness problem amongst present-day Indians is a reflection, not of increased genetically-determined susceptibility, but of the alcoholic excesses that their society tolerates.

It is worth considering that the contradictory reports of the effects of smoking cannabis by Eastern and Western observers might have a similar explanation by social learning processes and cultural modification.

Amphetamines

Amphetamines have been in clinical use for many years. They are stimulants and act via the sympathetic part of the autonomic nervous system. Originally developed for the treatment of asthma, a change of emphasis arose when their actions on the C.N.S. became clear.

It is believed that they act in the upper part of the reticular formation, causing or accentuating an alerting response. They lessen fatigue, increase wakefulness, and many lead to a subjective feeling of confidence, security, and enhanced ability. The effects of single doses have been extensively studied in animals and man, but the evidence conflicts as to the specific effects of psychological and physical functioning, and can be perplexing to interpret. Improvement in physical performance (e.g. swimming and running) appears to be best in those already fatigued, rather than those who are rested and fresh. This is also in general true of intellectual tasks. Amphetamines may help in solving problems with a cognitive content, particularly where speed is necessary, but more complex tasks may not be affected in the same way and there may be an increase in the number of errors made. In animal experiments, amphetamines have often been used to accelerate the acquisition of conditioned responses. Reaction times tend to be significantly reduced although there is great individual variation. A striking feature is the subjective report of increased ability to concentrate, even in the absence of objective evidence. Most people comment favourably on the subjective feeling, but some, particularly with higher doses, report increased tension feelings, restlessness, inability to concentrate and difficulty in thinking. These are perhaps features of "over-arousal", which reminds us of the relationship between arousal and performance, the inverted U-shaped Yerkes-Dodson curve. (As arousal and motivation increases, performance increases, but this eventually reaches a plateau, and further increase in arousal can actually decrease performance.)

Amphetamines have been claimed to be of benefit in depression, behaviour disorders in children, in the control of psychopathy and as appetite suppressants. In depression, the symptoms that respond are the neurasthenic ones—complaints of slowing down, weakness, loss of concentration, etc.—but other anti-depressants are now preferred. The indication in over-active children with behaviour disorders and in delinquents and adult psychopaths might seem surprising and is an example of a paradoxical effect (as in the same way tranquillisers may occasionally provoke an *increase* in aggression as monitored by psychological testing). Unfortunately, the beneficial effects usually prove to be short-lived. This is a characteristic of all amphetamine derivatives, and illustrates how tolerance develops fairly quickly. Animals on amphetamines lose both weight and appetite, but both of these increase again after only a short time. This is also true of appetite suppressants, most of which are related to amphetamines and which are used in humans in the treatment of simple obesity. They probably have no place whatsoever in the management of the overweight, and it would be equally true to say that amphetamines have no place in the management of any medical or psychiatric state. Schizophrenia, for example, can be intensified by amphetamines, and attacks of mania precipitated in those so disposed. The only exception might be the treatment of narcolepsy, a rare condition, related to epilepsy, in which attacks of normal sleep occur at repeated intervals during the day.

Amphetamine-barbiturate mixtures have been in vogue until recently. Amphetamines can be taken orally or by injection. Injections of methylamphetamine were commonly used to induce abreactions in neurotic patients, but the intravenous forms have disappeared from the market and there are in many parts of the country voluntarily operated bans on prescribing the oral forms too. No one should lament their passing, because of their harmful side-effects and their marked tendency to cause habituation.

LSD (lysergic acid diethylamide)

There are many examples in medicine of important discoveries made by accident. The effects of LSD were discovered in such a way when a Swiss chemist inadvertently experienced its effects whilst researching on ergotamine derivatives. Many more hallucinogenic drugs have now been described, including mescaline, which produces very similar effects to LSD and possibly acts centrally in the same way, although the structures of the two substances differ greatly. The effects of hallucinogenic drugs have many parallels with the psychotic features of schizophrenia, and the similarities of the effects of the two compounds stimulated great interest in a possible metabolic cause of schizophrenia.

As we have seen, no drugs are predictable in their effects, but some are less predictable than others, and may produce great distortions of mood, feelings and perceptions rather than simple accentuations of such experiences. LSD, mescaline, and psilocybin can do this and they produce their effects with only minute amounts, e.g. fifty to a hundred micrograms of LSD will produce the effects of an average "trip". The effects of a single dose of LSD, taken orally, come on after fifteen minutes, reach a maximum in two to four hours and pass off over twenty-four hours. Many of the observable and measurable effects are due to a stimulant action—a rise in blood pressure, sweating, dilation of pupils, increase in muscle tension, often accompanied by nausea, headaches and light-headedness—and it is likely that LSD, too, works on the arousal part of the reticular system, not directly, but by increasing the amount and variety of incoming stimuli.

No characteristic mood changes occur—indeed mood can be volatile, changing from second to second, from anxiety to elation or from contentment to depression. A characteristic feeling is of anxiety, occasionally of dread, and this may be accompanied by agitation, although this can be punctuated by attacks of incongruous laughter.

Thought processes can be disturbed in rate, form and content, and may be speeded up or slowed down. Concentration can be impaired and thought processes loosened, and extraneous ideas can begin to creep into thought-sequences. All these features may also be seen in schizophrenia, as may delusional mood—a strange phenomenon in which something is expected to happen, often with a very frightening implication. Actual delusions can occur in this state, although they are not common, but vaguely-formed paranoid ideas, persecutory or grandiose, are frequently described and misinterpretation of these phenomena can take on mystical or magical significance in the individual's mind.

Depersonalisation or derealisation phenomena are very characteristic. These are described in many ways, but intimate a change in experience, a feeling of unreality, a dreamy state in which external objects and bodily awareness are appreciated in a new way. Perceptual processes in all sensory modalities may be affected in some degree, from mild to severe, although occasionally they are not reported. Of these, visual changes are most common. Objects may appear to change in contour, two-dimensional figures can be seen in three dimensions or colour, shade and intensity may be altered. Macropsia—an increase in size, micropsia—a decrease in size, dysmegalopsia—distortion of size, are all commonly reported. Illusions of auditory, tactile and olfactory modalities may occur, or even hallucinations occasionally. These tend to be visual rather than auditory, and elementary rather than complex. Fully-formed visual hallucinations of people, religious figures, etc., tend to occur only in situations which would be expected to evoke strong emotions. Many experiences appear to be cross-modal (i.e. a sight causing a sensation of sound, etc.) and can be so elaborate and complex that it is difficult to express them in words, although many have exercised their literary talents in trying to do so in a meaningful way. Whilst many reports seem extravagant, carefully controlled studies have affirmed the breakdown of reasoning capacity, inability to gauge time, and a decrease in articulacy and the ability to plan ahead. A strange feature of LSD consumption is the "flashback" experience, which can be delayed as much as six months, when the experiences of taking the drug can be spontaneously re-lived, the event lasting from seconds to much longer periods. No explanation can be given for these episodes, which can occur without apparent provocation, although they may indicate a permanent organic brain change which can be triggered off, given the right circumstances.

It has been suggested that those who react most to LSD are the more artistic, more creative and more sensitive, but evidence for this is rather tenuous. It might be predicted that people suffering from pre-existing psychoses would be more susceptible to the effects, and certainly it is recorded that schizoid personalities, who are usually regarded as predisposed to psychoses, have developed frank schizophrenia after taking LSD. In spite of the obvious dangers, LSD has been used extensively in psychiatric treatment, but there is no hard evidence that it is of any help in schizophrenia, neurosis or personality disorder, and most doctors no longer prescribe it. There are some reports which suggest that alcoholics benefit because of the revealing insights it gives into their behaviour, and even suggestions that autistic children grow up to be less withdrawn, but the authors would suggest that scepticism is perhaps more appropriate than enthusiasm for a drug which has potentially very serious and uncontrollable effects even in normal people.

Cannabis

Cannabis is a generic term used to cover the products derived from the Indian hemp plant, *Cannabis sativa*. The dried leaves of the plant are generally referred to as marijuana, and the resinous exudate of the flowering tops as hashish, although there are many local names for the preparations. In the U.K., use of the resin form is usual, whereas in the U.S.A. marijuana, usually less potent, is much more commonly used. The activity of both forms is now known to be due to a group of chemicals known as tetrahydrocannabinols, or THCs. Both are normally smoked in cigarette form, the usual dose containing 3–5 mg of Δ^1THC with a probable dosage range of 0·5–10 mg. Plants vary greatly in the amount of active constituents they contain, the differences probably depending on genetic factors, soil factors, and exposure to sunlight, so that cannabis grown in the U.K. contains virtually none, whereas 100 g of plant grown in the East will yield 5 g of resin, of which five per cent or so is active.

Cannabis is absorbed by the lining of the respiratory tract after inhalation and up to 40–50 per cent of THC is transferred from a cigarette. It can be absorbed after oral administration but is rarely taken in this way. Tetrahydrocannabinols are broken down by a process of hydroxylation and excreted in the urine and faeces, but only slowly so that accumulation in the body is a real danger with repeated usage.

The physical effects of cannabis consumption are mild, comprising increased pulse rate, rise in blood pressure, dilation of the conjunctivae giving redness of the eyes, dilation of the pupils, occasionally breathlessness and choking, and neurological features such as unsteadiness, muscular twitches, tremor of the tongue, and changes in the deep reflexes. These are rarely noticed or complained of unless severe, but vomiting, vertigo, and collapse have all been recorded. The severity of the symptoms depends as much on the individual as the dose, but an intake of 10 mg of Δ^1THC would normally cause severe intoxication. Good and bad effects come on within half an hour, and last for three to four hours.

The psychological effects can be altered by learning experiences, so that the effects in naïve and habitual subjects can be very dissimilar. Anxiety and apprehension may be the first reported subjective feelings, followed by a dreamy state with euphoria and a loss of reality sensation. Predominantly the effects are agreeable, with distortion of time and space, body-image changes, depersonalisation, and illusions or even hallucinations. Observable changes can be hyper-activity, irritability, incoherence, agitation, silliness, suggestibility, and sometimes lassitude and sleepiness occur later.

It is alleged that cannabis improves non-verbal communication, but disorders of thinking are often evident, so that conversation can become unintelligible, and can even stop abruptly in mid-stream. This may be caused by a memory deficit which can be severe in many, yet negligible in others. In controlled studies, using placebo cigarettes, 5 mg of THC given to volunteers has caused clear decrements in mental and motor tasks, under both non-stressed and stressed conditions. Earlier tests had suggested impairment of intellectual ability in both speed and accuracy in naïve subjects, whilst in experienced smokers there was sometimes an improvement. There was evidence that simulated driving tests were less disorganised with cannabis than with alcohol, although there is a problem in defining equivalent doses. However, in a comparison of the effects of 70 g alcohol against 300 mg of cannabis resin, cannabis produced a significantly greater impairment in complex rather than in simple tasks, especially in problems requiring consecutive steps for their solution. Conclusions have recently been made that cannabis does have profound effects on the skills and judgments necessary for driving, so that motoring during cannabis intoxication may well be a hazardous undertaking. Cannabis may not have a great effect on information already stored, but it is possible that it blocks ultra-short-term memory in a profound way.

It is perhaps too easy to over-emphasise the deleterious *sequelae* of cannabis, when there are thousands of users who deny any serious effects on their functioning. Well-informed opinion states that tolerance and physical dependence do not occur, but experiments in chronically treated rats, albeit with large doses, have demonstrated abstinence signs after cessation. These include aggression, tremors, yawning, photophobia, anorexia and odd behaviours such as biting and licking of the paws, eating faeces, and even self-administration after abstinence has been observed. Miras believes that tolerance occurs in humans, describing Greeks who ingest large amounts by smoking through water pipes, becoming tolerant to 150 mg of Δ^1tetrahydrocannabinol, and gradually losing their abilities to undertake social and economic activities. Little is yet known about long-term consumption, but Eastern literature is clear about a syndrome of increasing physical and mental deterioration, to the point of total apathy and incompetence. Animal models have now been developed to study cannabis effects, but although there is as yet no evidence of an "a-motivational" syndrome from the laboratory, rats do lose their ability to continue working for rewards. Cannabis given to schizophrenic patients causes many to develop hallucinations and some to pass into stupor or catatonia, but it is not clear whether cannabis given to normals can precipitate a psychosis.

Cannabis has occasionally been used medically to treat those addicted to more serious drugs, but it is doubtful whether it will become universally accepted as an efficacious agent.

Opium alkaloids

Morphine is the most important of the many alkaloids derived from opium, the dried juice of the poppy, *Papaver somniferum.* Many other alkaloids, including heroin, methadone and codeine, are easily synthesised from morphine. Morphine is of great historical importance in medicine, having been used for centuries in the relief of pain. Perhaps the greatest benefit is the relief of the intense, constricting pain of a coronary thrombosis, but it is also of value in surgical emergencies, once they have been diagnosed. It is also useful in the treatment of certain kinds of heart failure, unproductive coughs, and for diarrhoea. Pethidine and heroin are also widely used for the relief of pain, but methadone has few indications other than its use in treating opiate addiction.

Medically, morphine is usually given by injection, but it can also be absorbed by mouth and by inhalation (as in opium snuff or opium smoking). Heroin, a synthetic opiate, is usually given by injection, whilst methadone is well-absorbed orally. The maximum effect is reached one to two hours after an intramuscular dose, and the effects begin to wear off after four or five hours. The onset and duration of heroin's effects are similar, but with methadone the onset of its actions is very slow, yet they persist for a long time. The mechanism of the action of morphine is uncertain, though it is the subject of a vast amount of research. Heroin is rapidly changed in the body to morphine, which probably accounts for the similarity of its activity to morphine. Most of a single dose of morphine is excreted in the urine within twenty-four hours, as the unchanged substance or as breakdown products, but traces can still be found even at forty-eight hours. If preparations containing codeine are taken (and this includes many proprietary headache tablets) traces of morphine can be identified in the urine, thus possibly leading to misinterpretation.

In small doses, morphine causes a depression of consciousness to the point of drowsiness, an inability to concentrate, and reduced physical as well as mental activity. The commonest mood change is a state of euphoria, although panic and anxiety reactions are not unknown. Morphine directly stimulates a part of the brain—the medulla—which contains an emetic centre and this may lead to nausea or occasionally vomiting, depending on the dose. This is not usually distressing, as the reaction to unpleasant events is reduced. Experiments have shown that morphine alters the pain-threshold, reducing the appreciation of pain in those suffering from it, or altering their ability to tolerate the discomfort. The response to other sensory inputs is not markedly affected, and patients often report that they feel the pain in exactly the same way, but it no longer worries them. An undesirable effect of morphine is its ability to depress the brain-centres responsible for respiration, and this can lead to unfortunate complications of administration in people whose respiratory functioning is impaired.

Since tolerance to morphine and heroin build up rapidly, far more quickly than to methadone, this is a feature which has important therapeutic implications for the latter drug.

Habituation to drugs in this group is sometimes horrifyingly easily acquired. In Britain, until quite recently, this often occurred as a complication of medical treatment—not uncommonly, the patient was dying from a painful terminal illness and pain-relief was more important than the theoretical considerations of addiction. It also occurred in those with ready access to the drugs, such as doctors, nurses and pharmacists. Nowadays, many addicts are young and have become "hooked" as a result of participation in the drug scene. The opium alkaloids are indispensable in medical practice, but otherwise they are to be avoided like the plague. There are people who can take them or leave them: we see the dreadful results of trying to do this ending in failure.

REFERENCES

Barr, T., *Psychopharmacology*, Williams and Wilkins, Baltimore, 1969.
Claridge, G., *Drugs and Human Behaviour*, Allen Lane, The Penguin

Press, London, 1970.
Joyce, C. R. B., "Cannabis", *British Journal of Hospital Medicine*, 4: 162–6, 1970.
Joyce, C. R. B. (ed.), *Psychopharmacology: Dimensions and Perspectives*, Tavistock Publications, London, 1968.
Kalant, O. J., *The Amphetamines: Toxicity and Addiction*, University of Toronto, Toronto, 1973.
Ley, P., Swinson, R. P. and Eaves, D., *et al.*, "A State-Dependent Learning Effect Produced by Amylobarbitone Sodium", *British Journal of Psychiatry*, 120: 511–15, 1972.
MacAndrew, C. and Edgerton, R. B., *Drunken Comportment: A Social Explanation*, Nelson, London, 1970.
Paton, W. D. M. and Crown, J. (eds.), *Cannabis and its Derivation*, Oxford University Press, London, 1972.
Reports on Public Health and Medical Subjects, No. 124: Amphetamines, Barbiturates, LSD and Cannabis, H.M.S.O., London, 1970.
Schachter, S. and Singer, J., "Cognitive, Social and Physiological Determinants of Emotional State", *Psychological Research*, 69: 379–99, 1962.
Shepherd, M., "The Classification of Psychotropic Drugs", *Psychological Medicine*, 2: 96–110, 1972.
Shepherd, M., Lader, M. and Rodnight, R., *Clinical Psychopharmacology*, English Universities Press, London, 1968.
Wallgren, H. and Barry, H. III, *The Actions of Alcohol*, Vol. I, Elsevier, Amsterdam, 1970.
Wootton report: *Report by the Advisory Committee on Drug Dependence: Cannabis*, H.M.S.O., London, 1968.
Wootton report: *Report by the Advisory Committee on Drug Dependence: The Amphetamines and LSD*, H.M.S.O., London, 1970.
World Health Organisation, *Expert Committee on Drug Dependence, Technical Report Series No. 116*, WHO, Geneva, 1964.
World Health Organisation, *Research in Psychopharmacology, Tech. Rep. Ser. No. 371*, WHO, Geneva, 1967.
World Health Organisation, *Expert Committee on Drug Dependence, Tech. Rep. Ser. No.* 407, WHO, Geneva, 1969.

4 Social influences in the causation of alcoholism and drug dependence

This chapter and the following one will describe influences which appear to operate in the onset and maintenance of various forms of drug dependence. The present chapter concentrates largely on social factors and the subsequent one on individual factors.

One of the difficult problems still requiring solution in the field of drug dependency is the delineation of relevant causative agents. There are many factors associated with alcoholism and drug abuse that have been put forward as being involved, causatively, with the addictive states. Rarely has work been carried out in which a young population has been studied over a long period of time to determine *in a prospective manner* those factors which are found to be important and *which existed prior to the onset* of the behavioural pattern involved in any form of drug abuse.

In the field of alcoholism, there have been a few such studies performed with varying degrees of success and these will be described fully in the following two chapters. In the study of drug dependence, there has not been time to respond to the emergent problem in the same way. It is only some ten years since any great concern was expressed about the British drug scene and there is a lot of scope for prospective research in this particular area.

In chapters 2 and 3 some of the factors involved in causation have already been discussed, although in a different context. The extent of the problem is determined apparently in large part by the availability of the particular drug in question and thus the cause is linked to supply. Without alcohol there would be no alcoholism. The people who develop alcoholism might, in those circumstances, develop another condition, but also to be considered is the aspect of the interaction between the drug and the person. To use the infectious disease model adopted by de Alarcon (1969), it is necessary for there to be an infecting agent (drug) and a host (person) for the possibility of the condition (addiction) to develop. Not everyone who comes into contact with an infective agent develops the condition and this can be due to a number of variables. Firstly, the infectiousness of the agent varies. Leprosy is much less contagious than cholera; similarly, alcohol is less likely to produce dependence, in our society, than heroin is when it is self-administered. Given enough heroin, or alcohol, or barbiturate, everyone will show signs of withdrawal if the drug is suddenly stopped. Physical dependence depends on the action of the drug. The taking of enough of the drug to produce physical dependence does, however, depend in turn on the person taking it. Variables in individual make-up that produce this form of behaviour are also important in the genesis of drug dependence.

A third variable is also of great importance. People do not act within an environment that they influence entirely by themselves. Everyone is part of some society, both in the restricted sense of the family in which he is reared, or the sub-group to which he belongs as an adult and, in the wider sense, he is part of a very large group of people with laws, unspoken restrictions and arbitrary class structures.

The interplay between the pharmacological action of a drug, the society that uses or forbids it and the make-up of the individual in that society, is very complex. The degree of importance of each factor will vary from inidividual to individual and a search for a single, abnormal personality type is bound to fail, since it is essentially an illogical task.

Within the fields of alcoholism and drug dependence there is such wide variation and so many people have found so many things related, however abstrusely, to the conditions, that Lester (1973) has produced an amusing list of the findings in groups of alcoholics. Although in retrospect the list is diverting, it also serves as a reminder of the tremendous amount of effort that has been put into finding a cause for these conditions; yet still there are times when the important factors seem as far from discovery as they have always been. Inspection of the list will reveal the disciplines and areas that have been involved in considering causative factors. It is not within the scope of this book to discuss the minutiae of all these areas and we shall concentrate on the more important of the findings to date.

This chapter will emphasise one side of a debate that has continued for many years: the issue of the relative effects of nature and nurture in the causes of many forms of deviant behaviour. The "nature" side emphasises the basic inherent qualities of the individual who becomes alcoholic or drug-dependent, whereas the "nurture" argument contends that upbringing and social influences are all-important. A recent conference on this topic was held by the National Council on Alcoholism of America (1972) and although the report is divided into the two camps, there was a general agreement at the conference that both sets of factors are relevant and that there is interplay between them.

The variables of age, sex, social class and marital status have already been discussed in Chapter 2. The present chapter will deal with the roles of large societies, i.e. national or religious groups, and small societies, i.e. families or peer groups, as regards the drug-taking habits of the members of these groups.

It is well known that different cultures have widely varying rates of alcoholism and drug-use and abuse. The rates vary from country to country and between ethnic and religious groups within countries. As already stated, the rates also vary with social class and marital status. Barry (1968) reviewed the role of socio-cultural factors in alcoholism and his remarks apply with equal relevance to other forms of drug-abuse. He stated that the motivation of the individual to get drunk is not sufficient by itself for the development of alcoholism. There are controls on the behaviour of each individual and these include legal restraint, disapproval from friends and neighbours, the possibility of conflict with a spouse or family members and the control consequent upon being a member of a special group such as a religious or professional body.

Addiction is a deviant pattern of behaviour shown by a minority of people. (This statement is typical of the position of the "absolutist" described by Young (1971) and is open to attack.) Using a statistical model, alcoholism and taking drugs such as heroin, speed and LSD are abnormal. The position as regards marijuana is becoming less abnormal in this respect as time goes on. Taking the viewpoint that drug dependence is *per se* abnormal forces the drug-dependent person to be viewed in terms of deviancy and his deviant behaviour as arising from a combination of strong personal motivation coupled with inadequate social controls. There is frequently a positive feedback system in such situations. People who have high personal motivation toward drug-taking tend to originate from groups which commonly produce inadequate, insecure, tense members, who are subjected to little in the way of effective controls against deviant behaviour. Such a system is bound to continue in a circular fashion, unless the controls can be changed or the individual removed from the situation. A society that does develop a big problem with a form of drug dependence may well tighten up the controls considerably, as Britain has done with opiates and amphetamines and as the U.S.A. did with the prohibition of alcohol. This response is likely to occur in a country which sees a growing problem with drug abuse, but will not happen within a small group, such as the "hippies", for whom drug abuse is an essential part of being a member of that group.

NATIONAL VARIATION

The Irish and the French have high rates of alcoholism, whereas the Italian and Jewish peoples have low rates. The Swedes have fairly high rates for alcoholism and had a considerable problem with stimulant abuse, which has also occurred in Japan. America as a whole has a large alcohol problem and in her big cities has a severe problem with heroin and other drug dependence. Britain also has a sizeable problem with alcoholism and has developed a heroin problem. It still does have a largely hidden barbiturate-dependent population. No doubt there is an increasing number of marijuana users in Britain, but the problems that they present, and suffer from, are minimal at present.

Why should there be this great variation both in the type of drug used and the extent of abuse of particular drugs between one country and another? The sources of the variation appear to lie in the availability of the drug, the attitudes towards its use and abuse and also, in primitive societies, to insecurity from future prospects.

The prevalence of alcoholism in pre-literate societies has been studied by Horton (1943), Field (1962) and Child and his associates (1965). Similar work in the field of drug dependence has been reported by Blum (1969). In his study of primitive societies, Horton found that alcohol was not freely available and therefore social controls against drinking were not very strong. Child and his colleagues found marked variation in the drinking patterns in the 139 pre-literate cultures that they examined. Some of the cultures displayed frequent prolonged drinking bouts, which included drunkenness, but others were found to drink large quantities of alcohol without displaying drunkenness. In Horton's study, increasing rates of drunkenness were found in societies with high levels of social anxieties related to insecurity about food supplies and also to threats of weakened kinship ties, which were due to acculturalisation to Western standards. The weakening of the ties was said to produce anxiety.

Field disagreed with Horton's conclusions and considered that the degree of drunkenness achieved at a communal drinking bout was related to individual variation rather than being a variable affecting the whole society. He also stated that rates of drunkenness were unrelated to cultural anxiety levels. In his study, certain factors were found that correlated with relative sobriety in primitive tribes. These were corporate kin-group structure, with continuity in time, patrilocal residence at the time of marriage, clan-community organisation, the presence of the custom of a bride-price, and village existence rather than nomadism. Field said that those measures which Horton took to be related to anxiety were, in fact, related to loose social organisation. It might, though, be more anxiety-provoking for an individual to live in a loosely organised society than a tightly regulated one, particularly if it appears that, as time goes on, the structure will become more disorganised. Lynn and Hampson (1970) attempted to correlate national levels of anxiety with alcoholism and found by their questionnaire method that high anxiety in a group of university students did correlate positively with high levels of alcoholism and with cirrhosis deaths. The main drawback to this study is that a measure of "national anxiety" has not yet been shown to exist.

Excessive drinking, that is, intoxication, in primitive societies is a group affair and is not subject to much censure, nor is the behaviour occurring under the influence of alcohol. In societies like our own, public drunkenness is heavily censured and legislated against. Even when intoxicated, a man is still supposed to behave correctly and not to become obnoxious, aggressive or too amorous. In Finland, drinking commonly results in drunkenness but the alcoholism rates remain low. Where excessive drinking to the point of public drunkenness is seen as being deviant, alcoholism is likely to be a problem (Kessel and Walton, 1965).

One way of guarding against some members of a society becoming excessive drinkers is to impose total abstinence on all the members. This has usually been done as part of the behaviour of religious groups, but also on the occasions that prohibition has been attempted, as in the U.S.A. and certain Scandinavian countries. Barry (1968) interpreted the need for total abstinence as being due to a conflict between the societies' requirements for strict self-control and the simultaneous absence of means for satisfying individual dependency needs in those societies.

Blum (1969) examined the use of drugs, including alcohol, in 247 non-literate societies. Earlier reports of drug use in these societies have been inconsistent, largely due to poor experimental methodology. Overall, the use of alcohol, tobacco, opium, cocaine and some stimulants was found to be common but use of hallucinogens was infrequent. Drugs were freely available in most of the societies, but there was rarely any problem with drug-abuse except in the case of alcohol.

The drugs were usually used in a social setting with a "cocktail party" effect; that is, the enhancement of social interaction and smooth interpersonal activities were produced by the use of the drugs. Stimulants, alcohol and tobacco tend to be used in this social way, hallucinogens being used in either religious or magical settings and opium to provide psychological escape. It was found that, in all societies, the use of drugs by males was never exceeded in amount or frequency by the use of any drug by females. Alcohol, hallucinogens and cannabis were particularly used to a greater extent by the men in the various cultures studied.

There was a relationship between social status and drug use. Alcohol, cannabis and opium were the drugs used by those of low social status. High-status groups used stimulants and, as might be predicted, the use of hallucinogens was restricted to special people, such as religious figures. The organisation of the cultures had an influence on the particular drugs used. Cultures organised into "states" had populations which used alcohol moderately, hallucinogens in groups and showed little use of cannabis. In hereditary chieftainships, there was high use of cannabis and moderate alcohol use. The choice of drugs used in any culture appeared to be related to both the social structure of the culture and also to the economic life-style in the culture.

Drug abuse was in evidence in societies in harsh environments, in those with class stratification based on wealth or occupational status and also in those that emphasised military glory and general bellicosity. Whilst the U.S.A. does not provide a harsh environment for many of its inhabitants it does rather fit the description of the other factors involved in societies showing drug-abuse. It can be argued that the black population in the U.S.A. also suffers from a harsh environment and that this might be part of the reason why drug-abuse is higher in the black groups than among Anglo-Saxon Americans. However, it is perhaps unreasonable to compare the U.S.A. with pre-literate societies.

Abuse of all drugs, including alcohol, was lowest in groups following the Christian ethic, in the groups where political activity was high and where the communication of news was good. This finding has been confirmed in modern societies in which drug-abuse was found to be low in people with strong religious faith and in people who identify with, and feel part of, the larger society in which they live.

Turning to civilised countries, the same wide variation in alcohol and drug use is noted. Attitudes to drunkenness differ in civilised societies and primitive ones. In primitive societies, drunkenness is part of the accepted behaviour at the time it occurs, whereas in English society, drunkenness is usually considered to be a deviant act occurring despite restrictions against it. Drunkenness in France is a common occurrence and it is also common in certain small groups of individuals in other societies. Part of being a "skid-row" alcoholic is being almost perpetually drunk. France has a terrible problem with alcoholism, having the highest rate of any of the Western countries. This is particularly caused by the economic dependence of the country on the wine industry. Approximately one person in three in France derives his livelihood directly from the operation of the wine or spirit trade. Bastide (1954) carried out a large survey into the opinions of people about drinking habits in France. He reported that approximately half the men interviewed considered that an intake of two litres of wine per person, per day, was quite reasonable. The National Council of Alcoholism of America in its list of criteria for the diagnosis of alcoholism presented a table showing the equivalent quantities of alcohol to a bottle of whisky in various drinks. There is little difference between two litres of wine and a bottle of whisky as regards the total alcoholic content and therefore half of the men in Bastide's study considered that an alcohol intake consistent with a diagnosis of alcoholism on this single measure was acceptable. It is not surprising, given such widely-held attitudes, that alcoholism is a grave problem in France. With a high intake in so many people, alcoholism is likely to affect large numbers of individuals who show no other form of psychiatric abnormality. Alcoholism in France is generally of the "failure to abstain" variety that commonly leads to long-term physical complications.

France is not the only country in Europe that depends to a great extent on its wine industry. Italy is in a similar economic situation but drinking patterns in Italy are very different from those in France. In general, Italians drink in the evenings, at meal times, in what is largely a formalised setting. Drinking is moderate in amount, circumscribed in time and place and, in addition, drunkenness is subject to marked disapproval. There is apparently very little alcoholism in Italy (Lolli, Serriani, Golder and Luzzatto-Fegiz, 1958) but the Italians as a race are not immune from the adverse effects of alcohol. The same investigators studied Italian immigrants in the U.S.A. and found that although the Italian immigrants had lower alcoholism rates than the American national average, these were eight times as high as the rates of Italians in Italy. In America, the immigrants changed the type of drink they consumed. In Italy, it is almost exclusively wine, but the immigrants included other alcoholic drinks and they also drank at times other than meal times. Another finding was that drunkenness occurred in immigrant women, a feature which is extremely rare in women in Italy.

In Chapter 2 it was pointed out that the prevalence of alcoholism varies throughout the British Isles. It is high in Scotland, particularly the North West, high also in Ireland and higher in cities than rural areas. In Scotland, part of the reason for the high prevalence of alcoholism may be the presence of the whisky trade, but there is some evidence that part of the apparent increase may be due to more complete identification of alcoholics in Scotland. The causes of the high prevalence of alcoholism in Ireland have been the subject of a number of studies. Bales (1962) considered that part of the cause of the Irish alcoholism problem lay in the fact that the Irish, in contrast to the Jews, had no form of ceremonial drinking. Drunkenness is tolerated by many of the Irish and they show high rates of arrest for drunkenness (Gath, 1969). In London, it was found that the proportion of men of Irish origin amongst a group of men arrested for drunkenness exceeded by ten times the proportion of Irish men in the general community. Skolnick (1954) also found that the Irish in America tended to have high rates of arrests for drunkenness. In the same study, the black American, the native American and Slavs were found to have high arrest rates and the Jews, Italians, Germans and Scandinavians low rates. In addition to the lack of ceremonial drinking and the lack of controls against drunkenness, Bales reported that the fathers in Irish culture have lost their dominant family position and that there is a very strong attachment between mothers and their sons, a feature which has been particularly true of the Irish in America.

Low rates of alcoholism are consistently reported in Jewish and Chinese groups (Snyder, 1962, Lin, 1953, Barnett, 1955), even though alcohol is fairly widely used by these nationalities. The Jews mainly drink at meal times and have very strong controls against drunkenness, which is seen as being a Gentile trait and therefore indicative of non-Jewish behaviour. The Jews certainly demonstrate considerable emotionality in the form of tension and anxiety and it might be expected under these conditions that alcoholism would be a considerable problem if appropriate controls were not imposed.

Bales outlined three ways in which societies influence their rates of alcoholism. A society can produce in an individual such feelings as anxiety, guilt or sexual tension. The inner tension can then be resolved in a number of ways. If alcohol is available and is used by the members of the society, then to prevent alcoholism the society also needs to proscribe heavy drinking and drunkenness, by making the thought of transgressing the society's code so anxiety-provoking that alcohol abuse does not occur. In such a circumstance, other forms of anxiety-relief have to be present and it was pointed out by Bales that both the Italians and the Jews tend to over-eat.

In the field of drug-dependence on drugs other than alcohol, the rates of use and abuse tend to follow the availability of the drug in the community. Cannabis grows wild in warm places and is easy to cultivate. It occurs in India, the Middle East, Northern Africa and Mexico. It can also be grown in the U.K., but under our climatic conditions it does not produce very good resin. Cannabis use is therefore a part of everyday life in those countries in which it commonly occurs. As was stated in Chapter 2 the use of cannabis is increasing rapidly in Britain and North America, particularly amongst the young, but increasingly in older age groups. This increase is occurring despite the fact that, in Western countries, its possession and use are illegal. The World Health Organisation (1967) reported that although the use of both opium and cannabis were widespread they were now beginning to decline. In Egypt, the main drugs of dependence are still opium and hashish and other areas that have a high intake of opiates are Hong Kong and Singapore. As everyone is aware, drug use is high in Vietnam and the neighbouring countries. Many of the servicemen returning to the U.S.A. after service in Vietnam had experienced the use of cannabis and opiates and this caused anxiety about what the return of a large number of young men with drug experience might do to the drug scene in America.

PARENTAL AND FAMILY FACTORS

There has been a considerable difference in the approach to the search for the causes of alcoholism on the one hand and drug abuse on the other. In our society, excessive alcohol drinking is statistically abnormal and also abnormal from the ideal position or from the health/disease viewpoint. Alcoholics are therefore viewed as being abnormal people, whose condition arises due to some variation or pathology in them which does not exist in the "normal" man, who does not get into trouble with alcohol. Drug use is not accepted as statistically normal either, although it patently is if one looks at the figures for barbiturate, amphetamine, tranquillisers and "over-the-counter" drug consumption. Drug abuse is commonly seen not only as being due to variables in the individual, but also to deviation in the society to which the drug-taker belongs. It is easy to hold these attitudes as long as the "drug-abusers" remain a small, distinctive group, particularly if it can be seen that harm comes to the people who are members of the group. This position will probably remain as it is for intravenous drug abuse for a long time, but a change is likely to occur in attitudes towards the use of marijuana.

"Normal" drinking and drug-taking have already been considered in Chapter 1. People drink alcohol because (almost) everyone else does, it is freely available and it is part of being sociable. Drugs are taken on the order of a doctor or for self-medication for headaches, constipation and so on. Marijuana is illegal, freely available and part of being sociable for a lot of young people in our society today. There is a dilemma in the investigation of marijuana abuse, because of its transient status. The use of marijuana does not parallel the use of alcohol or the use of drugs such as the stimulants or the hallucinogens. There are too many people using marijuana to dismiss them all as deviants or psychopaths who are taking it as part of a generally disturbed existence, arising from a disadvantaged upbringing. In Western society there as not yet been sufficiently widespread and prolonged enough use of marijuana for judgments to be made of the long-term effects on a normal population. It appears to the writers that with continued liberalisation of the laws on marijuana use, which seems inevitable, the users of marijuana will probably come to be divisible into groups similar to those of the present users of alcohol and tobacco. That is, there will be social users who are not particularly affected by their moderate use of the drug, excessive users, and "addicts" or people who suffer from the effects of the drug but are unable or unwilling to stop.

As has been indicated, the lines of research that have been carried out in alcoholism and drug dependence have differed. Since it has been accepted that alcoholics are different from other drinkers, there have been many investigations into the precise ways in which they are different and into what has caused these differences. In the area of drug dependence this sort of research is not so common as yet. Drug addicts are different from other people but the present viewpoint commonly held is that all that is needed is to remove the drug and the addicts will merge with society again, or perhaps stand out as non-specifically deviant.

Acts which are defined as deviant are generally considered to arise as a result of abnormalities in the personality of the doer. The kinds of personality abnormality will be discussed in the next chapter. Personality abnormalities can arise in two broad ways: they may be determined before birth, but the usually accepted position is that they are produced by adverse experiences early in life. However, the possibility of inborn abnormalities will be considered in the next chapter.

The families of alcoholics have been extensively investigated and, fortunately, there have been three prospective studies of the early occurrences in the lives of people who later became abnormal drinkers. This sort of work has not been done for drug addicts and the data in their case is retrospective and therefore usually less reliable and more open to interpretative bias.

Seldin (1972) has reviewed the findings of studies into the family of the addict and what he has to say about addicts applies also in the case of alcoholics. (He notes also that little has been written specifically about the families of addicts.) In his view, the normal functions of the family are to provide for reproduction, to give status to the members, to provide biological maintenance, to allow for socialisation, to impose sexual controls and to provide maintenance for the emotional life of the members. Families which fail to provide one or more of these functions are disorganised to some degree and, because of this, tend to produce members who are disturbed or deviant in some way.

The families of addicts have been shown to be abnormal in a number of ways. Broken homes caused by divorce, desertion or death, have been frequently shown to produce children who later become addicts or alcoholics. The McCords (1960), whose work will be discussed at greater length in this chapter, showed that in 97 per cent of young alcohol addicts, there was a history either of family disorganisation or of open hostility between the parents.

The mother has commonly been identified as the key figure in the development of the character traits that later predispose to addiction or alcoholism. In many of the families of addicts the father has either been absent or has been a background figure, playing an inconsistent role, but overall being generally unsuitable as a model for the developing (male) child. The mother has been described as alternatively over-possessive and rejecting, and over-protective and emasculating with seductive overtones. She has also been described as emotionally ill, guilt-ridden, hostile and controlling. These statements have been made about the mothers of opiate addicts as well as alcoholics' mothers.

The role of the mother in contributing to drug dependence was evident in Smart's (1971) study of the drug-taking behaviour of the mothers of young drug-takers. Having a parent who takes drugs of any kind on a daily basis influences to a tremendous degree the likelihood that the children in the family will also take drugs. One-third of the children in the study were found to take the same drugs as the parents, the rest obtaining a different drug either on prescription or illicitly. The attitudes of parents toward the drinking of alcohol also influence the subsequent behaviour of their children. When parents agree about the use of alcohol, the children tend to grow up to be abstainers or moderate users of alcohol (Jackson and Connor, 1953). In families in which the attitudes of the parents are inconsistent or conflicting, there appears to be an increased chance that the children will become alcoholics.

Parental deprivation has been implicated in the causation of many different psychiatric disorders since the pioneer work of Bowlby. In groups of alcoholics it has been found that parental deprivation has occurred in 30–50 per cent of cases. Some controlled studies (e.g. Oltman and Friedman, 1953) have failed to confirm these findings, but de Lint (1964) found this factor to be of importance, particularly in females deprived of one or both parents before the age of six years.

In two studies of young addicts in Britain it was found that parental deprivation was a very common feature. Hawks *et al.* (1969) found that almost half of a group of methylamphetamine abusers had had one or both parents die before the child was sixteen. A similar finding was reported by Mitcheson and his colleagues in a group of heroin addicts; in 52 per cent there had been separation from one or both parents for a period in excess of two years before the age of sixteen and in 32 per cent of cases the separation was from both parents. By way of contrast, McGrath (1970) investigated adolescent pill-users and found that, by and large, they came from stable homes with stable parents.

One of the many factors to be considered in the causes of alcoholism is that of ordinal position (i.e. by age) in a sib line. Schachter (1959) investigated affiliation tendencies in families and he found that first and only children need to affiliate with other people more than siblings born in other ordinal positions. Children in small families also affiliate more than siblings in large families, particularly in later ones in large families. Schachter suggested that alcoholics should come from the later-born in large sibships more frequently than would happen by chance. A study of 242 alcoholics was undertaken by Smart (1963) in order to test this suggestion. It was found that there were a lot of alcoholics who came from large families but there was no evidence that any particular birth position predisposed to alcoholism. Even the finding regarding alcoholics coming from large families was considered by Smart to be due to the make-up of the sample studied rather than a finding that could be generalised to all alcoholics. (The sample contained an excess of lower-social-class families who tended to have a large number of children.)

PROSPECTIVE STUDIES OF CHILDREN WHO BECOME ADDICTED IN ADULT LIFE

There have been a number of studies of children who, at the onset of the studies, did not display any abnormalities in the way of addiction to drugs or alcohol. Two of these were concerned largely with social factors (McCord and McCord, 1960, Robins, Bates and O'Neal, 1962) and will be described in this chapter. The Oakland Growth study has provided evidence regarding the antecedents of various drinking patterns in terms of personality correlates (Jones, 1968 and 1971) and these will be considered in the appropriate section of the following chapter. Genetic research has also been performed, using the prospective study method and the work of Anne Roe (1944) and Goodwin and his colleagues (1973) will also be discussed in the next chapter.

Some of the factors discovered by the McCords were of a psychological or physical nature, but for the sake of continuity they will be included here rather than in another section. This study was based on a sample of 255 urban, lower socio-economic-class boys, who participated in the Cambridge Somerville Youth Project. At the beginning of the study, no special attention was paid to the drinking behaviour of the boys or the families they came from and it was felt that although some information might have been lost in this way no bias could have been introduced into the study by concentrating to a great extent on the possible factors involved.

The boys were followed up closely until they were in their thirties, and during this time a proportion became alcoholic. A comparison of the pre-existing factors that had been measured was then made between the now-alcoholic group and the social drinking or abstaining group. An alcoholic was defined as a person whose repeated drinking of alcoholic beverages interfered with his interpersonal relations or his social or economic functioning. Operationally, a person was considered alcoholic if he lost a job through drinking, caused marital disharmony by drinking, had been identified by a social agency as a problem drinker, or had had treatment for alcoholism. In addition, conviction on the grounds of public drunkenness on at least two occasions was included as indicative of alcoholism.

The subjects at the time of the diagnosis of alcoholism were in their thirties and, therefore, some men who might have developed alcoholism later in life would go unrecognised and only the more disturbed ones would be identified. It is possible that alcoholics with a "failure to abstain" pattern would also go unrecognised using the above criteria. Even allowing for these possible sources of error, freely admitted by the investigators, some 10 per cent of the sample was diagnosed as alcoholic by the time they reached their thirties. The high rate was no doubt influenced by the original selection of the 225 boys, which was made on the basis of childhood maladjustment, so it may well be that the findings in this study are not applicable to middle or upper socio-economic groups.

Deviance, including alcoholism, was associated with a number of pre-existing factors. Intense parental conflict, which often produced physical violence in the families, or led to temporary separations, was found to be positively related to the development of alcoholism in the boys studied. There was a significant relationship between sexual deviance within a family and the later onset of alcoholism in the boys of the family. Sexual deviance was defined as incest or illegitimacy occurring in the family. It was suggested that such behaviour by the family members caused a loss of sense of security and did not allow the child to participate in normal affectional relationships.

Two broad factors were discovered which appeared to be highly significant in relation to alcoholism occurring in the boys as they became adults. These were dependency conflicts and role confusion.

Dependency conflicts were described as arising from six sources:

1. The alternation, by the mother, between active affection and rejection.
2. The withdrawal of the mother at times of family crisis into such behaviour as promiscuity or excessive drinking.
3. Deviant behaviour in the mother at times other than crises.
4. The presence in the family of a father who denigrated the mother. (A combination of this factor coupled with deviant behaviour in the mother produced the highest rates of alcoholism in the offspring.)
5. Antagonism in the parents.
6. Resentment by the mother of her role in the family.

Role confusion in the boys was also caused by a combination of six factors:

1. Parental rejection.
2. Escapist behaviour by the father.
3. The absence of high parental demands on the child.
4. Conflict with an outsider, usually a grandparent, over the family's expectations of the child.
5. Less-than-average restrictions on the child by the mother.
6. Lack of supervision of the child.

It was found that 83 per cent of boys became alcoholic when they came from families which were characterised by parental antagonism, or escapism, or a conflicting outsider combined with an absence of high demands. By combining factors, the McCords were able to identify four types of family that produced *only* alcoholic sons:

1. Families with mothers who were overtly ambivalent, deviant and not strongly Catholic, together with fathers who were antagonistic, escapist or who denigrated their wives, in combination with low demands on the son.

2. Families in which the mothers were escapist and who were not strongly Catholic, combined with a father who was antagonistic toward the son.
3. Families in which an outsider was in conflict with the values of the parents and in which the father was antagonistic and escapist.
4. Families having the combination of an outsider in conflict with the parents and an ambivalent, deviant or escapist mother.

The first two types of family were considered to produce alcoholism in the sons due to the mothers' causing dependency conflicts and the fathers' causing role confusion in the children. The third and fourth family types produced dependency conflicts and role confusion through the action of an outsider who was, as stated above, usually a grandparent.

There were similarities and also differences between the backgrounds of the boys who became alcoholic and those who showed other forms of deviance. Common features in the development of alcoholism and other deviations were parental conflict, sexual deviance and ambiguous family roles. Dependency needs were not coped with in either situation in a normal manner. In the pre-alcoholic group, dependency conflict occurred, but in the pre-criminal group dependency desires were said to be extinguished. Role confusion was not a feature of the backgrounds of the boys who became criminal.

The effects of having an alcoholic parent will be discussed fully in the following chapter, but in the McCords' study paternal alcoholism was not related to the development of alcoholism in the sons, whereas it was significantly related to criminality. The alcoholic sons tended to come from the stable, middle-class neighbourhoods in the study and the criminals from the lower-class, transitional neighbourhoods.

In a study of former problem children (Robins, Bates and O'Neal, 1962) childhood social status was also found to be a predictor of the occurrence of alcoholism. It was found to occur most commonly in children from the lowest socio-economic group. Heavy drinking in higher socio-economic groups did not usually lead to alcoholism, but when heavy drinking took place in people from the more disadvantaged groups, it tended to lead frequently to social or medical problems. The adequacy of parental care was studied and it was found that where the parents had not matched up to the traditional parental roles, then high rates of alcoholism were evident in the children of such parents. Parental failure in some cases was due to chronic illness, or absence, and was therefore "accidental", but in other cases the failure to perform in the traditional role was due to general neglect of the child, or excessive drinking on the part of one or both parents.

Fathers who were described as anti-social produced children who became alcoholic in 40 per cent of cases. Other factors correlating with high rates of alcoholism were lax parental discipline, excessive family mobility, broken homes and deprivation of food, shelter and supervision. Children who demonstrated deviant or anti-social behaviour when young tended to become alcoholic as they grew older, but there was no relationship between any particular symptomatology or form of the childhood deviance and the subsequent development of alcoholism.

The two studies described above did not set out to examine precisely the same factors, but many similarities are evident in the findings. Being brought up in a lower socio-economic group in a family that does not provide for a child's emotional growth or stability and does not provide adequate parental models, appears to be a fruitful source of alcoholism and of other forms of deviance in the children of such families.

A retrospective study, but one which contributes to the same area, was conducted amongst young urban black Americans by Lucy King *et al.* (1969). Drug abuse, and particularly narcotic abuse, is concentrated in this sort of social group in North America, but Lucy King's study dealt with alcohol abuse. Three main factors were chosen for study in relation to alcohol abuse. These were as follows:

1. Whether or not the father was present in the family.
2. The influence of socio-economic status.
3. Evidence of school problems.

The subjects were also divided into three groups: those showing alcohol abuse; those showing heavy drinking with no problems; and those with no evidence of heavy drinking.

It is frequently stated that alcoholism or drug dependence in adult life is merely an expression of deviant behaviour which begins in childhood. The conclusion from the above study disagreed with this view. It was found that alcohol abuse was independent of the backgrounds of the fathers, pressure on the subjects in childhood or achievement in school. Alcohol abuse was, however, seen as being predictive of social, economic and legal problems.

The occurrence of alcohol abuse in the father of a family leads to the development of a vicious circle. Subjects from broken homes were not likely to complete their education, but were likely to start drinking early and also to drink heavily. Having started heavy drinking early in life, common-law marriages were frequent which led to the birth of illegitimate children and subsequently to frequent failure of the union. With the break-up of the marriages the children were then at a greater risk of failing in their education and were also at risk from early heavy drinking.

Drug abuse other than alcohol is, as stated earlier, largely found in adolescent and young adult groups. The exceptions to this rule—the oral use of barbiturates, amphetamines, tranquillisers and "over-the-counter" drugs—occur in a predominantly female middle-aged group with drugs that are made freely available to them. There is some evidence that doctors prescribe mood-modifying drugs more frequently and for a wider range of complaints to their female patients than to their male patients. Women are expected to show more evidence of their emotional feelings than men and a lot of such emotional display is explained or dismissed as being essentially female in nature. They are also subject to recurrent hormonal change as part of the menstrual cycle that commonly leads to some change in emotionality. Nevertheless, it does appear that emotionally-based diagnoses may be made rather too frequently in women. On the other hand, Winokur and his colleagues (see Chapter 5) have shown that depression in women may be the equivalent of the expression of alcoholism in men. From the data presented in Chapter 2, it is evident that drug and alcohol consumption is dependent on the availability of the substance. There is a sequence of being a woman, being allowed emotional expression, having many complaints diagnosed as emotionally based and also having those complaints treated with tablets. It is not too surprising in these circumstances that drug-taking is commoner in middle-aged women than in middle-aged men.

DRUG USE IN YOUNG PEOPLE

Young drug-takers are construed as being deviant in terms of their social relationships, their interpersonal relationships, their general behaviour and their personality structure. Arising from this point of view, there has developed a system of interpretation of drug-taking behaviour based on individual deviancy, with consequent attempts to influence either the social setting of the individual (his family) or to alter his personality, usually by psychotherapy. Neither of these methods has proved to be very successful.

Drug dependence is not necessarily a form of deviant behaviour occurring in an individual who then becomes part of a deviant group. Indeed, it may be part of the requisite behaviour of an individual to enable him to identify himself as a member of a particular group. In his book on this topic, Young (1971) has compared the nature of drug dependency in various cultures and has shown how the features vary from country to country. The source of variation does not arise from the effects of the drugs but from the social influences acting on the individual in the different countries.

Three kinds of drug-taking groups differing from each other in their behaviour are described by Young. The first group consists of the individuals who indulge in the sort of drug-taking that is normal for the society, such as the use of alcohol and tobacco. The second group he terms the "tame" deviant group who act out a deviant role approved as such by the society. A provision of adopting this role is that these drug-takers agree to be labelled as "sick" in some way. The two groups just described are part of society and therefore cause little or no conflict to arise as a consequence of their activities. Conflict does arise, however, around the third group. Instead of adopting the social pattern of drug use or the "tame deviant" drug-use pattern, drugs are given a different meaning by certain people, who develop a sub-culture with particular methods of using drugs and with expectations that are at variance with the patterns of the use of drugs in their parent society.

It is contended by Young that such sub-cultures will evoke markedly antagonistic reactions from society in general. The reaction is, moreover, not seen as being a one-way event, but as an event producing changes in the target sub-culture that provoke further reactions in other groups within the general society. This sequence of events is termed a "deviancy amplification spiral" and Young gives a number of examples of ways in which such systems can develop and continue to operate. The origin of deviancy amplification spirals in drug dependence and in other phenomena such as criminality is described as arising due to faulty perceptions by both sides. This leads us straight back to the problem of the assessment of the number of alcoholics or drug-takers in any society. The commonly held stereotype of "young people who take drugs" is that of a layabout, dirty, unemployable, sexually acting-out group that starts with "soft drugs" and proceeds inevitably to "hard drugs" with high prospects of an early death. In America, the picture is completed by the addition of illegal activities such as stealing or prostitution, to raise money to pay for illicit drugs. The perception of society by the addict is also part of the spiral. The "man in the street" is seen as being "square", "straight" or ignorant of what life is really about. In addition, agents of society, usually policemen and others involved in the legal process, are viewed as being repressive and persecutory.

Klerman (1970) examined the social values with respect to drugs held by different people and described three broad groups. "Drug hawks" are the police and the legal agencies who see no difference between the use of marijuana by students and the use of intravenous heroin. This group tends to seek strong and punitive legislation to solve the drug problem. The "moderate" group consists of the helping professionals who agree with liberalisation of the laws relating to marijuana use. They tend also to be more concerned with people than the drugs they use. The "heads" are typified by people such as Timothy Leary and Allan Ginsberg, who espouse the complete liberalisation of all drug use in society.

The "hawks" are the holders of attitudes consistent with the "drug-fiend" hypothesis that Rubington (1967) discussed. According to this group, all illicit drug-use leads to physical and moral deterioration. Along with these features, the addict is seen as a weak person who becomes not only a sexual menace under the influence of drugs, but also a source of contagion that affects other young people who come into contact with him. Drug addiction is also viewed as being an irreversible process.

The origins of opiate dependence, at least in America, appear to go back a long way into the addict's history (Chein, 1966). In contrast to the view that few addicts can stop taking drugs, it has been shown that as many as 75 per cent of heroin users try to stop taking the drug at some time in their career and many people who try heroin do not go on to chronic use. The vast majority of servicemen returning to the U.S.A. from Vietnam have not had any problems stopping their drug-taking on returning back home. The chronic users come from the worst social backgrounds, in terms of both economic status and the amount of affection present in the home. Children in such circumstances are already bound into a spiral that confirms their worthlessness to society and their own mistrust of society outside their own group. Stephens (1971) examined the role of the street addict, again in the setting of North American society. This role supplies a meaningful life for him that, although deviant in terms of the general population, is acceptable to the addict's peers. A drug-using sub-culture provides a source of the drug and also knowledge of how to use it and how to obtain money to buy supplies. A further aspect of the drug-culture career is that it gives the addict a chance to live without stigma in his role.

The roles in a single, drug-using culture are commonly believed to be only two in number—the supplier who makes a lot of money from his activities and the drug-user who pays heavily for his supplies. Hughes and his colleagues (1971) investigated the various roles of individuals within a single drug-taking area in Chicago. (In Chicago and other cities there are a number of drug-taking communities that have been termed "copping communities".) Seven roles were found to exist in the area. These consisted of three dealing roles, from the big dealer to the part-time dealer. "Bag followers" were young women who helped the dealers and touts did the liaison work between the dealers and the takers. The takers were sub-divided into two groups: the hustlers who used illegal activities to support their habit; and the workers who obtained at least some of their money from part-time work.

There were 125 heroin addicts and two non-addicts in the community studied. Apart from the two non-addicts who were in the community for the money they could obtain, all the roles were filled by heroin-takers. Overall, about one-third of the individuals were involved in the supply of the drug, but only 56 per cent of all the members of the community were active in any role in each week.

The other members were often out of action, either due to being in treatment, or because they had been arrested. During the year of the study, 40 per cent of the addicts went into treatment at some time and of these 60 per cent stayed in treatment for at least six months.

In contrast to the view that big dealers in heroin live in luxury, the ones in this community were found to have a fairly low standard of living when compared with the general population. They did have a better standard of living than the people in the other roles, particularly the hustlers, who were in the worst situation. Amongst these people, one in two had no fixed abode and very few of them paid anything toward what accommodation they did have. The hustlers came off worst with regard to all the factors measured, including being the most severely mentally disturbed group within the community.

SUMMARY

In summary, alcoholics and addicts are found in all societies and from all strata in society. Certain factors appear to influence the proportion of addicts found in a particular setting. These are such things as national origin, religion, family structure and societies' expectations of the activities of some of its members. The next chapter will concentrate on variations in individuals, rather than groups, that have been found to correlate with the presence of alcoholism or drug dependence.

REFERENCES

Bales, R. F., "Attitudes toward Drinking in the Irish Culture", in Pittman, D. J. and Snyder, C. R., (eds.), op. cit.

Barnett, M., "Alcoholism in the Cantonese of New York City: An Anthropological Study", in Diethelm, O. (ed.), op. cit.

Barry, H. III, "Sociocultural Aspects of Alcohol Addiction", in Wickler, A. (ed.), op. cit.

Bastide, M., "Une Enquête sur l'Opinion Publique à l'Égard de l'Alcoolisme", *Population*, 2: 13–42, 1954.

Blum, R. H., *Drugs and Society: A Cross-Cultural Study*, Vosey-Brass Inc., San Francisco, 1969.

Bowlby, J., *Forty-four Juvenile Thieves: Their Characters and Home-Life*, Balliere, Tindall and Cox, London, 1946.

Chein, I., "The Chronic Addict and Why He Turned to Drugs", *Rehabilitation Record*, 7: 16–18, 1966.

Child, I. L., Bacon, M. K. and Barry, H. III, "A Cross-Country Study of Drinking", *Quarterly Journal of Studies on Alcohol*, No. 3, 1965.

de Alarcon, R., "The Spread of Heroin Use in a Community", *Bulletin on Narcotics*, 21 (3): 17–22, 1969.

de Lint, J. E. E., "Alcoholism, Birth Rank and Parental Deprivation", *American Journal of Psychiatry*, 120: 1062–5, 1964.

Diethelm, O. (ed.), *Etiology of Chronic Alcoholism*, C. C. Thomas, Springfield, Illinois, 1955.

Field, P. B., "A New Cross-Cultural Study of Drunkenness", in Pittman, D. J. and Snyder, C. R. (eds.), op. cit.

Gath, D., "The Male Drunk in Court", in Gath, D., Cook, T. and Hensman, Celia (eds.), op. cit.

Gath, D., Cook, T. and Hensman, Celia, (eds.), *The Drunkenness Offence*, Pergamon, Oxford, 1969.

Goodwin, D. W., Schulsinger, F., Hermanson, L., Guze, J. B. and Winokur, G., "Alcohol Problems in Adoptees Raised Apart from Alcoholic Biological Parents", *Archives of General Psychiatry*, 28: 238–43, 1973.

Hawks, D. R., Mitcheson, M., Ogborne, A. and Edwards, G., "Abuse of Methylamphetamine", *British Medical Journal*, ii: 715–21, 1969.

Horton, D., "The Functions of Alcohol in Primitive Societies: A Cross-Cultural Study", *Quart. J. Stud. Alcohol*, 4: 199–320, 1943.

Hughes, P. H., Crawford, G. A., Barker, W. W., Schumann, S. and Jaffe, J. S., "The Social Structure of a Heroin Copping Community", *American Journal of Psychiatry*, 128 (5): 551–8, 1971.

Jackson, Joan K. and Connor, R., "Attitudes of the Parents of Alcoholics, Moderate Drinkers and Non-Drinkers Towards Drinking", *Quart. J. Stud. Alcohol*, 14: 590–613, 1953.

Jones, Mary C., "Personality Correlates and Antecedents of Drinking Patterns in Adult Males", *Journal of Consulting and Clinical Psychology*, 32 (i): 2–12, 1968.

Jones, Mary C., "Personality Correlates and Antecedents of Drinking Patterns in Women", *J. Consult. Clin. Psychol.*, 36 (i): 61–9, 1971.

Kessel, W. I. N. and Walton, H., *Alcoholism*, Penguin, Harmondsworth, 1965.

King, Lucy, J., Murphy, G., Robins, L. N. and Darvish, Harriet, "Alcohol Abuse: A Crucial Factor in Social Problems of Negro Men", *Am. J. Psychiatry*, 125: 185–90, 1969.

Klerman, G. L., "Drugs and Social Values", *International Journal of Addictions*, 5 (2): 313–19, 1970.

Lester, D., "Self-Maintenance of Intoxication in the Rat", *Quart. J. Stud. Alcohol*, 22: 223–31, 1961.

Lester, D. and Freed, E. X., "A Rat Model of Alcoholism", *Annals of the New York Academy of Sciences*, 197: 54–9, 1973.

Lin, T., "A Study of the Incidence of Mental Disorder in Chinese and

Other Cultures", *Psychiatry*, 16: 313–36, 1953.
Lolli, G., Serriani, E., Golder, G. M. and Luzatto-Fegiz, P., *Alcohol in Italian Culture, the Centre of Alcohol Studies*, The Free Press, Glencoe, Illinois, 1958.
Lynn, R. and Hampson, S., "Alcoholism and Alcohol Consumption in Ireland", *Journal of the Irish Medical Association*, 63: 39–42, 1970.
McCord, W. and McCord, Joan, with Gudeman, J., *Origins of Alcoholism*, Tavistock Publications, London, 1960.
McGrath, J. H., "Adolescent Pill Users", *Int. J. Addict.*, 5 (2): 173–82, 1970.
Mitcheson, M., Hawks, D., Davidson, J., Hitchens, L., and Malone, S., "Sedative Abuse by Heroin Addicts", *Lancet*, i: 606–7, 1970.
National Council on Alcoholism Inc., New York, "Criteria for the Diagnosis of Alcoholism", *Annals of Internal Medicine*, 77: 249–58, 1972.
Oltman, J. and Friedman, S., "A Consideration of Parental Deprivation and Other Factors in Alcohol Addicts", *Quart. J. Stud. Alcohol*, 14: 49–57, 1953.
Pittman, D. J. and Snyder, C. R. (eds.), *Society, Culture and Drinking Patterns*, John Wiley, New York, 1962.
Robins, L. N., Bates, W. M. and O'Neal, P., "Adult Drinking Patterns of Former Problem Children", in Pittman, D. J. and Snyder, C. R. (eds.), op. cit.
Roe, Anne, "The Adult Adjustment of Children of Alcoholic Parents Raised in Foster Homes", *Quart. J. Stud. Alcohol*, 5: 378–93, 1944.
Rubington, E., "Drug Addiction as a Deviant Career", *Int. J. Addict.*, 2 (1): 3–30, 1967.
Schachter, S., *The Psychology of Affiliation: Experimental Studies of Sources of Gregariousness*, Stanford University Press, Stanford, California, 1959.
Seldin, N. E., "The Family of the Addict. A Review of the Literature", *Int. J. Addict.*, 7 (1): 97–107, 1972.
Skolnick, J. H., "A Study of the Relation of Ethnic Background to Arrest for Inebriety", *Quart. J. Stud. Alcohol*, 15: 622–30, 1954.
Smart, R. G., "Alcoholism, Birth Order and Family Size", *Journal of Abnormal Psychology*, 66: 17–23, 1963.
Smart, R. G., "Illicit Drug Use in Canada: A Review of Recent Epidemiology with Clues for Prevention", *Int. J. Addict.*, 6 (3): 383–405, 1971.
Snyder, C. R., "Culture and Jewish Sobriety: The In-Group—Out-Group Factor", in Pittman, D. J. and Snyder, C. R. (eds.), op. cit.
Stephens, R., "The Street-Addict Role, Implications for Treatment", *Psychiatry*, 34: 351–9, 1971.
Wikler, A. (ed.), *The Addictive States, Research Publications of the Association for Research in Nervous and Mental Disease*, Vol. XLVI, Wilkins and Wilkins, Baltimore, 1968.
Winokur, G., Rimmer, J. and Reich, T., "Alcoholism IV: Is There More

Than One Type of Alcoholism?", *British Journal of Psychiatry*, 118: 525–31, 1971.
World Health Organisation, *Services for the Prevention and Treatment of Dependence on Alcohol and Other Drugs, Technical Report Series No.* 363, WHO, Geneva, 1967.
Young, J., *The Drug Takers*, Granada, London, 1971.

5 Individual factors in the causation of alcoholism and drug dependence

The factors operating in an individual as opposed to the variables in the individual's society will be considered in this chapter. These factors can be categorised as physiological, genetic and psychological.

PHYSIOLOGICAL VARIABLES

The majority of studies in this area have been devoted to the field of alcoholism and although some of the findings might be applicable to drug dependency other than alcohol, this has not yet been confirmed.

The greatest difficulty in determining whether or not a factor plays any part in the causes of alcoholism is to produce evidence that it was influencing the person before the alcoholism was at an advanced stage. Many differences in physiological make-up have been found between alcoholics and non-alcoholics, but very few, if any, have been found that will separate the *pre*-alcoholic from the non-alcoholic.

Some of the supposed differences between established alcoholics and non-alcoholics have not stood up to investigation and hopeful leads have had to be discarded many times in the search for a pre-existing variable predisposing to alcoholism that would form some basis on which to construct a true disease model of alcoholism.

A purely physical basis has been adopted by Alcoholics Anonymous (A.A.) to explain the onset of alcoholism. Silkworth (1937) put forward the idea that alcoholism might arise due to an allergy to ethyl alcohol. Testing of the reactions of established alcoholics and non-alcoholics showed no difference in any measure of alcohol's allergic potential. Although this hypothesis was disproved many years ago, it is still put forward by many adherents to A.A. philosophy.

An elaborate theory of alcoholism was presented by R. J. Williams (1947), which was based on the assumption of metabolic individuality. The hypothesis was that, because so many enzyme systems are involved in everyone's physiology, then due to slight variations everyone must be unique in this respect. Following from this, a diet that is adequate for most people will be inadequate for some and thus in this minority a distinctive metabolic pattern may develop which predisposes to alcoholism. There have been many criticisms of this approach and it has largely been abandoned as a fruitful area for research.

A similar approach was proposed by Mardones and Onfray (1942) based on vitamin deficiency. It was found that rats raised or lowered their alcohol intake depending on the presence or absence of certain elements in the B vitamin group. By manipulating the solutions from which the rats could choose and adding an alternative supply of calories in the form of sugar (sucrose) it was found that the alcohol intake dropped again. In fact, the drinking of alcohol appears to have been in response to calorie restriction and not from any other need; investigations of human alcoholics have not confirmed the preliminary finding in rats. Many variables have been found to influence the alcohol intake of rats and other animals, but very few of the studies have shown that experimental animals have drunk sufficient alcohol to be termed alcoholic. As with humans, most animals that drink alcohol are "social" drinkers.

Disorders in the endocrine glands, particularly the adrenals and the thyroid, have also been said to form the basis of alcoholism but the disorders have all proved to be secondary to alcoholism rather than implicated in its causes. Investigations of factors related to tension and resentment (Fleetwood and Diethelm, 1951) found that "alcoholics" and non-alcoholics reacted to situations causing anxiety, tension and resentment in a different manner. The "alcoholics" in this study were chosen on questionable criteria but were reported to produce biochemical substances during these three emotional states in excess of the amounts produced by the normal group. Furthermore, alcohol was effective in reducing the level of "tension substance" and was the only agent that removed the so-called "resentment substance" from the blood of the alcoholic group. Although the results are superficially impressive, the way in which the cases were selected and the manner in which the emotional states were determined raises many doubts about the validity of the findings. They have not been reproduced by other researchers.

Alcohol is metabolised by the action of an enzyme called alcohol dehydrogenese (ADH). This enzyme exists in the lung, kidneys and intestines of the foetus and also in the liver, which is the site of its action in the adult. In man it has been found that three different forms of ADH exist. One of these forms, "atypical ADH", has been found to break down ethyl alcohol at a more rapid rate than the typical ADH. The atypical form exists in 2·5–20 per cent of normal individuals (according to the results found in various studies). It is tempting to explain the more rapid intake of alcohol in alcoholics as being in some way related to their ability to rid themselves of it more quickly than the rest of the population. As yet it has not been possible to show that there is any such relationship between alcoholism and this genetically-determined characteristic—a point to which we will return later.

Therefore, despite a tremendous amount of work, it has not yet been shown that alcoholics differ from non-alcoholics in any physiological sense before the development of alcoholism.

GENETIC VARIABLES

Alcoholism runs in families. The sons of alcoholic parents stand a greatly increased chance of becoming alcoholic as compared with the sons of non-alcoholic parents. Kessel and Walton (1965) dismissed genetic influences as being of no importance in the causes of alcoholism, but their outright dismissal appears to be, at least, premature.

Five approaches to the determination of a genetic involvement in the causes have been described. These are as follows:

1. Animal studies.
2. Family incidence studies.
3. Twin studies.
4. Studies of the adopted children of alcoholic parents.
5. The association of alcoholism or drug dependence with a factor known to be inherited.

Animal studies

A number of investigators (Rodgers and McLearn, 1962, Erikkson, 1968) have shown that drinking behaviour in rats with respect to alcohol can be passed on to the offspring. It has been possible to breed strains of rats that refuse alcohol, and other strains with a high alcohol intake. From studies that have been carried out, it appears that genetic make-up accounts for the greatest part of the variability in the drinking behaviour of different rat and mouse strains.

The dominant gene effect is toward non-drinking. A particular strain of high alcohol-intake mouse (Z C57 BL) is in general more active, aggressive and curious than strains showing low alcohol-preference. It may be that increased alcohol drinking in this case is merely part of a general behaviour pattern demonstrated by the animal.

By using sophisticated conditioning techniques, it is possible to make rats drink alcohol in such amounts and at such a rate that their alcohol intake equals their ability to metabolise it. In humans the metabolism of ethyl alcohol is less efficient and certainly in alcoholics the intake of alcohol outstrips their metabolism so that high blood-alcohol levels are reached. It is fairly easy to cause a rat to drink a great deal of fluid which may be alcohol in part and this factor has been investigated to see if there is, as yet, an animal model of alcoholism. (Lester and Freed, 1972).

Assuming that an animal model of alcoholism can be found, the animals in the study should drink alcohol for its psycho-pharmacological effects. Although it is possible to make animals drink large amounts of alcohol rapidly this has usually only been possible when the animals are food-deprived. Alcohol is therefore used by these animals for the calories it provides and not for its central nervous system effects.

Similar experiments have been reported by Nichols (1972) but the interpretation of the results is rather different. Early experiments in opiate addiction in animals centred round animals being administered the opiates, whereas Nichols points out that humans give themselves the drugs and this difference in administration has appeared to be critical in later experiments. It has proved possible to make rats administer morphine to themselves either by injection or by drinking morphine solution. A very important finding was that rats relapsed into drug-taking if re-exposed to opiates after a long period of abstinence. It was also found that the likelihood of relapse varied from rat to rat and, by selective breeding, high-relapse and low-relapse rats were bred. On exposing the different strains of morphine-trained rats to alcohol, slight differences in intake were noted but these later disappeared. However, on testing the relapse rates a second time to alcohol, the addiction-prone rats now drank twice as much alcohol as the addiction-resistant rats. "Addiction-proneness" to a variety of drugs seems to have a genetic basis which must, however, depend on initial exposure to the drug. Such exposure in humans is likely to be determined by social factors, at least in part.

Relapse in opiate-addicted rats was also produced by Wikler and his colleagues (1961). Rats in opiate withdrawal show a characteristic behaviour pattern described as "wet-dog shakes", a self-explanatory term. Rats which were experiencing withdrawal were repeatedly placed in a distinctive environment and after a number of such experiences were deprived of further opiate supply for some weeks. On being placed again in the distinctive withdrawal setting, the number of wet-dog shakes increased although there was no pharmacological basis for this behaviour. It appears that the experience of withdrawal symptoms is partly determined by the surroundings and it is possible that in humans relapse into drug-taking may be precipitated by the environmental cues. So it is necessary to persuade addicts to stay away from their addict friends, not only to restrict their future supplies, but also to reduce the environmental stimuli which might predispose to a relapse by producing conditioned withdrawal symptoms.

Family incidence studies

Alcoholism is found to occur in the family members of an alcoholic more than would be expected to occur on a chance basis. Roughly 1 per cent of the population is alcoholic. Table IX demonstrates the occurrence of alcoholism in various relatives of an alcoholic.

TABLE IX
Risks of alcoholism in relatives of alcoholics

Relative	*Alcoholic* (%)
Fathers	17–53
Mothers	2–12
Brothers	21–30
Sisters	1–4

It can clearly be seen that the rates of alcoholism in the relatives of alcoholics are markedly increased, especially for the male relatives.

Drug-taking also runs in families. Smart (1971) investigated the factors associated with drug-taking in school children and one of the major influences appeared to be parental drug use. If a child's mother was using tranquillisers, then the likelihood that the child would use such drugs as marijuana and opiates was increased. It was also found that *heavy* tranquilliser-use by the mother was associated with an increased likelihood of drug-taking in the child. The same association was found between the drug-taking of fathers and their children.

Parents who needed tranquillisers daily had children whose drug-taking was increased by between three and seventeen times over that of other children. The greatest increase was in the taking of opiates and barbiturates. Although drug-taking is familial, there is not usually any suggestion that it is genetically based but rather is considered to be more due to the effects of training occurring in the family setting.

Amark (1951) investigated over 600 Swedish alcoholics and as many of their family members as possible. Overall, 349 brothers, 371 sisters, 186 fathers and 200 mothers took part in the study. Although the rates for alcoholism differed between the fathers (26 per cent) and the brothers (21 per cent) the morbidity risk was considered to be the same, considering the age differences in the two groups. The female members of the families had rates of alcoholism much closer to the general population figures than did the male members.

An attempt was made to analyse the data with regard to the genetic components in alcoholism, psychopathy and criminality in the sample. It was found that hereditary factors played a part in the causation of psychopathy but that the role of genetic factors in alcoholism was unclear. In a small sample, it was found that "periodic alcoholism" showed a considerable degree of heritability.

Nylander (1960) confirmed the finding that alcoholism in a parent contributes to psychiatric and possible physical illness in the children. His subjects were of such an age that the offspring would not normally be old enough to have developed alcoholism, but two children, both aged thirteen, were showing signs of drug addiction, one to alcohol and one to solvent inhalation.

A great deal of very impressive work into the families of alcoholics has been carried out by Winokur and his colleagues (*see* Winokur, Rimmer and Reich, 1970, for further references). In a series of investigations, they have confirmed the occurrence of alcoholism as being more than that expected by chance in the close relatives of alcoholics. They have also studied the relationship between alcoholism and other psychiatric illnesses, which will be considered in more detail later in this chapter.

Very briefly, Winokur's findings were that a number of different types of alcoholism appear to exist and two distinct types were described in female alcoholics (Schuckit, Pitts, Reich, King and Winokur, 1969). Of 70 female alcoholics, 39 were described as primary alcoholics; the rest had pre-existing psychiatric disorders and the largest group of these (19) had affective (mood) disorders. An examination of the male relatives of the primary alcoholic and affective groups showed that those who were psychiatrically ill suffered from alcoholism. In respect to the female relatives, the two groups differed. The female relatives of the primary-alcoholic females suffered from alcoholism and those of the affective-alcoholic group suffered from affective disorder without alcoholism. A further group was described but was too small to compare with the others. This was the sociopathy-alcoholism group with a family history of both alcoholism and sociopathic behaviour. Sociopathy was defined as police involvement in ways separate from drunkenness offences.

In a separate study, 259 alcoholic patients and 507 first-degree relatives were investigated (Winokur, Reich, Rimmer and Pitts, 1970). The morbidity risk was calculated for alcoholism, depressive disorder and sociopathy in the first-degree relatives of both sexes of alcoholic patients. (Morbidity risk is the probability that a relative will develop a particular disease in his lifetime, assuming he survives the period of risk for the disease.)

Overall, it was found that of the relatives interviewed, between 26 per cent and 63 per cent were diagnosed as psychiatrically ill. The figures were higher for the relatives of the female alcoholics than for the male alcoholics. The morbidity risk for alcoholism in the male relatives of both male and female alcoholics was found to be about 33 per cent. For the same relatives, the risk for depressive disorder was about 6 per cent. In contrast, the female relatives carried a risk for alcoholism of between 0 and 16 per cent and for depressive disorder in the range of 20–30 per cent, except for the daughters of female alcoholics. In this case the risk of depressive disorder in the daughter's lifetime was 74 per cent. The risk for sociopathy in all groups was 6 per cent or less.

So, it seems that the male relatives of alcoholics suffer from alcoholism and the female relatives from depression. Combined data showed that alcoholism seemed to occur in three forms: primary alcoholism, affective (i.e. depression-linked) alcoholism and sociopathy alcoholism. The authors suggested that there may either be three quite different types of alcoholism or else there is just one illness, which is expressed in different ways by males and females.

Schuckit (1972*b*) adopted another approach to the study of the familial nature of alcoholism by investigating the half-siblings of 41 alcoholics; 98 half-siblings were traced and interviewed. Half-siblings of alcoholics have genetic material from one of the parents of the alcoholic and that material may come from either the alcoholic or the non-alcoholic side. They also make it possible to investigate the differential effect of being reared with an alcoholic or non-alcoholic parent, independently of the genetic make-up of the half-sibling.

By comparing the effects of being the biological child of an alcoholic and being raised in a family containing an alcoholic parent, it was found that genetic influences appeared to be of greater importance in the development of alcoholism in the offspring. But a word of caution is necessary. The number of subjects in the study was fairly small and because it is a report that stands on its own, without corroboration as yet, it has to be considered with some degree of reserve.

Twin studies

One of the ways in which the influence of a genetic component can be discovered in disorders is to study the prevalence of the disease in twins. Monozygous (MZ) twins come from the same fertilised egg, which splits to give rise to two (or more) individuals. In this case, the two babies produced are identical in every way and are, of necessity, of the same sex. Dizygous (DZ) twins come from two eggs fertilised by two sperms or from one egg that is fertilised by two sperms and which then splits. Such babies may be of the same or different sexes. Their genetic make-up is different from each other but they usually are exposed to very similar environments.

The twin who presents with the disease being studied is termed the *proband*. Concordance rates are a comparison of the proportion of twins of the probands who also exhibit the disease being investigated. If all the probands and their twins have the disease, the concordance rate is 100 per cent; if all the probands and half of their twins have it then the rate is 50 per cent. Because the genetic make-up of MZ twins is identical, then a genetically-determined disease should produce a concordance rate which is higher than that found in DZ twins or non-twinned siblings. Conversely, a condition which is mainly caused by the environment will produce similar concordance rates in both DZ and MZ twins and should also produce approximately the same rates for siblings or adopted children in the same family.

There have been a number of reports on the occurrence of alcoholism in twin pairs. As can be imagined, the difficulties involved in tracing the twins of alcoholics, who are probably middle-aged and may well have left their place of birth, is immense. Carrying out such a study in England would probably necessitate having to start with hospitalised alcoholics and this would bias the sample greatly. All the reports so far have come from Scandinavia. The reasons for this include the small population, its relative immobility, the detailed local records of births and the Temperance Board records of deviant drinkers.

By comparing twin-birth registers and Temperance Board records, Kaij (1960) studied 174 pairs of male twins born in Sweden between 1890 and 1939. The pairs were included in the study if one twin had a record of convictions for drunkenness or other alcohol abuse. The probands and the twins were all interviewed personally.

In the 48 MZ twin pairs a concordance rate for alcoholism of 54·2 per cent was found and in the 126 DZ pairs the rate was 35 per cent. A recalculation of the data by Slater and Cowie (1971) shows that the concordance rate for the DZ pairs was 32 per cent higher than expected and for the MZ pairs was 114 per cent in excess of that expected. From this evidence, Kaij concluded that genetic effects were of great importance in the causation of alcoholism.

Tienari (1963) included 17 twin pairs in his more general study of the genetic effects in psychiatric illness. The alcoholics were not treated separately, but were included as part of his study of sociopathy. The "abuse of alcohol" grouping produced a concordance rate of 34 per cent and "continued abuse" a rate of 24 per cent. In view of the contamination of this sample with patients showing other psychiatric disease, little reliance can be placed on the findings.

The third study was a monumental piece of work involving the investigation of 902 male twins aged between twenty-eight and thirty-seven in Finland (Partanen, Bruun and Markkanen, 1966). The investigation covered abstinence as well as drinking and also covered tobacco and coffee use. There was a very close check on the true zygosity of the twin pairs. Drinking behaviour was considered under three headings: *Density* referred to the frequency of the use of alcohol; *Amount* referred to the amount of alcohol consumed on a single occasion, to the duration of the drinking and to the degree of intoxication achieved; and *Lack of control* was used to describe dependency on alcohol and the ability to control the amount consumed.

The estimate of heritability of each factor was made in 172 MZ and 557 DZ pairs. The means by which the heritabilities were calculated were extremely sophisticated statistical techniques which need not concern us here. The results for the heritabilities were as follows:

Density	0·39
Amount	0·36
Lack of control	0·14

It was concluded that normal drinking, abstinence and heavy alcohol use show variation that depends upon heredity. However, an estimate of the social complications of drinking showed no evidence of a hereditary factor. Although "lack of control" showed no overall evidence of heritability, if the younger pairs were considered separately there was such evidence. The investigators concluded that if alcoholism is considered in terms of drinking behaviour and dependency on alcohol, then the differences between DZ and MZ pairs can be explained on an hereditary basis. On the other hand, defining alcoholism in terms of social consequences reveals no evidence for such a basis. (For a criticism of this study readers are referred to Popham, de Lint and Schmidt, 1967.)

The adopted children of alcoholic parents

It is incontrovertible that alcoholism and drug dependence run in families. The cause of familial conditions can lie in genetics or in environmental factors. The genes of an individual are defined at conception and cannot be altered, but the environmental factors are open to a great deal of manipulation and variation. In experimental animals, the environment can be altered at will, but in humans one has to wait for events to occur on a chance basis before they can be investigated. This may partly explain why, until very recently, there had only been one report of the development of alcoholism in the children of alcoholics raised in a home other than that of the natural parents.

Anne Roe (1944) investigated a group of 36 children who were the putative offspring of fathers who drank excessively and who also had repeated job-loss and episodes of disorderly conduct. The children were all white, non-Jewish children who were adopted before the age of ten and who were at least twenty-one at the time of the follow-up study. In addition to having alcoholic fathers only four of the mothers were considered normal. Overall, the children came from severely disturbed backgrounds.

A comparison of the alcoholic-parent group was made with a group of 25 children from a non-alcholic background. These children were illegitimate or orphaned. They fared better from the beginning in being placed very early in life and they also tended to be placed in homes with a number of advantages over the homes in which the "alcoholic" children were placed. One marked difference between the groups was that 92 per cent of the control children were ultimately adopted by their foster parents whereas only 56 per cent of the "alcoholic" children were adopted. On a strict methodological basis the control group was therefore not as well-matched to the experimental group as one would have wished.

However, at follow-up the drinking behaviour of the two groups was remarkably similar. The subjects were aged twenty-two to forty years, with the alcoholics being on average older than the controls (thirty-two years and twenty-eight years respectively). In neither group was there any evidence of serious alcohol abuse. Regular alcohol use was reported by 7 per cent of the "alcoholic" group and 9 per cent of the control group, occasional use by 63 per cent and 55 per cent respectively. Abstinence was unexpectedly high in both groups at 30 per cent and 36 per cent respectively. From this study it can be concluded that the genetic element in the development of alcoholism, if present at all, would appear to be of less importance than the environmental influences.

Until recently, those who hold a belief in possible genetic influences have had to rely on criticising Anne Roe's study for its various methodological defects. Recently, a similar study has been reported upon from Denmark (Goodwin *et al.*, 1973). Denmark was chosen because of the factors already noted as advantages for this kind of study in Scandinavian countries.

Investigations took place of 5,483 non-family adoptions, all of which occurred in or around Copenhagen between 1924 and 1947. The criteria for inclusion as a subject in the study were: being male; having a parent admitted to hospital with a primary diagnosis of alcoholism; being separated from the biological parents before six weeks of life; having no relation to the adoptive parents; and having no contact with the biological parents after adoption. A total of 67 subjects matched these criteria. Most of the alcoholic parents were the adoptees' fathers.

Two control groups were chosen which matched the "alcoholic" group in all but one factor. Neither control group had a history of having a parent admitted to hospital with alcoholism. One group (N = 70) had a history of parental psychiatric hospitalisation for a condition other than alcoholism. Schizophrenia was also excluded and most of the admissions were for depression or character disorder. Due to difficulties in tracing some of the selected cases, the final numbers were slightly lower than those stated above.

The control and experimental groups were well-matched on the vast majority of the demographic characteristics measured and the groups of adoptive parents were also well-matched. Two differences were found between the adult offspring of alcoholic parents and the control groups. In the "alcohol" group, the rate of divorce was significantly higher than in the control group and so was the occurrence of psychiatric treatment and hospitalisation. The "alcohol" group had five times the rate of psychiatric hospitalisation exhibited by the controls. Alcoholism played the major part in the increased rate of hospitalisation in the "alcohol" group.

The diagnosis of alcoholism in the two groups was based on being a heavy drinker and having problems in three of the following areas: social/marital, job/police, evidence of physical dependence, loss of control or morning drinking. Using these criteria, 10 out of 55 probands and 4 out of 78 controls (both groups of controls combined) were described as alcoholic. This difference is significant at the 2 per cent level. An investigation of psychopathology in general revealed no differences between the groups. In the study, the adoptees were aged twenty-three to forty-five years, with a mean of thirty years and it might be expected that ten years hence the prevalence of alcoholism would be higher in both groups.

The conclusion drawn by Goodwin and his colleagues is that although it appears that a "genetic predisposition" to alcoholism (and divorce) seems probable, it is not yet established. Taking the evidence presented earlier from twin studies and half-sibling research, together with this latest paper, there is some presumption that in at least severe alcoholism, genetic predisposition does play some part in the causes of the condition.

Association with a factor known to be inherited

There are a lot of factors that are known to be genetically determined and that are not influenced by environmental factors.

Height, which is genetically determined to a large degree, can be affected by nutrition or disease and therefore cannot be used in the way we shall consider next. Characteristics such as ABO blood groups, the ability to taste phenylthiocarbamide (PTC), the secretion of blood group (ABH) substance in the saliva and, finally, colour-vision are determined genetically and are apparently subject to little environmental influence.

This chapter has so far been heavily biased towards studies of alcoholism and it will have to continue in this same direction in the present subsection because all the work of this nature has been restricted to alcoholics.

The four characteristics listed above are all examples of a particular kind of genetic characteristic termed "genetic polymorphisms". This means that they all exist in a number of forms—for example there are four ABO blood groups, groups A, O, B and AB. The rarest of the forms occurs in a greater proportion than could be maintained by recurrent mutation and usually there is some advantage to the rarest form that keeps it in equilibrium with the rest. An example of this is a trait which occurs in some Africans called "sickling". Their red blood cells, instead of being round, at times form into sickle shapes and this can cause serious consequences. Possession of the sickle trait in its full form is not at all advantageous, but possessing one of the sickle-cell genes and one normal red-cell gene not only means the person will have normally-shaped red cells but also in some way is resistant to malaria. As would be expected the highest rates of the occurrence of the sickle-cell trait are in malarial areas where it is very advantageous. However, the advantages of some rare forms of genetic polymorphisms are not at all obvious.

With regard to alcoholism there have been a number of investigations into the relative proportions of the various phases of the polymorphisms in order to determine whether or not the proportions are changed when compared with the normal population. Assuming that such a change was found consistently, then this would be evidence that there might be a genetic component in the causes of alcoholism.

The findings with regard to ABO blood groups have been inconsistent. A review by Swinson and Madden (1973), has found that although there have been some reports of an excess of blood group

A or blood group B in alcoholic populations, overall no one blood group is represented with any greater frequency than would occur by chance. In the same review the reports of the secretion of ABH substance in the saliva were considered and further evidence was found to confirm the studies of Camps and his co-workers, that there was an excess of non-secretors of ABH substance in a large group of alcoholics. In the general population in the U.K., the proportion of non-secretors is approximately 23 per cent. In the alcoholic group studied in Chester the proportion was 36·49 per cent.

Looking at the blood groups separately, almost half the people of blood group A were non-secretors. This finding was statistically greater than for the general population. It might therefore be hypothesised that there is some genetic difference between alcoholics and the normal population, but Camps (1972) has argued that the change in the proportions of secretors and non-secretors may be secondary and be brought about by excess alcohol intake. If so, then the finding is one of an acquired change and not a pre-existing physiological difference. Camps's suggestion has not yet been confirmed.

A similar state of affairs exists with regard to the use of PTC-tasting as a genetic marker in alcoholism. Early reports suggested that the proportion of tasters and non-tasters of PTC amongst alcoholics was different from the general population proportions. One of us, (Swinson, 1973) confirmed the finding but it appeared that the inability to taste the bitter PTC was due to the effects of alcohol and there was no real evidence of any genetic difference between alcoholics and non-alcoholics.

The investigation of colour vision in alcoholism started with reports from Chile of a marked increase in colour-blindness amongst groups of alcoholics (Cruz-Coke and Varela, 1965). Since that time, a number of similar studies have been reported and their results have fallen into three fairly predictable groups: firstly, reports of an association between alcoholism and a genetic form of colour-blindness; secondly, reports of an association between alcoholism and colour-blindness acquired through the excessive use of alcohol; and thirdly, investigations that have reported no connection between alcoholism and colour-blindness. The Chilean workers have presented a lot of evidence supporting the hypothesis that alcoholism is part of a sex-linked genetic disorder, but in the opinion of one of the present authors (Swinson, 1972) this is not yet proven.

As yet, all that can be safely said about alcoholism and genetics is that alcoholism appears to be commoner in the close relatives of alcoholics whether or not they are reared in the same environment. Despite some reports to the contrary, it is not yet possible to use a definite genetic factor to predict the development of alcoholism in an individual. In the field of drug dependence apart from alcoholism, there is no comparable work. The genetic study of drug dependence seems at the present time unlikely to be a fruitful field of research. Until the relevant work is done, the possibility (however remote) cannot be entirely dismissed.

PSYCHOLOGICAL VARIABLES

The psychological factors in the causes of alcoholism and drug dependence have been studied very extensively. The evidence for a psychological component in drug dependency can be considered under three broad headings:

1. The addictive-personality hypothesis.
2. Personality correlates of alcoholism and drug dependence.
3. Learning-theory formulations.

The addictive-personality hypothesis

The idea of a particular personality structure which is the basis for addiction to any one of a range of substances has a certain appeal, but little support from the available evidence. If "personality" is defined in terms of behaviour with respect to certain chemicals, then all opiate addicts and all barbiturate addicts must have the same "personality" as all other opiate or barbiturate addicts.

What the proponents of the addictive-personality theory should be able to demonstrate to gain support for their hypothesis is that *prior* to the onset of drug dependence there was a particular type of personality or a particular constellation of personality traits in those people who later became drug dependent. Conversely, it should also be shown that the same personality structure is not very common amongst non-drug-dependent people. It has not yet been possible to find a particular type of personality that is related either to all forms of drug dependence or to all sufferers from any one kind of dependence.

Another of the difficulties to be answered by the proponents of the theory is that even though they may find similarities amongst the personalities of the drug-dependents in a particular study, these similarities may well not extend to the total population of drug-dependents, the majority of whom are not investigated.

It was possible a few years ago to consider all drug addicts as personality-disordered people, but if one includes the use of marijuana the illogicality of a search for an addictive personality becomes obvious. It is inconceivable that the 10 per cent of university students who admit to marijuana use all have the same pre-existing personality structure. Jellinek (1952) dismissed the idea of the alcoholic personality, but one still finds papers written on the subject (Berger, 1972). In putting forward the idea of the addictive personality again, Berger states that addicts can never cure their addiction but can only exchange it for another. Thus, he states that heroin dependents can only switch to methadone and alcoholics to almost-nightly meetings of Alcoholics Anonymous. Whilst what he says may be true of a proportion of the people in the group he considers, such behaviour is not typical of the whole group. Even in those in whom it does occur, nightly attendance at A.A. is usually a transient stage in recovery (or relapse).

There is no hard evidence to support the addictive-personality hypothesis, but this is not to say that particular personality abnormalities do not play a considerable part in the genesis of alcoholism and drug dependence. These factors will be discussed in the following section.

Personality correlates of alcoholism and drug dependence

The personality traits of alcoholics and drug-dependents have been described by many workers of varying orientation in psychiatry and other disciplines. These include psycho-analytical formulations, psychiatric descriptions of personality types, the results of formal psychological testing and the prospective study of children in whom a description of the personality before the onset of the condition was obtained.

Whatever the orientation of the investigation, and whatever the drug of dependence, the main difficulties in this area are to show that the method of assessment of personality traits is reliable, that the traits pre-dated the onset of dependence and that the traits delineated are typical of groups of drug-dependents who do not present for treatment. Few studies have matched up to these requirements.

Psycho-analytic reports of alcoholism and drug dependence have claimed that the drugs are used in an attempt to cure defects in the primitive conscience, or to satisfy infantile unconscious needs. Without this attempt at self-cure, which leads to alcoholism or drug dependence, it is hypothesised that there would be a more serious breakdown in the integrity of the personality. There is little evidence to support this point of view. In psycho-analytical terms, alcoholism is seen as arising as a result of difficulties in an early stage of psycho-sexual development—the oral stage. Due to fixation then, the child grows up with persistent oral-character traits, which are revealed in adult life by passivity, dependence, general intolerance of psychic tension and reduced ability to withstand pain and frustration. Whilst dependence (in an emotional and not a drug sense) and intolerance to tension and frustration typify many alcoholics and drug-dependents, they are certainly not common to all people in these categories.

Rado (1933) proposed the idea that certain people are excessively predisposed to respond actively to the pleasurable effects of any drug. Such individuals are also said to be intolerant to tension and stress and would always attempt to solve these symptoms by means of mood-altering agents. The predisposition was termed "pharmacothymia" and the use of alcohol (or drugs) was equated with a sexual act in which the effects of a pharmacological agent replaced normal sexual experience.

A recent psychodynamic study of narcotic addicts (Barnard and Ritch, 1968) described them as having a dependent, infantile character structure and an inability to tolerate tension. It was also stated that, because the conflicts in the development of the personality occur at a very early age before the development of language, the conflicts cannot be verbalised. Psychotherapy that relies on verbal communication is therefore considered by these investigators to be likely to fail.

Oral character traits were said by Knight (1937) to persist due to faulty upbringing in families with a particular make-up. In these families, the mothers are said to be over-indulgent and to shield the child from a harsh, inconsistent father. (The effects of parental attitudes and personality on addictive behaviour were discussed more fully in the last chapter.)

Psychiatric formulations of personality types have been offered by many authors, who have classified alcoholics and addicts into various sub-groups depending upon their own clinical judgment. The reliability of such judgments is open to question. Most of the personality types of alcoholics and addicts are covered by Williams' (1963) rhyming classification of alcoholics into the "good", the "bad", the "sad", and the "mad". "Good" alcoholics are the socially-adjusted ones who remain with the same group of friends, but gradually neglect their families. The "bad" ones are the people with psychopathic personality structures, the "sad" comprise the shy, tense people who use alcohol as a prop and the "mad" group is made up of people with psychotic disorders of either a manic-depressive or schizophrenic nature. This classification could just as well apply to the general population if we said that the "good" individuals are psychiatrically normal and those people who are psychiatrically ill fall into three large groups: the personality disordered, the neurotic or the psychotic. It is therefore possible to divide all addicts or any other group into similar categories but it does not help with delineating causatively important factors.

Studies of alcoholics tend to agree on findings of depression, isolation, low frustration-tolerance and inability to cope with anxiety and tension. Immaturity, or sexual problems, are also commonly found in groups of alcoholics. Another fairly common report is that alcoholics are excessively emotionally-dependent upon other people. One point that is made by Tiebout (1945) and others is that, whatever the initial personality structure, alcoholics tend to become similar in terms of behaviour as the condition progresses.

Kessel and Walton (1965) divided alcoholics into five groups, of which the dominant characteristics are contained in the above list. They described the immature, the self-indulgent, the person with sexual problems, the self-punitive and the stressed-personality types. The *immature* type is said to have difficulties in becoming independent of his parents and is also unable to form stable and meaningful relationships with other adults. The *self-indulgent* are seen as being the product of an over-protective childhood environment that leads to a persistence of childhood traits like the need for instant gratification and an inability to delay rewards. The *sexually-troubled* are subdivided into those with abnormally low sex-drive, the sexually shy and the sexual deviants, who are mainly homosexual. Many psycho-analysts have emphasised the homosexual nature of the drinking habits in male-dominated pubs and have explained the lack of overt homosexual activity by saying that the homosexuality remains latent. Deviant sexual thoughts which are unwanted by the person can either be anaesthetised by drugs or alcohol, or alternatively, by reducing inhibitions the deviant thought can lead to an acted-out deviant behaviour. The *self-punitive* personality is said to arise from an upbringing that punishes overt expressions of anger so that when the child grows up and feels angry at times, he is also bound to feel anxious. If alcohol is used to suppress the anxiety component, then the accompanying anger may well be expressed in a violent manner. The *stressed personality* might be termed the anxious personality (or in lay terms "highly strung") and because alcohol and barbiturates are efficient sedatives, they are commonly used as self-administered medication to control the anxiety when it is marked. Due to the development of tolerance, the danger of drug dependence developing in such a personality is obvious.

Very similar observations have been made in studies of drug dependence to those outlined above. Wikler and Rasor (1953) described the majority of narcotic addicts as having one of two forms of behaviour deviation, the *neurotic* and the *psychopathic*. A few addicts were also found to have normal personality structures, as in the case of people with painful illnesses, and a few were found to be psychotic. The "neurotics" were said to seek relief from anxiety and this was termed "negative euphoria". The psychopaths in contrast sought elation or "positive euphoria". In the normals, the main concern was the relief of pain and for the psychotics the relief of depression. A psycho-analytical analysis of narcotic addiction concentrated on oral satisfaction, sexual immaturity, self-destruction, hostility and depression of mood. The finding that narcotic addiction usually occurs in adolescent men was explained in terms of opiates being particularly effective in suppressing aggressive and sexual feelings, areas in which young men commonly develop conflicts. The actual drug of choice was seen by Wikler and Rasor as being accidental and it was postulated that there was not a pre-addiction "impulse" to use any drug or particular kind of drug.

Formal psychological testing of alcoholics and drug-dependent people has produced comparable results to the clinical observations described above. Personality assessment is based largely on two methods. The first, the projective-test technique, consists of presenting the subject with a vague picture or indeterminate pattern and asking him to say what he sees or to make up a story around the picture. The hypothesis is that, because the test material is unstructured and ambiguous, what the subject says will be representative of his inner feelings that are projected (hence "projective test") on to the material. The commonest of such tests is the Rorschach inkblot test. Although it is very frequently used and has been employed for decades, there is little evidence that the test is either reliable or valid. Interpretations of responses to the Rorschach cards are usually no more reliable than clinical interviews held without any attempted psychological testing.

Non-projective techniques usually consist of a questionnaire or a task which may be administered by the examiner or attempted by the subject. The most commonly reported test in the investigation of the personality structure of alcoholics and addicts is the Minnesota Multiphasic Personality Inventory (M.M.P.I.). The M.M.P.I. is a long and somewhat tedious test that is self-administered. The results are expressed in terms of the subject's position on a number of scales measured by the test. The test may reveal normality or an increase or a decrease on a scale when compared with the normal population. An "M.M.P.I. profile", which is a composite of all the scales, can also be determined.

Again, the scale scores that have tended to be elevated in alcoholics and drug addicts have been the psychopathic deviate (Pd) scale and the depression (D) scale. There have also been reports of an increase in the schizophrenic (Sc) scale scores. Alcoholic group studies such as those by Hewitt (1943) and Manson (1949) have mainly reported increases in the Pd scale. Several attempts have been made to construct scales especially designed to differentiate alcoholics from normals and from other psychiatrically-ill groups. MacAndrew and Geertsman (1964) examined the usefulness of three M.M.P.I.-derived alcoholism scales and found that the tests measured general maladjustment rather than alcoholism.

Due to the fact that most alcoholism scales were developed as a result of testing groups of hospitalised alcoholics, or of people with drinking problems who present themselves for treatment, it is not legitimate to attempt to use the scales in differentiating non-diagnosed alcoholics, either in the general population or in a group of psychiatric patients.

The M.M.P.I. has been used in a similar way in the investigation of the personality structure of drug addicts. Amongst infrequent drug-takers, very little is found in the way of personality abnormality. Studies of long-term takers, particularly from such institutions as the specialised hospital in Lexington, Kentucky, have confirmed the general similarity between heroin addicts and non-drug-taking psychopaths (Hill, Haertzen and Davis, 1962). Very close similarities were shown by hospitalised adolescent addicts and non-addict adolescent delinquents. Many of the studies of narcotic addicts were on those whose addiction was not so severe. In this circumstance, the finding of increased psychopathy scores in the addict population is to be expected. Gendreau and Gendreau (1970) compared a group of incarcerated addicts with a non-addict imprisoned group. The groups were controlled, as far as possible, for socio-economic level, criminal record, age, intellectual performance and opportunity to obtain narcotics. It was hypothesised by these investigators that the addiction-prone personality should be either inadequate, passive and neurotic, or psychopathic or sexually maladjusted or prone to anxiety and depression. Comparison of the addict groups however revealed no differences in M.M.P.I. responses. Both groups showed high Pd scores and the authors pointed out that after thirty years of unsuccessful search for the "addictive-personality", people might be well advised to stop looking.

One of the methods by which researchers may hinder themselves in the search for a typical personality make-up in addiction is the use of group-mean responses. Averaging the responses for a large group of addicts may obscure differences in individual make-up that are of importance. The addiction-prone personality was one of four causatively important factors in addictive disorders put forward by Sheppard (1972) and his colleagues. The other three factors were accidental exposure, peer pressure and sensation-seeking. They studied 336 male narcotic users in Centre Islip State Hospital, of whom 33 per cent showed sociopathic personality structure on the M.M.P.I., 30 per cent showed psychotic features, 16 per cent neurotic traits, 2 per cent organic brain disorder responses, while 6 per cent showed no psychopathology. This study simply confirmed the usual clinical findings in narcotic addicts.

In a less-disturbed group, the findings were quite different as might be expected. McAree (1972) and his colleagues reported on 100 student drug-users and 100 student non-users. All the people taking part in the study were granted anonymity and guaranteed immunity from the legal repercussions of identifying themselves as illicit drug-takers. By this means it was hoped that a representative sample of student drug-takers would be obtained. Due to the ingrained knowledge that drug-taking is punishable by law (and at times very severely) it seems unlikely that anxious or suspicious drug-takers would volunteer even under these conditions. Of the 100 drug-takers, 33 took only marijuana, 19 were multiple drug-takers and 48 gross multiple drug-takers. No difference was found between the personality structure of the normals and the marijuana group but multiple-takers, even if infrequent in their habit, showed marked divergence from normal responses. The greatest deviation of the M.M.P.I. scales in the multiple drug-use groups was found in the Sc (schizophrenic) scale.

Walton (1968) adopted the same approach in the area of alcoholism. He divided the alcoholics into "loss of control" and "failure to abstain" categories and then compared the responses of the groups on a variety of personality tests. Variations in drinking patterns are thought to be socially determined in the main, although Jellinek (1960, pp. 147–9) proposed a rather unsatisfactory hypothesis based on differences in cell metabolism. Walton's study was designed to investigate the possibility of a correlation between personality type and drinking pattern. The sample studied was small (N = 38) and was highly selected. Compared with normals, the alcoholics were found to be less stable emotionally, less cheerful, more inhibited and more tense. "Loss of control" alcoholics were found to have a great fear of their own impulses and they were also found to be more aggressive than the "failure to abstain" group, but the aggression was directed toward themselves. Walton considered that his findings showed that personality type and drinking pattern were inter-related, but suggested that some of the test responses were due to the patients' recalling and reporting upon their behaviour when intoxicated. "Loss of control" addicts suffer public drunkenness more frequently than "failure to abstain" alcoholics and for this reason they might fear their own impulses, which are a result of their drinking pattern, rather than that their fear leads to a particular way of drinking.

So far, most of the reports have related psychopathic, anxious or dependent-personality structures to the excessive use of alcohol and drugs. One other important factor appears to be depression of mood. An investigation of the psychopathology of narcotic addicts, reported to the Committee of Problems of Drug Dependence, 1971, made use of the M.M.P.I. and two depression-rating scales, the Zung Self-Rating Depression Scale and the Beck Depression Inventory. A 36-symptom check list was also used to study the 196 methadone-taking out-patients in the sample. The subjects were mostly male, 55 per cent were black Americans and they were typically hard-core, unskilled, unemployed narcotic addicts. The main finding in this group was of an increase in depression, though not as great an increase as is reported by psychotic or neurotic depressives. The addicts felt irritable and unable to cope with tasks and had a negative outlook on most things in their lives. A second study of the same group showed that the motivation to continue opiate use was relative to feelings of depression and mood-disturbance. The findings of Winokur and his colleagues with regard to alcoholism and depression have been presented earlier in this chapter, and these too find a close relationship between the disorders.

Fejer and Smart (1972) in a study of school children in three areas of Southern Ontario used a measure of anxiety based on the Taylor Manifest Anxiety Scale to assess the possible differences between admitted drug-takers and non-takers. The occurrence of problems needing psychological treatment at any time in the subjects' lives was also determined by the same questionnaire.

The proportions of school children using drugs in Ontario has been discussed in Chapter 2. In this study there was a highly significant difference between the groups with regard to the anxiety scores. All the drug-users were found to be in the top quarter of the anxiety scores. Glue and solvent abusers had the highest overall anxiety ratings, followed by the users of stimulants, tranquillisers and barbiturates. Tobacco, alcohol and marijuana users also fall into the highest quarter but were less anxious than the previous groups. Opiate and speed users also reported moderately high anxiety. Of the drug-using group, those using LSD as their major drug of abuse reported the lowest level of anxiety, although this was still higher than that found in the non-users.

There was also a significant link with the occurrence of psychological treatment in the drug-taking group. Marijuana, barbiturate and tranquilliser users had on average four times the prevalence of past psychological treatment as non-users. The increase for LSD, speed and opiate users was 500 per cent, for stimulants other than speed 300 per cent, and for tobacco and glue users 200 per cent. Of the non-users, 6 per cent had had treatment and of those using opiates, speed, tranquillisers and LSD altogether 20 per cent had had treatment. Not only was the proportion of drug-takers who had received treatment in the past higher, but they also underwent treatment for longer periods and on more occasions than the non-users. Amongst the drug users, speed users had the most frequent and most long-lasting psychological problems.

The problems presented by both users and non-users were related in the main to the family and school. LSD, speed and opiate users commonly went for help because of depression. In general, opiate and speed users were found to be highly anxious, to have had a lot of treatment for psychological problems and also to be depressed.

Wiener (1970) reviewed the findings of personality make-up in young drug addicts and concluded that infrequent takers often had no personality deviation, but that regular takers commonly were deviant. He included an assessment of "ego strength" in the questionnaires administered to his subjects but found no difference between drug-users and non-users. The drug-takers in Wiener's study were extremely mildly dependent, if at all, on the drugs they experienced. Of the 35 children who had experienced only the use of one drug, 26 had taken the drug less than five times and only one had used drugs at times other than the weekend. The two-drug users (N = 15) did not include a single regular drug-user and the 9 children who claimed experience of three or four drugs had had very limited experience both in time and frequency of use. Whether these subjects can be termed drug abusers is extremely doubtful.

In summary, it can be safely stated that there is no single personality type that can be termed addiction-prone. Some alcoholics and drug addicts show no personality abnormality at all and this is most likely to occur if alcohol or a particular drug is freely available in the population. There is an inverse relationship between the degree of psychopathology in addicts in any population and the availability of drugs, including alcohol, in that social group. People who are tense, depressed, emotionally dependent, psychopathic or uncertain of their sexual role, are particularly liable to become addicted.

Learning theory in relation to alcoholism and addiction

Under the heading of psychological factors in the causes of addiction one can include learning theory formulations. As has been stated above, people who are tense and anxious appear to run the risk of becoming alcoholic and one of the reasons for this may be that alcohol causes a reduction in anxiety and also causes disinhibition. The anxiety-reducing effect of alcohol can act as a powerful reinforcer of behaviour. Dollard and Miller (1950) have interpreted alcoholic drinking in terms of anxiety-reduction leading to the excessive drinking of alcohol. Drive-reduction has also been hypothesised by Wikler (1961) as being of great importance in maintaining opiate addiction. The drive in opiate dependence is derived from the changes that the addict felt on injecting the drug on earlier occasions. When these changes occur again, a connection is made between the perception of that state and the reduction in the unpleasantness of the state by a further injection. Once having discovered that a further injection causes a reduction in the unpleasantness produced by withdrawal, there is a greater likelihood that the next time the withdrawal state occurs it will be followed by yet another injection.

The choice of opiates as opposed to alcohol as the drug of dependence in a particular person has been explained in terms of the effects of opiates in reducing the primary drives of sex and pain. Individuals who have conflicts in these areas are seen as being more likely to choose relief from opiates, whereas people who "act out" when stressed are more likely to choose the disinhibition offered by alcohol. The actions of alcohol in reducing feelings of anxiety are very variable. When taken in small doses its results are inconsistent (Docter and Perkins, 1961) but in large doses alcohol produces a substantial reduction in mood-arousal (Carpenter, 1957). The effects on anxiety reduction are far from peculiar to alcohol. Meprobamate (a tranquilliser) and barbiturates have been shown to produce the same effect. Lienert and Traxel (1959) assessed basic emotionality some weeks before a study of the effects of alcohol, meprobamate and placebo on emotional response. They found that those subjects who exhibited high emotionality before the trial had a greater response to the anxiety-reducing properties of alcohol than occurred in the low-arousal or moderately-aroused subjects. Thus people who are initially, and perhaps pathologically, anxious, will find alcohol and similar drugs to be a greater positive reinforcer than those who are not so basically anxious.

Alcoholics and other addicts suffer greatly from their repeated drug-intake and for this reason it might be expected that the behaviour involved in drinking or drug-taking would be self-limiting, because it is so punitive. However, it has to be realised that a small immediate positive reinforcement for a piece of behaviour is much more powerful than a delayed negative consequence of great magnitude. The threat of failing an examination three months ahead is less effective in determining behaviour than being invited to the pub by a friend. Rather perversely, it has been reported by Tamerin and Mendelson (1969) that alcoholics given free access to alcohol become more depressed and anxious as they continue to drink. Bandura (1969) suggested that presenting the future consequences symbolically before drinking occurs may inhibit the initiation of drinking. Perhaps covert sensitisation works in this manner (*see* p. 230).

Animal models of alcoholism and drug dependence have been studied by many investigators. Probably the best known experiments in this field are those of Masserman and his colleagues. Cats that showed no inclination to drink alcohol before the experiment were conditioned to go through a series of steps to obtain food from a closed feeding box. When the pattern of obtaining the food reward was well established, the procedure was changed so that, on opening the box, the cats received a blast of air in their faces. This aversive stimulus produced a disruption of the conditioned response and resulted in an "experimental neurosis". On being given alcohol, the cats again approached the food box and persisted despite the aversive stimulation. In normal cats it had been shown that alcohol impaired the performance of conditioned responses but a number of "neurotic" cats chose an alcohol/milk solution in preference to plain milk. Further experimentation by Smart (1965) has confirmed that alcohol acts so as to reduce anxiety in this experimental situation.

The effects of alcohol in Masserman's study could either have been to reduce the avoidance behaviour or to increase the approach behaviour in what Conger (1956) considered was an approach-avoidance conflict. Conger similarly trained two separate groups of rats to discover which of the alternatives appeared to operate and found that the approach activity was unaltered but that after alcohol, avoidance behaviour was reduced. Not all experiments have confirmed these findings and Mildred Weiss (1958) was very critical of the interpretations of the results. In a series of experiments with rats she concluded that alcohol led to a recurrence of the food-approach behaviour, because it disorganised the most recently-acquired behaviour pattern—in this case avoidance.

Alcohol does affect the display of emotionally-determined behaviour. Normally, when a positive reinforcer such as food is withdrawn from the experimental situation, the response it previously elicited fades away. Comparing groups of animals under non-reinforcement conditions, Barry and his co-workers (1962) found that alcohol-receiving animals continued to perform the non-reinforced behaviour for longer than those animals receiving a placebo.

In contrast to the effect of anxiety on alcohol drinking, and vice versa, Lester (1961) caused animals to become intoxicated by rewarding the drinking of alcohol solutions in a random intermittent way with food. Keehn (1969) reported similar findings using positive reinforcement. His experimental animals drank sufficient alcohol to produce blood alcohol levels of 220 mg per cent, the sort of levels one finds in human alcoholics rather than in social drinkers. Keehn suggested that in human alcoholics, the environmental contingencies may be of greater importance in the development of alcoholism than the mere effects of drinking alcohol.

A commonly-used method to test the effects of alcohol or drugs in animals has been to administer the appropriate amount of the drug to the animal and observe the effects. Nichols (1972) has reviewed his earlier work and has defined the process of addiction in terms of "operant" conditioning. In this type of conditioning process, it is necessary for the experimental subject to make a variety of responses, one, or some, of which is followed immediately by a reward. The application of positive reinforcement following on a specific behaviour causes that piece of behaviour to occur more frequently. By placing rats that were in a withdrawal state in a situation where they could administer opiates to themselves, the reward for self-administering the opiates was of course the relief of the withdrawal symptoms. Nichols was also able to make rats relapse into morphine addiction by means of an operant-condition method.

Environmental stimuli were considered by Wikler as influencing relapse in opiate dependence. Opiate-dependent rats show both a short-lived and a long-lasting abstinence syndrome. In this latter state, which may persist for six months, rats show a number of physiological and behavioural changes including "wet-dog" shakes. Rats were made opiate-dependent and then at the time they were due to experience withdrawal symptoms, were placed in a distinctive environment. After pairing withdrawal experiences and the special environment on a number of occasions, the rats were then kept abstinent from opiates for some weeks or months. On being returned to the withdrawal environment after this time and without receiving any more opiates the rats exhibited withdrawal behaviour in the form of increased "wet-dog" shakes.

Wikler suggested that human addicts, returning during an abstinent phase to old haunts and companions previously associated with opiate-withdrawal experiences, might produce a conditioned relapse into further opiate addiction.

The effects of drugs on behaviour mediated by learning are complex, but it appears that, through their effects on anxiety and emotionality and their effect on the conditioning processes, drug dependence is a self-perpetuating process that should (and of course does) have a high relapse rate.

REFERENCES

Amark, C., "A Study in Alcoholism, Clinical, Social, Psychiatric and Genetic Investigations", *Acta Psychiatrica Scandinavica*, Suppl. No. 70: 1–251, 1951.

Bandura, A., *Principles of Behaviour Modification*, Holt, Rinehart and Winston Inc., London, 1969.

Barnard, G. W. and Ritch, Linda, "Psychodynamics of Narcotic Addiction", *Journal of the Florida Medical Association*, 55 (9): 831–4, 1968.

Barry, H., Wagner, A. R. and Miller, N. E., "Effects of Alcohol and Amobarbital on Performance Inhibited by Experimental Extinction", *Journal of Comparative and Physiological Psychology*, 55: 464–8, 1962.

Berger, H., "There are No Addictive Drugs, only Addictive People", *Postgraduate Medicine*, 51 (3): 269–70, 1972.

Camps, F. E., "Genetics and Alcoholism", *Annals of the New York Academy of Sciences*, 197: 134–7, 1972.

Carpenter, J. A., "Effects of Alcoholic Beverages on Skin Conductance: An Explanatory Study", *Quarterly Journal of Studies on Alcohol*, 18: 208–16, 1957.

Conger, J. J., "Reinforcement Theory and the Dynamics of Alcoholism", *Quart. J. Stud. Alcohol*, 17: 296–305, 1956.

Cruz-Coke, R. and Varela, A., "Colour Blindness and Alcohol Addiction", *Lancet*, ii: 1,348, 1965.

Docter, R. F. and Perkins, R. E., "The Effects of Ethyl Alcohol on Autonomic and Muscular Responses in Humans", *Quart. J. Stud. Alcohol*, 22: 374–86, 1961.

Dollard, J. and Miller, N., *Personality and Psychotherapy*, McGraw-Hill, New York, 1950.

Erikkson, K., "Genetic Selection for Voluntary Alcohol Consumption in the Albino Rat", *Science*, 158: 739–41, 1968.

Fejer, D. and Smart, R., "Drug Use, Anxiety and Psychological Problems amongst Adolescents", *The Ontario Psychologist*, 4 (1): 10–21, 1972.

Fleetwood, M. F. and Diethelm, O., "Emotional and Biochemical Findings and Alcoholism", *American Journal of Psychiatry*, 108: 433–8, 1951.

Gendreau, P. and Gendreau, L. P. "The 'Addiction-Prone' Personality: A Study of Canadian Heroin Addicts", *Canadian Journal of Behavioral Sciences*, 2 (i): 18–25, 1970.

Goodwin, D. W., Schulsinger, F., Hermanson, L., Guze, J. B. and Winokur, G., "Alcohol Problems in Adoptees Raised Apart from Alcoholic Biological Parents", *Archives of General Psychiatry*, 28: 238–43, 1973.

Hewitt, C. C., "A Personality Study of Alcohol Addiction", *Quart. J. Stud. Alcohol*, 4: 368–86, 1943.

Hill, H. E., Haertzen, C. A. and Davis, D., "An M.M.P.I.-Factor Analytic Study of Alcoholics, Narcotic Addicts and Criminals", *Quart. J. Stud. Alcohol*, 23: 411–31, 1962.

Jellinek, E. M., "Phases of Alcohol Addiction", *Quart. J. Stud. Alcohol*, 13: 673–84, 1952.

Jellinek, E. M., *The Disease Concept of Alcoholism*, Hillhouse Press, New Haven, Connecticut, 1960.

Kaij, L., *Alcoholism in Twins: Studies on the Etiology and Sequels of Abuse of Alcohol*, Almqvist and Wiksell, Stockholm, 1960.

Keehn, J. D., "Voluntary Consumption of Alcohol by Rats", *Quart. J. Stud. Alcohol*, 30: 320–9, 1969.

Kessel, W. I. N. and Walton, H., *Alcoholism*, Penguin, Harmondsworth, 1965.

Knight, R. P., "The Psychodynamics of Chronic Alcoholism", *Journal of Nervous and Mental Diseases*, 88: 538–48, 1937.

Lester, D., "Self-Maintenance of Intoxication in the Rat", *Quart. J. Stud. Alcohol*, 22: 223–31, 1961.

Lester, D. and Freed, E. X., "A Rat Model of Alcoholism", *Ann. N.Y. Acad. Sci.*, 197: 54–9, 1972.

Lienert, G. A. and Traxel, W., "The Effect of Meprobamate and Alcohol on Galvanic Skin Response", *Journal of Psychology*, 48: 329–34, 1959.

MacAndrew, C. and Geertsman, R. H., "A Critique of Alcoholism Scales Derived from the M.M.P.I.", *Quart. J. Stud. Alcohol*, 25: 68–76, 1964.

Manson, M. P., "A Psychometric Analysis of Psychopathic Characteristics of Alcoholism", *Journal of Consulting and Clinical Psychology*, 13: 111–18, 1949.

Mardones, R. J. and Onfray, B. E., "Influence de una substancia de las levadura (elements au complejo vitaminico B) sobre el consumo de alcohol en ratas en experimentos de auto selecion", *Rev. Chilena de Hig. y Med. Prev.*, 4: 293–7, 1942.

Masserman, J. H. and Vum, K. S., "An Analysis of the Influence of Alcohol on Experimental Neuroses in Cats", *Psychosomatic Medicine*, 8: 36–52, 1946.

McAree, C. P., Steffhangen, R. A. and Zhentlin, L. S., "Personality Factors and Patterns of Drug Use in College Students", *Am. J. Psychiatry*, 128 (7): 890–3, 1972.

Nichols, R., "The Children of Drug Addicts, What Do They Inherit?", *Ann. N.Y. Acad. Sci.*, 197: 60–5, 1972.

Nylander, I., "Children of Alcoholic Fathers", *Acta. Paediat. (Upps)*, 49 Suppl. No. 121: 1–134, Part 1, 1960.

Partanen, J., Bruun, K. and Markkanen, T., "The Inheritance of Drinking Behaviour: A Study on Intelligence, Personality and Use of Alcohol of Adult Twins", *Journal of the Finnish Foundation for Alcohol Studies*, No. 14, Helsinki, 1966.

Popham, R. E., de Lint, J. E. E. and Schmidt, W., "Review of Partanen, J., Bruun, K. and Markkanen, T., (1966)" *Alkoholpolitik*, 3: 146–9, 1967.

Rado, S., "The Psychoanalysis of Pharmacothymias (Drug Addiction)", *Psychoanalytic Review*, I: 396–413, 1933.

Rodgers, D. A. and McLearn, G. E., "Mouse Strain Differences in

Preference for Various Concentrations of Alcohol", *Quart. J. Stud. Alcohol*, 23: 26–33, 1962.

Roe, Anne, "The Adult Adjustment of Children of Alcoholic Parents Raised in Foster Homes", *Quart. J. Stud. Alcohol*, 5: 378–93, 1944.

Schuckit, M., "The Alcoholic Woman: A Literature Review", *Psychiatry in Medicine*, 3 (1): 37–43, 1972 (*a*).

Schuckit, M., "Family History and Half-Sibling Research in Alcoholism", *Ann. N.Y. Acad. Sci.*, 197: 121–5, 1972 (*b*).

Schuckit, M., Pitts, F. N., Reich, T., King, Lucy J. and Winokur, G., "Alcoholism I: Two Types of Alcoholism in Women", *Arch. Gen. Psychiatry*, 20: 301–6, 1969.

Sheppard, C., Fracchia, J., Ricca, E. and Merlis, S., "Indications of Psychopathology in Male Narcotic Abusers, Their Effects and Relations to Treatment Effectiveness", *J. Psychol.*, 81: 351–60, 1972.

Silkworth, W. D., "Alcoholism as a Manifestation of Allergy", *Medical Record*, 145: 249–51, 1937.

Slater, E. and Cowie, V., *The Genetics of Mental Disorder*, Oxford University Press, London, 1971.

Smart, R. G., "Effects of Alcohol on Conflict and Avoidance Behaviour", *Quart. J. Stud. Alcohol*, 26: 187–205, 1965.

Smart, R. G., "Illicit Drug Use in Canada: A Review of Recent Epidemiology with Clues for Prevention", *International Journal of Addictions*, 6 (3): 383–405, 1971.

Swinson, R. P., "Colour Vision Defects in Alcoholism", *British Journal of Psychiatry* (*opt.*), 27 (1): 43–50, 1972.

Swinson, R. P., "Phenylthiocarbamide Taste Sensitivity in Alcoholism", *British Journal of Addictions*, 68: 33–6, 1973.

Swinson, R. P. and Madden, J. S., "Blood Groups and the Secretion of ABH Substance in Alcoholism", *Quart. J. Stud. Alcohol*, 34 (i): 64–70, 1973.

Tamerin, J. S. and Mendelson, J. H., "The Psychodynamics of Chronic Medication: Observations of Alcoholics during the Process of Drinking in an Experimental Group Setting", *Am. J. Psychiatry*, 25: 886–99, 1969.

Tiebout, H. M., "The Syndrome of Alcohol Addiction", *Quart. J. Stud. Alcohol*, 5: 535–46, 1945.

Tienari, P., "Psychiatric Illness in Identical Twins", *Acta Psychiatr. Scand.*, Suppl. No. 171, 39: 1–195, 1963.

Walton, H. J., "Personality as a Determinant of the Form of Alcoholism", *Br. J. Psychiatry*, 114: 761–6, 1968.

Weiss, Mildred, "Alcohol as a Depressant of Psychological Conflict in Rats", *Quart. J. Stud. Alcohol*, 20: 439–51, 1958.

Wiener, R. S. P., *Drugs and Schoolchildren*, Longman, London, 1970.

Wikler, A. *et al.*, "On the Nature of Addiction and Habituation", *Brit. J. Addict.*, 57: 13–79, 1961.

Wikler, A. and Rasor, R. W., "Psychiatric Aspects of Drug Addiction", *American Journal of Medicine*, 14: 566–70, 1953.

Williams, L., *Tomorrow will be Sober*, Cassell, London, 1963.

Williams, R. J., "The Etiology of Alcoholism; A Working Hypothesis Involving the Interplay of Hereditary and Environmental Factors", *Quart. J. Stud. Alcohol*, 7: 567–87, 1947.

Winokur, G., Reich, T., Rimmer, J. and Pitts, F. N., "Alcoholism III: Diagnosis and Familial Psychiatric Illness in 259 Alcoholic Probands", *Arch. Gen. Psychiat.*, 23: 104–11, 1970.

Winokur, G., Rimmer, J. and Reich, T., "Alcoholism IV: Is There More Than One Type of Alcoholism?", *Br. J. Psychiatry*, 118: 525–31, 1971.

6 Medical complications of alcoholism and drug-taking

Alcoholism

The medical complications of alcoholism are many and varied. They can be divided into acute and chronic effects and it is the long-term effects that will be considered in this chapter. The acute effects have already been discussed in Chapter 3.

The long-term effects of the abuse of alcohol become evident in all systems of the body and range from very dramatic occurrences, such as delirium tremens, to insidious but no less dangerous conditions, such as cirrhosis of the liver. These two conditions, delirium tremens and cirrhosis of the liver, are probably the two states that come to mind when lay people think of alcoholism. Certainly, they are both of importance but delirium tremens is, at least in England, not all that common at the present time.

The acute withdrawal effects will be discussed separately from the effects of long-term consumption of alcohol, but obviously the conditions described in each group can co-exist with those in the other.

WITHDRAWAL EFFECTS

Alcohol produces physical dependence in animals that are exposed to it and it has been said that ethyl alcohol causes the most prevalent form of physical dependence. The physical dependence produced by the repeated administration of alcohol, or any other dependency-producing drug, becomes evident on stopping the drug abruptly. Alcoholics who stop drinking suddenly suffer from a withdrawal syndrome but, fortunately, few of them develop the full-blown picture of delirium tremens. It is not necessary for the alcoholic to stop drinking completely to precipitate a withdrawal illness, as a reduction in intake will commonly produce the same effect.

The different patterns of alcoholic drinking give a clue as to the likely frequency of withdrawal symptoms in the various types of drinker. The "bout-drinking", "gamma" alcoholic is very likely to suffer withdrawal effects due to his repeated episodes of very heavy drinking, followed by a period of abstinence which he may choose to enter, or which may come about through events beyond his control.

The "delta" alcoholic on the other hand, usually keeps his blood alcohol level fairly high and although he may be a little shaky in the mornings, he does not usually have a severe withdrawal spell unless he is cut off from his alcohol supply unexpectedly. This may come about through an illness, or a traffic accident causing the alcoholic's admission to hospital. If he is forewarned about his admission, then the hiding of a bottle or two in the bedside locker will stave off the withdrawal effects. The sudden onset of a delirium or epileptic convulsions in the delta alcoholic who has not made such arrangements causes alarm and, unfortunately, still causes too much diagnostic confusion amongst the attending physicians. A complete history of all patients' drinking and drug-taking habits is far more useful than emergency neurological investigations in the midst of a preventable medical emergency.

The withdrawal syndrome in alcoholism has been recognised for many years and was described by Trotter almost two centuries ago. The early symptoms are described as "the shakes" and consist of a tremor, general nervousness and anxiety. A feeling of weakness and loss of appetite may be associated with vomiting. Sleeplessness is also common. This state is often self-treated by the patient by having another alcoholic drink. If this does not happen, then a more serious condition may develop in which the body temperature increases. Hallucinations in the visual and auditory fields occur and tend to be frightening (in contrast to the traditional friendly pink elephants!). Typical of this frightening aspect was one patient who had hallucinations of unpleasant faces in the wallpaper and interpreted the green pattern in the carpet of his room as poisonous green gas seeping across the floor. Along with their hallucinations, patients are disorientated in terms of knowing the time and date and as to where they are. In some cases convulsions of an epileptiform nature occur.

The typical symptoms of delirium tremens due to alcohol withdrawal are superimposed on the more frequently seen picture of delirium from any cause. Delirium, in general, consists of a lowered level of consciousness resulting in disorientation for time and place, co-existing with fleeting attention and disconnected thinking, which is concerned with fantasy rather than reality. The hallucinatory and illusory experiences have already been mentioned. Also evident are motor disturbances consisting of general restlessness and over-activity, which may appear purposeful but in fact are not goal-directed. In delirium tremens due to alcohol withdrawal, there tends to be considerable motor restlessness combined with difficulties in balancing and walking.

It is difficult to gain the attention of the patient in delirium and even when it is gained, it tends to be fleeting so that the topic of conversation is quickly lost by the patient. To compound the difficulty of carrying on a conversation, the speech may be affected and words are slurred or are produced incorrectly or incompletely.

Usually, delirium tremens is treated in hospital and since it carries with it a certain risk of death, it is better treated in a general hospital rather than in a psychiatric hospital, even though the patients may be quite disturbed and noisy, particularly at night.

The cause of delirium tremens is primarily due to the cessation or reduction in alcohol intake, but this is far from the sole precipitant. Vitamin deficiencies, head injury and infections such as pneumonia appear to be responsible for the onset of delirium in a considerable proportion of alcoholics who continue to drink. On the other hand, when morphine dependents have been allowed to drink excessively, they develop convulsions and delirium on stopping their alcohol intake, despite being on a full diet and being otherwise in good health. As with many conditions in psychiatry or general medicine, the body reacts to non-specific insults of varying kinds in similar ways and delirium tremens can be seen as the end result of a combination of insults in differing proportions in individual cases.

In the vast majority of cases, delirium tremens clears up with treatment in a matter of a week or so, at the end of which time a terminal prolonged period of sleep occurs, after which the patient's state is greatly improved. In a very small proportion of cases the condition deteriorates due to such complications as pneumonia or heart failure. As will be explained later in this chapter, alcohol has a deleterious effect on the heart muscle and the risk of circulatory failure is frequently present in delirium tremens. If any additional physical illness complicates delirium tremens, the possibility of a fatal outcome is greatly increased. Even in an apparently healthy person who has developed delirium tremens, the seriousness of the condition should not be underestimated, as is confirmed by the experience one of us had with a man in his twenties who suddenly collapsed and died a few hours after admission to hospital in alcoholic withdrawal. The treatment of delirium tremens is discussed in Chapter 8 below.

Although the majority of patients recover from a withdrawal phase with no apparent long-term problems, it has been shown that their memory and ability to learn new pieces of information is reduced for at least a three-week period after the withdrawal. This finding may be of great importance in timing the teaching of alcoholics about their problems and the modern trend to very short in-patient stay may be disadvantageous in this condition. The average patient, however, appears to recover clinically after a few days. He can hold a coherent conversation, is fully-orientated and is physically fairly fit. For some patients, the course of events is not so smooth and instead of the delirium completely clearing up, they go into a sub-acute delirious state, in which the disorientation and confusion return, particularly at night, over a period of weeks and then gradually subside to leave the patient well again.

LONG-TERM EFFECTS ON THE BRAIN AND NERVOUS SYSTEM

Korsakoff's psychosis

Longer-lasting cases of disorientation and memory disturbance also occur and were originally described in 1887 by Korsakoff. This type of state may arise out of a delirium, or come on gradually with little in the way of initial confusion or lowering of consciousness. The main feature is the impairment of memory. The syndrome is well described by Talland (1968) and according to this author many of the patients with "amnesic" (or Korsakoff's) syndrome are so confused initially as to appear demented.

A concomitant of Korsakoff's psychosis may be Wernicke's encephalopathy. This syndrome consists of difficulty in walking (ataxia), disorder of the muscles that move the eyes (ophthalmoplegia) and peripheral nerve damage (neuropathy). Over a short space of time, usually weeks, the Wernicke's component subsides, to leave the patient with a chronic disorder of memory and learning. There may be other signs of abnormality, such as apathy and fatigue, but these are minor compared to the memory disorder.

The striking feature of the amnesic syndrome is the loss of recent memory. Although events occurring many years ago are clearly and correctly recalled, a patient with the amnesic syndrome may well deny ever meeting someone to whom he was talking five minutes earlier. Talland has shown that new information is learnt and retained at least briefly, provided there are no distractions during the task, but if any distraction does occur, as commonly happens, the information is irretrievably lost.

Due to the failure of recent memory processes, the patient is continuously disorientated for time and place, though not for who he is. Upon being pressed to give details about the events of the previous few hours, the sufferers from the amnesic syndrome will frequently produce stories of travelling or going to work which in themselves are plausible but are not compatible with being in hospital. This filling in of memory gaps is termed "confabulation".

The Korsakoff state is due to a deficiency of Vitamin B_1 (thiamine) and is reversible, provided the alcoholic will abstain from further alcohol intake and will also take a full diet and vitamin supplements. Even in this case, the recovery to full intellectual functioning is likely to take many weeks or months.

Alcoholic dementia

In some alcoholics there is a gradual falling off in all fields of intellectual functioning, which occurs over years without any dramatic episode, although the picture may come to light rather dramatically at the time of a withdrawal episode. In dementia, there is a diminution of the ability to learn and to make judgments that is accompanied by changes in behaviour. The behaviour changes may be remarked upon and noticed by relatives of the patient before there is any awareness of the degree of intellectual failure. The dementing alcoholic's social behaviour deteriorates, his memory is less efficient and his emotional responses to situations can become callous or otherwise inappropriate. In a severely-demented state, the patient is reduced to a condition in which he is unable to care for himself, shows little in the way of spontaneous speech or behaviour, has large gaps in his memory and has grossly limited emotional response. This state is irreversible and fortunately it is not common.

Cerebellar degeneration

Alcoholism may cause a more localised form of brain damage in which the cerebellum is affected. The cerebellum is located at the back of the brain below the cerebral hemispheres. It acts as a feed-back centre for the control of the muscles, and thus movement, including eye movements and speech. Damage to the cerebellum produces a picture in which the large muscles are flaccid and the gait is a wide-based reeling and staggering one. At the same time, there is a tremor of the hands and feet, and impairment of co-ordination of movement. The speech becomes irregular and may be slurred or produced in explosive bursts. Examination of the eye movements reveals that, in contrast to the normal smooth movements, the eyes jerk across the range of movement and cannot be held fixed on a point at the edge of the field of vision (nystagmus).

Peripheral neuropathy

This condition has already been mentioned in connection with the clinical picture of delirium tremens. It is quite common in a mild form in alcoholism, particularly if there has been a vitamin-deficient diet for any length of time. It can occur in any ailment causing B_1 (thiamine) deficiency or in other B vitamin deficiencies.

It presents as a symmetrical affection of the distal part of the limbs. The patients complain of tingling or numbness in the feet or hands and also of clumsiness of the hands and difficulty in telling where their feet are when walking. There is often a peculiar feeling described as "walking on cotton wool". Particularly in alcoholic peripheral neuropathy, there is often pain in the calf muscles which can be very tender to pressure. The arms and legs are weak and there may be wrist-drop or foot-drop. In these states, the hand or foot hangs from the end of the outstretched limb instead of being held in line with it. The tendon jerks are diminished or lost. Due to the association of alcoholism with heavy cigarette consumption, there may be painless burns on the hands. The feet may also suffer injury which goes unnoticed. This arises due to the nerves that carry pain and touch being damaged and causing a type of anaesthesia termed "glove and stocking" anaesthesia because the area of loss of feeling coincides with that area covered by gloves or stockings of varying lengths.

The administration of a full diet and vitamin supplements produces a full recovery in a few weeks.

Alcoholic delusions of jealousy

The conditions described so far in this chapter are all physical complications of the excessive intake of alcohol over a long period. Alcoholic delusions of jealousy involve some of the physical effects, namely, lessened inhibition and decreased powers of judgment. It also includes, and is usually based upon, the unwillingness of the wife of the alcoholic to continue in a sexual relationship with her recurrently-drunken husband, who is probably having difficulties with his sexual potency. The refusal of a woman in this situation appears perfectly reasonable to us, but is not interpreted in this way by the alcoholic husband. He sees her refusal as a rejection of him, to which he reacts with suspicion and violence. The violence may be of an extreme nature and can end in a fatal assault on the wife. It is reported (Slater and Roth, 1969) that 14 per cent of recorded cases have made a potentially fatal attack on their spouse. In a recent study (Madden, 1973) it has been shown that accusations of infidelity are common in both male and female alcoholics. (It has also been recognised for some years that paranoid reactions, with jealousy as a major symptom, occur without an alcoholic background.)

As the condition develops, the alcoholic becomes convinced that he is the only sexual partner that his wife is rejecting. He accuses her of having intercourse with many men and may try to find evidence of such behaviour. One of our patients, a man in his late forties, who had always had an unsatisfactory sexual life, began to suspect his wife of bringing men into the house whilst he was asleep. He regularly inspected his wife's clothing for signs of sexual intercourse and stayed away from work to follow her throughout the day. He reached the stage of insisting that his wife go to bed before him each night and he would then search the garden, lock all the doors, search each room and cupboard and finally search the loft space before he went to bed. His suspicions were eventually confirmed, when he was woken one night by what he interpreted as stones being thrown at his bedroom window and on getting out of bed he saw a man walking down the road. Although it was dark, he was certain the man was someone who lived next door to them in a town where they had previously lived.

Reasoning and persuasion have no effect on the maintenance of the delusion. Medication with major tranquillisers or antidepressant drugs may alleviate the symptoms, but in the case above no change was brought about over a two-year period. He agreed to live away from his wife and, fortunately, no violence was ever reported to have occurred.

In another very similar case seen at the same time, an alcoholic man who had a very active and promiscuous sexual life began to suspect his wife of infidelity. His wife had a gynaecological complaint which necessitated her seeing her male general practitioner. The doctor performed a vaginal examination during the investigation of the disorder. At the time the wife was unaware of the jealousy her husband felt and she told him she had seen the doctor and about the examination. She was astounded at the outburst of rage which followed and it became necessary to inform the doctor that one of his patients' husbands was considering the best way to attack him. Fortunately, this particular patient responded well to medication, although he insisted later that his wife's operation be performed by a female gynaecologist.

It is always difficult to advise a woman to leave her husband, particularly if he needs someone to care for him, as the alcoholic man does. In the case of the jealous alcoholic husband who has attacked his spouse, the wife should be informed that the possibility of serious physical injury, or even death, exists as long as the paranoid state persists. Alternatively, the husband may have to be admitted to hospital against his will until the danger lessens.

A variation on the above cases was referred to the alcoholic outpatient clinic as a case of pathological jealousy and appeared to have all the hallmarks of such a condition. On interviewing the wife, however, she fully admitted to many extra-marital sexual encounters that she felt justified in pursuing, because her husband neglected her. Not all accusations of infidelity are delusional!

Alcoholic hallucinosis

As was previously discussed in Chapter 5, in some alcoholics there appears to be a close relationship between the development of alcoholism and the pre-existence of another psychiatric disorder. In alcoholic hallucinosis, a clinical picture occurs which is very difficult to distinguish from schizophrenia.

The picture in schizophrenia is very varied at the onset and the following description is very brief and incomplete. In schizophrenia the sufferer may present with hallucinatory experiences, usually in the auditory field, whilst he is fully conscious. Stimultaneously, or later on, there are also changes in the thought processes, so that the form or content of the thought becomes disturbed. The normal emotional responses to situations become bizarre or absent and there can also be abnormal motor (muscular) behaviour.

Alcoholic hallucinosis is one of a number of drug-induced states (LSD, cocaine and amphetamines may produce similar effects) that presents as an acute hallucinatory condition and is therefore clinically similar to schizophrenia. In alcoholic hallucinosis, the patient experiences the acute onset of voices talking to him or about him. Initially, the hallucinatory noises may be indistinct and only become clear as voices at a later stage. This state may occur as part of a withdrawal picture, or may persist after an attack of delirium tremens but, if so, the hallucinations are of a different kind than those experienced in delirium tremens. The voices in acute hallucinosis are nearly always threatening or abusive. Typical of patients with this condition was a fifty-year-old sailor, who heard the voices of his companions coming through the ventilation shafts on the ship. He locked himself in his cabin for three days and kept an axe ready to defend himself against the attack he expected. At times the voices order the patient to kill himself and suicide by violent means presents a grave risk.

The acute hallucinatory state is very similar to some schizophrenic illnesses and the similarity is increased by the false ideas held by the patient secondary to the hallucinations. The areas of difference between alcoholic hallucinosis and schizophrenia are in the emotional response, the form the thought processes take and the motor behaviour, all of which are normal in alcoholic hallucinosis.

Usually, the condition subsides rapidly and completely with hospitalisation and the use of the major tranquillisers. A large follow-up study by Benedetti (1952) revealed that 90 of 113 cases cleared up in less than six months; 10 became demented and only 13 developed the syndrome of schizophrenia. Although the viewpoint of American psychiatrists is that alcoholic hallucinosis represents schizophrenia that has been precipitated by alcohol, there is little evidence to support this point of view.

EFFECTS ON THE GASTROINTESTINAL TRACT

The central nervous system and the gastrointestinal tract are the systems most commonly affected by the effects of chronic alcoholism. The common gastrointestinal disorders produced are alcoholic gastritis, peptic ulcers, cirrhosis of the liver and pancreatitis. Less common, but very serious conditions, are cancer in the upper alimentary canal and also in the liver. These conditions may not be due so much to the consumption of alcohol, but to the concomitant excessive use of tobacco.

Alcoholic gastritis (inflamed stomach)

The social drinker who celebrates too heartily over a weekend may well experience the effects of a mild gastritis. Gastritis causes pain in the upper central abdomen, associated with flatulence and loss of appetite. Inspection of the inside of the stomach shows it to be inflamed with enlarged blood vessels and to have the walls covered with mucus. The condition responds rapidly to stopping drinking and taking a bland diet for a day or two.

Peptic ulcer

Peptic ulcers also present with upper abdominal pain, flatulence and at times nausea. This pain does not, however, disappear after a few days abstinence from alcoholic drinks.

The pain is typically present for a few days and then disappears for a variable length of time, but gradually the spells between the attacks of pain become shorter. Frequently the pain is felt before eating and may either increase or decrease the desire for food. Some patients are woken in the middle of the night by severe pain, which is typical of an ulcer in the duodenum. The pain may be relieved by eating or taking a glass of milk and antacid tablets. In some patients vomiting gives relief from the pain.

Peptic ulcers can present dramatically with severe pain and collapse from an acute exacerbation of the ulcer, which may be associated with a perforation from the stomach to the abdominal cavity. In this circumstance, the stomach contents can cause severe irritation of the lining of the abdomen, the condition known as peritonitis. Another serious consequence of peptic ulceration can be bleeding from a blood vessel in the ulcer crater. A small amount of bleeding may be missed completely, but a large bleed is life-threatening and requires immediate management in hospital.

The treatment of peptic ulcer initially is medical, with bed rest, a bland diet consisting of frequent small meals and the administration of antacids. The consumption of tobacco and alcohol should be prohibited. A lot of patients with peptic ulcers appear to develop them at times of stress and for this reason they are given tranquillisers, a practice which is not to be encouraged in the alcoholic, or any other patient with a tendency to abuse drugs.

Surgical treatment is indicated if medical treatment fails or if there is an emergency situation such as a perforated ulcer. Alcoholics are notorious for failing to stick to diets and this fact, coupled with the recurrent abuse of alcohol and tobacco, may partly explain the high prevalence of alcoholics who have had gastrectomies for peptic ulceration. In a recent study of 222 alcoholics, we found that 21 (9·4 per cent) had had gastrectomies and many more had had treatment for ulcers or indigestion.

Cirrhosis of the liver and fatty liver

Alcoholism commonly causes damage to the liver in the form of fatty liver and, less commonly, goes on to cause actual cirrhosis. Other diseases such as infective hepatitis cause cirrhosis and only a minority of deaths from cirrhosis are reported to be alcohol-related. As already mentioned, physicians are loth to report alcohol-related deaths from whatever final cause and thus the proportion of deaths due to alcoholism may well be underestimated. Even so, the number of deaths from alcoholic cirrhosis has been steadily increasing over the last few years.

Acute intoxication has an effect on the liver. It causes cell damage and increases the fat content of all the liver cells. In an alcoholic, the accumulated damage arises from a combination of excessive alcohol intake and a diet deficient in protein and essential food factors. Certain of these food factors are amino-acids that ordinarily prevent the build-up of fat in the liver.

Due to the collection of fat in the cells, the liver becomes large and can be felt below the rib margin on examination. As well as an excess of fat, the enlarged liver contains an excess of iron due to the increased absorption of iron in the presence of alcohol and the high iron content of alcoholic drinks. If the assault by alcohol on the liver goes on, then the phase of fatty degeneration is replaced by diffuse scarring in the liver. The scarring and hardening of the liver is cirrhosis and is irreversible. The liver which was initially enlarged shrinks, and it may not be discovered until a post-mortem examination reveals that the patient had liver disease.

The type of cirrhosis in alcoholism is termed portal cirrhosis (the other types are biliary cirrhosis and post-necrotic scarring). The symptoms which present in portal cirrhosis are due to disturbances in the blood flow through the portal blood vessels in the liver or to the liver being unable to carry out its normal functions (hepatic insufficiency).

The blood flow through the liver is obstructed due to the scarring and this causes pressure effects and results in portal hypertension. The effects of portal hypertension are wide-reaching and include nausea, vomiting, flatulence and pain over the liver. Part of the cause of cirrhosis is malnutrition and it will be appreciated that anyone with the preceding symptoms is not likely to eat very well and so the liver condition is made worse.

The blood vessels in the liver are widely connected, particularly to the spleen and to veins throughout the abdomen. With increasing pressure in the veins they swell and protrude. The spleen enlarges but this does not cause very many symptoms. However, danger arises from the swollen blood vessels. These may be seen as haemorrhoids, or as dilated vessels on the abdominal wall around the umbilicus, but the hidden ones at the lower end of the oesophagus and in the stomach are of particular concern. The veins in these situations are exactly similar to varicose veins in the lower leg and are termed oesophageal varices. All varicose veins are liable to rupture and the first sign of cirrhosis of the liver may be a massive haemorrhage from the stomach or oesophagus which can be rapidly fatal. The vomiting of blood in anyone, of any age, calls for emergency treatment and investigation in hospital. In 20 per cent of cases with portal cirrhosis, death results from a haemorrhage (Davidson, 1970). Due to repeated bleeding, anaemia is a common complication of cirrhosis.

The liver destroys many poisons in the body and also produces essential substances that are needed for normal functioning. Hepatic insufficiency is shown by an accumulation of toxic substances and by progressive deficiency states. Jaundice is produced in only a few cases of cirrhosis and is due to accumulation of bile pigments in the blood. Oestrogens (female hormones), usually present in small amounts in men, also accumulate and give rise to enlarged breasts, redness of the palms and the appearance of spider-like blood vessels on the face, neck and arms.

The liver produces proteins that circulate in the blood and decreasing levels of these results in fluids being drawn out of the blood into the tissues where it appears clinically as oedema (dropsy). In addition to the dangers from bleeding from oesophageal varices, a failing liver produces insufficient amounts of a number of factors necessary to control the clotting of blood which therefore increases the tendency to bruise or bleed.

The poisonous substances which accumulate include a number containing nitrogen compounds and when these reach a certain level they produce mental changes which may be acute in onset.

Pancreatitis

About one-fifth of all cases of acute inflammation of the pancreas are associated with alcoholism. It is a serious condition that can present dramatically as an emergency with severe abdominal pain and collapse. Many of these cases are operated on with the provisional diagnosis of perforated ulcer.

The actual treatment consists of relieving the pain and treating the collapse of the patient. Usually recovery is complete, but some patients die in the acute phase and others go on to develop chronic pancreatitis. These patients also suffer from abdominal pain with nausea and vomiting occurring on and off and lasting for a few days on each occasion. The pancreas normally produces enzymes that are used in the digestion of food. In chronic pancreatic disease the production of these substances is decreased and this results in faulty absorption of food with loss of weight and chronic diarrhoea.

The treatment of this condition is to provide a high carbohydrate, high protein, low-fat diet, and replacement medication for the pancreatic enzymes.

CARDIOVASCULAR SYSTEM

In chronic alcoholism, a disorder of the heart muscle can occur that may be due to a deficiency in thiamine (Vitamin B_1). This condition is termed alcoholic cardiomyopathy. It may present with the signs of increasing cardiac insufficiency. These include breathlessness, tiredness, swelling of the feet and a cough. It may also present as sudden death, occurring with no warning signs.

On examination, the patient's heart is found to be enlarged and to have signs of disturbances in the blood flow through the heart. The treatment, as for all the long-term complications of alcoholism, is to make the patient abstain from alcohol and to take a balanced diet. It may also be necessary to help the heart to function more efficiently by administering drugs such as digitalis and diuretics.

Medical complications of drug-taking

It has been pointed out in previous chapters that the effects of drugs can be very unpredictable, particularly in single dosages. But with large dosages, and with continued consumption, the general rule is that drugs have more predictable actions. Unfortunately, as drug usage is not confined to single drugs, but, as is so often the case, occurs as poly-drug abuse, the picture becomes, as ever, more complicated.

INTOXICATION

It has been suggested that there are three global categories of drugs. With *stimulants* varying degrees of excitation are seen, ranging from restlessness and cheerfulness, to an alarming overactivity associated with hallucinations and delusions. Mental changes predominate, and there is a lesser degree of physical effect, a feature which is quite different from the depressant substances. Intoxication due to *depressant* substances is characterised by a change in the level of consciousness, varying from mild drowsiness to deep coma, together with, characteristically, slurring of speech, inco-ordination, and an ataxic gait. Behaviour disturbances are likely to occur with barbiturate intoxication, giving a picture that is identical to alcohol intoxication. With morphia there is a lack of responsiveness to outside stimuli, a condition often referred to as "on the nod". With chronic consumption, the level of consciousness varies generally with the serum level of drug, so that a changing picture of confusion, disorientation and drowsiness may be interspersed with periods of evidently normal behaviour, but the larger the consumption the more severe the effects on emotional control, appearance and behaviour, and on the whole personality. These general features of intoxication do not generally result from taking *hallucinogens*, but mild degrees of inco-ordination, and instability of gait occur with cannabis and slurred speech and ataxia may rarely be seen with LSD.

OVERDOSE

For several years there has been a progressive decrease in the number of successful suicides, but an alarming rise in the number of individuals attempting suicide. The greater part of this rise is due to younger people, especially young women, taking excesses of drugs, rarely with the true intent of killing themselves, but usually to draw attention to their emotional problems. The vast majority cannot be labelled as neurotic or psychiatrically ill, but are torn by adolescent identification crises, difficulties in interpersonal relationships, or, more commonly, are simply trying to persuade their boyfriends to return to them. A proportion have been experimenting with drugs, when clearly the overdoses are accidental. In established cases of addiction, overdoses are often seen, and it can be a major difficulty defining whether they are accidental or purposeful. Overdoses tend to occur in those who do not know the dose they are taking, and are therefore most likely to occur in novitiates. Addicts who have been withdrawn from drugs sometimes miscalculate the dose if they relapse, and inject a greater amount than necessary, as tolerance has disappeared in the drug-free period.

Barbiturate overdose is perhaps the most dangerous, as serious consequences can result from the consumption of only ten times the normal sleeping dose. If a large dose has been taken, there is deep coma, with lowered blood pressure and respiration rate, increased pulse rate, and often the picture of "shock". The pupils are constricted in the early stages of coma, but dilate later. With morphine or heroin there is coma, pin-point pupils, and depressed respiration. Opium alkaloids have a specific depressant effect on the brain centre for respiration, and death from respiratory arrest is a common complication, accounting for many addicts who are found dead in the streets.

Alcohol intake increases the depressant effect of barbiturates, and is dangerous when in combination, but taken alone, even in great excess, it is rarely fatal. The odour of alcohol can be detected in the breath, and the patient is usually stuporose, with a full pulse and deep respiration. The pupils will be dilated, except in deep coma, but they usually dilate if the patient is shaken. Amphetamines only threaten life if taken in very large quantities when they can cause convulsions and collapse, and overdosages of hallucinogens rarely cause difficulties unless, as occasionally occurs, they are taken in huge quantities. Overdoses of non-barbiturate sleeping tablets, particularly of the benzodiazepine group only rarely cause death unless taken in combination with other drugs.

PHYSICAL DEPENDENCY AND WITHDRAWAL

Characteristic withdrawal syndromes of a serious nature are associated with alcohol, barbiturate and opiate administration.

Physical withdrawal syndromes can be seen after chronic consumption of nearly all drugs, however, if subtler rather than grosser changes are searched for, and with refined experimental methods tolerance can be demonstrated to occur even with single doses of drugs. The time taken to develop clinically observable effects after withdrawal varies with the type of drug, the frequency and dosage, and several other factors.

Barbiturate addiction develops when four to six times the sedative dose is taken for more than one month, the range for addicts being usually 600–1,600 mg each day. Although tolerance develops rapidly, it is unusual to find people taking more than this upper limit of 1,600 mg. For twelve to sixteen hours after withdrawal there are few untoward effects, but after this "honeymoon" period of well-being, apprehension and anxiety set in, with headaches, muscle twitching, nausea and abdominal cramps. Muscular weakness, and postural faintness, evident on sitting or standing suddenly can persist from three to fourteen days. Epileptic fits occur in 80 per cent of cases (Wikler, 1968), these being up to four grand mal attacks after the second day, but rarely after the eighth day. The height of adverse effects is seen in the 60 per cent or so who develop a toxic psychosis, this being ushered in with a fever heralding the onset of delirium or fits, or both.

With heroin and morphia, the abstinence syndrome begins much earlier, after four or five hours. The first manifestation is a craving, accompanied by anxiety, and followed later by irritability, shivering, and running of the eyes and nose. Insomnia is the rule, accompanied in severer states by nausea, which can progress to vomiting, abdominal cramps and diarrhoea. If the fluid loss is severe, blood pressure can fall, to induce a state of collapse. Gross effects can persist for a week, the same time as for the barbiturate syndrome, but subtler effects may persist for months. This is almost equally true of the amphetamines, as electro-encephalographic changes can be measured months after the drug has been discontinued. It has been a subject of debate as to whether amphetamine withdrawal has physical effects, but undoubtedly the severe depression and profound tiredness so often seen does have an organic basis, and it is extremely persistent. Other behavioural effects, such as irritability and tension feelings, so often seen months after drug cessation, may be correlated with brain-wave changes. Haider and Oswald (1970) reported restlessness, insomnia, delirium, and epileptic-type electroencephalographic changes in ten patients who had taken overdoses of hypnotics. These sometimes occurred many days after apparent recovery, and complete restoration to normality took up to eight weeks. The abstinence syndrome associated with methadone is similar to that of heroin and morphia, but is much less serious, and comes on usually after two or even three days.

Cannabis withdrawal does not appear to be associated with any profound changes, but chronic consumers have reported tiredness, anxiety, and insomnia after withdrawal. LSD also causes no problems. It is important to remember that addicts may be addicted to several drugs, and epileptic fits occurring after heroin withdrawal are more likely to be due to concomitant barbiturate abstinence, than to heroin itself.

DRUGS AND PSYCHOTIC ILLNESSES

Psychotic illnesses are described under the headings of functional and organic, acute and chronic. The organic psychoses are those with an underlying physico-chemical basis, as opposed to the functional, where no such known pathology exists. The distinction is far from being a clear one, and similar symptom-sign complexes are common to each group. Drug-induced psychoses show a clear relationship to drug ingestion, and usually terminate shortly after drug ingestion stops.

Psychoses where the level of consciousness is impaired are termed delirious states, or toxic confusional states. The deliria related to barbiturate and alcohol withdrawal have already been mentioned. Deliria can also supervene even when drugs are continually taken, particularly with high dosage and continued use.

If the level of consciousness is moderately lowered, disorientation of time, place and even person occur. Whilst delirium with such features and loss of memory is very rare with cannabis, it has been reported, although Weil (1970) believes that adverse reactions to marijuana do not include disorientation. The delirium of barbiturate withdrawal is very similar to that of alcohol withdrawal, including the coarse tremor of the hands and the characteristic affective change of absolute terror, but occasionally these are absent. If the anxiety is not accompanied by visual and auditory hallucinations or delusions of persecution, the state will resemble an acute panic reaction rather than a psychosis, and at times may resemble schizophrenia if the lowering of consciousness is not marked. Occasionally a gross deficiency of recent memory is present, resembling the Korsakoff's state of alcoholism.

Idiosyncratic reactions to low dosages of drugs are well documented, and recently we saw a young girl who had taken one Dexedrine tablet, and was brought into the hospital casualty department in a state resembling delirium tremens. She was terrified by hallucinations of snakes, rats, mice, and spiders, seeing them at the end of her bed crawling towards her. She was unable to quote the day or date, and her confusion persisted for three days, eventually clearing to leave her with only a limited recollection of her experience. Delirium tremens has now been recorded with chloral hydrate, paraldehyde, glutethimide, ethchlorvynol, meprobamate, and more recently methaqualone, a constituent of a proprietary methaqualone-diphenhydramine combination ("Mandrax") (Ewart and Priest, 1967).

Amphetamine psychosis is usually set in clear consciousness, with florid visual and auditory hallucinations. It closely resembles schizophrenia of the paranoid type, but is distinguished by the modality of the hallucinations, visual ones being less common in true schizophrenia, and by the absence of emotional flattening. Mood changes may suggest a manic or depressive component. Thought disorder of the formal kind does not occur, nor does it occur in paranoid schizophrenia, so that differentiation can be very difficult or even impossible without a history of drug taking, or confirmatory evidence of drugs in the urine. Cocaine psychosis is very similar, but sensations of insects crawling under the spine (a tactile hallucinatory phenomenon known as formication) is common. Paranoid ideas develop, with the addicts misinterpreting people's actions, feeling that they are spying on them, or that police agents are following them. Assaults resulting from delusions of persecution are not unknown, aggressive acts often being impulsive, sudden, and (fortunately) poorly-planned and executed.

Cognitive changes are associated with LSD and cannabis psychoses. Thought disorder of the mildest kind consists of loosening of the association of ideas and a vagueness or woolliness of thinking. In more severe forms of thought disorder there can be interruptions or sudden switches in thought sequences, an interweaving of multiple thoughts destroying concentration, or less commonly, a total and chaotic disruption leading to total incoherence. Misinterpretation of external events can lead to paranoid ideas, accompanied by mood changes of elation, panic, terror, or depression. Suicide has very rarely been reported in these states, and indeed drug-induced psychoses as a whole amount to only a minute proportion of hospital admissions. Keup (1970) found that cannabis-induced psychoses accounted for only two out of 2,126 hospital admissions in one year. It is disputed by some that cannabis can cause a psychotic reaction, but a picture of excitement, incoherence, persecution and hallucinosis has been described. Catatonic changes, especially of mutism, negativism and abnormal posturing have been observed with both LSD and cannabis, but are uncommon. Visual hallucinations as such are uncommon with LSD, but bizarre descriptions have been given of the perceptual distortions occurring, such as halo effects, blurred vision, shimmering lights and colours, tunnel vision and increased visual imagery. The experiences give the user new "understandings" which are not readily grasped or understood by others (Frosch *et al.*, 1965) and which border on delusions. We treated reports of people with delusions of grandeur somewhat lightheartedly, until we came across a young girl who dived off a building thinking she could fly, and suffered appalling neurological damage and head injuries. Such episodes are very infrequent, but personal experiences of such tragedies are never forgotten.

Cannabis "flashbacks" have been reported, but not so commonly as LSD flashbacks, and they rarely amount to full blown psychotic episodes and are transient. Horowitz (1969) has described the symptoms of the LSD phenomenon that can occur up to six months after taking the drug, but they are essentially similar to other LSD experiences, except that they are intrusive and unpleasant, often provoking anxiety as if they have a "will of their own". Woody (1970) described three cases where the recurrent visual effects caused driving hazards and it is possible that LSD can cause permanent damage to the retina, or to the central brain pathways responsible for vision from the optic nerve to the occipital cortex.

Drug-induced psychosis usually settles within a week, and rarely persists. If it does, then it is possible that the underlying condition was a functional psychosis of the schizophrenic type. There is no convincing evidence that LSD can cause a permanent psychosis, but drugs given to psychiatrically-ill patients can cause exacerbations. Amphetamines have induced manic episodes in hypomanics, severe depressive reactions in melancholics, and catatonic changes in schizophrenics. Cannabis is known to have precipitated episodes of mania, hyperactivity, stupor and catatonia in schizophrenics who previously had not shown such behaviours.

Psychotic reactions are often seen in morphine and heroin addicts, but are related to a pre-existing illness or to the consumption of other drugs. Persistent drug use leads to many personality changes, but a common picture is one of narrowing of interest, irritability, querulous and aggressive change, often with paranoid ideas. Such states are usually described as paranoid personality developments, although the distinction from schizophrenia is not a clear one. Hallucinations and thought disorder never occur, and a gradual change occurs over many years in which delusion-like ideas become firmly held delusions, though these are often circumscribed, leaving some personality features more or less intact. The delusions are systematised and commonly are of a sexual nature, involving the imagined misdemeanours of the individual's spouse or cohabitee. An identical picture can occur in chronic alcoholism, as described above (*see* p. 139).

DANGERS OF INTRAVENOUS DRUGS

Heroin is the drug most commonly taken illegally by the intravenous route, but morphine, other opioids, amphetamines, and barbiturates can be taken this way too. Favourite injection sites are the antecubital fossae (the elbows), because of ease of access and concealment. The next most popular sites are the backs of the hands and forearms, whilst feet and thighs are used as a last resort. "Railroad tracks" of injection marks identify chronic addicts, who always have multiple scars and often pigmentation over the veins at injection areas. Dorothy Vollum (1970) has reviewed the skin lesions of drug addicts. Thrombosed veins are common and often extensive, and nasty necrotic ulcers are seen in those who inject barbiturates. These drugs are dissolved in tap-water from capsules before injection, and if they escape into the tissues from the vein they provoke an intensely painful local reaction. The tissues affected break down to leave ulcers which heal very slowly, if at all.

The syringe technique of addicts is never impeccably hygienic, so that a whole host of infective complications can arise. The complications of opiate addiction have been extensively reviewed by Louria (1967) and Cherubin (1967). Superficial skin infections and abscesses are common, as is infected thrombosis, in which the clot accompanied by infection can travel along the vein, with a risk of breaking off and passing as an embolus into the circulation. When emboli settle in the lungs, abscesses or pneumonia can develop. If the infection passes through the lungs and into the general circulation, any organ of the body can be infected, although the heart is especially vulnerable, and septic endocarditis is a very serious complication. In the U.S.A., injected heroin almost always contains adulterants, and if these include talc or starch they will not dissolve in the blood but lodge in the lungs, causing a local fibrous reaction that, if generalised throughout the lungs, can seriously affect lung function, and eventually result in the addict becoming a respiratory cripple. Up to 30 per cent of American addicts have enlarged livers, and three-quarters of British addicts have impaired liver function tests. This impairment is invariably due to serum hepatitis, a viral disease transmitted by syringe sharing. This is rarely fatal, but the inefficiency of a vital organ contributes to the physical deterioration that inevitably accompanies chronic addiction.

DEATH IN ADDICTS

Studies have shown that the mortality rate in opiate addicts is 2–2·5 per cent per year, and a generally accepted figure is that the risk of dying in any one year is thirty times higher in a heroin addict than for a normal person of similar age. In the U.S.A., heroin addiction is one of the most important causes of death in the fifteen to thirty-five age group.

Approximately half of the American addicts who die do so from overdosage or from an "acute reaction". This latter is not seen in this country, and commonly involves pulmonary oedema, a great flow of fluid into the lungs, literally causing the person to drown in his own fluid. This may be due to toxic substances in American heroin, thus accounting for its rarity in the U.K. Other causes of death include suicide, death from infective complications such as septicaemia, liver failure, accident, murder, concomitant alcoholism, tuberculosis and even tetanus, and of course, complications occurring during withdrawal.

Glue sniffing is an important cause of death in drug abusers in the U.S.A., but not in the U.K. Bass (1970) reported no less than 110 deaths in American teenagers, where at autopsy no physical abnormalities were found. Death had occurred very suddenly due to cardiac arrest. Other serious dangers from solvent sniffing are liver and kidney damage, brain damage, and irreversible damage to the blood-forming organs. The mortality rate for other drugs is low, except for barbiturates. Apart from suicide, which kills over 3,000 per year in Great Britain, many die from accidental overdoses, including some who, after taking a sleeping dose, wake and take several more tablets in an "automatic" state.

DRUGS AND GENETIC DAMAGE

The effect of drugs in causing cellular and genetic damage, and damage during pregnancy is currently a topical subject. There have been several reports of LSD causing congenital abnormalities in humans, and there is experimental proof in hamsters that adverse genetic effects are seen if LSD is given in the early stages of pregnancy. Abnormal chromosomes have been identified in women who have taken LSD and given birth to abnormal children. Some of these children have been born without limbs. However, it would be unwise to ascribe the cause to LSD, even though the drug has been shown to cause chromosome damage in chronic users. It may be that the abnormalities are due not to LSD but to other drugs, or to the impurities contained in the LSD. LSD abusers frequently take excesses of alcohol, heroin, cannabis and other hallucinogens. In laboratory situations, LSD has caused chromosomal changes in white blood cell cultures in dosages similar to those taken by illicit users, but other drugs are well known to cause similar effects (e.g. several antibiotics). We know of a case of one 23-year-old man who abused LSD and who developed leukaemia; a causal relationship has been suggested but not proven.

MISCELLANEOUS DRUGS

It would be unwise to discount the possibility that drugs of abuse are related to congenital deformities, but further research will no doubt elucidate this. Certainly it is known that pregnant LSD-users have a higher spontaneous abortion rate than normals. This of course could be due to other factors, including the intake of other drugs, to nutritional problems, and so on. Many drug-takers tend to focus on the drug to the exclusion of their own health, and weight loss, features of malnutrition, vitamin deficiency, scabies and lice infestation are often found.

Heroin and opiates depress appetite and sex drive, perhaps through an effect on the hypothalamus, and loss of libido, impotence in males, and sterility in females are complications. If pregnancy does occur, there is a chance that an abstinence syndrome will occur in the newborn child. Similarly, barbiturates pass the placenta, and children born to addicted mothers are very listless and have initial feeding difficulties; 36 per cent of pregnant heroin addicts have toxaemia of pregnancy, and 47 per cent have premature labours.

The full range of dangers of chronic illicit drug consumption is not really known. It is understood now that cannabis is excreted very slowly, and can be deposited in fatty tissues, having a potentially cumulative effect. Suggestions that cannabis smoking can enhance the risk of developing lung cancer will obviously have to be explored. It has been suggested that opiates and hallucinogens can cause permanent brain damage, and a report from Bristol drew attention to this possibility (Campbell *et al.*, 1971). Special investigations to demonstrate brain tissues showed cerebral atrophy in ten cannabis smokers who had used the drug regularly for three to eleven years. Some were asymptomatic, but several presented at hospital because of poor concentration, failing memory, headaches, amnesic blackouts, and depression. A causal relationship between the drug and these symptoms was suggested, but by no means demonstrated.

Another area of interest is concerned with drug interactions, the way that two or more drugs when given together profoundly alter the normal effects of the other. Some interactions are beneficial, but most are not, and systematic research is only just beginning to bring to light what promises to be an immense amount of data. Of the psychotropic agents, barbiturates and alcohol have been shown to be amongst the most powerful in influencing and potentiating the actions of each other and of other drugs.

REFERENCES

Bass, M., "Sudden Sniffing Death: 110 Sniffing Deaths in the U.S.A. in the 1960s", *Journal of the American Medical Association*, 212: 2,075–9, 1970.

Benedetti, G., *The Alcoholic Hallucinoses*, G. Thieme, Stuttgart, 1952.

Campbell, A. M. G., *et al.*, "Cerebral Atrophy in Young Cannabis Smokers", *Lancet*, ii: 1,219–24, 1971.

Cherubin, C. E., "The Medical Sequelae of Narcotic Addiction", *Annals of Internal Medicine*, 67: 23–33, 1967.

Davidson, S., *The Principles and Practice of Medicine*, Livingstone, Edinburgh, 1970.

Ewart, R. B. L. and Priest, R. G., "Methaqualone Addiction and Delirium Tremens", *British Medical Journal*, iii: 92–3, 1967.

Frosch, W. A., Robbins, E. S. and Stern, M., "Untowards Reactions to LSD Resulting in Hospitalization", *New England Journal of Medicine*, 273: 1,235–9, 1965.

Haider, I. and Oswald, I., "Late Brain Recovery Processes after Drug Overdose", *Br. Med. J.*, ii: 318–22, 1970.

Horowitz, M., "Flashbacks: Recurrent Intrusive Images after the use of LSD", *American Journal of Psychiatry*, 126: 565–9, 1969.

Keup, W., "Psychotic Disturbances due to Cannabis", *Diseases of the Nervous System*, 31: 119–26, 1970.

Louria, D. B., *et al.*, "The Major Medical Complications of Heroin Addiction", *Annals Intern. Med.*, 67: 1–22, 1967.

Madden, J. S., Personal Communication.

Slater, E. and Roth, M., *Clinical Psychiatry*, Cassell, London, 1969.

Talland, G. A., *Disorders of Memory and Learning*, Penguin, Harmondsworth, 1968.

Trotter, T., "Essay, Medical, Philosophical and Clinical on Drunkenness and its Effects on the Human Body", cited by Hunter, R., and McAlpine, I., *Three Hundred Years of Psychiatry, 1535–1860*, Oxford University Press, Oxford, 1963.

Vollum, D. I., "Skin Lesions in Drug Addicts", *Br. Med. J.*, ii: 647–50, 1970.

Weil, A. T., "Adverse Reactions to Marihuana", *N. Engl. J. Med.*, 282: 997–1,000, 1970.

Wikler, A., "Diagnosis and Treatment of Drug Dependence of the Barbiturate Type", *Am. J. Psychiatry*, 125: 758–65, 1968.

Woody, G. E., "Visual Disturbances Experienced by Hallucinogenic Drug Abusers While Driving", *Am. J. Psychiatry*, 127: 683–6, 1970.

7 Social complications of alcoholism and drug abuse

Alcoholism

Alcoholism is not by any means a clearly defined entity. It is a complex condition, varying in severity, and progressing through stages. The end stage is death, but the development of the illness may be arrested or fixed at any point on the downward course. Some of the factors which affect the expression of alcoholism appear to be the age, sex and personality of the alcoholic, and there may also be a genetic influence as to whether or not the excessive drinker develops one or more of the possible physical complications.

Despite the individual variability of an alcoholic's progress, some generalisations can be made and clinically identifiable phases have been described. These have been termed excessive drinking, addictive drinking, and chronic alcoholism by Kessel and Walton (1965). In contrast to these three phases, Jellinek (1952) described four phases, namely the pre-alcoholic, the prodromal, the crucial, and chronic alcoholism. Jellinek's classification separates the excessive drinking stage of Kessel and Walton into two sub-phases, but the last two stages of the two classifications appear to be identical.

A major problem of medically-oriented descriptions of the

development of alcoholism is that people who present at treatment facilities and who have been studied extensively are not representative of all alcoholics. Many early alcoholics probably recover without any formal help, and their constellation of symptoms has not been fully documented. They may indeed differ in many ways from alcoholics who seek help. Jellinek's study was derived from a sample of alcoholics not only limited to the "loss of control" typology, but also to those who attended Alcoholics Anonymous. In spite of this sampling bias, Jellinek's delineation of stages and also his classification of alcoholism has proved of enormous practical benefit in clinical settings.

Jellinek used the first five letters of the Greek alphabet to label the sub-types of alcoholism (alpha, beta, gamma, delta, epsilon). There is nothing sacrosanct about this classification and many objections have been raised against its validity in strictly scientific terms. Each of the categories in the classification progresses from a fairly general early stage onwards, but the end point of the development differs from one category to another. Many alcoholics, probably the majority, appear to stay within one category of alcoholism, but others may change, for example from alpha to gamma or from gamma to a delta pattern of drinking.

TYPES OF ALCOHOLISM

Alpha alcoholism consists of psychological dependence on the effects of alcohol to control anxiety, tension, depression or other emotional or physical distress. There are no symptoms of loss of control or failure to abstain from alcohol as in gamma or delta alcoholism. Many people drink at times of stress of course, and therefore the term "alcoholism" is restricted to those who drink consistently and excessively over a prolonged period.

Case 1

Margaret, an alpha alcoholic, was aged forty at the time she came to hospital. She was divorced after an unhappy, sexually unfulfilled marriage. She had attempted unsuccessfully to solve her sexual problems by a series of hopeless love affairs. She became obese by over-eating and for years had drunk approximately one-third of a bottle of spirits every night to get to sleep. She presented at hospital because of continuing unhappiness. She was physically fit apart from raised blood pressure and did not show any signs of withdrawal.

Beta alcoholism presents with the physical complications of alcoholism (*see* Chapter 6) without the signs of either physical or psychological dependence on alcohol. It does not appear to be very common in the U.K.

Case 2

One of us was asked to see a man of thirty-six who was admitted to hospital after a gastric haemorrhage had left him with a blood count that was only 20 per cent of the normal value. He had marked liver damage with grossly swollen feet and abdomen (ascites) and oesophageal varices (*see* Chapter 6). His drinking pattern was to visit friends from Friday to Sunday each week and to drink all weekend, but not during the week. He showed no signs of psychological or physical dependence on alcohol but, considering his age, was the sickest alcoholic we had ever seen.

Gamma alcoholism is "Anglo-Saxon" alcoholism, loss of control, "binge" drinking, the drinking pattern upon which the philosophy of Alcoholics Anonymous is based. It accounts for more than half of all alcoholics who present for treatment in the British Isles. The symptomatology of gamma alcoholism includes increased tolerance to alcohol, metabolic changes at a cellular level, withdrawal symptoms on stopping or reducing alcohol intake, and loss of control over the amount drunk on any one occasion. Both gamma and delta alcoholism lead to serious consequences, but gamma-variety alcoholics appear to suffer more than any other group. The symptoms include repeated drunkenness, repeated attempts at social drinking or abstaining, repeated breaking of promises to the spouse and therefore considerable conflict.

Case 3

Sam was forty-five and married for the second time. His wife was losing her patience with him, and his son's disabling asthma worsened whenever he disappeared for a day or two. A heavy drinker for many years, he had a small circle of friends who met regularly at a Service Club. Sam was the first to arrive and the last to leave. Often his first drink of the day was at 7.00 a.m., neat whisky which he swallowed with difficulty, and after which he frequently vomited. His hands shook until two doubles stayed down. A concerned father and husband when sober, he was now unemployed, although three years ago he had a good work record. After a period of abstention, he promised himself that he would have only two or three drinks each evening, and for a few days kept his promise. On the last occasion he went out to buy an evening paper, he stayed out until 3.00 a.m., consumed 1·5 litres of whisky, and was arrested for drunken driving.

He presented for treatment because of acute abdominal pain, caused by pancreatitis. He admitted that his bouts of drinking were lengthening, and the intervals between them shortening. His early morning shakes had become full-blown panic attacks, and he was concerned about gaps in his memory during the drinking sprees. At the time of his admission to hospital, he had been abstinent for three days but two days after discharge was again drinking two bottles of whisky each day.

Delta alcoholism is also known as "failure to abstain" alcoholism. The symptomatology is very similar to that of gamma alcoholism but instead of "binge" drinking, the delta alcoholic typically drinks excessive amounts of alcohol steadily every day. The French drinking pattern is a delta-alcoholic pattern. It used to be thought that delta alcoholism was rare in Britain, but as Ritson and Hassall's (1970) study showed, there may be as many delta alcoholics as there are alcoholics of the gamma variety.

Case 4

John, aged fifty-six, entered hospital for the second time in five years. After his first admission, he had remained abstinent for two years, but relapsed and had been drinking continuously for three years. Drinking progressively more during this time, he fell into old habits of consuming half a bottle of spirits each day, and more at the weekends. He had recently lost his job, prematurely retired from a senior executive position in a major company. Following his dismissal, his drinking increased even further, since his wife was away from home during the day. No one had suspected he was drinking so heavily, but soon after admission he showed a marked withdrawal syndrome. He complained that he could not feel his feet when he walked. The walking difficulty, due to a peripheral neuropathy, cleared up after a few weeks on a high vitamin diet.

Epsilon alcoholism, a rare condition, is also termed dipsomania or periodic alcoholism. When it does occur, it takes the form of a bout of drinking which is interspersed with months or years of total abstinence or light social drinking. The authors have no personal knowledge of a patient with this condition.

THE DEVELOPMENT AND PROGRESSION OF ALCOHOLISM

The development of alcoholism differs from person to person in terms of the time taken for various symptoms to appear and the order in which the symptoms do appear. Some people go on for years drinking socially and only develop alcoholism relatively late in life. Excessive drinking patterns commonly begin early in adulthood and develop into alcoholism in the sufferers' thirties or forties. There are a few unfortunate people whose alcoholism develops in the space of a year or two from either abstinence or social drinking.

The average development of the disease of alcoholism is as follows:

Pre-alcoholic phase

In this phase alcohol is used as any other tranquilliser, to provide a temporary solution for anxiety, tension and other unpleasant emotions. The use of alcohol in this manner becomes more and more frequent and is precipitated by progressively lower stress. An increase in tolerance for alcohol produces a decrease in the effectiveness of alcohol as a tranquilliser. To overcome this, there is an increase both in the amount taken and the rate of consumption.

Prodromal phase

After using alcohol as a means of providing relief for some years, the drinker usually finds that he is spending more time drinking, more time thinking about drinking and that he is also needing increasing amounts to achieve the same effect. He is still drinking with his original group of friends, but unless they are all excessive drinkers he finds that his glass is the first one to be empty after each round of drinks. There is a great deal of pressure to drink at the same rate as one's friends and apart from changing one's drinking group (which may happen later) there are a number of ways out of this situation. The alcoholic may have a few drinks before joining the usual group; he may visit another bar in the same pub between rounds, or he may have a standing order with the barman to put a whisky in each pint of beer. The sneaking of drinks is typical of the excessive drinker in the prodromal phase of alcoholism and accentuates the pre-occupation of the drinker with the effects of alcohol. It also demonstrates how early on in the development of alcoholism the drinker tends to adopt abnormal behaviours other than just concerning the amount drunk. Research into the drinking behaviour of established alcoholics has shown that they drink faster than non-alcoholics, gulp rather than sip, and drink straight spirits rather than beer or mixed drinks, all of these features allowing more alcohol to be consumed in a given space of time.

The excessive drinker attempts to conceal his drinking, but inevitably there is a change in his life style and behaviour which others notice. His tolerance of alcohol increases, more time and money is spent in the pursuit of drink, and this leads to family quarrels, the breakdown of old friendships and difficulties at work. These events are often accompanied by guilt feelings and depression.

A symptom that causes a great deal of anxiety in excessive drinkers is the occurrence of transient loss of memory for the events of a few hours or even a day or more. This symptom may occur in non-alcoholics once or twice in a lifetime, but the regular occurrence of the symptom is a warning signal that may or may not be heeded. Typically, the day after a night's heavy drinking, the alcoholic can recall the first few hours of the evening before, how he went out, who he was with, but the later part until he wakes the next day is a complete "blackout". Unwilling to admit a memory lapse, by surreptitious questioning he can discover what really did go on without arousing suspicions about his behaviour. Occasionally, the alcoholic may wake up a long way from home, or more rarely, as one of our patients did, in a police cell, having been charged with indecent exposure on the way home. It is unknown how many people heed this warning and regulate their drinking but most realise that something is very wrong, and some make strenuous efforts to stop drinking, whilst for others the motivation proves temporary.

Glatt (1970) has drawn attention to the problem of the man who drives after drinking over the legal limit. The law regarding drinking and driving is that it is a punishable offence to drive with a blood alcohol level of 0·80 mg of alcohol per 100 ml of blood (the rule of thumb is that three small drinks in three hours is the absolute limit if you are going to drive). No doubt people do drink much more than that amount and drive home without causing an accident but repeated driving with an excessive amount of alcohol in the bloodstream may well be an early sign of dependence on alcohol.

The crucial phase

It is in this phase that the key symptom, loss of control over drinking, occurs. The alcoholic is spending ever more money and more energy obtaining and devouring a supply of alcohol. He is certainly aware of the process, and may express a fear that he is about to go mad. He is no longer able to conceal the effects of his drinking from people around him. He can no longer stop drinking, but continues until he is so sick or drunk he can drink no more, or as he runs out of money and people from whom to borrow.

Loss of control may initially be countered by the alcoholic's rationing himself to a number of drinks, perhaps by taking with him only a restricted amount of money or by going out later in the evening. Many of these strategies fail, because the alcoholic is able to borrow money as the evening goes on, or he belongs to a club that allows prolonged drinking till the early morning. In the early stages of loss of control, drunkenness may be restricted to evenings, weekends and holidays. In the fully developed state, the loss-of-control alcoholic alternates between binges of very heavy drinking and periods of total abstinence.

After a period of abstinence he may show insight into his abnormality, and make an attempt to regain control and to begin socially-acceptable drinking again. By an ultimately painful process of self-deception, he rationalises that the next time will be different. Many attempts are made, but all ultimately fail. He may attempt various manipulations to change his drinking habits, such as going on a holiday or moving house. Many doctors and counsellors may propose or reinforce such changes, instead of facing the core issue.

Living with an alcoholic who goes on bouts of drinking lasting several days at a time is very stressful for the wife and children in the family, and changes are necessary in the way the family operates, if it is to survive as a unit. In fact, many families do not survive the onset of addictive drinking in either parent.

Accompanying the guilt over his actions, there is a massive amount of rationalisation on the part of the alcoholic. He is able to see reasons in his marriage, his job and his social situation why he should go on drinking heavily. The shifting of the blame on to other people or circumstances is commonly accompanied by aggressive outbursts. Ideas of his wife's infidelity occur at this stage and at times can become absolutely fixed in the alcoholic's mind. These ideas may lead to bizarre behaviour in the form of checking on the wife, or even to brutal physical attacks (*see* p. 139).

Profound disruptions occur in the family, especially through a reduction of social interactions. Friends no longer call; the children prefer to play at a neighbour's house; the wife refuses invitations to go out lest her husband should accompany her and become drunk in public. It is important to realise how overpowering is the craving for another drink. The victim is totally engrossed in obtaining and protecting his supply, in the face of others who oppose him. An alcoholic will conceal drink from his wife, so that she will not pour it away, or attempt to obtain it whilst in hospital even if he professes motivation for cure. Although he is bent on obtaining alcohol at almost any cost, the alcoholic is not unfeeling. He is subject to spells of intense depression, remorse and self-pity and alcoholics at times present a severe suicidal risk.

As the crucial phase develops, the alcohol addict spends more and more time drinking and neglecting everything else about him. Many of the physical problems of alcoholism are due to a failure to eat nutritious foods, particularly those containing vitamins. The typical day of an alcoholic in this advanced crucial stage will follow a pattern of waking in the morning with little memory of where he was the night before. He will feel sick and have a feeling of shakiness inside himself, which also affects his hands and feet. His first thought is to find a drink and he will either have to go out to get one, or will probably have one in the house somewhere. Initially, he will be unable to pour a drink and may be unable to hold either glass or bottle to his lips. Having got the first drink down he will vomit and then have another one and, after a few minutes, gradually begin to feel calmer and be able to shave and get dressed to go to work. Breakfast is skipped, but he will check to make sure he has enough money to buy drink through the day, which may necessitate taking money from his wife that she sorely needs to pay debts. There is not likely to be much in the way of social interaction and pleasantry with the family before he leaves the house.

Depending on the type of job he is in, the day's supply of alcohol may be in a desk drawer, the car, or be available in pubs or on an outside job. Such an alcoholic will have a few drinks in the morning but may put in quite a reasonable morning's work. At lunchtime he heads for a bar and stays longer than he should, with a group of friends who also drink heavily. Rather than going back to work late, someone may suggest a visit to a club that opens at pub-closing time. From there, the alcoholic may well return to the pub in the evening and then finish off the night in another club.

By this time he is drunk, he has no money, he has not told his wife where he is, he may have lost his job, he has consumed over a bottle of spirits in the day, has had no food and has the problem of getting home, which he may do by driving himself if he can find his car. His main thought, however, will be to obtain a bottle to have available for the morning.

The chronic phase

With the appearance of physical disorders due to the effects of alcohol, the alcoholic enters the final stage of alcoholism. All the normal social controls against drunkenness are ineffective and repeated daytime drunkenness occurs. Whereas previously he could drink enormous amounts of alcohol and remain fairly sober, he now experiences loss of tolerance to alcohol. After only two or three drinks he finds himself very drunk and unable to continue drinking. Any pretence of clinging to his previously-held social position disappears. Money is in short supply and the choice of drink deteriorates and usually cheap wine is the chronic alcoholic's drink of choice. A few alcoholics go on to add methylated spirits, or shaving lotion, to cheap wine, and consume these very cheap substitutes by themselves. Drinking with people who were socially inferior to the alcoholic's original social position is further evidence of his gradual decline in all areas of functioning.

Along with the behavioural changes, there are changes in physical and mental health which are described in Chapter 6. Thinking becomes unclear, there is often an air of anxiety and perplexity, with general disinterest in everything that is not related to alcohol. Having reached this stage the alcoholic does not have many choices left. He realises that he cannot stop drinking, but he also realises that drinking is the cause of his problems. A few (or it would seem to be a few) make a supreme effort and stop drinking entirely unaided; the majority seek help either directly for their drinking problem or indirectly for one of the physical or psychiatric consequences of alcoholism. A few more just go on drinking without seeking help and drift inexorably towards skid row.

The progression of alcoholism is outlined above and the effects of the abuse of alcohol on an individual and his family have recently been closely scrutinised. Alcoholism is a very serious disorder and for that reason it is important that its diagnosis should be based on definite criteria. To tell a person that he has alcoholism and therefore should stop drinking is a major decision, but one that has to be taken for the good of the patient. To say this to a man who is not an alcoholic would cause him some concern, but undergoing the treatment would do him little, if any, harm. To tell an unrecognised alcoholic that he is *not* an alcoholic is very dangerous to his future well-being. Alcoholics are masters at deceiving both themselves and people about them.

In order to highlight the problem of recognition and to attempt to lay down strict criteria for diagnosis, the National Council on Alcoholism of America has published a paper detailing symptoms and signs of alcoholism that occur at various stages in the condition and in different aspects of a person's functioning. The criteria are divided into Physiological and Clinical manifestations as one group, and Behavioural, Psychological and Attitudinal manifestations for the second group. Each symptom is scored 1, 2, or 3 with 1 being the most significant. The symptoms are also divided into "early", "middle" and "late" manifestations of alcoholism. The list is exhaustive and extremely useful as a standard by which to make the diagnosis. Interested readers are advised to obtain and study this list of symptoms closely.

The general practitioner is one of the first people to whom the alcoholic turns for help and the diagnosis of alcoholism, before it becomes glaringly obvious, is one area in which the general practitioner could be of great help to the early alcoholic. Wilkins (1972) has drawn attention to what he termed the "alcoholism gap"; that is the failure of communication between the alcoholic and his family doctor. By means of an "Alcoholic at Risk Register", patients in a general practice identified as being at risk from alcoholism were asked to complete a questionnaire regarding frequency of alcohol intake, their opinion about their own drinking, problems caused by alcohol abuse and symptoms of alcohol addiction. By means of the questionnaire the identified abnormal drinkers were divided into heavy drinkers, problem drinkers, and alcohol addicts. Comparing a group defined as "at risk" with a "no risk" group, the diagnosis of problem drinker and addict occurred ten times as frequently in the "at risk" group as in the controls (28 to 2·8 per cent). Several items correlating with being an alcoholic were identified by the survey. Any patient who asked for help with an alcohol problem, or had a history of a drunkenness offence, had 100 per cent risk of being an alcoholic. Smelling of alcohol at a consultation carried a 75 per cent risk of the patient being an alcoholic.

As the likelihood of someone being alcoholic dropped to 50 per cent, so the indices became superficially less related to alcoholism. This category included suffering from peptic ulcer or gastritis and asking for a sick note when there was no evidence of a significant illness. Common events, such as having a road accident or any accident at work, indicated that one of every two such people had an alcohol problem. Also included in this category was living in a hostel for the homeless. Symptoms of anxiety and depression carried a 25 per cent probability of alcoholism, as did working in a brewery or the catering trade. Being a single male over forty years old, being divorced or separated, or having a history of marital disharmony, also carried a 25 per cent risk. It would almost appear that, if each general practitioner looked for such features, he would be questioning each and every patient he saw about his or her drinking habits. This may appear unnecessary, but ignoring these findings will only lead to a continuation of the *status quo*, in which far too many early alcoholics are not identified and go on to damage themselves, their families and other people because of a condition which, if not preventable, is frequently treatable. In these circumstances, it is better for the doctor to be suspicious and wrong, than to be incurious or too embarrassed to enquire.

So far, we have mainly considered the effects of abuse in the male alcoholic, taking into account his family, social situation, employment and, in the previous chapter, his physical health. Alcoholism also affects females and we will now consider the female alcoholic.

THE FEMALE ALCOHOLIC

The female alcoholic differs in a number of ways from her male counterpart. Alcoholism is less common amongst women than amongst men and a number of reports have described the female alcoholic as being, in many ways, sicker than the average male alcoholic. There have been studies showing that women in general start to drink later in life than men who become alcoholic, but once women do start to drink heavily they develop the physical complications of alcoholism relatively earlier than males. Certainly, complications such as cirrhosis of the liver occur much more commonly in female alcoholics than in males.

There are strict social controls on drunkenness in women in all Western societies and it is not too surprising that women who present for treatment with alcoholism usually appear to have marked personality disturbances. One of the consequences of this disturbance is that the results of the treatment of female alcoholics are in general worse than those for men. Another reason for the poor results may be that there are many controls on the behaviour of men through the day, both at home and at work, whereas women are alone a great deal of the time and can fairly easily indulge in secret, daytime drinking.

A review of the literature on the female alcoholic was published by Schuckit (1972). One of the main points he made was that many of the reports from which the above composite picture of the female alcoholic has been drawn have failed to state clearly the nature of the sample being studied and the methods by which the diagnosis was reached. Schuckit agreed with the contention that a woman becomes alcoholic about eight years later than the average male, and that she is hospitalised at the same age as the man, and therefore comparatively earlier in her illness. Sexual problems are frequent and approximately one half of their marriages end in breakdown. A high proportion, about one-third, have a husband who is also an alcoholic. As mentioned in Chapter 5, there appears to be a close connection between affective (mood) disorders in females and the development of alcoholism, one of the concomitants of this feature being the increased suicide risk in female alcoholics.

THE WIFE OF THE ALCOHOLIC

The wives of alcoholics are the daughters of alcoholics, or the previous wives of other alcoholics, much more often than would be expected by chance. For these and other reasons that will be detailed below, it has been hypothesised that the wife of the alcoholic is not just a hapless woman caught in an impossible situation but in some way needs to be in such a situation to satisfy her own unconscious neurotic needs. There is no doubt that the wife of an alcoholic takes continual punishment from her husband, as do the children of the family. The divorce rate amongst alcoholic women is higher than that amongst alcoholic men and this could be construed as evidence that the wives of alcoholics have an emotional need to stay in the situation. It may be, however, that it is easier for a man to walk out on his alcoholic wife and start a new life than it is for a woman with children and little or no financial support to leave her alcoholic husband, no matter how uncomfortable the situation is.

A number of highly impressionistic descriptions of alcoholics' wives is contained in the literature. The wife of the alcoholic becomes the dominant partner when the man is drinking and she has to fulfil many of the roles of both sexes. These women have been described as frigid, sadomasochistic and dependent. At times, it appears that when the husband makes attempts to stay sober then the wife goes out of her way to sabotage his attempts so that she can retain control over the household. Another feature reported in alcoholics' wives has been the relapse into neurotic or psychotic illness of the wife when the husband does manage to regain sobriety.

Recently, the hypotheses concerning the personality and reactions of the wives of alcoholics have been examined and many of the hypotheses have been found to be lacking in supportive evidence (Edwards, Harvey, Whitehead, 1973). The evidence from the psychological testing of these women has shown them to have normal, or only slightly abnormal, personality structures, when compared with the wives of non-alcoholics. The hypothesis of decompensation into neurotic or psychotic states received no support and in fact it was found that the severity of the disturbance in the wives was directly related to the severity of the alcoholism of the husband. As the husbands became abstinent so the wives improved. The wives of alcoholics abstinent for six months showed markedly less disturbance than the wives of alcoholics who were still drinking. No particular type of personality structure was found amongst these women, who are for the most part essentially normal women reacting to a markedly stressful situation.

THE CHILDREN OF ALCOHOLICS

The children of alcoholics face many problems that are known to be powerful factors in the production of emotional disturbance in both childhood and later life. Assuming that the results of the genetic research detailed earlier are valid, then the child of the alcoholic has an inborn disadvantage, as far as his long-term prospects are concerned. Whether or not this factor is of importance, he faces the likelihood of a very unstable upbringing. A great deal depends upon the ability of the non-alcoholic parent to compensate, both materially and on an emotional level, for the unpredictability of the alcoholic.

Children do best, in general, when raised in a family that provides material comfort, stable parents with whom the children can identify, and definite roles for the children in the family. In the families of alcoholics, material comforts are usually met through the efforts of the non-alcoholic spouse. The relationships between the children and both the alcoholic and non-alcoholic parent are difficult. The alcoholic parent is usually unpredictable. When drinking, he is absent, aggressive, depressed, or physically sick. He may be cruel both to the children and his wife. The children may feel humiliated by him and may well be unable to bring their friends home because they never know whether their father will be sober or drunk. (Somewhat perversely, some children of an alcoholic father may prefer him to their sober mother. The reasons for this include the fact that the mother has to take over the role of the disciplinarian and when the alcoholic is sober he may be extremely generous and affectionate, due to his guilt about drinking.) The families of alcoholics often break down due to divorce or the death of the alcoholic, and the children have to face the problems of parental deprivation. Very many of the children of alcoholics, however, manage to become mature stable adults despite their upbringing.

Nylander (1960) reported on the findings from two studies into the effects of having an alcoholic father. He found that, although the children of alcoholics were admitted to hospital for suspected physical diseases only slightly more often than the children of a control group, the diagnosis of a physical cause for the admission was made in two-thirds of the control group children but only one-quarter of the alcoholics' children. In the remaining three-quarters, the precipitant for admission had an emotional basis. The children of the alcoholic parents were also considered by their teachers to be problem children in almost half the cases. In the control group, only one child in ten was similarly considered to be a problem child.

A fairly large study into the effects of parental alcoholism was carried out by Margaret Cork (1969) in metropolitan Toronto. Starting with the files of 3,813 patients from the Addiction Research Foundation and the Bell Clinic in Toronto, a total of just over 1,000 patients were contacted for permission to interview their children. One-third of the patients could not be traced, a further third did not reply and after various other exclusions 62 sets of parents accepted the idea of having their children interviewed for the study. From this source, 115 children were finally interviewed by the investigator. The account produced is a very evocative record of the feelings of a number of the children and although it can be criticised for its sampling techniques, its judgment of damage to the children and whether it has applicability to other groups, the report is well worth reading for the descriptive passages alone.

Not one of the 115 children between the ages of ten and sixteen who were interviewed felt that they had been unaffected by their parents' alcoholism. All but two felt the relationship in the family had been affected. The vast majority worried about lacking confidence and felt easily hurt. Many of the children were anxious and were worried about being different from other children. All but three felt unwanted by at least one parent and three-quarters of the children described themselves as being angry towards their parents and other people.

An attempt was made at determining whether or not the children had been damaged by their parents' behaviour. This was done by reading through the interviews and taking note of the child's responses to questions about vital areas in their lives. This method of assessment is not very satisfactory, since it depends almost entirely on the investigator's subjective interpretation of information obtained in a non-structured interview, by the same investigator. The damage suffered by the children was classified as none, slight, fairly serious and very serious. None of the children was classified as not damaged. Nine were considered to be only slightly damaged, 56 as fairly seriously and 50 as very seriously damaged. The slightly damaged children still maintained some relationship with one parent and felt that things might improve within the family. Most of the children in this group were at the younger end of the sample studied and it was hypothesised that they might well progress to the more seriously damaged categories in time. The children in the fairly seriously damaged group (half the total sample) did not have a meaningful relationship with either parent and although they had lost hope that things would improve, they still felt some ties to the family. The very seriously damaged children were emotionally isolated from all their family members and felt hatred and resentment to their parents and frequently to people in authority. The two commonest concerns expressed by the children about their family lives were related to parental quarrelling and lack of interest by the parents, and were not directly about drinking.

Whether or not Margaret Cork's study is representative of the effects of alcoholism on children it does show what can happen to these children. Glatt (1967) raised an important point with regard to the complications of alcoholism when he said that the social complications of alcoholism occur much earlier in the condition than the physical complications. To be able to influence the effects of alcoholism on the children it is essential that alcoholism be identified early in its course. By the time the alcoholic gets to hospital with physical complications, he is on average forty years old and his children are teenagers. In Glatt's study there had been friction between the parents for at least seven years previously, coinciding with the early years of their children's lives.

SUICIDE AND ALCOHOLISM

The relationship between suicide and alcoholism can be considered in two different ways. Alcoholism has been said to be the equivalent of slow suicide (Menninger, 1938) and there is also an increase in the proportion of alcoholics who both attempt and complete suicide when compared with non-alcoholics. Menninger, who did not define what he meant by alcoholism, interpreted the symptoms of excessive drinking as a maladaptive, self-destructive attempt to avert an even more threatening self-destructive impulse. This other impulse was said to be derived from feelings of aggression with which the person is unable to deal. Guilt was thought to arise, due to the aggressive feelings, and the suicide aspect, from a need to be punished, to deal with the guilt.

Kessel and Grossman (1961) investigated the deaths from suicide in two groups of alcoholics. No woman in either series, from a total of 46 cases, committed suicide. Of the men, 8 per cent of one group and 7 per cent of the other committed suicide. These rates were between 75 to 86 times as high as the rates for men of similar age in the general population of Greater London. Although there were no particular identifying features from which the suicidal alcoholics could have been picked out during their stay in hospital, those who later committed suicide had all (except one) reverted to heavy drinking.

A similar study was reported upon by Ritson (1968). Eight suicides occurred amongst the first 300 admissions to the alcoholism unit at the Royal Edinburgh Infirmary. Control groups comprising the same-sex patient admitted immediately before and after the suicide patient was admitted were compared on eighteen measures with the suicide group. The main differences between the suicides and the control groups were that the alcoholics tended to be last in their sibship, were very attached to their mothers, reported a previous suicidal attempt and were very self-critical. Unlike the stereotype of the high-suicide-risk patient, the suicides in this study were living with their families and were not socially isolated. They also had good work records. The follow-up in this study was short compared with Kessel and Grossman's groups, who were followed for up to eleven years, and it is probable that more suicides would occur in time.

ALCOHOLISM AND CRIME

Drunkenness is an offence which in 1969 was responsible for over 80,000 convictions in England and Wales. This represents an increase of over 70 per cent since 1950 but the greater part of this increase had taken place by 1961 and since that time the figures have been fluctuating around 80,000. Of all the men in prison in 1969, 5·9 per cent were serving sentences for drunkenness offences and 13·4 per cent of all the women in prison were similarly convicted of drunkenness offences.

Gath (1969) conducted an intensive survey into the characteristics of the male drunk appearing in court in London. Each man was interviewed by an investigator in the team, immediately after appearing in court. The investigation excluded drunken driving offences; 70 per cent of the sample were charged with being drunk in a public place, 22 per cent with being drunk and disorderly and 8 per cent with a variety of other drunkenness offences. A total of 151 men were interviewed. Men of lower social-class, Irish origin and Roman Catholic faith, were significantly over-represented in the sample, as were the separated and single. During the preceding year, 50 per cent had been arrested at least once for drunkenness and 4 per cent had been arrested over 25 times in that year; 45 per cent had also been in jail at least once in their lives; 24 per cent of the sample were thought not to have a serious drinking problem but 50 per cent showed evidence of addiction to alcohol and the other 26 per cent had a serious drinking problem, without being physically dependent.

Very few of the men had any stable social contacts. Only 17 per cent were married and living with their wives. The majority were without accommodation in terms of a house, flat or room and 45 per cent were unemployed at the time of arrest. The overall picture of the male drunk charged with an offence in London emerges as one of a man in a lamentable state of affairs, who is alcoholic, homeless, unemployed, separated from social contact and is being repeatedly charged with minor offences. As Gath stated, the methods of dealing with such people that are at present employed by the courts seem totally inappropriate, and only by providing half-way houses and hostels instead of giving small fines following repeated arrests, could one hope to see any change in the situation.

Gath's study dealt with the characteristics of the male drunk who was charged with a minor offence and not jailed. Celia Hensman (1969) carried out a survey into drinking problems in male recidivists serving short-term sentences, not necessarily related to drinking. She interviewed 188 short-term recidivists. The population tended to be young, with a preponderance of Irish- and Scots-born. Again a very small minority (19 per cent) were married and cohabiting at the time of imprisonment. Half the prisoners had been in jail five times previously and they were mostly of low socio-economic status. Although the sample was not selected on the basis of drinking problems, only 30 per cent had no previous history of drunkenness offences and 40 per cent had six or more previous drunkenness offence convictions. The majority of the sample were drunk at the time of the offence for which they were imprisoned, 68 per cent were drinking immediately before the offence and 12 per cent said they couldn't even recall the offence.

An assessment of alcohol as a problem in the recidivist group showed that 17 per cent of the prisoners felt drinking had been a problem before they turned to crime and 29 per cent were criminal before drinking became a problem. More than one-third of the sample had symptoms of physical dependence on alcohol. In men who had had six or more arrests for drunkenness, over 75 per cent were physically dependent on alcohol and there was a 29 per cent chance that such men had drunk crude spirits at some time.

This group was in as serious, if not a more serious state, than the group of non-imprisoned drunkenness offenders. Both had few social contacts, few were married and of those arrested more than six times, the majority were addicted to alcohol and, just as important, were not receiving any treatment for their alcoholism.

The relationship between alcoholism and crime is complex. Both forms of behaviour are over-represented in men as compared with women, in people from lower socio-economic groups, in people with personality disorders and in men coming from broken, unsatisfactory homes, often with a previous family history of either criminality or alcoholism. Both conditions can occur in a single person as differing aspects of a single factor, such as a personality disorder, or they may arise consecutively. An alcoholic who has slipped down the social scale and has no income may turn to crime to obtain money for alcohol, as the American narcotic dependent is forced to do. Alcoholics sometimes also embezzle money when still employed, but this kind of offence is not covered by the study of Hensman. In her work, more of the recidivists admitted to being criminals before drink became a problem than admitted to being alcoholic before turning to crime.

Drinking and driving presents a specific problem that has come to light over the last few years with the introduction in the U.K. of the breathalyser and the accurate checks of blood alcohol concentration (B.A.C.) now employed. Apart from the change to an accurate method of measuring B.A.C.s, the other factor that (at least temporarily) affected drivers' behaviour was the institution of the law which allowed compulsory and immediate testing of a driver suspected of impaired driving. After the initial disagreement between those wholeheartedly in favour of the 1967 Act and those who feel it involves an invasion of privacy, the situation appears to have settled down into one of acceptance of the Act as useful. Perhaps it should even be tightened up by allowing random testing of drivers or by lowering the permitted level of blood alcohol from its present 80 mg of alcohol per 100 ml of blood to 50 mg per 100 ml.

Conviction under the Act allows for varying penalties but, in practice, conviction means disqualification from driving for a year plus a variable fine. People charged with a second or third offence run a very high risk of being sent to jail for some months. Following the introduction of the Road Safety Act 1967 the number of prosecutions for drunken driving more than doubled in the first year and initially there was a drop in the number of fatal casualties on the roads. As time goes on, there has been less of a perceived threat from the breathalyser and the accident rate has risen again. Reports of the proportion of drivers involved in fatal accidents with high B.A.C. vary from one country to another. A rate of 15 per 100 was reported in Britain in 1967 for drivers in fatal accidents with B.A.C. over 80 mg per cent. In Australia 50 per cent of drivers involved in fatal accidents have B.A.C.s over 100 mg per cent and in single vehicle accidents the rate was 80 per cent. (Many of this latter group may well have been suicides.) Alcoholics tend to drive for many years before being admitted to hospital for their alcoholism and it is surprising how many of them escape so frequently whilst being grossly impaired, without being caught or seriously injuring themselves or someone else.

ALCOHOLISM AND INDUSTRY

Alcoholics are, in general, men in the middle of life who have been drinking excessively for up to twenty years. They are typical therefore of the young to middle-aged working man of all social classes. They miss time from work, they are inefficient and they cost a great deal of money by being fired and thus necessitating someone else to be trained for their position. They also cause accidents at work and they cost the legal, health and welfare services large amounts in caring for both them and their families.

Until recent years, industry was content to ignore the problem (and to dismiss anyone who drank so heavily that it affected his work) to the point that some notice had to be taken of the situation. Glatt (1970) quotes the investigation by a director of a large company into drinking problems amongst the employees of a number of businesses. He was unable to find any evidence that employers considered alcoholism an issue to be dealt with in any other way than by dismissal of the affected employees. Recently, there have been considerable changes in the attitudes of employers to their alcoholic staff, as exemplified by the co-operation between the Merseyside Council on Alcoholism (M.C.A.) and a shipping line in Liverpool. The arrangement which exists is that any employee of the shipping line with a drinking problem can ask for help and be referred to the M.C.A. for assessment, and possible referral to other agencies for further treatment. As long as the alcoholic employee follows the prescribed treatment regime, he is guaranteed to have a job to which he can return. That this approach works is shown by the sustained sobriety rate of over 75 per cent amongst men going through the programme.

The problem of alcoholism in American industry is very large. Von Weingard (1972) reported that over 5 per cent of the labour force suffers from alcoholism and that the cost to industry due to the illness of these 6,500,000 people is between 6 and 8 billion dollars annually. Industries likely to have a higher than average proportion of alcoholics are those with a high male to female employee ratio, an older than average group of employees and a permissive attitude to absenteeism and general job performance. Von Weingard made the point that, although particular jobs attract alcoholics, it is not that the job causes alcoholism but rather that the alcoholic is able to survive in these particular areas of employment because there are lax controls on job performance. The areas of employment having especially high rates of alcoholism are seafaring, bartending, dishwashing and labouring jobs. In a three year survey of Merseyside Council on Alcoholism clients, the largest single "employed" group was housewives, with 133 out of 1,186 cases! The next largest groups were labourers (121) and seafarers (62) followed by drivers, dock labourers, shop owners and clerks. The largest group of all was the unemployed or casual workers, with 185 people in this group.

Industry has many advantages to gain from following a programme designed to treat and return to work as many alcoholic employees as possible. Von Weingard showed that the New York Transit Authority spent 65,000 dollars a year on its alcoholism programme, but saved $1\frac{1}{2}$ million dollars on sick-leave payments in one year alone. There are many suspicions and mistaken ideas to be tackled on both sides of the employment fence. Many employers may still wish to dismiss an alcoholic employee rather than face the prospect of having the employee intermittently ill for a period of years. The individual employee and his union may feel that a man's health and his drinking habits are all part of his private domain and not part of his employer's concern. However, a policy based on identifying the alcoholic by his Monday-morning absences, poor work performance and occasional smell of alcohol, which then leads on to treatment, pays dividends. The employee may feel he is being pressured to have treatment, but may also welcome the opportunity to talk to someone about his problem and still be guaranteed an income and a job with no demotion as a reward for trying to cope. The employer is unlikely to lose by adopting such a policy. He is ultimately in control of the situation by having the power of dismissal; it is merely the reasons for dismissal that vary. The alcoholic may lose his post when his performance deteriorates, as he becomes more and more ill, or he may be fired for failing to co-operate with a treatment programme carried out on behalf of the organisation for which he works. In the first instance, the alcoholic is pushed further down the road to total social breakdown; in the second, he may be started on a rehabilitative route that will be all the easier to travel the less he has progressed in his illness. The sooner the idea disappears that an alcoholic has to reach "rock bottom" to be motivated to seek treatment, the better will be the prospects for many early alcoholics.

Drug abuse

Quite a lot of information is now available about the numbers of people who take drugs, although much of this is of little value as it is based on unrepresentative or small samples. Braucht *et al.* (1973) have reviewed the sociocultural and personality correlates of deviant adolescent drug-abusers and these workers review a wide range of research which they too consider to have many shortcomings. A critical issue they highlighted was the lack of co-ordination among alcohol, narcotic and psychedelic researchers, and a neglect of the examination of common factors in their various fields. With regard to the natural history of drug abuse, there has been hitherto a lack of long-term studies, and in particular prospective studies, so that it is difficult to piece together the events in the life of a drug abuser.

In an excellent review, Russell (1971) has traced the natural history of cigarette smoking, and much emerges that is of direct relevance to drug abuse as a whole. Only a tiny proportion of people begin smoking before the age of ten; for most it is a phenomenon of adolescence. The onset of smoking is mediated by many social influences, but by far the most powerful is the number of friends who smoke. Smoking is a precocious activity occurring in those orientated towards out-of-school activities, such as cinemas, coffee-bars and other outlets of pop-culture. Smoking occurs in an environment of smokers, who characterise smoking as mature and tough. Russell describes the archetypal English smoker as a lower working-class male, aged twenty-five to thirty, educated at secondary modern school, who prefers chasing girls and drinking to quieter pastimes. A few cigarettes in adolescence, and progression to habitual smoking is almost inevitable, for only the teenagers who have had one cigarette or less in adolescence have much chance of becoming non-smoking adults. Ignoring the variety of internal and external cues that trigger the habitual repetition of smoking, and the complex interplay of these pressures, in three to four years the adult type of smoking regularly takes over from smoking confined to social situations in nearly 70 per cent of males. A high proportion of smokers use tobacco because of an "inner-need factor", which suggests that earlier motivations to smoke are replaced in adult life by the dependency-producing properties of nicotine. Smoking is then continued in the face of financial disincentives and the risk to health. The withdrawal symptoms of irritability, craving, difficulty in concentration and mood changes are well known. After the age of thirty, some smokers will try to stop smoking, and 18 per cent of smokers will become ex-smokers. This is not a stable state, and a high proportion will relapse to regular smoking. As with drug abuse generally, the longer the period of abstention, the less the likelihood of relapse, so that 37 per cent relapse within the first year, whilst only 5 per cent who have not smoked for two years relapse.

Altogether 77 per cent of smokers wish to stop smoking, or have tried to stop, but only 25 per cent will do so permanently. The threat of lung cancer will not stop smokers, for it is only when they personally experience physical ailments, such as shortness of breath, cough, sore throat and indigestion that they will become motivated. It has been estimated that smoking is responsible each year in the U.S.A. for the loss of 77 million man-working days. It is impossible to conceive the social consequences of such a loss, but the bare statistics of the long-term effects of smoking are quite frightening. Smokers have a mortality rate 30 to 80 per cent higher than that of non-smokers, the mortality increasing with higher cigarette consumption, and for those who start smoking early. Not only this, but the mortality is highest in those in the prime of life, when career goals have been achieved, and whose lives would otherwise have been materially comfortable.

Only 2 per cent of adult smokers can be described as occasional smokers (McKennell and Thomas, 1967), so that regular smoking is a habit easily learned but not so easily lost. The fact that four out of every five people who have smoked one cigarette become regular devotees might act as a pointer to what could happen eventually if public attitudes to drug abuse were to change, as indeed there is some evidence that they are changing.

The numbers of young people taking drugs have been reviewed earlier, as have the figures for multiple drug-use and the factors governing the abuse of more than one drug. There are huge gaps in our knowledge about the progression of drug-taking, many of them due to methodological problems. Wiener's (1970) original intention in his school survey was to employ a longitudinal design, and to follow up schoolchildren for several years after leaving school. Such a project would require many investigators, and for practical reasons he abandoned his idea. He was primarily interested in contributory factors in drug-taking, rather than the complications of drug abuse. He did show that the 5 to 10 per cent of children who had sampled drugs had poorer school records, more delinquent histories, poorer relationships with their parents, and indulged in more adult leisure activities than non-drug-takers with peer groups whose members tended also to take drugs as well as drink and smoke. Samples of drug abusers are likely to contain an over-representation of social misfits, so the "typical" drug addict emanates from a fragmented family in a disturbed community, is aggressive, impulsive, lacks concern for others, is insecure, depressed and has low endurance, and has shown these predominantly psychopathic traits long before taking drugs. Many changes attributed to drug-taking may, really, be causally related to pre-existing abnormalities, or even to changes concomitant with drug-taking, such as heavier alcohol intake, alterations in life style and changes in friends and acquaintances. Any statements made about the social consequences of drug-taking should therefore be tentative rather than dogmatic.

It is certainly true that a high proportion of college students take drugs. (For example, 26 per cent in an American study (Mizner, G. L., *et al.*, 1970), and an equally high figure from a British study (Hindmarch, 1970)), so that many drug users must be, essentially, of normal personality and from normal backgrounds. Graham Blaine (1969) classified drug users into three groups, which he called "experience seekers", "oblivion seekers", and "personality-change seekers". The largest group comprise the experience seekers, youthful experimenters with an excess of energy who enjoy taking risks, breaking rules, and who show the healthy rebellion of adolescence. Three-quarters of Weiner's group were occasional users only, and only a tiny proportion of this young age-group could be described as habitual drug-takers. Occasional use of drugs seems to have few untoward consequences for the users, and most spontaneously give up taking drugs, some because of the legal consequences, some because they consider drugs to have harmful physical and genetic effects, and many because they gain little from their drug-taking experiments. The following brief case history is typical of the experience seeker's behaviour:

Case 5

Jim was twenty-three and worked as a labourer in a factory. In the summertime, he attended week-end pop festivals, but rarely missed work. He smoked and drank, but took other drugs only at week-ends, in the company of drug-taking friends. He found that smoking cannabis resin made him feel relaxed, and saw nothing wrong with the practice. He had taken LSD at pop festivals, and once was treated in a hospital casualty department for an adverse reaction, the main features of which were anxiety and bizarre visual experiences. He had appeared in court once on a charge of drug possession, and stated that if caught again might well give up smoking "pot". He lived at home, where he had constant arguments with his father, who objected to his "long-haired attitudes". His mother hoped he would marry and move out.

Blaine's group of oblivion-seekers find the drugged state a pleasant respite from the ordeals of life, and take drugs consistently. Cohen and Klein (1970), in a study of psychiatric patients, confirmed the generally accepted view that there are two groups of moderate users, one abusing many drugs, and one restricting their use to cannabis. Becker (1963) believes that most marijuana users show no abnormalities. He describes the progression of usage from learning the technique to learning to perceive the effects, to learning to enjoy the effects. Interaction with others is important in appreciating the experience and in accepting that the drug is "safe", but it involves moving into a society that approves of drug-taking, which process alters one's social needs and identifications. Kaufman and his colleagues (1969) believe that marijuana acts as a unifying force, bringing together people with similar spiritual values. Drugs give them a magical escape into romanticism, a pilgrim's road away from the crippling technological progress of modern society. They inspire ideals of creativity, beauty, freedom and self-expression, and yet suppress the flow of energy that made the "green rebellion" self-destructive. Cannabis use is so often associated with a rebellion against institutions, politics, war, power, and gives relief to the anger and insurgence of youth. LSD usage in Kaufman's view is the "pharmacological sacrament", giving a divine insight into the pacifist mystique, the supreme experience of an alienated minority.

Case 6

Bill was twenty-one, a third-year university student referred by the university counselling service, to whom he had presented because of inability to cope with his courses. He smoked several "joints" each day, and complained of being "spaced out", a condition that prevented him from concentrating on his work. He had been a member of a left-wing student group, but found the militant attitudes of his fellow members distasteful. He was disillusioned with materialist values, and the hypocrisy of his teachers. He felt generally dissatisfied and tended to blame others for his situation. Close questioning revealed that he suffered from premature ejaculation, and that he had been humiliated in several sexual encounters with women. He reluctantly agreed that his real dissatisfaction was with himself, and that he used drugs and rationalisation processes to escape from intense feelings of sadness and inadequacy.

Many youngsters hold a variety of "alternative" values, which in only a minority have resulted in the establishment of a new life style, seen in its extreme in the hippie communal movement. In the U.S.A., thousands of runaways have evolved naturalistic alternatives to technocratic cultures and have united in groups with less-structural social form. Few have had strong sustaining ideologies, and the majority therefore have proved fragmentary, and the lack of social integration has brought these societies to premature ends. An attempt has been made by some of the more successful ones to bring up a second generation with similar ideals (Smith and Sternfield, 1970), but the seeds of rejection appear to be present even there.

Blaine believes that those who reject materialism and competitiveness are burdened with feelings of incompetence and inadequacy. They believe in conventional goals, but do not believe personally that they can achieve success. They cannot live up to their own or their parent's expectations and drug-taking provides an avoidance response. The group of personality-change seekers are those who are profoundly disappointed and frustrated, and who become permanently incapacitated by drug use. They include a large number who are psychiatrically ill: manic-depressives, gross neurotics, psychopaths and schizophrenics. Hekimian and Gershon (1968) considered that 50 per cent of drug abusers admitted to hospital were schizophrenic before taking drugs of the marijuana and amphetamine type—a high figure which does not receive support from other sources.

Case 7

Tom was nineteen, single, and came from a working-class housing estate, where drug-taking was rife. He had a tumultuous home life, with an over-concerned but weak mother, and an extraordinarily punitive father. For a week he had been sleeping in a garden shed, as he had been refused entry to the house. He began smoking "pot" and taking amphetamines from the age of fourteen, and by sixteen had left home (Liverpool) to live in London. At that time he was already taking heroin daily. He was now taking 60 mg of heroin daily, and methadone from the clinic. He had been admitted to hospital three times already for withdrawal, but relapsed quickly, obtaining black-market drugs until he returned to a clinic. He had not worked for a year, and had not held any job for more than two months. His only friends were "junkies". He constantly importuned for drugs and was surly and unco-operative. When he could obtain amphetamines he became threatening, and talked of the police following him wherever he went, a statement probably not totally untrue. He had taken two near-fatal overdoses of barbiturates, and had received treatment for hepatitis, pneumonia, abscesses, and numerous minor complications. He had a vague intention to change his life-style, but expressed a great fear that he would die very soon.

ESCALATION

Evidence about the progression of drug-taking has been almost wholly derived from retrospective studies of delinquent or hospital attenders. Amongst notified addicts, the most frequently used drugs in the early stages are amphetamines and cannabis (Bransby, 1973). Cannabis use at an early age has been confirmed in methylamphetamine abusers (Hawks *et al.*, 1969), non-registered heroin users (Kosviner *et al.*, 1968) and amongst delinquent girls (Noble and Barnes, 1971). Bransby found that at the age of fifteen, 28 per cent of the males in his series had smoked cannabis, compared with 35 per cent who had taken amphetamines, whilst at the age of twenty-five almost all had used cannabis and stimulants, and had extensive experience of other drugs. It seems that potential heroin-takers start taking drugs very early, rapidly progress to poly-drug abuse, and begin taking heroin or other opiates at an early age. In Bransby's study one-quarter of the males had taken opiates by the age of seventeen, and three-quarters by the age of twenty. The youngest age that patients had taken opiate drugs was twelve for males and thirteen for females. In Hawk's study, problem drinking had ante-dated drug-taking in almost one-quarter of the patients, but there was a suggestion that heavy drug-usage led to a decline in alcohol consumption.

In many drug abusers, drug-taking is unsystematic, and many are not even aware of the exact nature of what they are consuming.

For many, being seen to take drugs is as important as experiencing the effects, and for some a diffuse intoxication, no matter how achieved, is the aim. Heroin addicts regularly take non-opiate drugs in large numbers, the reasons for this action being many. If heroin or opiates are in short supply, then alternative drugs are taken to fill the gap. Cocaine was commonly taken to reverse the soporific effects of heroin, but is rarely prescribed by clinics now, so that amphetamines are taken instead. Amphetamine use can result in insomnia, so that regular use of sedatives, tranquillisers and hypnotics, often of the barbiturate type, is to be expected.

In the U.K., heroin-takers use the intravenous route almost without exception from the first use. It is not known what proportion of those who take heroin on one occasion progress to regular use, but of those who do, most progress from intermittent to daily use within one to six months. There is usually simultaneous exposure of groups of young people, connected by age, geography and interests, so that drug-taking can spread rapidly. De Alarcon and Rathod (1968) have traced the spread of an epidemic in Crawley New Town. Commercial pushing did not exist, but initiation and sharing amongst friends was the rule, and only heroin surplus to the individual's personal needs was sold by the users. Hawks felt that a significant proportion of methylamphetamine users were members of a delinquent sub-culture and that this contributed to their later adoption of drugs, but once they were using drugs regularly they associated almost exclusively with other drug-users in wholly drug-regulated activities. Drugs provided a currency to buy friendship, and were mostly passed on to acquaintances, although a number obtained drugs from sellers they did not previously know. De Alarcon showed that a high proportion of heroin-takers were not known to the authorities, and in Bransby's study one-half of the patients claimed to have started using heroin, methadone, or cocaine two years before attending hospital. They may not have used drugs continuously over these periods, but clearly many of them become enmeshed in a cohesive sub-culture that supports their drug-taking habit, and often provides support in other ways too. Whilst there are few signs of a highly organised British drug "racket" on the American model, there is increasing evidence of non-using pedlars providing imported opiates for adolescents, who may present more quickly to the drug dependency clinics now that prescribing is available. Even in the U.S.A., pushers are themselves likely to be drug users. An interesting account of amphetamine peddling in Oklahoma is given by Griffith (1966) whose work suggests that valuable information can be gained from field research. Few of the amphetamine-takers were gainfully employed, and most derived their incomes from crime, selling drugs, or from prostitutes.

Noble and Barnes found that the items which marked out a group of delinquent girls in their susceptibility to progression to narcotic drugs were: more frequent use of non-narcotic drugs; involvement in a drug milieu; high incidence of personality abnormality; and poor work-record. During a short stay in a remand setting, those who had progressed to narcotic use proved to have poor interpersonal relationships and found it difficult to concentrate on academic and household tasks. A two to four years' follow-up of girls admitted to a London remand home showed that over 20 per cent who had taken non-narcotic drugs at admission progressed to narcotic use, but only 1 per cent of non-drug-taking controls similarly progressed. An earlier study of boys in a remand home (Noble, 1970) had shown that of a group of soft-drug-takers 19 per cent progressed to narcotic use in a very short follow-up period. Unfortunately, Noble does not say in detail what distinguishes those who progress from those who do not, but he says that they tended to be worse-off in the degree of their personality abnormality, the incidence of psychiatric morbidity within the family, and in having poor work-records. These features were exactly the ones that differentiated the "soft" from the "hard" drug-takers in the sample.

The most controversial issue about escalation of drug usage is the relationship between cannabis smoking and the progression to heroin usage. Mirin and colleagues (1970) have described in detail a group of casual and heavy cannabis smokers. A few of the heavy smokers who were thought to have become true abusers, associated cannabis use with the use of amphetamines and hallucinogens. Work and social adjustment were very poor, but none progressed to heroin use. There can be no denial that a proportion of cannabis smokers do go on to heroin addiction, and some distinguished people have pointed to the statistical relationship between the rise in cannabis offences and the increase in heroin addiction (Paton,

1968), but there is an equivalent relationship between heroin, and stimulant and tranquilliser, misuse. There have been suggestions that cannabis intoxication reduces self-control, so making heroin-taking more likely, although a more realistic suggestion about the missing link was by Forrest (1970), who reported that many U.S.A. soldiers in Vietnam used marijuana soaked in heroin solution. The amount of heroin absorbed in this way is probably small, and tolerance is unlikely to develop at this low concentration. A direct, causal link between heroin and cannabis is unlikely, and the fallacy of the escalation theory has been exposed by Michael Schofield (1971), who feels that a theory predicting that cannabis-smoking protects against heroin addiction is just as tenable. To summarise, there is not a well-delineated continuum of use from cannabis to heroin, but a multitude of drug-taking pathways that lead in different directions, many of which result in some degree of social infirmity.

LIFE STYLE

Anyone who has worked in a drug-dependency clinic quickly realises how extraordinarily disorganised are the lives of their clients. Addicts' inability to form meaningful relations, their hollowness and isolation, together with a poor comprehension of their effect on others, can lead to a chaotic environment for those closely related to them. There have been many psycho-analytically-oriented studies of mother–child and father–child relationships, but few dealing with wider family aspects. Many addicts come from "broken homes", but in turn they so often contribute to deterioration of family life by their behaviour. Typical complaints from mothers are of their adolescent sons associating with undesirables, coming home late or not coming home at all, losing jobs, coming home drunk or "high" on drugs, being rude and petulant or using foul language, or behaving badly in front of other children. Answering complaints are of parental lack of concern and interest, preoccupation with old-world values, over-restriction or undue interference in the adolescent's life. Nowhere is the "generation gap" better illustrated than in the families of drug addicts, although a high proportion of unmarried addicts have remained in close contact with their families until their presentation at treatment centres

(Blumberg *et al.*, 1973). Often, the attitudes of the parents and their deviant offspring are so out of accord that any schisms between the parents are widened and the parent–child position intensified. Parents, no matter how indulgent initially, invariably become hostile to their drug-taking children, although this may remain as smouldering resentment rather than outright rejection, and proportionally few actually evict addicts from their homes. Many addicts undoubtedly leave home prematurely, and life histories of addicts testify to their periodic migrations and numerous changes of address. A high proportion have slept "rough" at one time or another, and many have no fixed abode, but the number of these may be inflated in the U.K. by London figures, because of the tendency of people to drift there from the provinces.

For many, the first index of instability is truancy in the later years of schooling, which has occurred in serious degree in nearly half of registered drug addicts. This is followed by ventures into employment, with most involved in work less skilled than that of their fathers. Two-thirds of those entering apprenticeships fail to complete them and, overall, there is a downward drift in occupation, the rate varying with the extent of the drug-taking. The social-class distribution of the fathers of male patients in the U.K. is much the same as the national distribution, but the parents of English female addicts contain a very high proportion working in the professions, so that the discrepancy in occupation of their addict daughters is more marked. Bransby was surprised to find in his first study that 40 per cent of male addicts were working, mostly full-time. The second report confirmed this figure as accurate, but no details are given of the length of time in work so that, for many, full-time employment could conceal numerous job-changes in a short space of time. In the U.S.A., the employment rates for addicts are as low as 10 to 13 per cent, a figure that implies the totally different life-style of the American from the British addict.

A very interesting paper by Taylor and her colleagues (1966) commented on the wives of American addicts. Of a large number of patients, 43 per cent were married, a figure higher than Bransby's (23 per cent) but similar to Blumberg's (39 per cent). In the latter figure were included common-law spouses, so that the incidence of marriage is probably lower in English addicts, almost certainly due to the younger age of present-day opiate addicts in the U.K. In the American group, 22 per cent were divorced or widowed, a strikingly high proportion for a group of young people, but substantiated in English addicts, where one-third of the women and one-seventh of the men had broken marriages. The wives of addicts, like the wives of alcoholics, seem to function more adequately and have stronger egos than their husbands. It is possible that they seek out men whom they can control and dominate, and certainly they tend to deprecate their own fathers and identify with their mothers, even though they often show stronger feelings of antagonism toward them. Some may have entered marriage as an act of rebellion and many were warned not to do so, but few did so precipitously and many had known their intended spouses long before marriage. Some knew of their husbands' drug usage before marriage, but felt they could cope with it. The major attractions were their husbands' gentle, sweet, passive disposition—qualities that so often proved to be illusory.

Families in which there is an addict-member rarely escape from a series of economic, medical, legal and social crises. Many addicts have acted in a violent way towards their wives (half in the Taylor study), yet surprisingly few of the wives are overly concerned by this. More will complain of the passive behaviour of their husbands, feeling that drugs have given them an escape from responsibility, so that the burden of every-day living falls on their shoulders. Most have to work, or rely on social security, and they become resigned to leading a semi-independent life. It is perhaps surprising that so many continue to live with their husbands, whilst constantly ignored. Even those who separate usually remain in contact.

Drugs such as heroin have an effect on every aspect of human functioning. Many addicts are promiscuous before addiction, and of those who marry most will have extra-marital affairs, but the drugs have an insidious effect on sexual behaviour. Sexual intercourse decreases in frequency and satisfaction and other appetites are equally diminished. Weight loss and inadequate diet lower resistance to disease, so that medical complications ensue which in turn cause further social consequences. Addicts, particularly those who knew drug users and mixed in their circles before taking opiates, increasingly mix with addicts, so that their connection with the "straight" world diminishes. Life activities become the buying, borrowing and selling of drugs, stealing, receiving, moving from place to place, attending clinics and hospitals, and confronting the law. In a group of people approaching drug treatment centres in London, 46 per cent had been involved in illegal activities in the previous year, and most had sold drugs or received stolen goods, if they had not themselves stolen property. Few of those on intravenous drugs had abstained for more than a short period since beginning regular "fixing". It seems that many are reluctant to attend treatment centres, so that it is not known at all what happens to the great numbers who do not. The course of those who come into contact with treatment agencies has been discussed elsewhere, but one sadly neglected area of study has been the way some addicts cease taking drugs. Winwick (1962) commented that there should be as much interest in the cessation of heroin addiction as in its genesis, and remarked on the absence of data. He derived his information from the files of the Federal Bureau of Narcotics, which is concerned with regular users of opium derivatives and synthetic opiates only, excluding marijuana, cocaine, and barbiturate addicts. The average age of inactivity (defining inactivity as a five-year period of non-abuse) of a huge group of addicts was 35·12 years, with a standard deviation of 8·675. There was a substantial concentration of addicts becoming inactive in their thirties, a proportion not dependent on the total number of addicts in that age group, in the total active-addict population. He had earlier noted in a study of addicted jazz musicians that there were very few over the age of forty still using the drug (Winwick, 1962).

Winwick speculated that addicts "matured out" as the need for drugs became less salient and less urgent. If the use of narcotics is to evade or mask the social pressures, sexual demands, and vocational contributions of adolescence, addicts may feel that less is expected of them later, or else the emotional homeostasis of simply growing older may stabilise them without need for narcotics. The obvious parallel is between delinquents and psychopaths who, in equivalent ways, mature, with consequent decline in their criminal or antisocial activities. The maturation of psychopaths may have a biological basis, as the abnormal brain-wave patterns they show in adolescence are known to decline to normal levels and, of course, many addicts can clearly be classified as psychopaths. A further possible explanation is that the life cycle of the addiction process has a limited span, and the maturing out is not related primarily to age but the length of the addicts drug-taking history. In Winwick's sample, the average length of addiction was 8·6 years, most became inactive under 10 years, and very few after 15 years.

In a test of the maturation hypothesis, Ball and Snarr (1969) found that only one-third of the addicts in their sample matured out by the age of forty. Not only were two-thirds still taking drugs 13 years since the onset of the opiate abuse, but the extent of social impairment and criminality tended to increase. They suggested that two major patterns existed. In one, the addict's dependence is progressive, and he is dragged into a mesh of criminal behaviour from which he finds it impossible to extricate himself. In only a small minority can the addict assume a legitimate role in society, but if he can remain abstinent for 3 years, then the chances of relapse are virtually nil, and chances of arrest significantly decline. These workers' conclusions were that there is no evidence to support the interpretation that years of drug use, or the ageing process, themselves contribute to abstinence.

Vaillant (1966) agreed that addicts did not "burn-out" in their mid-thirties, but he found that between the age of twenty and forty, 2 per cent became abstinent per year. Stephens and Cottrell (1972) cited as reasons for abstinence the patient's desire to stay "clean", the effectiveness of therapy, the emotional support of the family, and fear of continued involvement in the sub-culture. The rate of abstinence was high for those over thirty, but these authors felt that there was little overall support for either of Winwick's hypotheses.

DRUG ABUSE AND CRIME

Most drug abusers are not criminals, but drug-taking in many of its aspects is a proscribed activity, and therefore there is a direct relationship between drug-taking and criminality. The number of prosecutions and convictions for drug offences in Britain has spectacularly increased over the last ten years or so, as may be seen from Table X.

Drugs covered by the Drugs (Prevention of Misuse) Act 1964

and the superceding Misuse of Drugs Act 1971 include lysergic acid and amphetamines, and the offences comprise unlawful possession and larceny for the most part. Convictions under the Dangerous Drug Act 1965 (again replaced by the 1971 Act) have also risen dramatically: by far the greater number of convictions involve cannabis, mostly relating to possession, rising from 51 in 1957 to 9,219 in 1972; but offences of unlawful possession and unlawful supply, larceny and unlawful import of all drugs, including heroin and opium, have also shown substantial increases.

TABLE X

Conviction under Drugs (Prevention of Misuse) Act 1964*

Year	*No.*
1966	1,216
1967	2,486
1968	2,957
1969	3,762
1970	3,885
1971	5,516

* Note: convictions after 1971 were carried out under the Misuse of Drugs Act 1971, which repealed the earlier Act.

The extent of the illegal abuse of drugs in the U.K. and the U.S.A. is such that huge amounts of money can be made by importing and distributing them. In the U.S.A., the big dealers belong almost exclusively to the criminal sub-culture, and are involved in the syndicates that control gambling and prostitution. The lower down the scale, the greater the likelihood of drug abuser involvement in selling and distributing. Undoubtedly, large-scale drug rackets exist in the U.K. but are by no means as important or well-organised as their trans-Atlantic counterparts. Heroin addicts in the U.S.A. may need from $50.00 to $100.00 each day to buy the requisite quantities of drugs, depending on their developed need, and it is impossible for them to obtain such sums through legal activities. As drug-tolerance rises and their need increases, drugs, or money for drugs, are obtained by petty thieving, forgery, embezzlement, or prostitution. Inevitably, there is contact with the law, and this in turn brings the criminal underworld closer to the addict. Addicts in prison congregate together, induce the novice into criminal behaviours, and the stigma of imprisonment prevents rehabilitation, so pushing the addict into more deviant activities. In the U.K., theoretically at least, addicts do not have to resort to criminal activities, as they can obtain drugs from treatment centres. However, the majority of registered addicts have criminal histories, involving both drug and non-drug offences. In Willis's group of heroin addicts (Willis, 1971) 76 per cent had been arrested at least once, including 70 per cent for drug offences, and 62 per cent for non-drug offences. In almost all groups of drug abusers, from cannabis smokers to those taking LSD, amphetamine and heroin, there is a higher incidence of criminal behaviour than in controlled groups of non-drug-takers from similar backgrounds. The question of a relationship is not in doubt; what is in question is the exact nature of the relationship. Is drug-taking one manifestation of delinquency, or is drug-taking a causal factor in delinquency and can it predispose to certain crimes, or do both result from an underlying personality disorder? Which comes first, delinquency or drug-taking?

Cockett (1971) found in a series of young offenders remanded in custody that in 71 per cent delinquency coincided with or preceded drug-taking, James (1969) noted that 76 per cent had been convicted of offences before addiction, while Willis reported that 54 per cent of London addicts and 48 per cent of New York addicts had been convicted before drug use began. It does seem that drug-taking can lead to delinquency, but only in a tiny proportion. Drug-takers as a whole, in Cockett's series, began their criminal careers later than non-drug-takers, and he found that soft-drug-takers began their criminal careers later than hard-drug-takers. In regard to the qualitative aspects of past criminal behaviour, Cockett separated violent and non-violent crimes, and found no differences in drug-takers as opposed to non-drug-takers. Those more heavily involved in drug-taking committed fewer offences than chronic addicts but the ratio of type of crime remained exactly the same (six drug offences to four crimes against property to one crime against the person) and it was considered that criminality-type did not distinguish the two groups. In the U.S.A., addicts are five times more likely to be arrested than ex-addicts, although of course most arrests are for drug offences.

Kolb, overy forty years ago (Kolb, 1935) carefully documented the relationship of drug addiction to crime, and his words are just as relevant today: "Addicts are so often criminal in the sense that they violate drug laws, not in the sense that their actions are harmful to others, and criminals behave in criminal ways because they are so disposed, rather than because they take drugs". A causal connection between cannabis and crime is a very tenuous one. It has been suggested that heroin addiction may predispose toward violent crime, but it is likely that the sense of well-being and good temper that heroin produces may even protect a group of otherwise aggression-prone individuals by inhibiting their drives. Clearly, much more work needs to be done, but there certainly are theoretical reasons why drugs could predispose towards crime, and there are many unvalidated reports to suggest a relationship between specific drugs and certain crimes. Connell (1958) noticed that one-fifth of the amphetamine psychotics he had seen had shown aggressive behaviour. Drugs which can precipitate psychoses can also precipitate aggressive actions in response to the panic, misinterpretations or delusions due to the psychosis. Ellinwood (1971) reported thirteen cases of homicide under the influence of amphetamines. He felt that the drug-induced paranoia, emotional lability and lowered impulse-control were more important in evoking abnormal behaviour than environmental factors and personality predisposition, and he considered amphetamines to have increased the incidence of assault, rape, kidnap and attempted murder. Barter and Reite (1969) looked at the connection between crime, especially murder, and LSD consumption and suggested criteria that had to be met in an individual case for implicating LSD as a causal factor. Surprisingly, reports of murder associated with LSD abuse are quite rare.

The relationship between alcohol and crime is not disputed, and is exactly analagous to the situation with drugs and crime. Alcohol does not generate crime-orientated behaviour, but it is often consumed by those who are at least considering crime, and a drug which alters people's perceptions or inhibits their control, also increases the risk of criminal involvement. Drugs therefore seem to act as catalysts rather than as causative agents.

REFERENCES

Ball, J. C. and Snarr, R. W., "A Test of the Maturation Hypothesis with Respect to Opiate Addiction", *Bulletin on Narcotics*, 21: 9–13, 1969.

Barter, J. T. and Reite, M., "Crime and LSD", *American Journal of Psychiatry*, 126: 531–7, 1969.

Becker, H. S., "On Becoming a Marijuana User", in Becker, H. S., *Outsiders: Studies in the Sociology of Deviance*, The Free Press, New York, 1963.

Blaine, G. B., "Drug Abuse in Young People", *Journal of the Iowa Medical Society*, 59: 37–42, 1969.

Blumberg, H., *et al.*, "British Opiate Users I: People Approaching Drug Treatment Centres", a Paper presented at the Second International Conference on Alcoholism and Drug Dependence, Liverpool, 1973.

Bransby, E. R., "A Study of Patients Notified by Hospitals as Addicted to Drugs", Second Report, *Health Trends*, 5: 17–20, 1973.

Braucht, G. N., *et al.*, "Deviant Drug Use in Adolescence: A Review of Psychosocial Correlates", *Psychological Bulletin*, 79: 92–106, 1973.

Cockett, R., *Drug Abuse and Personality in Young Offenders*, Butterworth, London, 1971.

Cohen, M. and Klein, D. F., "Drug Abuse in a Young Psychiatric Population", *American Journal of Orthopsychiatry*, 40: 448–55, 1970.

Connell, P. H., *Amphetamine Psychosis*, Chapman and Hall, London, 1958.

Cork, M., *The Forgotten Children*, General Publishing Co., Don Mills, Ontario, 1969.

de Alarcon, R. and Rathod, N. H., "Prevalence and Early Detection of Heroin Abuse", *British Medical Journal*, ii: 549–53, 1968.

Edwards, P., Harvey, C. and Whitehead, P., "Wives of Alcoholics: A Critical Review", *Quarterly Journal of Studies on Alcohol*, 34 (i): 112–32, 1973.

Ellinwood, E., "Assault and Homicide Associated with Amphetamine Abuse", *Am. J. Psychiatry*, 127: 1,170–5, 1971.

Forrest, D. V., "Marijuana to Heroin ... A Missing Link?", *Am. J. Psychiatry*, 127: 704–5, 1970.

Gath, D., "The Male Drunk in Court", in Gath, D., Cook, T. and Hensman, Celia, (eds.), op. cit.

Gath, D., Cook, T. and Hensman, Celia (eds.), *The Drunkenness Offense*, Pergamon, Oxford, 1969.

Glatt, M. M., "Complications of Alcoholism in the Social Sphere", *British Journal of Addiction*, 62: 35–44, 1967.

Glatt, M. M., *The Alcoholic and the Help He Needs*, Priory Press, Royston, U.K., 1970.

Griffith, J., "A Study in Illicit Amphetamine Drug Traffic in Oklahoma City", *Am. J. Psychiatry*, 123: 560–8, 1966.

Hawks, D., *et al.*, "Abuse of Methylamphetamine", *Br. Med. J.*, ii: 715–21, 1969.

Hekimian, L. J. and Gershon, S., "Characteristics of Drug Abusers Admitted to a Psychiatric Hospital", *Journal of the American Medical Association*, 205: 125–30, 1968.

Hensman, Celia, "Problems of Drunkenness Amongst Male Recidivists", in Gath, D., Cook, T. and Hensman, Celia, (eds.), op. cit.

Hindmarch, I., "Drugs and their Abuse. Age Groups Particularly at Risk", *Brit. J. Addict.*, 67: 209–14, 1972.

James, J. P., "Delinquency and Heroin Addiction in Britain", *British Journal of Criminology*, 108–24, 1969.

Jellinek, E. M., "The Phases of Alcohol Addiction", *Quart. J. Stud. Alcohol*, 13: 673–84, 1952.

Kaufman, J., Allen, J. R. and West, L. J., "Runaways, Hippies and Marihuana", *Am. J. Psychiatry*, 126: 717–20, 1969.

Kessel, W. I. N. and Grossman, G., "Suicide Amongst Alcoholics", *British Journal of Medical Psychology*, 41: 235–42, 1961.

Kessel, W. I. N. and Walton, H., *Alcoholism*, Penguin, Harmondsworth, 1965.

Kolb, L., "Drug Addiction and Its Relation to Crime", *Mental Hygiene*, 9: 74, 1935.

Kosviner, A., *et al.*, "Heroin Use in a Provincial Town", *Lancet*, i: 1,189–92, 1968.

McKennell, A. C. and Thomas, R. K., *Adults' and Adolescents' Smoking Habits and Attitudes: A Report on a Survey Carried Out for the Ministry of Health*, H.M.S.O., S.353/B, London, 1967.

Menninger, K., *Man Against Himself*, Harcourt Brace, New York, 1938.

Mirin, S., *et al.*, "Casual Versus Heavy Use of Marihuana", a Paper presented at the 123rd meeting of the American Psychiatric Association, California, 1970.

Mizner, G. L., "Patterns of Drug Use Among College Students", *Am. J. Psychiatry*, 127: 15–24, 1970.

National Council on Alcoholism Inc., New York, "Criteria for the Diagnosis of Alcoholism", *Annals of Internal Medicine*, 77: 249–58, 1972.

Noble, P. J., "Drug-taking in Delinquent Boys", *Br. Med. J.*, i: 102–5, 1970.

Noble, P. and Barnes, G. G., "Drug Taking in Adolescent Girls: Factors Associated with the Progression to Narcotic Use", *Br. Med. J.*, ii: 549–53, 1971.

Nylander, I., "Children of Alcoholic Fathers", *Acta Paediat.*, (*Upps.*), 49, Suppl. No. 121 Part I: 1–134, 1960.

Paton, W. D. M., "Drug Dependence—A Socio-Pharmacological Assessment", *Advancement of Science*, 200–12, Dec. 1968.

Ritson, E. B., "Suicide Amongst Alcoholics", *Br. J. Med. Psychol.*, 41: 235–42, 1968.

Ritson, E. B. and Hassall, C., *The Management of Alcoholism*, Livingstone, Edinburgh, 1970.

Russell, M. A., "Cigarette Smoking: Natural History of Dependence Disorder", *Br. J. Med. Psychol.*, 44: 1–16, 1971.

Schofield, M., *The Strange Case of Pot*, Penguin, Harmondsworth, 1971.

Schuckit, M., "The Alcoholic Woman: A Literature Review", *Psychiatry in Medicine*, 3 (1): 37–43, 1972.

Smith, D. E. and Sternfield, J., "The Hippie Communal Movement" and "Effects on Childbirth and Development", *Am. J. Orthopsychiatry*, 40: 527–30, 1970.

Stephens, R. and Cottrell, E., "A Follow-Up Study of 200 Narcotic Addicts Committed for Treatment Under the Narcotic Addict Rehabilitation Act (NARA)", *Br. J. Addict.*, 67: 45–53, 1972.

Taylor, S. D. and Osnos, R., "The Wives of Drug Addicts," *Amer. J. Psychiat.*, 123: 585–9, 1966.

Vaillant, G. E., "A Twelve-Years Follow-Up of New York Narcotic Addicts IV: Some Characteristics and Determinants of Abstinence", *Am. J. Psychiatry*, 123: 573–85, 1966.

Von Weingard, R. A., "Alcoholism in Industry (USA)", *Br. J. Addict.*, 67: 181–7, 1972.

Wiener, R. S. P., *Drugs and School Children*, Longman, London, 1970.

Wilkins, R. H., "The Detection of The Abnormal Drinker", a Paper read at the symposium *Alcoholism in General Practice*, University of Manchester, May, 1972.

Willis, J., "Delinquency and Drug Dependence in the U.K. and U.S.", *Brit. J. Addict.*, 66: 235–48, 1971.

Winwick, C., "Maturing Out of Opiate Addiction", *Bulletin on Narcotics*, 14: 1–7, 1962.

8 Medical management of alcoholism and drug dependence

HOSPITAL MANAGEMENT

All hospitals, not only psychiatric hospitals, are becoming increasingly involved in the communities they serve. In-patient care has had to be organised more efficiently as a result of spiralling costs, so that day-hospitals, out-patient departments and community clinics are beginning to flourish. General hospitals as a rule have never had a favourable attitude towards alcoholism or addiction, but nevertheless they do have an important role to play. Hospital admission may form one link in a chain of therapeutic activities, and may occur as a first-stage procedure, or follow after other services, particularly when the family practitioner has initiated treatment.

Alcoholism

EMERGENCY TREATMENT

Every busy hospital casualty department is involved on a daily basis with problems related to alcoholism and addiction, although more with the former than the latter.

The commonest presentation is drunkenness, but rarely as a straightforward matter, for most drunks who appear this way are middle-aged men, without families or jobs, or without homes to return to. Many are brought in by police, after an altercation or accident, when there is the suspicion of trauma, mental disorder, or a medical condition. Reassurance from the doctor that there are no medical complications may mean removal of the patient to a police cell for the night, a course that is unsatisfactory and potentially dangerous. It is hoped in the near future to develop detoxification units in all major British cities, where drunks, young and old, can sleep off the effects of their imbibing in comfort and safety. Handled with discretion, drunks rarely cause trouble, but a few become rowdy and violent, and have attacked nurses and doctors. Experienced casualty sisters rarely need medical aid, as a firm yet kindly stance quells all but the most rebellious. Skid-row alcoholics often make regular visits to casualty departments, seeking warmth, a hot meal, or a comfortable bed for the night. Many are either fed or evicted, according to the whim of the staff involved. Detoxification centres could help greatly in distinguishing those who need prolonged aid from those who simply require time and space to recover from a drinking bout.

A major medical responsibility is to identify whether drunkenness alone accounts for an alcoholic's symptoms. Aggressive patients may require sedation, but also special nursing observation if there is a possibility of head injury. Aggression or bizarre behaviour may be related to brain trauma, to the epilepsy of acute alcoholism or chronic brain disease, or to hypoglycaemia (low blood sugar) that occasionally occurs during a drinking bout. Drunkenness may be simulated by various metabolic disorders, notably the overdosage effects of insulin in diabetics, a potentially fatal condition. Epilepsy may be the first sign of impending delirium tremens, so all patients should be observed for withdrawal signs; delirium tremens constitutes a serious emergency, and is a threat to life in those cases not adequately treated. As noted earlier, in the initial stages there are the "shakes", developing usually on the second or third day, then a phase of increasing tremor, restlessness, and malaise progressing to the florid picture of gross agitation, confusion and hallucinations.

The treatment of delirium tremens should always be carried out in a hospital setting. Different clinicians adopt their own favourite methods of handling the withdrawal phase, but they are all designed to prevent possible complications. General health has to be maintained or restored by way of a full diet and vitamin supplements, and frequently dehydration has to be counteracted by intravenous infusion of fluids. Care has to be taken that concurrent chest and other infections are promptly treated by antibiotics.

The basis of the modern treatment of delirium tremens has been the use of large doses of the minor tranquillisers such as chlordiazepoxide (Librium) or diazepam (Valium). Not only does such medication calm the patient but it also serves to reduce the risk of withdrawal fits. An alternative and very effective way is to use chlormethiazole (Heminevrin), either in tablet form or by means of an intravenous drip. This substance is extremely sedating and because of this, patients have to be nursed in bed. If they are allowed to walk around, they run the risk of falling and adding a fracture to their problems.

It was taught for many years that patients in delirium should be nursed in a dimly lit room. However, in view of the well-known outcome of sensory deprivation experiments, it is now the practice to nurse patients in an environment with continuous stimulation of all forms but at a low enough level for them to tolerate. Repeated reassurance should be given, with information as to the individual's whereabouts and length of stay in hospital. Preferably a small number of nurses should treat a patient, so that there is constancy in his environment. In this way it may be possible for on-going relationships to form between the patient and staff treating him in the early part of his hospital stay.

The majority of patients recover uneventfully. A prolonged confusional state is not characteristic of delirium tremens, but it can occur in the Wernicke-Korsakoff syndrome (Victor, Adams and Collins, 1971). In this state hallucinations are rare, but fatigue, apathy, poor concentration and perceptual derangement accompany a profound confusional state, with disorientation and an impairment of recent memory. Massive doses of B vitamins may arrest the disorder and prevent neurological complications, but some residual damage is invariable.

Another group of patients who present as emergencies are those who have psychiatric symptoms, especially of depression. If they are threatening to take their own lives, or have made some modest attempt to do so, they can pose very real assessment difficulties. Sheer weight of numbers precludes admission for observation in all cases, and many are discharged precipitously, without adequate investigation or arrangements for follow-up in psychiatric clinics. A few research studies have stressed that the emergency treatment of alcoholics leaves much to be desired, and that intensive early intervention by a team of psychiatrists, nurses and social workers increases the chances of many alcoholics remaining in contact with community facilities, with good results (Chafetz *et al.,* 1962).

GENERAL HOSPITAL CARE

Alcoholics in general wards may have been admitted from emergency departments, but often are referred by family doctors, who notoriously under-diagnose alcoholism, so that they are investigated and treated for medical conditions the underlying cause of which is not suspected. Such conditions include acute gastritis, stomach ulcers, intestinal haemorrhage, cirrhosis of the liver, and degenerations of peripheral nerves. The training of specialist physicians in a narrow, organic approach means that, even when the cause of the symptoms is acknowledged, there is merely resort to moral exhortation, or to bland statements about the dangers of abuse. It is not uncommon to find a degree of intolerance, shared by nursing staff, directed towards alcoholics who occupy beds needed by far more "deserving" cases who have not inflicted disease processes on their persons by sheer lack of regard. Such attitudes are surprising when one considers that the incidence of the two major causes of mortality in hospitals—coronary thrombosis and lung cancer—would fall dramatically if there was greater self-control of smoking and over-eating! Rarely are such patients condemned for their behaviour, which by the same criteria is equally irresponsible.

Fortunately more and more physicians are becoming enlightened, and directing heavy drinkers to the attention of their social work and psychiatric colleagues. Many admit alcoholics to general wards for drying out, to give them much needed rest and a nourishing diet for a week or two, allowing them to reflect on their life situation in a sober state. A convalescent period can be critical in an alcoholic's life, enabling him to recognise his problem, and to acknowledge a need for help in coping with it. Staff who are around him each day can help enormously by their patience and understanding, but abruptness or hostility incubates feelings of anger, which can push the idea of further treatment away.

GENERAL PSYCHIATRIC UNITS

General psychiatric wards are the sole treatment situations for large numbers of alcoholics, because specialised facilities often do not exist, or provide inadequate numbers of places. Many alcoholics are withdrawn from alcohol under psychiatric rather than general medical supervision, and most units have evolved special regimes for withdrawal. The treatment of the withdrawal phase is essentially the treatment of delirium tremens, but on a less intensive scale. Patients may be confined to bed for three or four days before gradual mobilisation. Heavy sedation with tranquillisers is the rule, with gradual dosage reduction over a seven-day period.

Ideally, general psychiatric units should be expected to cope with patients whose alcoholism conceals an underlying mental illness. Schizophrenia rarely presents primarily as alcoholism, and can easily be diagnosed, but depression, which is extremely common, can present in many guises and may be very difficult to recognise. Endogenous forms of depression, if identified, respond well to antidepressant medication, or electro-convulsive therapy in the most severe cases. Many cases of reactive depression are better dealt with in general units, because emphasis in treatment is placed on the environmental causes of the mental state rather than the factors that lead up to the drinking. Organic states, such as the dementing conditions associated with drinking, obviously need neurological investigations in addition to psychiatric management. However, for many alcoholics general psychiatric wards offer no long-term solutions. When there is no focus on the harmful effects of the drinking itself, or the harmful effects are viewed in the wrong context, alcoholics can become disheartened if they view themselves as psychologically normal, while everyone around them is mad, deranged, mentally disturbed, and therefore quite different from themselves.

SPECIALISED UNITS

Since 1962 there has been a development of specialised centres, emanating from the pioneering work at Warlingham Park in the U.K. There are now several regional units, which although they may differ in many ways, tend to offer a therapeutic "package-deal" comprising group and individual psychotherapy with the addition of an assortment of chemical and behavioural adjuncts.

Almost all have careful selection criteria, and expect abstinence during the stay in hospital, which can range from one to three months, or occasionally longer. The focal point of most specialised units is group therapy, which displaces other treatments in importance. The assumption is that this is the most appropriate way to treat alcoholics, and therefore the basic selection requirement is a willingness to undertake this form of therapy. Very few units have a non-discriminatory admission policy, and there is a tendency to admit patients of higher social class, with good educational status and verbal fluency. Almost all the units attempt to provide a comprehensive facility, however, with both in-patient and out-patient programmes, although liaison with outside agencies may be far from ideal, and some units are geographically isolated from the populations they serve. Ritson and Hassall (1970) describe a typical programme in a specialised alcoholism unit.

THERAPEUTIC RELATIONSHIPS AND STAFF ROLES

Therapeutic communities emerged from a belief that the traditional hierarchical structure of the medical and nursing professions have impaired communications in hospitals rather than helped them. Important individual therapeutic roles have been replaced by the team approach, and this has meant that staff roles have changed and to some extent overlapped and become blurred. Therapeutic communities do not abandon structure and professional staff tend to retain control over major aspects of treatment, but decision-making becomes more democratic and there is usually a high degree of patient participation in this aspect. Most specialised alcoholism units have endorsed to some degree the therapeutic community principle.

Individual psychotherapy is rarely excluded, and may have an important place as an adjunct to the group process, or as the major form of therapy for those who have difficulty in contributing to a group situation. Traditionally, the therapist is a psychiatrist, but he may have a psychoanalytic, Rogerian, or purely eclectic viewpoint. It is virtually impossible to pinpoint exactly what the essential qualities of the therapist are, and which techniques are best, but it would appear that the greatest degree of change is effected by therapists who are warm, emphatic, and genuine, irrespective of their technical training. If this is so, psychotherapy need not be the prerogative of psychiatrists and, indeed, nurses in alcoholic units now play a major role in a less formal capacity. Almost all units devise educational programmes about alcoholism in all its aspects, and nurses are trained to exploit their unique situation in having close, constant contact with patients. An important function is to monitor behaviour change on the ward, and to observe the number and type of contributions made in group situations. To this end, in our wards, they are taught time-sampling techniques and objective, rigorous methods of observation. Obviously this should be done unobtrusively, as the very fact that behaviour is being monitored is well known to alter that very behaviour. We believe that all therapeutic situations are also experimental situations, but this does not mean that patients should be allowed to see themselves as guinea pigs.

Patients who enter hospitals that diverge from traditional policies may feel insecure and highly anxious, and those who have been previously exposed to more formal wards tend initially not to tolerate new situations too well. Nurses can reduce these anxieties, forming continuity links from the external to the internal community. Therapeutic communities are never microcosms of the outside world, no matter how many attempts are made to reduce the differences, and the fact that everyday, outside life is also highly structured and formalised should not be ignored. If it is, the internal community is likely to foster attitudes and behaviours that are highly maladaptive to external contingencies, and great care must be taken to guard against this. Hospitals can pose very stressful situations, with many of the patients being highly emotional and labile. Obviously there are often parallel stresses within the families of alcoholics, so that ability to cope with and control these situations, learned in hospital, should, one hopes, generalise to the family situation. Nurses should note the stimuli that evoke inappropriate behaviours, and feed these items back to the group and to the patient himself, so that he develops insight. We do not believe that insight alone is enough to modify such behaviours, so that nurses should be taught to mobilise group forces to shape and modify more adaptive behaviours, and extinguish those that act against rehabilitation. Nurses often become centrally involved in minor "skirmishes" and crises on the ward, and must develop the ability to resolve these if possible by utilising and directing the therapeutic resources of patients on other patients.

Changing roles create anxieties for staff too, and these have to be faced in confrontation with one's colleagues. The role of the psychiatrist in a group situation is largely to educate, to encourage communications amongst all staff members, and to elicit the maximum effort from each member. Morale can be tremendously high, but as communities are ever-changing, day-to-day difficulties must be promptly dealt with. Above all, there must be an underlying acceptance of all members of the group, no matter what the momentary shifts of feelings are, for without this acceptance great hostility, shame and guilt can be engendered. Individuals find that groups can cause intolerable stresses, and they will turn to nurses and doctors in face-to-face situations to solve these, often revealing highly-charged and confidential matters. It should always be stressed that confidentiality must be interpreted in a new way, as loyalty is to the group, rather than to the individual. Patients will resent leaks of information if this is not made clear, and this will cause lack of co-operation or inhibition in both group and individual psychotherapy.

Patients who give vent to their emotions in a group may regret their outbursts, and turn to the psychiatrist rather than to the group, because of guilt about their actions or the content of their outburst. If it is the psychiatrist's role to ameliorate these guilt feelings with regard to the individual's situation in the therapeutic group, it is the social worker's role to perceive the relevance of the group interactions with regard to the patient's external milieu and particularly to his family. Reactions of the group which approximate to reactions of the family should be explored in great detail with the individual and his family, both separately and together. By the time an alcoholic reaches hospital, his family life, if it still exists, is often grossly disrupted, and relationships between the patient and spouse have reached a low ebb. Wives have to change their conventional family role, and often become the dominating, decision-making member, through no wish of their own. Many are highly competent, fulfilling both parental functions, so that their children do not suffer in any material way. When the alcoholic husband enters a treatment situation, the delicate family balance is altered, with ensuing anxieties and uncertainties for the wife. She often feels left out of the treatment situation, may be jealous of the attention paid to her husband and resentful of the label "sick" placed on him by his hospitalisation, and may even feel that she is held to blame for her husband's situation. Wives need help to understand the alcoholism process and the nature of treatment, so as to overcome rivalry feelings and to understand the nature of their relationships with their husbands and the possible influence they might have on the drinking pattern. They often need initial encouragement to participate, but can then become very enthusiastic, and studies have shown that the favourable outcome of an alcoholic's treatment can be related to his wife's attendance at group meetings specially arranged for spouses. Vital information can arise in such groups, and can be channelled through unit meetings.

Involvement of the family is clearly imperative, and has given rise to "family therapy" where treatment is directed not towards an individual, but to the entire family of which he is a member. Individual dysfunctions are viewed as arising from abnormal processes in the whole family, so that no individual malaise need necessarily be singled out. Specific interactional difficulties are only dealt with in the family context and with the family present, the therapist serving to balance the session and heal any past or present schisms. Family therapy in many ways therefore diverges from the therapeutic community concept, and indeed many alcoholic units have evolved their own individual formulae by a natural process. Even groups that begin in a totally unstructured way develop a natural order, although this need not be a therapeutic one, and in fact a central problem of groups is the avoidance of focusing on irrelevant issues. Commonly encountered groups are those with a psychoanalytic orientation, or whose theoretical formulation is in group analysis. Groups with shifting leaders are exemplified by the

Alcoholics Anonymous model, where accentuation is not on unconscious dynamic processes, but purely on the adverse social consequences of the drinking itself. Here, abstinence is held to be the only worthwhile goal, and detailed accounts are given by members of their success or failure in achieving that goal. Success receives peer-group adulation, and the abstinent alcoholic becomes a model for the group. Failure to abstain is not censured, but group pressures incline to alter the individual's situation and motivate him to abstinence. Most units have close contact with A.A. and groups are either run in the hospital or visits are made to local A.A. meetings from the hospital. Some groups within hospital, whilst independent of A.A., use direct extensions of its principles. Dissension often arises when different orientations clash, and it is therefore essential for successful units that there is a general acceptance of the team design, and a belief in the major goals of the treatment programme.

OUT-PATIENT DEPARTMENTS

Broadly speaking, out-patient departments have three kinds of functions: assessment, treatment and observation, and follow-up, which includes a preventive aspect.

Referral can be from general practitioners, from social agencies, or from other medical specialists. Alcoholics offered immediate help tend to stay in treatment rather than those offered help sometime in the future, so this must be an important factor in planning a treatment programme. Assessment is largely made by psychiatrists, but even in an out-patient setting the therapeutic team must be fully involved and indeed the best clinics provide a comprehensive service very similar to that of an in-patient service. Assessment involves discovering the reasons for attendance, the patient's motivation for treatment, a careful history of his mental and physical state, his socio-economic status, and his attitudes toward, and likely response to, therapy.

After initial evaluation, decisions have to be made regarding the best form of therapy. In-patient management would normally be indicated for those with severe physical dependence or physical complications, with profound psychiatric illness, or for those who might benefit from intensive daily psychotherapy. In-patient therapy would not normally be appropriate for those likely to be uncooperative, those unwilling to enter hospital, people in regular employment with no impairment at work, and for chronic alcoholics who have not benefited from numerous previous admissions.

A study in London (Edwards and Guthrie, 1967) compared in-patient and out-patient management, and found the response to each very similar. This does not mean that they are equally effective for all patients, or that in-patient treatment is not really necessary. The study did not show who was likely to benefit from one or the other treatment, and whether the groups who responded were similar in their socio-cultural or psychological characteristics.

Indeed, it is likely that both approaches are valid in given circumstances, but there are distinct advantages of management in the community. If alcoholics withdraw from alcohol, slowly, outside hospital, they find it easier to adjust to sobriety, and their wives can be more involved in treatment, so that the latter feel their roles are not devalued, and they can take some of the credit for success. It can be easier to mobilise support, and close liaison with Alcoholics Anonymous, advisory councils and the family, which are very important, are more easily available.

Specialised aspects of treatment such as aversion therapy and group therapy are often available on an out-patient basis, as well as personal psychotherapy and drug treatment. After treatment, careful follow-up is essential to provide further help as indicated, and to allow emergency intervention in crisis situations. Alcoholics often react poorly to stress and prompt help often prevents relapse, or other unfortunate escape responses. There are many authorities who believe that crises offer a major opening for therapeutic interventions and that total support should be organised to become effective in these situations.

ANTABUSE

"Antabuse" (disulfiram) has come to be widely used in preventing relapses in abstinent alcoholics. How it works is not known with certainty, but a severe bodily reaction occurs if a person consumes alcohol when taking a daily, oral dose of Antabuse. When the drug was first introduced in 1948, large doses were given that caused severe side-effects, including at times a psychosis, but it is absolutely safe in the currently-used small doses (0·25–0·5 g daily). The alcohol-Antabuse reaction consists of facial flushing, headache, a choking sensation, weakness, palpitations, anxiety, nausea, and faintness due to a lowering of the blood pressure. Extreme hypotension has led to shock and death in a few cases, but only with the larger doses of drug. There have been several reports, covering many thousands of patients treated (e.g. Hoff, 1955) with apparent success and few problems. Antabuse slows down the breakdown of alcohol by oxidation, leading to the accumulation of acetaldehyde in the tissues. It was considered that this must cause the symptoms, but acetaldehyde injected into volunteer subjects does not alone cause a similar state.

Antabuse therapy, to be effective, requires the fullest co-operation from patients. The provision of accurate information about the drug's action is a crucial matter, but it is not necessary to frighten the patient. It should be explained that commitment to a daily dosage regime will help him to withstand sudden, otherwise overpowering, impulses to drink. Side-effects of depression, headaches and fatigue, fortunately uncommon, may reduce the motivation to take regular medication, but patients should be left to take it themselves unless they feel that external pressure, say from spouse or social worker, is helpful. Recently, implants of disulfiram have been enthusiastically introduced; they are implanted in the abdominal wall and were thought to give up to six months protection. However, there is recent evidence (Malcolm, 1973) that the drug disappears from the tissues very quickly, perhaps in a matter of days. If blood levels drop to insignificant levels, success in treatment must therefore depend on the effectiveness of the warnings given before treatment commences, or, in other words, there must be some degree of placebo effect.

It was common practice to give patients test doses of alcohol to demonstrate the effects of Antabuse under controlled conditions, but in many centres this practice has been discontinued. Some patients learn to tolerate the symptoms and continue drinking despite the drug, but when it proves helpful it is normally given for a long period, rarely less than three months and often more than twelve months, until it is felt that the patient has gained sufficient self-control.

Citrated calcium carbide (Abstem) has similar effects to disulfiram, but is less widely used. Metronidazole (Flagyl), a drug used in the treatment of a form of venereal disease in women, has been used with the same rationale as disulfiram, but is now thought to decrease alcohol consumption by making alcoholic drinks less palatable.

AVERSION THERAPY

Aversion therapy can never be a total treatment for alcoholism. It could not be expected to be effective where there is a strong physical dependency and craving for alcohol, or where anxiety predominates in the clinical picture and alcohol gives relief from the anxiety. Before aversion therapy commences there is normally withdrawal from the drug, and prior or concomitant reduction of an anxiety factor if present, often by relaxation training and reciprocal inhibition of anxiety responses (systematic desensitisation).

Aversion therapy is usually directed, not at the primary reinforcer (alcohol), but at some of the innumerable secondary reinforcers that serve to maintain the habit. These can include stimuli related to the beverage itself (e.g. a wine glass or the sight of a drink), or more distant, but nevertheless important stimuli, such as the social reinforcement of one's drinking companions or the setting of a hotel bar. The hypothesis is that, if a noxious response (nausea or vomiting) is induced by, let's say, the sight, smell, or taste of a drink, the incentive properties of the alcohol itself (a delayed positive reinforcer) would be outweighed by negative reinforcement of the preceding activities. Most aversion therapies are based on, or interpreted as, classical conditioning paradigms. The treatment situation is reminiscent of Pavlov's early experiments, where an unconditioned stimulus is repeatedly paired with a conditioned stimulus, until a conditioned response is elicited independently of the unconditioned stimulus by the conditioned stimulus.

A typical treatment would be to inject apomorphine (the unconditioned stimulus) to evoke nausea and vomiting (the unconditioned response) and to associate this with the taste, smell or thought of an alcoholic beverage (Voegtlin and Lemere, 1942). Treatment sessions might be given on alternate days for ten to fourteen days, whilst the patient is carefully supervised in hospital, followed by booster treatments whenever necessary, over a long follow-up period. Another emetic that has been used is emetine hydrochloride, which is longer-acting than apomorphine and may therefore be more effective (Lemere and Voegtlin, 1950).

In classical conditioning, the temporal sequence of events is of vital importance and, optimally, the conditioned stimulus should precede the unconditioned stimulus. In many aversion treatments, the conditioned stimuli have been presented after the unconditioned response (nausea or vomiting), a procedure not likely to produce a strong conditioning effect. It is not clear whether the nausea or the vomiting is the most appropriate response, but several dubious experimental methods have been shown to be effective, and some conditioning occurs, irrespective of the correctness of the approach.

Chemical aversion is no longer quite so fashionable a procedure since it is inelegant and replete with potential hazards, and it is so difficult to control the relevant events. Electrical aversion therapy is safer, quantifiable, and easier to administer in a controlled way. A typical procedure would be to deliver high voltage, low current shocks to a patient's arm or leg whilst alcohol is being sipped.

In "covert sensitisation" the aversive event is an internal one, and is even more difficult to control than emetics. After initial training in relaxation, the patient is asked to imagine specified drinking activities, and to report when the image is clear. He is then asked to associate this image with a fantasy which has a strong negative connotation, such as vomit or faeces. Electrical aversion does not yet have an established place in the treatment of alcoholism, and is never likely to prove very popular, and high drop-out rates may well reduce it to a subordinate role in management. Covert sensitisation may prove to be a more acceptable technique.

Drug Dependence

EMERGENCY REFERRALS

Emergency presentations of drug withdrawal, adverse reactions, and overdosage are becoming increasingly common in hospitals.

"Withdrawal" is as often a complaint or a ruse to obtain drugs as it is a genuinely observed phenomenon. If there is no objective evidence of abstinence such a presentation should be firmly dealt with, lest an unwise prescription should lead to many subsequent and similar complaints. Genuine barbiturate withdrawal can seriously endanger life, so that hospital admission is advisable. Opiate withdrawal in uncomplicated cases needs only small doses of methadone as a palliative measure, followed by urgent referral to a specialised treatment centre where this exists. It is illegal for other than licensed prescribers to order heroin for patients, even if they are registered as addicts, unless there are purely medical reasons for doing so.

Typical of adverse reactions to drugs is a teenager being brought into a hospital casualty department suffering from a hallucinogenic crisis. Seccombe (1971) believes that youth workers with some medical knowledge are best suited to treating young people on "bad trips". Mild adverse reactions present with anxiety or fear as the major symptom, with possibly confusion, doubt and suspicion adding to the picture. Fear reactions can be intensified in hospital because of the noise and bustle. A few quiet words of reassurance and explanation can calm all but the most disturbed patients. Adverse reactions are most likely to occur in inexperienced drug-takers, or where emotional problems were present prior to the drug-taking. An acknowledgment by the drug-taker that the therapist has the capacity for participating in his feelings and situation can rapidly alleviate anxiety. Treatment should be in a quiet room with diffuse, soft lighting, a relaxed informal atmosphere, with the therapist using non-verbal as well as verbal techniques to gain rapport. Conversation should be directed by the patient, but should not extend beyond a superficial level in an emergency situation. There is often impairment of attention span, memory and thought integration that precludes in-depth intervention at that stage. Cannabis adverse reactions can be similar to LSD reactions, but are usually less intense and self-limiting, requiring the minimum of intervention unless there is a related and treatable psychiatric state.

Medical intervention is indicated where there is multiple drug-consumption and/or excessive alcohol intake causing complications, where there is affective (mood) change, particularly of suicidal intent, where behaviours become unstable and impulsive, or where there is loss of contact with reality. In a full-blown psychosis there is a danger to health, but admission for observation is rarely needed. Pharmacotherapy has a limited place, and a small dose of a minor tranquilliser can rapidly terminate a crisis. Solursh and Clements (1968) advocate the use of diazepam and other benzodiazepine drugs. They accentuate the dangers of using major tranquillisers (normally used for schizophrenia and organic psychoses) in hallucinogenic drug crises, and report the risk of cardiovascular shock or even death with phenothiazine drugs having an atropine-like action. Atropine is a drug that releases nervous control on heart-rate and contraction, and most psychotropic drugs share many of its properties. Street drugs may contain atropine or similar compounds and the addition of a phenothiazine drug with atropine-like side-effects can turn an hallucinogenic crisis into a major, medical, life-threatening emergency.

OVERDOSAGE

Self-poisoning is so commonplace now that up to one in six admissions to general medical beds is for "attempted suicide". In spite of the enormous number of admissions, few hospitals make special provisions for those who deliberately or accidentally have taken an excess of drugs. The medical profession is very sensitive to the physical needs of patients, but not so adept at providing for their emotional needs. It is generally accepted that, whenever possible, all suspected overdoses should be admitted to hospital for a minimum of twenty-four hours. This is obviously necessary for those who are unconscious or semi-conscious, but difficulties arise with patients whose conscious level is unaffected or minimally affected, and who do not wish to stay for treatment. Occasionally, patients who refuse treatment can be detailed under the Mental Health Act 1959, if they are aggressive or uncontrollable and if their mental state poses a threat to their own or others' safety and health. It should be remembered that quite a few apparent overdoses are found actually to be suffering from other states, such as head injuries or intra-cranial haemorrhages.

Accidental overdoses are most likely in beginners, who may take a handful of pills, often not knowing exactly what they are taking. Drug sub-cultures build up a fund of knowledge about drug effects and dosages, but sometimes even experienced drug-takers make mistakes. Miscalculations can occur when tolerance to a drug has been reduced, for example after an abstinence period, when a mixture of drugs are taken and there is a multiple reaction, or even when alternative drugs have been substituted for the supposed ones.

A high proportion of those who attempt suicide are young people, and a proportion of these have experimented with drugs. Immediately after taking the tablets many will inform their parents, friends, or perhaps a social worker about their action. It is helpful in treatment to know what tablets have been taken (if possible the container and remaining tablets, if any, should be taken to hospital), when they were taken and how many there were, whether they induced vomiting, and whether any changes have occurred in the patient's condition. Common medications can be readily identified from colour charts and by markings, and poison centres have been established in various areas to give advice on the most appropriate action to be taken with uncommon substances. Improved specialist care of massive overdoses, with intravenous infusions, gastric lavage, artificial or assisted ventilation, and methods of extracting poisons such as forced, peritoneal, or artificial renal dialysis has resulted in an ever-decreasing mortality rate, despite the huge rise in numbers of overdose cases.

Only a few overdose patients need intensive rescuscitation, and the majority recover uneventfully. Only a small number of people will see a need for, or accept, help after recovery from the medical complications, but it is vital to offer it, and to offer it in the right way. For some it is their first admission to hospital, their first contact with a caring system. Suicidal attempts are largely gestures of despair, coming from youngsters temporarily overcome by feelings of hopelessness and frustration, making pathetic attempts to bring their distress to notice. Such a statement is not to deny that overdoses can also be construed as manipulating devices to achieve certain aims, to blackmail or to bring pressure to bear, so that compassion always has to be qualified by objectivity.

GENERAL HOSPITALS

General hospitals have a more limited role in addiction than in the treatment of alcoholism. The infective complications of drug-taking can usually be dealt with by consultation without admission, and cases of mild jaundice can be looked after at home, but severer cases, and especially patients with spreading infections, thrombophlebitis, lung infections and septicaemia will require intensive care. Withdrawal therapy is rarely indicated for young opiate addicts in general hospitals, as they can be so disruptive in that setting, although older barbiturate addicts, especially if they also have alcohol problems, may safely be treated in general wards.

PSYCHIATRIC ASSESSMENT

Since 1968, special treatment centres have been established in the U.K. in all areas for dealing with drug abusers. The major need was to deal with the explosion of heroin users which occurred at that time, but medical teams now have increasing experience in all fields of drug abuse.

It is important to appreciate that drug abusers present to clinics for numerous reasons, many of them having little to do with the drugs they are taking. Often patients present under pressure, and attention should be focused on the pressure points. The following anecdote illustrates the need for careful assessment of a presenting "drug" problem:

> A headmaster telephoned, asking if appointments could be made to see three boys, who had been caught smoking "pot" in the toilets. On questioning it was evident that all the boys were eminently stable, with good school records, and there was no evidence of previous drug consumption. All were from good homes. Drug-taking *per se* is no indication for intervention, unless it is accompanied by features of personal or social disorganisation or impaired health and a discussion about the effects of drugs allayed the anxieties of the headmaster, who dealt with the matter internally as a disciplinary issue. A fruitful result was a small series of educational seminars with staff and parents about aspects of soft drug-taking in schools.

Parents often become anxious when they discover their children have been taking drugs—again, in the absence of pathological effects, treatment is by reassurance and explanation to the parents. It follows naturally that drug centres must have an educational role, and this can be as important as the therapeutic role. Parents envisage their children drifting into a drug-haunted underworld, becoming addicted to "hard" drugs, and acquiring all the features of the "junkie" stereotype. Often, though, parents are concerned for good reason, because their son or daughter has altered in ways that cannot be viewed as the temporary turmoils of adolescence. As drug abuse is so prevalent amongst teenagers nowadays, many cases should be dealt with by general practising psychiatrists and physicians rather than by experts in addiction, unless drugs dominate the presentation and are of much more than coincidental significance. History-taking should attempt to relate drug-taking with any physical illness and psychiatric symptoms, with socially maladaptive behaviour and deteriorating socio-economic functioning. Key matters are the duration of drug-taking, the types of drugs taken, the mode of administration and recent changes in the pattern and amount suggesting physical dependence. It is important to assess the pre-drug-taking personality, work record, sexual and interpersonal relationships, and to evaluate the changes that are attributable to the drugs. Although there is wide individual variation, milestones of deterioration stand out very much like the milestones of an alcoholic's progress. Not only do they have therapeutic, but also prognostic importance and their significance should be increasingly appreciated.

DIAGNOSIS

As drug-abusers' histories are highly unreliable, it is imperative to obtain confirmation of the history from a reliable source, such as the spouse, parents or employers, if the patient is agreeable that they should be approached. Physical dependence should be confirmed systematically. Physical examination may show evidence of neglect, of diet deficiences (rare in early cases), or of intravenous injections. There are no invariable diagnostic signs, but features of general intoxication (for example, slurred speech or staggering gait) may be present and jaundice, enlarged glands, and multiple injection scars, new and old, will suggest heroin or other opiate dependence. Excitability and psychotic features possibly indicate amphetamine, cannabis or LSD, and generalised depression of function, either barbiturates or opium alkaloids. Dilated pupils can occur with stimulants, and pinpoint pupils with opiates, but these signs are unreliable. Urine or blood tests can reveal the presence of opiates, barbiturates and amphetamines, but methods for identifying LSD and cannabis are not generally available.

It can be exceedingly difficult to distinguish true opiate addicts from casual users, who can become adept at simulating withdrawal signs when they want a "fix", and have been known to present to clinics with hundreds of injection marks, which can fortunately be recognised by all but the most naïve as being of recent origin rather than the result of injecting over a long period of time. One answer is to admit the person into hospital to observe carefully for the withdrawal syndrome, check the cardiovascular system (blood pressure and pulse changes) and watch for temperature alterations, but this is a cumbersome solution. Urine tests using new techniques of thin-layer chromatography are becoming widely used, and such facilities are essential in any treatment centre. An injection of the drug nalorphine will precipitate an abstinence syndrome in an addict, but interpretation can be hazardous because the side-effects of nalorphine may be severe, and can be mistaken for evidence of opiate withdrawal. A small amount of nalorphine (3 mg) given subcutaneously will cause a dilation of the pupil of more than 1·25 mm, measured by a pupilometer, in 85 per cent of heroin addicts. This is a valuable method of diagnosis, and a fairly reliable way of checking for relapse after treatment. Urine tests should always be interpreted cautiously, because they merely show consumption over the previous twenty-four hours, and therefore single positive or negative tests are of limited value.

HEROIN

The dilemma of treatment

When addicts present at a clinic, almost without exception they are seeking drugs rather than help or treatment. They rarely stay in a therapeutic situation unless they are prescribed drugs, and usually only if they are prescribed heroin. The approach to treating heroin addiction in the U.K. has evolved in an entirely different way to that in the U.S.A. In the U.S.A., until recently, addiction has been viewed as criminal behaviour, punishable by compulsory detention in State institutions. In the U.K., the addict is labelled as "sick", and clearly comes under the medical "umbrella". The essentials of the British approach are that heroin addicts should be treated in specialised units, by experts who can prescribe heroin and maintain addicts on drugs until such time as they request withdrawal. Persuasion rather than force are the keynotes, the onus being on the addict to develop motivation for cure. Free prescribing is intended also to prevent the need for a "black market" in drug-trading, so that the criminal world will not profit by, nor influence, the course of the addict's illness. The system incorporates aspects of control and prevention in addition to treatment. It is based on apparently rational elementary premises, but these cause an immense number of practical problems that raise doubts as to the fundamental validity of the approach. Above all, it is virtually impossible to assess the amount of drug that an addict needs to prevent him from turning to a black market supply, and yet will not give him a surplus to pass on to uncommitted acquaintances. The large surge in British heroin addicts in the 1960s was due, as already mentioned, to the irresponsible prescribing of several London doctors, who gave out opiates to patients in amounts far in excess of their requirements. Whilst no-one should question the motives of the licensed prescribers, there is little evidence that they can accurately quantify an addict's needs, and they are therefore likely to overprescribe. A surplus tends to create further addicts and the cycle repeats itself. Addicts always ask for more than they need, and to halve the dose they ask for is simply an invitation to them to double the requested amount. Such a basic weakness in the treatment system hardly suggests that it is a viable approach in present-day circumstances.

Heroin maintenance

If it is established that a patient is addicted to an opiate and not just taking drugs sporadically, a decision has to be made as to the suitability of a treatment programme. If he refuses withdrawal, which almost invariably he will, the choice generally lies between prescribing heroin or methadone, the amount being gauged by the appearance of the addict, the number of injection marks, and the credibility of his history, all compounded by the gullibility (if present) of the doctor. The doctor of course, can always refuse to prescribe drugs if he so wishes. It has been suggested that a decision to prescribe should never be made unless there are at least three positive consecutive urine tests. A heroin maintenance programme can only work if the prescribing doctor is firm and resists the manipulation of the patient to increase the dose, and takes advantage of every possible opportunity to cut down the drugs. There are serious drawbacks with heroin maintenance. The drug has a profound euphoriant action and depresses motivation, so that prescribing it does not lead to a better conventional adjustment. Also, the withdrawal effects come on after a short time and are severe, so that there is a rapid transition from a "high" state where there is generalised lethargy to a "low" state, where the only motivation is to obtain more heroin. Only a very few patients, perhaps those with the least disturbed personalities, can maintain equilibrium and adjustment whilst on heroin. The higher the dose, the more likely the disorganisation—the commonest dosage range for the British addict is 80–120 mg of heroin per day, about twice that of his American counterpart. And, as has already been noted, in the U.S.A. the heroin contains impurities such as lactose and caffeine, together with other substances that increase the risk of taking it. A heroin maintenance programme requires a consistent approach by all prescribers, otherwise a drift will occur from clinics, where doctors prescribe conservatively, to clinics where doctors are more liberal. Unfortunately, prescribing habits are as likely to be determined by the personality characteristics of the doctors as the psychological and physical needs of the patients.

Drug withdrawal

Griffith Edwards (1969) enumerated six central hypotheses underlying the British approach to treating heroin addicts. The three relating to treatment are:

1. That addicts will need to be prescribed drugs for variable periods of time, some permanently.
2. That motivation to withdraw will come through contact with clinic staff; and
3. That successful treatment ultimately depends on the patient's own motivation, so that there is no place for compulsory treatment.

It is our view that not enough attention is paid to preparing an addict for withdrawal. So often his motivation evaporates at the first withdrawal symptom, and his stay in hospital is fleeting. Out-patient withdrawal is not a practical proposition, but neither is in-patient withdrawal, if it is the result of a momentary impulse on the part of the addict, or calculated coercion or pressure on the part of the therapists. Withdrawal is wrongly viewed as the first essential act of treatment, whereas it ought to occur at an optimal time in a patient's planned therapeutic progress. Mutual trust and a genuine and deep-rooted conviction of the need for withdrawal are essential ingredients for success, together with an anticipation that some discomfort is inevitable for the addict.

"Cold turkey" withdrawal is a harrowing experience for an established addict, and is sometimes self-imposed, although it need never happen in hospital. Several methods are used to reduce the suffering of the withdrawal process, the best perhaps being the rigorously standardised method of Dole (1972). Immediately, 20 mg of methadone are given, followed by a twice-daily, reducing dosage over a seven day period (in mg):

Day 1	*Day 2*	*Day 3*	*Day 4*	*Day 5*	*Day 6*	*Day 7*	*Day 8*
20, 20	20, 10	10, 10	10, 10	10, 0	10, 0	10, 0	0

The methadone is given orally in liquid form in almost all cases, the method having been perfected in the treatment of over 22,000 addicts admitted to New York City jails. A few addicts on very high dosages of heroin may need higher dosages of methadone, whereas adolescent addicts are not normally given more than 20 mg on any day of withdrawal. There are few complications and side-effects are uncommon, apart from constipation. Decreasing heroin dosage is more hazardous, because it is a much shorter-acting drug. Other drugs, including steroids, hypnotics and tranquillisers have also been used in the withdrawal phase, but anxiolytic drugs and night sedatives ought to be used with caution in addiction-prone people. It is reasonable to use them to settle the common residual symptoms after the acute withdrawal stage, but not to prolong their use.

Withdrawal from morphine or other opiates can be effected in much the same way but without the need for methadone. Withdrawal from barbiturates is also similar, with decremental reduction over a period of not less than two weeks. Some physicians use long-acting barbiturates such as phenobarbitone during withdrawal but the kind of preparation is really immaterial. A standard procedure is to give amylobarbitone sodium to the point of mild intoxication (say 200–400 mg six-hourly in most cases), and to reduce the amount given by no more than 100 mg daily. Withdrawal fits should not occur with such a regime, and a delirium is unlikely. If fits occur, they can be controlled by increasing the barbiturate slightly. A toxic delirium can also be controlled in this way, or by the use of major tranquillisers such as chlorpromazine, although this and similar drugs should be used cautiously as they can sometimes increase the likelihood of fits occuring. Insomnia and irritability can persist after withdrawal, and can be lessened by the controlled use of minor tranquillisers such as diazepam. Withdrawal from stimulants (cocaine, amphetamine, etc.) can be abrupt as there are no serious physical withdrawal features. However, increased somnolence and depression are well known to follow cessation, and if they occur may be improved a little by antidepressant drugs such as imipramine.

Methadone maintenance

There have been many comparisons of the American and English approaches to treating narcotic addiction, the most comprehensive being that of Schur (1968). Heroin maintenance has never been considered a realistic model in the U.S.A., because of the enormity of the problem. It is impossible to maintain addicts on stable dosages, over-prescribing leads to a spread of drug abuse, and under-prescribing leads to increased crime. New addicts are created faster than established ones are cured, and thrice-daily attendances at clinics for heroin create an intolerable burden on clinic staff.

It was these considerations, and the view that heroin addiction is a metabolic disease, that led Dole and Nyswander (1966, 1967) to introduce methadone treatment on a large scale in the U.S.A. The advantages of methadone over heroin were thought to be as follows:

1. It has a longer action, and therefore attendances at clinic need be less frequent, no more than once per day.
2. Withdrawal symptoms are delayed and less serious.
3. It does not have a strongly euphoriant action, and leads to a more stable mental state.

4. It is medically safer, with fewer side-effects.
5. There is less likelihood of abuse outside the clinic.

Methadone has been used in various ways. It is strongly favoured as the method of choice for withdrawal from heroin, but is also acceptable to addicts as a transitional maintenance vehicle prior to withdrawal. In this way it may be used for several weeks up to several months, or low-dosage methadone maintenance may become a more permanent situation. The commonest use, however, is in high-dosage "blockade", normally with a dosage from 80–120 mg per day. In this dosage it has been proved to neutralise the euphoriant action of heroin injected intravenously, therefore eliminating the need for extra drug-taking.

Guidelines for the usage of methadone maintenance have been published by the American Psychiatric Association (1971). In order to qualify, heroin addicts should normally be over the age of twenty, should give evidence of at least two years of addiction and failure of the conventional treatments such as detoxification, incarceration, psychotherapy, etc. The starting dose of methadone is 10–20 mg, dissolved in fruit juice (rarely 30–40 mg may be necessary), taken in the presence of clinic staff. The effects are carefully noted, and this low dosage is maintained daily for three days. Thereafter a 10 mg increase in dosage occurs each week until the optimum level is reached. Daily consumption in the clinic is mandatory for the first three months, following which weekly prescriptions may be allowed. There should be regular urine checks for the presence of heroin, methadone and other drugs. The optimum dose of methadone is assessed by "challenging" with intravenous heroin, and by careful observation of the effects.

Methadone maintenance means the replacement of one form of addiction by another. It runs counter to the stereotyped attitudes of those who hold abstinence as the only worthwhile goal. It has been harshly criticised as a form of artificial "enslavement", damaging the prospects of future social progress. Any form of drug maintenance can turn a doctor into a detective, as Szasz (1972) points out, blunting the ethical sensibilities of his profession. Even urine testing for scientific purposes is denounced by Szasz, as a stage in transforming the medical relationship with a patient from concern and compassion into deception and coercion, in the interest of controlling his will. But proponents claim that the end result of a stabilised addict with a good work and social adjustment is amply justified, and gives the addict the chance to opt out of active participation in a dangerous and potentially violent criminal system that is no less a form of enslavement.

Unfortunately, methadone has not proved to be as safe as it was originally considered. To many addicts methadone is not euphoria-blocking but euphorigenic. Because of this, much legally prescribed methadone has been diverted into illegal channels on the street, some of the numerous and even ingenious methods of black-market and acquisition having been described by Weppner and Stephens (1973). Most commonly, methadone was diverted from clinics that dispensed multiple dosages, whilst other techniques of obtaining tablets have been to conceal them in the hand whilst pretending to swallow them, to conceal them under the tongue, to steal them from the clinics, or to feign illness to obtain extra prescriptions. Some physicians are known who actually provide methadone to "pushers"; methadone has been stolen from pharmacies or obtained by forging prescriptions, by addicts registering with several clinics, and even by illegal manufacture in laboratories.

The side-effects of methadone maintenance have been described by Dobbs (1972). These include the following:

1. Slight overdosage leading to lethargy ("nodding") or euphoria.
2. Severe constipation.
3. Excessive sweating.
4. Sexual dysfunction, with menstrual irregularities in females.
5. Insomnia and nightmares.
6. Difficulties in urinating.
7. Exacerbation of peptic ulcers.
8. Skin rashes.
9. Overdosage and death, which has been reported in many cases.

There is also the possibility of harmful genetic effects and damage to the unborn child of a female addict. It has now become apparent that the babies of methadone-addict mothers are more likely to suffer from withdrawal syndromes, and need more intense care at birth than the babies of heroin-addict mothers.

One justification for methadone programmes is an economic one. Induction into high-dosage maintenance does not require costly in-patient care. It can be effected quite safely from an out-patient clinic, at much lower cost. A critical question to answer is, whether simply giving out methadone is enough or whether there is a need for costly counselling services. An attempt to answer this was made by Ramer, Zaslove and Langan (1971). They originally contemplated a comparison between addicts given methadone alone, and addicts given access to group or individual therapy, vocational guidance, crisis intervention and the like in their San Francisco centre for special problems. Their plans quickly broke down as those given methadone demanded all kinds of ancillary help, and one-third needed extensive aid. Of the whole group, at some stage during their attendance, 79 per cent needed crisis intervention, 48 per cent vocational guidance, 34 per cent medical treatment, 23 per cent individual, and 30 per cent group, therapy. This raises the matter of the demands addicts make on clinic staffs, and what particular issues are posed in psychotherapeutic interventions with addicts.

PSYCHOTHERAPY

In psycho-analytic terms, an addict has insufficient ego strength and is overwhelmingly threatened by ego disintegration. He regresses to a primitive, undifferentiated state where he can only attempt to satisfy his unfulfilled oral needs: the needs to eat, to be eaten, and to exist in a semi-stuporous state. He has an unresolved Oedipal complex in which he feels neglected, denied of affection, abandoned, and where there is a symbolic equation of drugs with milk from his mother's breast, giving temporary respite from an insatiable desire for food, warmth and maternal love. Like a newborn child he cannot tolerate delayed gratification, nor can he tolerate tension, anxiety or depression. His interpersonal relations are at a primitive level and he has not learned to control desire, or experience love as a sharing process. Opiates temporarily restore the integrity of the ego but for an ever-shortening period of time, so that the need for the drug drives the addict inexorably towards his next injection.

It is not necessary to endorse this psycho-analytic explanation to accept that addicts often have extraordinarily disordered relationships with their mothers prior to the onset of drug-taking. Little and Pearson (1966) see the major factor in addiction-proneness as a sado-masochistic relationship with one's mother, and a perversion of the interdependence phenomenon. Not only do drugs reduce tension, but taking them is an expression of hostility towards those who deny his needs. The hostility is readily tolerated by this particular female, whether it be the mother or a symbolic substitute. She may even promote addiction, as a manifestation of her own "masochistic surrender", using the mechanism of denial to opt out of guilt feelings. This is therefore the use of the "addictor" concept similar to that found in the literature on the wives of alcoholics.

The aim of analytic psychotherapy is to give insight into these subconscious processes. Not surprisingly, addicts have great difficulty in accepting such explanations, and psycho-analysis is only a practical proposition in a minority of addicted persons. They rarely recognise the insidious influence of the "addictor", preferring to see that person as someone deeply involved in helping them. They can perceive the process of injecting as punishment, or as a prolonged form of self-destructive, suicidal behaviour, but rarely equate the intravenous injection as sexual intromission leading to an orgasm! To our mind, psycho-analytic formulations in this field are ill-founded and mystical, but do contain vital references to the needs of addicts which any therapist would ignore to his detriment.

It is only too easy to view addicts in over simple terms as manipulating, malevolent individuals wholly guided by self-interest and uncontrollable hedonistic drives. Treatment staff finding themselves the recipients of trickery and deception can respond by erecting a wall of counter-deception and intolerance that creates an insurmountable barrier. The addict's existence may appear a chaotic one, but it is one to which his adaptive mechanisms have made some adjustments. He may see a clinic as an extension of "authority", hypocritically offering therapy and care, whilst really demanding uniformity and conformity. Certainly clinics do have a dual role in offering a service to individual patients and yet being responsible to the needs of public health. This dual role can lead to a conflict of interests and inconsistencies in approach that an addict will be delighted to exploit.

Addicts have an extraordinary capacity for provoking disagreements and eliciting rejection, perhaps to cause a discordancy consonant with their perception of human relationships. A disequilibrium caused by bribery, corruption and belligerency is intolerable to staff, yet is a natural situation for addicts. If they see clinics as Establishment-orientated and the staff as out of touch with their view of reality, they will try to perpetuate a situation whereby their stereotype is maintained. And yet they avoid alienating to an extent that threatens their supply of drugs and they will go to any lengths to demonstrate their chemical needs.

Doctors, nurses and social workers must, if they are to be effective, question their own beliefs and value-systems, exposing themselves to situations that are dangerous or upsetting, but nevertheless often challenging and productive. To empathise with a way of life so different from one's own is not easy, but it is essential that there is a real understanding of the addict's frustrations and needs. Occasionally, this process of self-examination has proved damaging to the therapists themselves, in that they have over-identified with the addict's sub-culture. It is enough to acquire the language skills to appreciate the addict's attitudes and self-defeating mechanisms: it is more than unwise to acquire the behaviours themselves.

The justification for intervening in the addict's life is the conviction that at some stage he will genuinely regret the course his life has taken. We have met many addicts who have acknowledged the futility of their situation, yet so often they lack the inner resources to escape from their chemical confinement. Much of the antagonism they display can be resolved in therapy by clearly defining the guidelines along which relationships can develop, and by explaining the goals and policies of the clinic and the rules that operate. The less ambiguity there is, the greater the possibility of developing mutual respect and tolerance. If there is one common factor that characterises addicts it is their lack of trust and their suspiciousness, a trait often emanating from their disturbed relationships with their own parents. They act in ways which elicit feelings of hostility, so creating a situation where their sense of rejection is heightened and their self-justifying lack of trust seems justified.

Addicts often highlight the clash between themselves and authority, and this may obscure the defective social skills that impair them in their relationships in all aspects of their lives. They may have daily conflict with their parents, wives, girl-friends or their peer group. We have scarcely met a family that has not been deeply divided by its addicted son's or daughter's behaviour. We have never regretted spending time with the family, and consider that it may be more appropriate in many instances to direct much of the therapeutic effort towards the parents.

When rapport has been established, addicts may reveal that their outward aggression and assertion conceal powerful feelings of inferiority and inadequacy. There may be deficiencies in the sexual area, which they initially deny but may willingly discuss later. Opiate drugs depress sexual drive and can cause impotence in males or delayed orgasm in both sexes. Preoccupation with searching for drugs takes precedence over exploratory sexual behaviour, but a careful history may reveal longstanding feelings of sexual inadequacy, poor performance, or identification problems from long before the drug-taking began. These will be accentuated if drug-taking ceases, and may trigger relapses if not anticipated and included in plans for treatment.

NARCOTIC ANTAGONISTS

A narcotic antagonist is a substance that inactivates any opium alkaloid when administered at the same time. If given to a narcotic addict it will elicit the characteristic withdrawal syndrome. The rationale is similar to that for Antabuse in alcoholics, to discourage addicts from taking opiates, once they have been withdrawn.

The first drug of this type to be used clinically was cyclazocine, introduced in Lexington, Kentucky. In using this, normally an addict is withdrawn from heroin or morphine by using methadone over a three to six day period, then after a short drug-free time a small test dose of cyclazocine is given to determine whether an induced withdrawal syndrome can still occur. If not, cyclazocine is given orally in gradually increasing doses to a level of 4 to 8 mg. Patients are normally kept in hospital for a six-week period, then discharged as out-patients to attend daily for several weeks or months. The antagonist drug is dispensed daily by the clinic, until the addict can be trusted to attend at longer intervals. Cyclazocine, unfortunately, has a very short duration of action, so it is given in divided doses, but even then many addicts find that they can obtain a heroin "lift" if they inject when the antagonist is wearing off. Cyclazocine has therefore serious limitations, and the side-effects can be very distressing. These include nausea, loss of appetite, constipation, loss of sexual drive, and mental symptoms of anxiety, irritability and depression. These may disappear in time, as the body becomes tolerant to the drug and a physical dependence to it develops. A characteristic abstinence syndrome can occur, with loss of appetite, sleepiness, dizziness and muscular twitching when cyclazocine is discontinued, but the potential for abuse is considerably lower than for most narcotic drugs. A survey by Laskowitz (1972) of thirty-five patients showed a high incidence of distressing side-effects, and many had dropped out of treatment. After three years only 40 per cent could be regarded as successful; 20 per cent being opiate-free and off cyclazocine, and 20 per cent opiate free but still on cyclazocine.

The search for a more suitable narcotic antagonist led to the introduction of naloxone (Zaks *et al.,* 1971). An oral dose of 1,500 mg will effect a narcotic "blockade" against an injection of 20 to 50 mg of heroin. Side effects at this dosage are not substantial, but one patient was described who became apathetic and depressed, although his symptoms resolved with a slight dosage adjustment. Again, naloxone has a very short duration of action, and may prove to be unsuitable with prolonged clinical testing.

BEHAVIOUR THERAPY

Despite the learning-theory explanations of addictions, little attention has been paid to a comprehensive treatment approach based on behaviour modification and behaviour-therapy techniques. What little work has been done has been a translation of research in the areas of alcoholism and sexual deviation, using paradigms of aversion and desensitisation.

Thomas and Rathod (1968) described seventeen heroin addicts treated by aversion therapy in a very interesting experiment, using essentially a classical (Pavlovian) conditioning model. The addict prepares to "fix" an injection of heroin, and is then given an injection of a muscular relaxant drug, by an anaesthetist, to render him totally paralysed but fully conscious. The addict injects the heroin as the muscular twitchings preceding the paralysis commence. In his paralysed state, unable to breath, he is told in vivid terms of the dangers of addiction. He is artificially ventilated until he recovers (which occurs in a very short space of time). Doubtless, this is a very unpleasant procedure, but it has not deterred most treated addicts from relapsing in a short space of time.

The aim of treatment is to counteract the positive qualities of the injecting process, a small but vitally important aspect of the addict's life and electrical stimuli have been used to this end with apparent success. Many people have ethical doubts about this type of overt aversion therapy, but a technique of "covert" sensitisation seems to be a useful alternative. Also known as "aversive imagery", a deviant stimulus is followed, not by an unpleasant electrical shock or any other such stimulus, but by an unpleasant imaginary situation. The method has been used with sexual deviants, alcoholics, and addicts (Kolvin, 1967), and is possibly most successful with those patients who can evoke vivid visual or olfactory imagery. It is a very adaptable technique, having no physical dangers, and has a great advantage in that it can be used *in vivo,* as people can be trained to administer it to themselves in "tempting" circumstances.

Where addiction is mainly controlled by escape from, or avoidance of, aversive stimulation (as is often the case), a punishment, or aversion, technique might not be as important as some form of desensitisation. In desensitisation there is training in relaxation, followed by gradual, controlled exposure to anxiety-provoking stimuli. The details are described by Wolpe (1966) who has been largely responsible for popularising the method and demonstrating its wide areas of application. Success has been claimed in desensitising patients to anxiety-inducing interpersonal situations, from which many addicts and alcoholics seek refuge through intoxication. It is probably true to say that behavioural treatments only offer partial solutions to addicts' problems, and that combination procedures are necessary to achieve permanent improvement.

REFERENCES

American Psychiatric Association, "Position Statement on Guidelines for Methadone Maintenance Treatment by Private Psychiatrists", *American Journal of Psychiatry,* 128: 254–5, 1971.

Brill, L. and Lieberman, L. (eds.), *Major Modalities in the Treatment of Drug Abuse,* Behavioural Publications, New York, 1972.

Chafetz, M. E., *et al.*, "Establishing Treatment Relations with Alcoholics", *Journal of Nervous and Mental Disease,* 134: 395–409, 1962.
Dobbs, W. H., "Methadone Treatment of Heroin Addicts", *Journal of the American Medical Association,* 218: 1,536–41, 1971.
Dole, V. P., "Detoxification of Sick Addicts in Prison", *JAMA,* 220: 366–9, 1972.
Dole, V. P. and Nyswander, M., "Heroin Addiction—A Metabolic Disease" *Archives of Internal Medicine,* 120: 19–24, 1967.
Dole, V. P., Nyswander, M. and Kreek, M. J. "Narcotic Blockade", *Arch. Intern. Med.,* 118: 304–9, 1966.
Edwards, G., "The British Approach to the Treatment of Heroin Addiction", *Lancet,* x: 768–72, 1969.
Edwards, G. and Guthrie, S., "A Controlled Trial of In-patient and Outpatient Treatment of Alcohol Dependence", *Lancet,* i: 555–9, 1967.
Hoff, E. C., "The Use of Disulfiram (Antabuse) in the Comprehensive Therapy of a Group of 1,020 Alcoholics", *Connecticut State Medical Journal,* 19: 793, 1955.
Kolvin, I., "Aversive Imagery Treatment in Adolescents", *Behaviour Research and Therapy,* 5: 245–8, 1967.
Laskowitz, D., *et al.,* "Cyclazocine Intervention in the Treatment of Narcotic Addiction", in Brill, L. and Lieberman, L. (eds.), op. cit.
Lemere, F. and Voegtlin, W., "An Evaluation of the Aversive Treatment of Alcoholism", *Quarterly Journal of Studies on Alcohol,* 11: 199–204, 1950.
Little, R. and Pearson, M. M., "The Management of Pathological Interdependency in Drug Addiction", *Am. J. Psychiatry,* 123: 554–60, 1966.
Malcolm, M. T., Personal Communication.
Ramer, B. S., Zaslove, M. O. and Langan, J. "Is Methadone Enough? The Use of Ancillary Treatment During Methadone Maintenance", *Am. J. Psychiatry,* 127: 1,040–4, 1971.
Ritson, E. B. and Hassall, C., *The Management of Alcoholism,* Livingstone, Edinburgh, 1970.
Schur, E. M., *Narcotic Addiction in Britain and America: The Impact of Public Policy,* Indiana University Press, 1968.
Seccombe, I., "Illusionogenic Crisis and Effective Intervention", *Addictions,* 18: 28–40, 1971.
Solursh, L. P. and Clements, W. R., "Use of Diazepam in Hallucinogenic Drug Crises", *JAMA,* 205: 644–5, 1968.
Szasz, T., "Drugs, Doctors and Deceit", *New England Journal of Medicine,* 286: 111, 1972.
Thomas, I. E. and Rathod, N. H., "Aversion Therapy for Heroin Dependence", *Lancet,* ii: 382–4, 1968.
Victor, M., Adams, R. D. and Collins, E. H., *The Wernicke-Korsakoff Syndrome,* F. A. Davis Co., Philadelphia, 1971.
Voegtlin, W. L. and Lemere, F., "The Treatment of Alcoholic Addiction: A Review of the Literature", *Quart. J. Stud. Alcohol,* 2: 717–803, 1942.

Weppner, R. S. and Stephens, R. C., "The Illicit Use and Diversion of Methadone on the Street as Related by Hospitalized Addicts", *Journal of Drug Issues,* 42–5, Winter, 1973.

Wolpe, J. and Lazarus, A., *Behaviour Therapy Techniques,* Pergamon Press, Oxford, 1966.

Zaks, A., *et al.,* "Naloxone Treatment of Opiate Dependence", *JAMA,* 215: 2,108–10, 1971.

9 The social management of alcoholism and addiction

COMMUNITY CARE

The interest of the medical profession, and particularly hospital doctors, in the therapy of addiction is a relatively recent phenomenon. Prior to the last twenty years or so any concern most doctors had was in treating either the physical or the psychological *sequelae* of addiction, but not in dealing with its basic problems. This attitude is still prevalent, but is lessening as the knowledge that alcoholics and addicts can be helped increases.

Hospital doctors see only the tip of the addiction iceberg. Admissions to psychiatric hospitals in England and Wales for alcoholism, either as a primary or secondary diagnosis, account for approximately 8,000 admissions annually. The number of such admissions has been increasing by 20 per cent each year over the last few years but this only reflects a similar increase in all psychiatric admissions over the same period. Alcoholism admissions make up 3·6 per cent of all psychiatric admissions annually (Zacune and Hensman, 1971). In Scotland, alcoholism is responsible for approximately 14 per cent of all psychiatric admissions, which probably reflects the higher prevalence of alcoholism in Scotland. The combined total for England, Wales and Scotland for alcoholism produces a total of 12,000 or so admissions annually. Compared with the estimated prevalence of 300,000 to 400,000 alcoholics in the country, the proportion requiring and getting admission is clearly very small. The same general picture holds true for dependence on other drugs beside alcohol. Many alcoholics are never recognised, many more do not receive treatment for their addiction and of those that do, it is a minority who enter special units for the treatment of addiction.

The agencies coming into contact with addicts of all kinds can be classified as those agencies with the express aim of helping addicts, agencies that have a broader clientele but one that includes a lot of alcoholics, and agencies that treat specific problems not including addiction but whose clients may arrive for help because they themselves are in difficulties as the result of contact with an addict. The following list is not exhaustive, but the examples given are representative of the majority of the facilities available.

Agencies designed to help addicts

Alcoholism

Alcoholics Anonymous
- AlAnon
- Alateen

Regional councils on alcoholism
Detoxification centres
Hostels for alcoholics, including halfway houses

Drugs other than alcohol

Synanon
Daytop
Phoenix house
Regional advisory centres

Agencies whose clientele includes many addicts

Social and welfare services
Salvation Army hostels
Jails
Probation services
Ex-convicts rehabilitation services
Church organisations catering to the "down-and-out"

Agencies dealing indirectly with problems of addiction

Local authority services

Courts
Lawyers
Clergymen

AGENCIES DESIGNED TO HELP ADDICTS: ALCOHOLISM

Alcoholics Anonymous

Alcoholics Anonymous almost always comes to mind when the problem of dealing with an alcoholic arises. It has probably helped more alcoholics than any other single organisation and continues to help many thousands of them throughout the world. Alcoholics Anonymous was formed in 1935 in Akron, Ohio, through the efforts of two men, Bill W. and Dr. Bob. Both men were alcoholics who, having gained sobriety themselves, worked to help other alcoholics who, at that time, were receiving no organised help from anywhere else.

A.A. developed slowly at first. Four years after its start the membership had reached only 100. From its small beginnings A.A. has gradually come to be accepted as an important helping agency by clergymen, doctors, hospitals and prison workers. By 1942 it was still a fairly small organisation, but had become established in a few mental hospitals and had a group operating in San Quentin prison in California. About that time the membership increased to some 8,000 people following the publication of an article about A.A in the *Saturday Evening Post.* Soon after, it began to spread outside America, initially into Canada. From 1939 onwards it published a number of books and pamphlets and by the time the book *Alcoholics Anonymous Comes of Age* was published in 1957 the membership had risen to 200,000 and the organisation had spread to 70 countries, having begun in Britain in 1947.

At present A.A. has groups in most sizeable towns in the U.K. In cities such as Liverpool, an alcoholic can attend a different group each night of the week if he wishes and a social club or coffee shop at the weekends. Anyone who has a problem with alcohol can go along to an A.A. meeting and ask for help. The organisation is based on the concept of an anonymous, self-help group with no allegiance to any other political, social or religious body. The principles of its operation have been formalised into twelve steps and twelve traditions.

The twelve steps outline a programme by which an individual can live a satisfying life without the use of alcohol. Although A.A. is at pains to say that their programme is not orientated toward any particular religious belief, it is strongly based on the concept of some kind of God whom each individual member is free to choose for himself. This orientation towards a deity and towards spiritual awakening as an aid to sobriety often hinders the acceptance of A.A. by an alcoholic who needs help but has no religion of his own. The twelve traditions cover the aims of the organisation and the ways in which A.A. sees itself as being a totally independent, self-supporting agency, with no affiliation to, or opinions on, any outside matter or organisation. The anonymity insisted upon by A.A. is due to a wish to play down individual personalities and to stress the principles of the organisation, and it also allows some protection against the possible ill-effects of identifying oneself publicly as suffering from a socially undesirable condition.

The aims of A.A. are admirable and the success it has achieved is immense. It cannot, however, be all things to all men and a large number of alcoholics find that they cannot fit into the techniques practised by the groups that they attend. Different groups in A.A. adopt differing styles of operation dependent on the clientele they serve and the areas in which they are situated. Some groups operate on the traditional basis of having people stand up in the gathering to relate their life story, showing how they came to be dependent on alcohol, the effects of this dependence on their life and, if appropriate, their steps toward recovery with the help of A.A. Other groups have evolved into regular discussion forums and the occasional one has considered using group psychotherapy without the assistance of a professional group leader. Another development in A.A. has been the holding of open meetings at which A.A. members, their families and anyone else interested in the problem of alcoholism can attend.

Apart from its group sessions, A.A. arranges that anyone who wishes can have the help of a sponsor. Each sponsor is a member of A.A. who has been successful in remaining abstinent and who is well-versed in the practice of the Twelve Steps. The sponsor will make him- or herself available to the new member of the association *at any time* the alcoholic requests help. Apart from the psychological support of having an understanding person available whenever required, the alcoholic may also derive a great deal of practical help from his sponsor in sorting out problems at home and at work.

The fellowship of A.A. is available to anyone who will take the first of the Twelve Steps: that is, to admit that he is powerless over alcohol and that his life has become unmanageable. Having gone to A.A. and taken this first step, the alcoholic is provided with a way of understanding both his own behaviour and the condition from which he is suffering. The people who tell him about his illness are all self-confessed alcoholics and the regular attenders and the sponsors are those who have been successful in attaining sobriety by means of the programme they are offering to the new member. A.A. can be considered as a form of group psychotherapy, which is very directive and supportive. In a study of the curative factors in group psychotherapy in general, Yalom and his colleagues asked patients undergoing treatment to rate the factors that they felt had been important in helping them recover.

The important factors, as assessed by the patients, related mainly to the interaction between themselves and other patients in the group. They included seeing themselves in all the ways that others saw them, accepting unpleasant things about themselves and learning that, no matter how much support and help is given, each individual is still responsible for the way he lives. These were all factors that were rated as highly therapeutic. The realisation that other people could reveal embarrassing facts about themselves and benefit from doing so, helped the observers of this phenomenon to do the same themselves. Being able to develop trust in a group was also felt to be important to the individual participant in the group. Examining A.A.'s methods of operation it can be seen that in many ways A.A. groups can provide the circumstances in which important curative factors can develop.

All groups, whether social, therapeutic, religious or otherwise, must accept that some people will drop out of the continuing process of the group. Most people who begin to attend a group and are going to drop out do so within a few days or weeks of the beginning of its operation. A.A. is no exception to this occurrence and there are many people who attend for a few meetings and then never go back or attend only infrequently. Other alcoholics "tune in" to A.A. almost immediately and are able to derive great satisfaction from their involvement in its activities.

Although A.A. can, theoretically, appeal to all alcoholics from any social class it tends to attract, at least in London, the middle-aged, middle-class alcoholic (Edwards, G. *et al.,* 1966*b*). A.A. has a philosophy of the causation of alcoholism based on an allergic response to alcohol, coupled with a psychological predisposition to dependence, and has always appealed more to the gamma alcoholic (*see* p. 160) than to the sufferers from the other subtypes of alcoholism. Groups in both working-class and upper-class areas have been deliberately started, to widen the range of people that A.A. can help. There has also been a recognition of the varying age groups involved in alcoholism and groups designed to appeal to the alcoholic in the twenties and thirties have been started. These have had varying degrees of success and such a young group in Liverpool had a great deal of difficulty in continuing to function due to a very low membership while a similar group in Toronto attracts more people than can comfortably be accommodated in one meeting.

The efficacy of the treatment provided by A.A. and the other therapeutic regimes will be considered in the next chapter but a brief mention about this is appropriate at this time. There is, in fact, no really hard evidence on its effectiveness. In 1944, Tiebout reported that 75 per cent of those people really trying the programme were successful in becoming abstinent and recovering from alcoholism. It seems unlikely that this very high rate of success is achieved by A.A. now that it has grown to be such a large organisation. It is not possible to say that it does *not* achieve this rate of success with those who really try the programme because it is almost impossible to define what is meant by "really trying". It is possible to say that A.A. is not able, by itself, to provide a comprehensive successful treatment for all alcoholics and there is evidence that A.A. reaches only a small minority of alcoholics in the community.

AlAnon groups

AlAnon family groups are comprised of the relatives of alcoholics, both the sober ex-alcoholics and those who are still drinking. Family groups began to meet soon after the foundation of A.A., but AlAnon did not begin to function widely until about 1950. The relatives of alcoholics are in a difficult situation and being able to share experiences with a group of people who have similar problems may provide for the family member what A.A. provides for the alcoholic. AlAnon operates according to the same principles as A.A. and AlAnon members are taught to regard alcoholism in the same way as A.A. members. This internal consistency provides a framework within which both the alcoholic and his spouse can operate and be aware of the rules governing the relationships between themselves and the two organisations.

Alateen groups

Alateen is another organisation separate from, but allied to, A.A. It also operates according to the basic principles of A.A. and it was begun in 1957 in California by the teenage son of an alcoholic father. So far it is growing only slowly as a worldwide organisation. The membership of Alateen comprises the teenage, or approximately teenage, children of alcoholics who meet together to solve the common problems they have in living with one or two alcoholic parents. Usually the meetings are supervised by a member of A.A. or AlAnon.

Many children of alcoholics are cut off from social contacts and they can derive a great deal of benefit from mixing with children trying to cope with the same sort of problems.

Regional councils on alcoholism

The National Council on Alcoholism was founded in 1963, with the aims of educating the British public about alcoholism and providing agencies to which the alcoholic, or anyone concerned about him, could go for advice. There are a number of Regional Councils on Alcoholism throughout Britain, most of them being situated in large cities. Initially they began to operate solely as information and referral agencies but some have developed a wider range of activities as time has gone by.

The Merseyside Council on Alcoholism is an example of a very active and successful Regional Council. It began in a small way in 1963 with a part-time operation in one office in central Liverpool. Originally, this was an information centre but under the direction of its Executive Director, W. H. Kenyon, it grew and widened its range of activities greatly. The M.C.A. now has a number of full-time counsellors and several part-time counsellors who operate a service in Liverpool, two nearby towns and a growing area of the surrounding County.

The M.C.A. still provides an information service to alcoholics, their families, friends and employers and to anyone else who is interested. Over recent years, there has been an increasing demand for information by school teachers and school children. As part of their interest in education on alcoholism and drug dependence, the M.C.A. joined with the Merseyside Council on Drug-Taking and the Department of Psychiatry of the University of Liverpool, in organising two International Conferences in Liverpool that attracted over 400 participants at each conference. In addition, 1,000 school children attended a one-day seminar at each of the conferences.

The M.C.A. now offers advice and treatment, or referral to specialised treatment agencies, for approximately 600 new cases of alcoholism each year and it has an even greater client load of repeat attenders. It has extremely good connections with the medical, social and legal agencies on Merseyside and can offer, either directly or indirectly, a fairly comprehensive service to the alcoholic. The main drawback, so far, in the system is the absence of any hostel or halfway house accommodation in the Liverpool area. The great advantage of the system lies in the development of a two-way flow of referrals between the M.C.A. and other agencies. The Council has always kept in contact with the local general practitioners and this has paid dividends, because medical practitioners in the area have learnt of the expertise of the M.C.A. staff and now refer patients directly to the Council. By the means of a Medical Committee, the M.C.A. keeps directly in touch with doctors in the Regional Alcoholism Unit at nearby Moston, Chester, with doctors in both general and psychiatric hospitals, and with local industrial medical officers. As was mentioned earlier, the M.C.A. runs a programme for employees of a shipping line that has been able to promote a very high sobriety rate for those going through treatment.

All Regional Councils on Alcoholism are dependent on financial donations to enable them to continue functioning. The M.C.A. has been able to show to the local authorities in its region that it is providing a useful service that is not provided elsewhere by statutory organisations and it has been fortunate in obtaining financial support from local councils, businesses and individuals. In their study of the clients of Information Centres, Edwards and his colleagues (1967) suggested that the financing of the centres should be put on a stable footing because of the numbers and the range of alcoholics being reached by them. They studied 300 clients, all but 34 of them men, 100 each being drawn from Glasgow, Gloucester and Liverpool. The largest single source of referral was by doctors (23 per cent), followed by self-referral in 20 per cent of cases. A number of agencies such as A.A., the Marriage Guidance Council and others were responsible for 29 per cent of all referrals. In their social characteristics, the clients were much the same as those people attending A.A. They were mostly middle-class, but showing a downward drift in socio-economic status, middle-aged and still fairly well in contact with their families. The women had suffered less severely than the men, both in terms of the direct effects of their drinking and also in its social consequences.

There was no doubt that people presenting to the centres were suffering from alcoholism. Of the men, 90 per cent suffered severe morning shakes and 76 per cent of them had regularly taken a morning drink to counteract the withdrawal symptoms. In the field of employment, only 50 per cent currently held a job although most of them had held a steady, long-term job earlier in their work careers. In the year prior to the survey, only 2 per cent had not had time off work; 88 per cent claimed to have been drinking before going to work, and 75 per cent had lost a job as a direct result of drinking. The loss to industry from this small fraction of the total alcoholic population is immense. As the investigators pointed out, it may not be reasonable to extrapolate from these 300 cases to the total alcoholic population but there is probably a fairly close relationship between the alcoholics in the study and the other alcoholics in the U.K., in the way alcoholism affects at least their job performance. A further study by the M.C.A. (which has not yet been completed) confirms that, five years later, the alcoholics who present to an Information Centre have lost as much time off work as indicated by the Edwards study and have cost very large amounts in Social Security payments.

We have written earlier of the "alcoholism gap" between general practitioners and their patients and although doctors accounted for only a quarter of the referrals to the Information Centres, 74 per cent of the clients said that they had sought help from their family doctors in the last year. The medical profession appears at present to represent to alcoholics the main source from which they feel help can be sought, but whether or not doctors are matching the expectations of the alcoholics is doubtful.

The Information Centres have a unique situation in providing services for alcoholics in the community. They are community-orientated and they lack the possibly forbidding aura of statutory agencies. Although they deserve stable financing, it would seem a pity to lose the entrepreneurial aspects of at least some of the centres.

Detoxification centres

"Sobering-up stations" in Poland and "hang-over clinics" in Finland have been in use for years but the concept of detoxification centres has only recently made any impact on the alcoholism situation in Britain. The drunk who is arrested on the street is liable to have to spend at least a night in jail and the chronic drunk may be sentenced to a few weeks or months in jail. This system is undesirable in many ways but it does have the advantage that the chronic drunk spends a night under shelter instead of possibly in the open and he will also be fed, assuming he is able to eat. The disadvantages are, that the police and courts are involved in a lot of time-consuming tasks totally unrelated to crime as such, and the police are also made responsible for the care of someone who might be seriously ill. Most of the clients of detoxification centres are not physically ill and provided the centres are close to hospital facilities, they can be run by social workers and non-professional staff.

"Detox" centres usually keep clients for one or two days in order to clean them up, allow time for the alcohol to be metabolised and, if possible, start a therapeutic relationship. Under this system, the chronic drunk is deprived of the relatively long-term stays in jail which he intermittently requires to get back on to his feet and for these people a possible unfortunate alternative is to drink heavily every day and so become a regular detox client, thereby obtaining long-term care in frequent daily doses.

The problem of the detox "revolving door" has been discussed by Fox and his colleagues (1972). Their unit in Boston, Mass., consists of a 10-bedded ward, which operates more as a short-stay facility in a hospital than as the very short-stay detox unit which it is envisaged will be operating in numbers in Britain soon (e.g. at Leeds). Patients stay for up to ten days in the Boston unit undergoing a standard withdrawal programme of treatment. The first 100 patients admitted were followed for up to two years. During that time, half the patients were re-admitted to the unit, three as many as five times in the period of study. An encouraging finding was that 40 per cent of the patients kept in touch with the unit when sober, those maintaining the most contact remaining the most frequently sober. Sixteen of those admitted remained abstinent for at least six months. Although the outcome of treatment in alcoholism is relatively independent of length of stay as an in-patient, the possibility of building up a relationship between patient and therapist is obviously much greater over ten days than over twenty-four hours. It would seem unlikely that the detox units operating on a very short-stay principle would obtain, of their own accord, long-term results comparable with those in Fox's study.

Hostels for alcoholics

The treatment of alcoholics has been traditionally centred around hospitals with little in the way of residential follow-up. Many of the people entering hospital are homeless and without families and they frequently need a great deal of aftercare, which could be provided by hostels. In view of the variability of the damage caused by alcoholism on the basic personalities of the people affected, the ideal after care system would contain a number of hostels, allowing for a progression from a very dependent existence to one of total independence. For a minority of the alcoholic population, a prolonged period of almost total dependence on an institution might be necessary and even desirable.

The type of alcoholic who is most likely to need prolonged hostel care is the vagrant or the chronic-drunkenness offender. Ingram-Smith (1969) divided hostels into three groups: large hostels of up to 1,000 beds where the alcoholic could live and continue drinking; secondly, hostels of about 40 beds with greater therapeutic activity;

and thirdly, hostels designed to deal with specific conditions such as addiction or delinquency. The smaller hostels would aim to provide an atmosphere in which drinking was forbidden, together with provisions for material welfare, physical health and social rehabilitation. This is an extremely tall order but many writers have pointed out that the operation of a series of such hostels would probably be cheaper than repeated prison and hospital admissions and from the point of view of the individual alcoholic, the hostels would offer the possibility of a much more stable life pattern.

The characteristics of the skid-row alcoholic in London have been described by Edwards *et al* (1966*a*). The total number of people "on skid row" throughout Britain is probably in the region of a few thousand and these tend to be found in the dilapidated areas of cities, where they live in small, loose groups in derelict buildings. Of 51 men interviewed at a Stepney soup-kitchen, 63 per cent had had no shelter apart from that provided by derelict buildings during the previous week and only two of them had had anything substantial to eat in the previous twenty-four hours.

Compared with the clients of A.A. and the information centres, the alcoholics who reached skid row had been exposed to a much less stable upbringing. They were from lower socio-economic groups, none had had any higher education and 58 per cent had experienced prolonged, early, parental deprivation. Less than one-third of the men had had any period of job or family stability after leaving their parents' home. Most of them had been labourers and only two had held a job for a period of five years or more. As a group, the men had no social contacts outside the skid-row area and only three had been in touch with their relatives within the previous year.

On average, these men developed a drinking problem at about the age of twenty-nine, they were first jailed at thirty-three and they reached skid row at thirty-eight. Although the stereotype of a skid-row alcoholic is that of a crude-spirit drinker, there were actually two distinct groups—those who did drink crude spirit and those who drank wine or cider. The men from either group did not appear simply to be alcoholics who had slipped right down the social scale through a series of misfortunes. They were seen as being men with life-long personality disorders, combined with chemical dependence on alcohol. They had made a pathological social adjustment that was a futile way of fulfilling the needs of their damaged personalities.

The treatment of a long-standing personality disorder is a notoriously difficult and unrewarding task and the combination of such a disorder with dependence on alcohol makes the task even more difficult. Rathcoole House in the U.K. was begun in an attempt to provide a rehabilitation facility for the vagrant alcoholic and its method of operation and clientele have been described by Cook *et al.* (1968), Pollak (1969) and Cook and Pollak (1970). The men who become residents in this hostel match the description of the skid-row alcoholic very closely, but the results obtained by the hostel over its first two years were extremely encouraging, with approximately one-third of the men who entered the hostel staying for over three months. Nor did these men remain in a state of passive dependence. It was found that they rapidly developed, or re-disovered, a wish to go to work and they managed to do this for some months on a steady basis. The men also stayed sober for several months, the results in this respect being very comparable with those produced by hospitals earlier in these particular clients' drinking careers.

Rathcoole is only one of many such hostels now operating throughout Britain. The Helping Hand Organisation and the Simon Community have both opened a number of hostels which deal with various types of alcoholics. The Simon Community appears to have a clientele that consists mainly of vagrants who are allowed a great deal of freedom within the hostel.

A halfway house differs from the hostels described above in that, as the name implies, it is intended for the alcoholic who is not down and out, but is halfway back to being an independent member of society. Cahn (1969) found the residents of halfway houses to be similar to those in psychiatric facilities. They were middle-aged, middle or lower-middle class, with good work histories and having work skills. Although the majority of halfway-house residents were unemployed at the time of entry to the house, they had usually been employed to within a few months prior to admission and were keen to go back to work. Few of the men needed rehabilitation in a job sense and they were usually able to secure employment by their own efforts. It was found that men with skid-row characteristics did badly in the milieu of a halfway-house system and it was felt that individuals in a group do better when the group comprises members of similar socio-economic status.

Although the outlook for the homeless, under-socialised alcoholic is poor if he is treated in hospital and then discharged to fend for himself in the community, the provision of hostels or halfway houses for such people can considerably affect the prognosis for at least some individuals. Facilities for the rehabilitation of alcoholics are still woefully lacking in the greater part of the country, and, for example, Liverpool does not have a single hostel or halfway house despite having a large alcoholism problem and many active hospital and community resources for the treatment of alcoholics. At a very rough estimate, Liverpool itself probably has enough vagrant alcoholics to fill four hostels. Until sufficient facilities are provided, certain groups of alcoholics will not obtain anything like the most suitable treatment and will continue to make expensive and time-consuming demands on the present overburdened services.

An old idea has been resurrected by the Ontario Addiction Research Foundation (A.R.F.) in the treatment of severely-damaged alcoholics. Years ago, most large mental hospitals had a farm that provided work for the patients and reduced the overheads of the hospital by producing food. The use of patients as farm labour was gradually discontinued over the 1950s and most of the farms sold off. Anecdotally, many of the long-serving nurses in the large institutions saw this process as a retrograde step, mainly because some patients were not provided with alternative rehabilitation or work. Bon Accord farm, run by the A.R.F., was opened in recent years to serve men from skid row with a record of drunkenness offences. It was originally planned to run Bon Accord as a farm but instead, it has developed a programme in which the residents build furniture of a very high standard and also benefit from the rehabilitation programme.

Some alcoholics do not appear to fit into, or benefit from, any of the provisions made for them and they continue to drink, be arrested and become repeatedly ill. The Mental Health Act 1959 in the U.K. allows for the involuntary treatment of people with mental disorders who are not willing to be treated and yet who need protection and treatment to prevent their harming themselves or others. Alcoholics are usually admitted to hospital on an involuntary basis only because of something as serious as a suicide attempt or psychotic breakdown. Not many are admitted compulsorily for treatment of the alcoholism itself and perhaps more of those who do not respond to any of the treatment and rehabilitation methods should be required to enter into a long-term programme. The psychiatric hospital would not appear to be equipped to tackle this problem and some form of community-orientated organisation, with powers of compulsory admission, would need to be developed if, on investigation, sufficient people were found to be in need of such treatment. This subject is fraught with difficulty since many people would complain that if an agency could compulsorily admit alcoholics, then why should it not begin to admit the obese, the excessive gamblers and the heavy smokers? This argument is a little specious, since such categories are much more able to determine their destinies than the small and rather pathetic group we have just been discussing.

AGENCIES DESIGNED TO HELP ADDICTS: DRUGS OTHER THAN ALCOHOL

There is no equivalent organisation to Alcoholics Anonymous in the realm of drug dependence. The treatment of drug-dependents is centred on hospitals and the special prescribing clinics described in the last chapter.

Organisations such as the Association for the Prevention of Addiction provide information and act as referral agencies for addicts and their families. In Liverpool, a sister organisation to the M.C.A., the Merseyside Council on Drug-Taking, has acted as a part-time information centre and it is hoped that it will develop its activities into a much more comprehensive service in the Merseyside region.

The educational aspects of drug dependence have been well covered by the A.P.A. and the Society for the Study of Addiction, which publishes the *British Journal of Addiction,* and by books and articles appearing over the last few years. However, the rehabilitation of addicts is not even as far advanced as the inadequate state of the comparable services for alcoholics. There are fewer drug addicts and they do not present the problem of repeated public intoxication. There are many people, particularly the young, who are charged with drug offences and who could probably benefit from contact with an advisory service designed to help in cases of drug dependence. In this case, the probation officer is in the best position to offer advice but apart from making a referral to a specialised drug clinic, he can probably offer little else at present.

The community resources offering aid to addicts consist of a very small number of hostels and day centres. The most interesting developments in this field have originated in America. Synanon, Daytop, Phoenix House and Odyssey House are all organisations that are community-based and run by ex-addicts or alcoholics without professional help.

Synanon

Synanon was founded in 1958 by Charles Dederich, and was the first of the therapeutic communities operated by laymen providing treatment for addicts and alcoholics. Synanon does not aim to rehabilitate addicts back into general society, but instead retains them in a society based on Synanon principles. It accepts addicts on the understanding that they will remain drug-free and work toward an acceptance of their own responsibility for their drug problem. The society is non-permissive and residents gain in seniority by staying in Synanon. Each member has an obligation to work in a job that is relevant to his recovery. The staff members who direct operations are usually individuals who entered Synanon to deal with their own drug problem.

Initially, Synanon's stated aim was to produce "graduates" from the rehabilitation programme who would then leave and live in the general society. More recently, this idea was dropped and the founder is on record as saying his aim had always been to keep addicts within the Synanon framework. A further change has been the acceptance of non-addicts, who are not seeking rehabilitation but a change in their life style.

The milieu of Synanon is designed to be therapeutic but within the overall operation a special kind of group psychotherapy called "Synanon" is used. These groups are held about three times a week, with a small number of members, and the membership of the groups changes for each meeting. The basis of the operation of the groups is verbal attack. One member is put in the "hot seat" and is then verbally attacked about any aspect of his behaviour that the rest of the group members wish to raise. The group encounter is intended to be performed with total honesty and openness. The member in the "hot seat" is not allowed to retaliate with physical violence, although the temptation to do so must be great, considering the virulent content of the verbal attack which has been reported by Yablonsky (1965) and others.

The value of Synanon in treating and rehabilitating addicts has not been measured with any accurancy and probably it could not be measured. The usually accepted criteria of recovery, which are to be off drugs and be stabilised in society, do not hold when Synanon is considered. Many people are unable to stay in its milieu longer than a few weeks and should properly be included in any assessment of the efficacy of the method. By changing its aims from being a traditional rehabilitation agency to providing care on a long-term basis, possibly life-long, Synanon has compounded the difficulties of assessment.

It does appear to be a very successful agency in taking people off drugs and keeping them off, so long as they remain within the community. In itself, that is quite an achievement. The acceptance of individuals as life-long members has been criticised, on the grounds that this policy fosters the growth of excessive emotional dependence on the institution. The people who leave Synanon were initially reported to be staying off drugs, but more recent evidence has shown that less than 10 per cent have managed to remain abstinent for any length of time. Even this low success rate has to be viewed in the light of the fact that the addicts who selected themselves for the treatment must have had very high motivation towards abstaining to have gone through the programme for weeks or months.

Daytop Village

This community was begun by an ex-Synanon member in 1964 in Staten Island. In turn, one of Daytop's graduates started Liberty Park Village in New Jersey. Daytop operates a number of centres in and around New York in a very similar way to the Synanon operation. It attempts to make people return to the community and relies on non-professionals to carry out its treatment programme. According to the Le Dain Commission Report (1972), Daytop has had 177 people graduate and only 19 of these were considered to have failed.

The Liberty Park Village community has been described by Brecher (1972). The assessment of the results of the Village has been a little more complete than for most of the other therapeutic communities, but even so was lacking in detail. After selecting 272 promising addicts, only 22 had managed to stay in the community long enough to "graduate" back to society. What happened to the 22 people subsequently is not known due to lack of follow-up. It was known that four had relapsed in one way or another and therefore the highest possible success rate in terms of total abstinence could only have been about 7 per cent of the original total.

Phoenix House

The Phoenix House community is a residential organisation in New York City, drawing on much the same clientele as Synanon and Daytop, but it attracts a particularly high proportion of young people. It runs in very much the same way as Synanon with encounter groups three times a week, and it insists on its members working as part of their treatment. The house is drug-free and anyone bringing in or using drugs in the house is treated very harshly and may have their heads shaved although, as in Synanon, violence is otherwise forbidden.

Christie (1973) has reported on the operation of Alpha House in Portsmouth, U.K., which is run broadly on the lines of Phoenix House.

Odyssey House

This is another New York-based facility which opened in 1967. Before an addict is admitted to Odyssey House he goes through a phase of induction that is designed to inform him of the method of operation of the community and to assess his suitability for it. By way of contrast to the other communities, Odyssey House employs both psychiatrists and psychologists and carries out daily urine checks for drug use. The group meetings occur daily and are encounter groups. On discharge from the house, or "re-entry", the addict has to agree to a prolonged follow-up period, including two sessions of group therapy per week for two years.

Mahon (1973) has criticised the operation of the above therapeutic communities, comparing the techniques used with brainwashing methods. There is a lack of re-socialisation into a role acceptable by the general public by all these communities, except for Odyssey House which has a prime aim of returning people to society. Mahon feels that by failing to prepare their clients for life outside the community, Synanon and similar organisations are really doing their clients a disservice.

AGENCIES WHOSE CLIENTELE INCLUDES MANY ADDICTS

The Department of Health and Social Security

The Department of Health and Social Security in the U.K. deals with many alcoholics and addicts by virtue of their being unemployed and in need of financial support. As such, the Department does not offer care but is responsible for maintaining and operating Reception Centres. These Centres are the remnants of the Casual Wards or "spikes", described vividly by George Orwell in 1933. A census of the largest remaining centre in Britain was carried out by Edwards *et al.* (1967). Approximately 300 people stay at the Centre in Peckham each night, most of them only for an overnight stay but some on a more permanent basis.

Of the 279 men interviewed, some 20 per cent were found to be chemically dependent on alcohol. At the time of the survey, drug dependence was minimal: 3 per cent of the sample reported taking an amphetamine/barbiturate mixture on a regular basis but only two subjects had taken opiates. One-quarter of the men had been in mental hospitals for conditions other than alcoholism and almost 60 per cent had been in jail, usually for minor offences.

A number of subgroups were identified in the sample. Those men born in London had held on to social contacts longer and were less likley to be pathological drinkers than the immigrants to London. It was suggested that the London-born men might be in the Centre as a result of personality inadequacy, plus stress, whereas the immigrant men were there because of more marked psychopathology, which could be compounded by a drinking problem. Another group consisted of those arriving late in life, again largely due to social inadequacy rather than real psychopathology.

In many ways, the alcoholic in the Reception Centre is like the skid-row alcoholic. According to Tidmarsh (quoted by Zacune and Hensman, 1971), 500 new alcoholics pass through a single reception centre each year. The recognition of these men as alcoholics and the availability of a rehabilitation programme based on hostels might well prevent the total breakdown of a proportion of them and return them to society.

The Salvation Army

The Salvation Army has operated hostels for homeless men and women for many years. They also run a two-level system for semi-permanent residents and for people staying for one night. In Toronto, the Salvation Army is involved in running a detox centre and three residential centres are being specifically opened for women over the age of sixteen.

Prison service

The prison service receives people into prison convicted of offences that in many cases are related directly or indirectly to alcoholism. Arnold (1969) stated that of 160 men being received at Pentonville each month with sentences of three months or less, 56 per cent had committed a drunkenness offence. Some 280 men per month enter Pentonville with sentences of longer than three months and of these approximately one-quarter have a drinking problem. Pentonville is the only prison designated to receive men serving short sentences and has a largely recidivist population. From the study of Hensman (1969) it follows that the prison population is likely to contain a large proportion of alcoholics.

Although prison would seem to be an unlikely choice for anyone contemplating the treatment of alcoholics, Arnold put forward his view that a prison setting offers many advantages over a hostel system. The advantages he detailed were the enforced sobriety, the motivation of the prisoner to abstain and the presence of interested full-time staff. A.A. is a part of the Pentonville treatment plan and is also available in many other prisons throughout Britain.

The advantages of the prison system are not to be found solely in prisons. The broad characteristics of the clientele and the staff are comparable to those found in addiction units. Sobriety is enforced in these (though presumably not so completely as in prison), the patients are well-motivated and the staff usually interested in helping the alcoholic. There would appear to be no specific advantage to the treatment of alcoholics in prison and perhaps treatment in a special unit under a Probation Order (Section 4 of the Criminal Justices Act 1948) would be appropriate for some recurrent drunkenness offenders. Naturally, where society has to be protected for a time whilst a prisoner is rehabilitated, then prison is the appropriate place but the therapeutic advantages do not lie in the setting of prison being conducive to treatment. The benefit of the system described by Arnold accrues to the individual alcoholic prisoner who is fortunate enough to be committed to an institution that has a programme run by interested people.

Ex-convicts rehabilitation services

Ex-convicts rehabilitation services already fulfil a very useful purpose and are well-placed to develop services for the alcoholic returning to society. The recidivist alcoholic is likely to need a great deal of intensive rehabilitation aimed at re-socialising him. Without this rehabilitation he will return to the outside world as a homeless, jobless man with no family. It is well known that the less well-socialised an alcoholic is, the more likely he is to return to drinking and, in this group of men, to jail.

Addicts to opiates and other substances may spend time in jail for such offences as the possession and the selling of illicit drugs. In Britain, such individuals are managed along with the rest of the prisoners. In the U.S.A. two federally-run farms were opened at Fort Worth, Texas, and Lexington, Kentucky. Lexington was opened in 1935 and Fort Worth shortly after. The farm at Lexington holds about 1,000 people, both men and women, and although it was termed a farm and officially named a Public Health Service Hospital, it is actually a prison. Approximately one-third of the patients go to Lexington voluntarily. The facility has an international reputation for its work on the treatment and rehabilitation of narcotic addicts and is presently being run by the National Institute for Mental Health.

The majority of the inmates in Lexington have been either black American or Puerto Rican in origin. The results from treatment in the hospital were initially announced to be very promising, but a follow-up study by Vaillant (1965) showed that of 100 patients provided with aftercare, all of those who did not die in the follow-up period of twelve years had begun to take narcotics again. A group of 53 Puerto Rican addicts, followed up by De Fleur and his colleagues (1969) over an average period of sixteen years, relapsed in 75 per cent of cases. Relapse was found to be closely related to life patterns. One group was characterised by deviancy in early life and arrests before addiction, little employment and arrests for pushing narcotics: of these people all returned to taking narcotics. Another group with few arrests, good adjustment after treatment and a record of steady employment, had a prolonged abstinence period in 66 per cent of cases. A third group that fell between the other two in terms of its social characteristics had a recovery rate of 28 per cent.

A point to which we shall return in the next chapter is that it is not usually very helpful to describe the effects of a given programme of treatment for a group if the treated group consists of a heterogeneous mixture of many subgroups. The above programme worked well for one group and was a total failure for the other. A change in a programme aimed at improving the overall rate of success may lessen the very good results in the socialised group but still give rise to a better total result. It is arguable whether this represents a beneficial outcome.

Probation service

The probation service comes into contact with alcoholics and addicts in a number of ways. Drunkenness and drug offenders are referred for follow-up and for rehabilitation to the probation service, and alcoholics who go to Information Centres have frequently also sought the help of the probation service. A probation officer will often be responsible for the care of undiagnosed alcoholics and excessive drinkers who are beginning to commit offences under the influence of alcohol, or of people already embarked on a criminal career whose drinking is becoming out of hand. A study of the clients of the probation services along the lines of the Wilkins general practice study (*see* p. 167) would probably identify many people at risk of developing alcoholism.

Despite their lack of formal psychotherapeutic training, probation officers support many thousands of alcoholics and addicts. A survey of the affiliation of delegates attending the First International Conference on Alcoholism and Drug Dependence in

Liverpool in 1971 revealed that the largest single group was composed of probation officers and there was also a considerable proportion of prison and police officers. The probation service has recognised the problem it faces with its alcoholic clientele and appears to be taking steps to obtain more education and training in the field.

AGENCIES DEALING INDIRECTLY WITH PROBLEMS OF ADDICTION

Practically any service that deals with the public can be categorised under this heading. With one per cent of the population being alcoholic and thousands more being dependent on other drugs, every community service must come into contact with either the person who is drug-dependent or with one of his family.

The local authority social services were reorganised as a result of the Seebohm report (1968). The recommendations of the Seebohm committee were that the newly-organised social services departments under a Director of Social Services should take over the functions of virtually ail the statutory social work agencies. Their work now includes that carried out by the former childrens departments, services for the old and disabled, welfare and child guidance, home helps, mental welfare, adult training centres, day nurseries and some work done by housing departments. By centralising the services it was expected that anyone in need of local-authority social work help would know precisely where to go to obtain it and thereby the services would probably reach a greater proportion of people in need. A single service looking after the needs of an area of 50,000 to 100,0000 from infancy to old age could, with appropriate facilities, identify the effects of the development of alcoholism or drug dependence in those people presenting for help. The social service departments have contact with the schools and with family medical practitioners and can call upon the services of consultant psychiatrists and paediatricians. Such an array of contact with a family should make it possible for a family that is experiencing difficulties to be recognised before it reaches the crisis stage. Whether or not this happens depends on a great many factors and unfortunately at present it is being seriously inhibited by lack of resources contingent on financial restrictions.

Few local authority social workers have had special training in the field of addiction and to expect them to be able to identify the alcoholics on their case-load, without further education, is unrealistic. The trained and interested social worker is in the ideal position to identify the early alcoholic or addict, to recommend a treatment agency or institute a referral to an Information Centre, and then to assist in rehabilitation should it be necessary. We must hope that a spirit of mistrust and competition for the care of the addict will not arise between the voluntary agencies in the field and the statutory agencies but, instead, they will co-operate to use their respective expertise to the advantage of the addict.

Other agencies to which the alcoholic or his family may turn include marriage guidance councils, citizens advice bureaus and the N.S.P.C.C. Clergymen fairly frequently come into contact with addicts or their wives who go to the Church for aid at times of crisis, and alcoholics quite often report that they have attempted to become involved in religion as a way of solving their drinking problems. The recovering alcoholic, particularly if involved in the spiritual aspect of A.A., is likely to have a bias towards becoming involved in religion as an aid to his rehabilitation. Clergymen can be of great help to the alcoholic if they adopt an open-minded approach to his problem but interpreting alcoholism or addiction in terms of "sin" will usually alienate the person who is making a determined effort to gain, or keep, his sobriety. Practical help is provided directly to alcoholics by some churches in large cities, by means of soup kitchens or overnight hostels in church crypts. One of the most successful hospitals in the field of the treatment of drug dependence in Britain is the nursing home at Spelthorne St. Mary, in Surrey, which is an Anglican community for female alcoholics and addicts.

The prison and police forces have already been mentioned as having a great deal of contact with alcoholics. Lawyers could sometimes detect alcoholics, not only because of their criminal activities but also as a result of information gained in the process of the application for legal separation and divorce proceedings. Instead of simply continuing with the process of law necessary to obtain a divorce, an interested lawyer could offer advice for dealing with the root of the problem in marriages that are breaking down because of one partner's addiction. This fortunately is happening in an increasing number of cases.

SUMMARY

At present, alcoholics who are fairly intact socially appear to turn to the medical profession when looking for help with their drinking problem. Doctors could do a great deal more in recognising both early and late alcoholics and referring them for expert treatment. With regard to drug dependence, the medical profession is undoubtedly responsible for creating many addicts, particularly with the almost indiscriminate prescription of barbiturates and tranquillisers.

Social work agencies are well equipped to complement the medical profession both in detection and management. However, doctors and social workers have to appreciate that dealing with the physical or social complications of alcoholism does not help to the extent that tackling the roots of these problems could do. Despite the increasing acceptance of addicts as being sick, many people in the helping professions find themselves unable to deal with the problem directly. The feeling that addicts and alcoholics are weak-willed and deserve all they get still lingers amongst doctors, nurses and social workers. There is also the feeling that addicts never recover and therefore are not worth the very considerable effort that goes into treating them. This is certainly true of the response of addicts to a disorganised, uninterested approach to their problems, but as we shall see in the next chapter, the results of well-planned, broadly-based treatments can be beneficial to the client and gratifying to the therapist.

An informal inquiry, but one which has gone on for some years, into the opinions of medical students, trainee psychiatrists, social-work students and laymen about their expectations of success in treating alcoholics, has revealed that most of those questioned expect something like a 5 or 10 per cent recovery rate. This probably reflects the experience these people have had in observing the effect of alcoholics being ineffectively treated. In fact, a programme designed to produce prolonged sobriety nowadays is usually able to obtain at least a 30 per cent recovery rate. Persuading people who come into contact with alcoholics that they can significantly help one-third to a half of their clients may well affect their attitudes in a positive way and thus increase the chances of the patient obtaining appropriate treatment and achieving lasting sobriety.

A recent study by Hunt and Azrin (1973) has demonstrated how manipulating the social deterrents to drinking can affect the chances of an alcoholic's staying dry. These workers postulated that alcoholic drinking would be affected by the postponement or withdrawal of events or factors that ordinarily act as positive reinforcers. The reinforcers they used were events such as sexual intercourse, mixing with friends and being paid for working.

Each alcoholic in the study group had the benefits of help with job finding, legal counselling, vocational counselling, marriage and family counselling, social counselling and the provision of facilities such as a telephone, radio and newspapers at home. The first month's payment on all of these facilities was provided, but it was up to the alcoholic to keep up subsequent payments. The other people concerned with the alcoholic were involved in the treatment that was based on their degree of co-operation. For example, the wives of all the alcoholics made sexual interaction dependent on total abstinence from drink. Whilst the alcoholics were sober, they could enjoy a full social and family life, but if they drank, the benefits would immediately be removed.

A comparison of the reinforcement group with a control series over a six-month period showed that the active-treatment group did significantly better in relation to the time spent drinking, time employed, time away from the family and the time spent in institutions. The groups were admittedly very small, only eight patients in each and the effort required was fairly massive, but only one patient in the reinforcement group did not respond. He was of low I.Q., single, lived with an alcoholic father and had very few social contacts.

The treatment described was based on a hospital group but only because they had happened to be admitted for drying out. After the initial withdrawal period, the whole of the treatment was in the hands of counsellors and social workers. Although the treatment group was very small, the study demonstrated how social agencies might use their resources and those within the patient's family in order to influence pathological drinking. This study will have to be confirmed by others before it can be declared a successful method of treatment, but it does point to one means by which the social worker could be of great help to the alcoholic and his family.

REFERENCES

Arnold, A., "Alcohol in Prison: Pentonville", in Gath, D., Cook, T. and Hensman, Celia, (eds.), op. cit.

Brecher, E. M., *Licit and Illicit Drugs,* Little, Brown and Co., Boston, Mass., 1972.

Cahn, S., "Alcoholism Halfway Houses: Relationship to Other Programs and Facilities", *Social Work,* 14 (2): 50–60, 1969.

Christie, I. G., "Alpha House, Synanon, Phoenix House, U.S.A., British Alcoholism and Psychopathic Units: A Comparison of their Principles and Practices", a Paper read at the Second International Conference on Alcoholism and Drug Dependence, Liverpool, April, 1973.

Cook, T., Morgan, H. G. and Pollak, B., "The Rathcoole Experiment: First Year at a Hostel for Vagrant Alcoholics", *British Medical Journal,* i: 240–2, 1968.

Cook, T. and Pollak, B., *In Place of Skid Row: The Rathcoole Experiment—The First Two Years,* National Association for the Care and Resettlement of Offenders, London, 1970.

De Fleur, L. B., Ball, J. C. and Snarr, R. W., "The Long-Term Social Correlates of Opiate Addiction", *Social Problems,* 17 (2): 225–34, 1969.

Edwards, G. and Guthrie, S., "A Controlled Trial of In-Patient and Out-Patient Treatment of Alcohol Dependence", *Lancet,* i: 555–9, 1967.

Edwards, G., Hawker, A., Williamson, V. and Hensman, Celia, "London's Skid Row", *Lancet,* i: 249–52, 1966(*a*).

Edwards, G., Hensman, Celia, Hawker, A. and Wilkinson, V., "Who Goes to Alcoholics Anonymous?" *Lancet,* ii: 382, 1966(*b*).

Edwards, G., Kellog-Fisher, M., Hawker, A. and Hensman, Celia, "Clients of Alcoholism Centres", *Br. Med. J.,* 4: 346–50, 1967.

Fox, R. P., Graham, Marie B. and Gill, M. J., "A Therapeutic Revolving Door", *Archives of General Psychiatry,* 26: 179–82, 1972.

Gath, D., Cook, T. and Hensman, Celia, (eds.), *The Drunkenness Offence,* Pergamon, Oxford, 1969.

Hensman, Celia, "Problems of Drunkenness Amongst Male Recidivists", in Gath, D., Cook, T. and Hensman, Celia, (eds.), op. cit.

Hunt, G. M. and Azrin, N. H., "A Community Reinforcement Approach to Alcoholism", *Behaviour Research and Therapy,* II: 91–104, 1973.

Ingram-Smith, N., "Prospects for the Future in the Community", in Grath, D., Cook, T. and Hensman, Celia, (eds.), op. cit.

Le Dain Commission, *Cannabis: A Report of the Commission of Inquiry into the Non-Medical Use of Drugs,* Information Canada, Ottawa, 1972.

Mahon, T., "Therapy or Brainwashing?", *Drugs and Society,* 2 (5): 7–10, 1973.

Orwell, G., *Down and Out in Paris and London,* Gollancz, London, 1933.

Pollak, B., "Rathcoole House—An Experiment in Rehabilitation", in Gath, D., Cook, T. and Hensman, Celia, (eds.), op. cit.

Seebohm committee, *Local Authority and Allied Personal Social Services*, H.M.S.O., London, 1968.

Tiebout, H. M., in *A.A. Comes of Age*, A.A. World Services, New York, 1944.

Vaillant, G. E., "A Twelve Year Follow-Up of New York Narcotic Addicts", *American Journal of Psychiatry*, 122: 729, 1965.

Yablonsky, L., *The Tunnel Back: Synanon*, Macmillan, New York, 1965.

Yalom, I. D. (ed.), *The Theory and Practice of Group Psychotherapy*, Basic Books, New York, 1970.

Yalom, I. D., Tinklinberg, J. and Gilula, M., "Curative Factors in Group Therapy", in Yalom, I. D. (ed.) op. cit.

Zacune, J. and Hensman, Celia, *Drugs, Alcohol and Tobacco in Britain*, Heinemann, London, 1971.

10 Outcome of treatment

Alcoholism

In this section of the chapter we will consider the natural history of alcoholism, the aims of treatment, treatment methods, the success rates of the different methods and the prediction of the outcome of treatment. The treatment of withdrawal states has been discussed earlier and will be omitted here.

NATURAL HISTORY

The progression of alcoholism, from social drinking through the stages of excessive drinking to chronic alcoholism, was detailed in Chapter 6. The natural history of a disorder describes the events that take place in untreated cases of the disorder and in alcoholism there is a paucity of information in this area.

It is well documented that alcoholics die earlier than expected, from a variety of causes. Lemere (1953) in a retrospective study examined the outcome of alcoholism in 500 deceased alcoholics who had not received treatment. He found that the average age at death was fifty-two. He also found that a considerable proportion of the alcoholics had stopped, or controlled, their drinking before they died. This study has the disadvantage of being retrospective and of being based on second-hand information from relatives, but according to his findings, Lemere reported that only 28 per cent of alcoholics drank themselves to death, 33 per cent stopped altogether, though most of these were in a terminal illness at the time and 10 per cent regained some degree of control. For the remaining 29 per cent, drinking was a problem throughout the rest of their lives.

Considering the effectiveness of treatment solely in terms of abstinence, a treatment regime should be able to improve on the 11 per cent rate of those who stopped drinking without being in a terminal illness, or it cannot be said to have had any effect on the natural course of the illness.

AIMS OF TREATMENT

The aims of treatment in alcoholism have to be formulated in terms of the aims for the individual, for his family and for society in general.

Individual aims

At present the basic aim in treating an alcoholic is to make him stop drinking, which is fairly easy, and then having done that, prevent him from returning to drinking, which is more difficult.

From Lemere's study it can be seen that a small proportion of alcoholics appear to be able to control their drinking within social limits, instead of having to abstain totally. Lemere's work can be criticised on many grounds, but others have also shown that some alcoholics do seem to be able to revert to controlled drinking. Davies (1962) reported eleven cases of patients suffering from apparently genuine alcoholism who became social drinkers and did so without prolonged treatment or alteration of their basic personality. Gerard and Saenger (1966) found that 35 of their 797 patients were drinking in a controlled manner at the end of a year's follow-up. The patients studied were, with one exception, people who had had severe drinking problems at the time of intake, as shown by repeated drunkenness, physical ill-health due to drinking, problems at work or at home due to alcohol, and drunkenness arrests. Thus it is highly likely that they were true alcoholics. Davies (1973) stated that the recovery to normal drinking in alcoholics who present for treatment is in the region of 7 to 14 per cent of cases and in those who do not present, it may well be higher.

Why, then, insist on abstinence? Clinical experience shows that most alcoholics who try to go back to social drinking are not able to control their drinking for any length of time. As was stated earlier, most gamma alcoholics have tried to control their drinking and have failed on many occasions before they reach treatment. Perhaps those who present for treatment are a selected group who come for treatment primarily because they cannot regain control, whereas others may succeed in controlling their drinking and thus never do need to present for treatment.

Role expectancy may play a part in alcoholics' losing control again, after a period of abstinence. In A.A., alcoholics are taught that the first drink inevitably leads on to others and the same implication is made by most people treating alcoholics. That behaviour under the influence of alcohol varies with the expectation of the peer group and general society has been clearly demonstrated by MacAndrew and Edgerton (1969); we have already discussed this topic in some detail in Chapter 3. It is part of the folklore of alcoholism that having one drink sets off a train of events that inevitably leads on to a physical craving for more alcohol. Controlled experiments have failed to confirm that "craving" occurs, or that alcoholics are precipitated into a bout of uncontrolled drinking by drinking alcohol, even in fairly considerable amounts (Mendelson, Mello and Solomon, 1968).

The concept of "loss of control" has been debated most eloquently by Keller (1972). He argues that to consider "loss of control" to be simply the inevitable precipitation of a bout of alcoholic drinking by the consumption of one, or a few, drinks is limited and erroneous. "Loss of control" for Keller includes the inability to abstain, the inability to stop and, most importantly, the inability to choose whether or not to take a drink. It is this last point that he considers to be indicative of alcoholism as a disease. He points out that it is common knowledge that addicted alcoholics can and do drink in an apparently controlled manner for long periods, but that when some unknown factor affects them, then they demonstrate loss of control. The factors that finally precipitate the bout may be a psychological upset, a constellation of social occurrences, or a response to certain blood-alcohol levels, which become the cue for an addictive response.

State-dependent learning, in which the response shown by an organism depends on the internal state of the organism, may partly explain the phenomenon of loss of control (Storm and Smart, 1965). The experimental evidence for the effects of state dependency is inconclusive at present, but it can be shown to occur in normal humans under the effects of various drugs (Ley, Jain, Swinson *et al.,* 1972). The idea that further drinking might be dependent on the blood-alcohol concentration (B.A.C.) gives rise to the possibility of being able to train alcoholics to recognise when they have a high B.A.C. and to stop drinking at that point. Lovibond and Caddy (1970) have demonstrated that alcoholics can learn to drink up to a point when their B.A.C. is 70 mg/100 ml. The subjects in the study were told that self-control in drinking was important and they were given electric shocks if their B.A.C. went over a level of 65 mg/100 ml.

Drinking behaviour in terms of the types of drink, the length of time spent drinking each one, and the size of the sips taken, are all facets of alcoholism that may be conditionable and thereby allow alcoholics to return to social drinking patterns. Some of these aspects are now under investigation.

Aims for the family

Merely to stop, or control, his drinking is not enough of a change for the alcoholic to make. For example, the patient we called Sam in Chapter 6 did become abstinent with the aid of oral Antabuse and has so far remained dry for three months. However, he is not yet working and is not making any attempts to look for work. He is still not at home much, but is spending his time with his old drinking friends at the Service Club. In short, all he has done so far is to stop drinking. His marriage is no better, he is not working on his reasons for drinking, and it would seem almost certain that he will start to drink again.

The alcoholic has to re-adjust to a paternal role in the family over a period of time. This has far-reaching implications for the mother and the children and they usually need a period to accept this change. There is likely to be a delay in the acceptance of the sober alcoholic because the families know only too well that on previous occasions, spells of sobriety have always been followed by further spells of alcoholic drinking. Many alcoholics have lost their families and some attempt to reunite the family when they regain sobriety. The adjustments necessary in such families are even greater than in those that managed to stay together through the drinking spells.

General adjustment

The norm for middle-aged men in Western society is to be married, living with a wife and two or three children and to have a steady job. The norm for the sober alcoholic includes all of these factors, so the well-adjusted, sober alcoholic should be able to hold down a job, support his family, not fall into trouble with the police, not gamble excessively, and so on.

In setting the optimal aims for an individual alcoholic, the therapist has to take into account the proposed future drinking behaviour (usually total abstinence), the patient's social and family situation, his intellectual ability, his personality make-up, job skills, physical ailments and possible psychiatric disorders, in addition to his alcoholism. Great emphasis is put on abstinence as a measure of the success of any particular treatment and in many studies this is the only factor measured. This stress on abstinence as the basis for success is not misplaced because, unless an alcoholic does stop drinking, it is unusual for him to make adjustments or gains in other areas. The hypothesis that solving an alcoholic's problems so that his drinking will come to an end as a consequence has little support in practice. But with some alcoholics (it is not yet possible to predict which) it may be necessary to accept that total abstinence is an unreasonable goal and the therapist has to settle for aiming to achieve a more stabilised, if not totally controlled, pattern of drinking.

TREATMENT METHODS

Drugs

The drugs used specifically to prevent the alcoholic from drinking are Antabuse (disulfiram), Abstem (citrated calcium carbide) and Flagyl (metronidazole). The use of these drugs has been discussed in Chapter 8. Antabuse and Abstem are useful for the patient who wants to stop drinking but finds he is unable to stay dry for more than a few days at a time. Giving Antabuse is not enough in itself as treatment. The therapist has also to take advantage of the spell of sobriety to help the alcoholic find ways of remaining abstinent.

Flagyl was suggested as a treatment for alcoholism by Taylor (1964). Initially, a number of uncontrolled trials appeared to support the usefulness of the drug but most of the later controlled trials showed that it was little more effective than a placebo. A double-blind study by one of us (Swinson, 1971), confirmed the usefulness of the drug in a group of 60 male alcoholics but the place of Flagyl in the treatment of alcoholism is still questionable.

LSD has been used extensively in the past in the treatment of many psychiatric disorders, including alcoholism. Many claims were made of its outstanding usefulness in this setting and it was hypothesised that, under the influence of LSD, alcoholics would gain insight into their psychic mal-functioning, which could be used to advantage in psychotherapy. The usefulness of LSD was critically examined by Smart and his co-workers (1967) who found that the drug offered no advantages over the other forms of treatment employed in their trial and since it has itself so many dangers its use does not appear justified.

Psychotherapy

The term "psychotherapy" has been applied to so many different methods of treating so many varieties of patients that a review of its use in the treatment of alcoholism is almost meaningless. The problems of assessing the outcome of treatment become even greater in considering the effects of psychotherapy. With a drug there is comparatively little variation in the treatment from one therapist to another, although admittedly the depth and quality of the doctor-patient relationship is still very important. In psychotherapy, the treatment is based almost entirely on the relationship between the therapist and the patient and is therefore open to endless variation, depending upon the characteristics of the therapist. The schools of psychotherapy all have different theoretical orientations, which might be expected to produce some variation in the efficacy of their treatments although research has shown that this is a less important factor than the personal characteristics of the therapist.

A great deal has been written about the efficacy, or lack of efficacy, of psychotherapy in general, following Eysenck's critical review in 1952. Eysenck was unable to find support for the idea that psychotherapy was superior to no treatment at all. Needless to say, his observations did not go unchallenged and a review of the present situation regarding the efficacy of psychotherapy in treating psychiatric illness as a whole has been published by Bergin (1971). Bergin's conclusions were that psychotherapy was probably helpful in some cases but that other cases were not affected by the process of treatment and in a number of cases, actual harm was done to the patient.

The efficacy of therapists has been found to vary widely and the pairing of particular therapists with particular patients has also been found to affect the outcome of treatment. Although therapists from different schools, for example, client-centred, psycho-analytic and existential schools, have different theoretical methods of operating, examination of what they actually do with patients reveals that they tend to operate in very similar ways. Successful therapists are characterised by warmth, the ability to be genuinely sympathetic and understanding, and are people who give help quickly and constructively. Truax and Mitchell (1971), who have reviewed these findings, also consider that the therapist's personality is of more importance than his techniques, in predicting the outcome of therapy. The techniques of psychotherapy are not unimportant since, at the very least, a therapist needs a conceptual framework within which to practise, which provides consistency for himself and his patients. He should not, however, allow the framework to become more important than those parts of the therapy that have been shown to be effective.

Reports of the efficacy of psychotherapy in the treatment of alcoholism have produced widely-varying results. This is not surprising, considering the variation in clientele, the stages of alcoholism reached, the type of alcoholism, therapist variables, outcome assessment variables and the length of the follow-up. The reliability of the assessment methods used has also varied greatly and has at times bordered on the naïve.

Hill and Blane (1967) reviewed 49 studies that examined the effects of psychotherapy in alcoholism. The vast majority of the studies were retrospective in nature and therefore open to considerable bias. Only two studies were prospective and of the 49 only three could be described as meeting the demands necessary for a properly controlled trial. None of the studies used a "no-treatment" control group, and because of this and the various other uncertainties, Hill and Blane said that they could reach no definite conclusion about the effects of psychotherapy, beneficial or otherwise.

Group psychotherapy

This form of treatment has become the cornerstone of therapy for alcoholics in recent years, particularly for those alcoholics who are admitted to the special addiction units.

Group psychotherapy also varies in the way it is conducted, the number of times a week the group meets, the length of treatment and so on. An overview of the efficacy of group psychotherapy in alcoholism would produce little in the way of meaningful results due to the averaging of all these variables.

Treatment in groups is commonly used as part of the in-patient treatment of alcoholics and this will be discussed below. It may also be used as the main mode of managing alcoholics who do not need admission to hospital. In either situation, the usual arrangement is to have a therapist, and perhaps a co-therapist, in a group together with about eight patients. Depending on the therapist and the type of patients, the group may concentrate on discussion and deal with practical problems in the everyday life of an alcoholic, or it may be set up to deal primarily with the emotional problems of each member as these become evident in the group setting. For an easily-read explanation of many facets of group psychotherapy the interested reader is referred to Walton (1971).

Hypnosis

Hypnotherapy has been widely used in the treatment of psychiatric disorders. It does not appear to have any advantages over other forms of treatment and it has not been shown to be particularly effective in alcoholism.

Behavioural therapy

Psychotherapy is concerned with uncovering reasons for a patient's difficulties and persuading him to change his behaviour as a result of the understanding of feelings and behaviour that he gains through insight.

Behaviour therapy, on the other hand, is concerned with modifying behaviour as a primary aim and the methods used are based on the work of a number of learning theorists. Behaviour therapists and traditional psychotherapists have frequently clashed over the relative effectiveness and correctness of their respective therapies. Behaviour therapy is experimentally-based and offers hypotheses of the causes of abnormal behaviour which are tested out in clinical practice. Traditional psychotherapists tend to feel that human beings cannot be understood in terms of laws derived from animal experimentation and consider that people are unique individuals requiring individual understanding. The measures used by behaviour therapists to show that treatment does have an effect have often been criticised by psychotherapists as being irrelevant and superficial.

The most frequently used form of behaviour therapy in alcoholism has been aversion therapy. The aim of aversion therapy is to pair an unpleasant occurrence (aversive stimulus) with the piece of behaviour that it is wished to eliminate. The aversive stimulus can be an electric shock, a very loud noise or the onset of nausea. Also, as described in Chapter 9, the technique of covert sensitisation may be used.

Voegtlin (1940) described the use of apomorphine to produce vomiting in close temporal association with the drinking of alcohol. The onset of paralysis in full consciousness by means of a curare-like drug was similarly used by Madill and his co-workers (1966). Group aversion therapy has also been employed (Miller and colleagues, 1960).

Aversion therapy of itself has not, so far, offered any great advance in the treatment of alcoholism. It works as well, in those cases reported, as other forms of treatment and frequently is quicker to perform. The emphasis of behaviour therapy in alcoholism is moving away from a simple, straightforward aversive treatment, to the use of aversion in a broader treatment setting which pays attention to other aspects of the patient's total behaviour (McBrearty, Dichter, Garfield and Heath, 1968) and also to non-aversive training procedures.

Hospital treatment

Many alcoholics receive short-term treatment in hospital that may appear to be too superficial and brief to have any effect on the course of the condition, but many authors have found that even a very brief hospital stay can have a positive effect on the progress of the alcoholic (Pattison, 1966).

The progress of the patients treated in a general psychiatric ward and followed for two years was studied by Davies, Shepherd and Myers (1956). The therapy was on an individual basis and included the use of drugs, A.A. and close contact with the therapist. After two years 36 per cent of the 50 patients were totally or almost totally abstinent and 42 per cent were improved in that they performed better in their jobs and family setting, although they continued to drink. Rathod and his colleagues (1966) also followed up a series of patients for two years in whom the main treatment employed had been group psychotherapy. Of the series of 111 patients admitted to the Alcoholism Unit at Warlingham Park, U.K., 106 were followed up, of whom 52 per cent remained abstinent for at least a year; 43 of these 56 abstainers remained "dry" for the whole of the follow-up period.

Out-patient treatment has been found by Edwards and Guthrie (1967) to compare well with in-patient treatment in a one-year follow-up trial comparing 8 to 9 weeks of in-patient care with 7 to 8 weeks of intensive out-patient treatment. However, the patients in both groups were fairly well integrated socially and had family contacts. The out-patient treatment of alcoholics was evaluated by Gerard and Saenger (1966) who examined the methods and outcome of eight treatment programmes in the U.S.A. The programmes varied widely in enthusiasm, orientation and the facilities available and the treatment personnel variously included psychiatrists, physicians and social workers. The report is a very detailed account of a massive piece of work in seeing and following up almost 800 alcoholics and only an outline of the findings can be mentioned here. Of the 797 patients initially in the study, 602 were available for follow-up. The investigators found that many of the patients had changed during treatment and the change was often in the direction of improvement; but at the time of follow-up, only 18 per cent were abstinent or were able to control their drinking, 13 per cent were in institutions and 2·4 per cent had died by the time of follow-up. Overall, it appeared that more patients had improved in the year after intake than had deteriorated and Gerard and Saenger considered that had treatment not been received, then perhaps more patients would have deteriorated. But as mentioned above, Lemere found that a proportion of alcoholics do improve without treatment and since there was no comparison with a "no-treatment" group in this study it is not possible to state that treatment helped to any great degree. However, Gerard and Saenger did find that patients having a lot of contact with the treatment agency were likely to do better than those having little contact but they noted that the number of visits was of more importance in predicting outcome than the total time in weeks in contact with the agency.

The treatment of alcoholics in special addiction units has been described by many authors (Glatt, 1959; Evans, 1967; Ritson and Hassall, 1970). The Edinburgh unit is typical of the 14 units currently existing in the U.K. in that its treatment is based on short-term withdrawal, followed by a period of in-patient group psychotherapy and milieu therapy, with the administration of Antabuse, and then follow-up for a year. Such units tend to attract a specific kind of patient who is fairly well intact socially, is in the upper half of the social scale, is not too psychopathic and is well-motivated to abstain. Given the characteristics of the patients, the prognoses can be expected to be quite good.

A comparison was made between 50 patients admitted to the Edinburgh unit and 50 patients treated solely as out-patients, followed up for twelve months; 48 per cent of those treated as in-patients remained abstinent for a year as did 42 per cent of the out-patients. As already described, a number of studies have reported achieving equally good results from out-patient as from in-patient treatment and the special units have not as yet shown that they improve the prognosis of a particular kind of alcoholic. It can be hypothesised that the staff of an in-patient unit will be highly motivated to treat alcoholics and that the non-specific enthusiasm and expertise will rub off on those patients treated in the out-patient programme of a special unit and this may well be true. The special units tend to have developed or attracted many community resources around themselves and these are available for the out-patient. For example, in the Liverpool region, the unit at Moston

Hospital directed by Dr. J. S. Madden was in existence before, and was instrumental in the establishment of, the Merseyside Council on Alcoholism which is now a successful treatment agency in its own right. The efficacy of the special units cannot therefore be judged solely in terms of how many alcoholics they assist to remain abstinent for one year. Their influence in setting up other services and in educating the public and other professionals has also to be taken into account.

Alcoholics Anonymous

The efficacy of A.A. is impossible to assess in any rigorous way. Those people who stay in the programme for any length of time appear to do well but they are a highly-selected group. A.A. carried out a survey of over 11,000 members in North America in 1968; 60 per cent of the respondents said they had been abstinent for over a year and 25 per cent claimed to have been abstinent for more than five years. These rates have to be considered against the general expectation of members of A.A. that they and other members should be abstinent and in this kind of survey there is the possibility of a great deal of bias towards reporting abstinence where it does not exist. Also, one would expect the successful abstainers to respond; the unsuccessful would either ignore the survey or be unreached by it.

PREDICTORS OF OUTCOME

Treatment probably does have a favourable effect on the outcome of alcoholism and can be expected to produce long-lasting abstinence or improvement in 30 to 50 per cent of the patients treated. The different types of treatment do not appear to produce markedly different success rates unless the clientele to which the treatment is applied is a selected one. Kissin and Platz (1970) have gone some way in determining which patients do best in which treatment. They found that psychotherapy was most effective for the socially and psychologically stable, drug therapy helped the socially stable but psychologically unsophisticated patients, and the socially unstable but intellectually intact did best in an in-patient rehabilitative setting.

Straus and Bacon (1951) in a study of 2,000 male alcoholics

found that outcome in alcoholism could be related to four measures of social and occupational stability:

1. Having held a steady job for over three years.
2. Living in the same town for over two years.
3. Living in one's own home or that of friends or relatives.
4. Being married and living with the spouse.

Alcoholics who fulfilled only one or none of these criteria did badly, while the rest did fairly well in the long term.

In Ritson and Hassall's study, the good prognosis out-patients were married, had attended A.A., were sober at the time of the first interview and had a long history of "loss of control" alcoholism. Older patients who started drinking late in life, and particularly those from classes I and II, did well in both in-patient and out-patient treatment. Poor prognosis was associated with previous suicide attempts and arrests, which probably indicates that the basic personality structure was of an impulsive type.

In Gerard and Saenger's study, outcome was independent of age, sex, race and educational status, whereas social stability at the time of entry into treatment was a good predictor of outcome. Patients with a high degree of social stability improved three times as readily as patients of low initial social stability. The other main factors indicating good prognosis were: continued and extensive contact with a clinic, the use of Antabuse, and being treated by a general physician rather than by any other professional. This last factor may be related to the finding that treatment designed to assist in behavioural change, especially with regard to drinking, seems to be more effective than trying to produce psychological change. In the U.K. more psychiatrists and social workers are more amenable to the concept of inducing practical behavioural changes than in the U.S.A., where the study was performed, and where the need for fundamental psychological change is stressed.

The motivation of alcoholics is frequently used as a reason (or excuse) for allowing patients into a treatment programme, or to explain their success or failure. The assessment of the motivation of a given patient towards treatment is very difficult. An apparently highly-motivated patient may present in this manner because of undisclosed pressures from external sources and a patient who appears low in motivation may do so through fear that he is not able to be helped, so rather than risk having his hopes dashed he presents in a superficially uninterested manner. Rosenberg (1973) has shown how the offering of frequent brief contacts with a therapeutic situation can influence the apparent motivation in a positive direction.

A frequent finding in the treatment of alcoholics is that many of them drop out after fewer than five sessions. This is a feature of all psychiatric treatment programmes. Rosenberg found that the patients who drop out of therapy exhibit low social stability, are young, are referred for treatment by other people, and have either hysterical or acting-out personality disorders. The therapists who experience the highest drop-out rates tend to be moralistic and reject people, offering a fragmented treatment programme that they do not explain to the patients. Therapy that is likely to have high drop-out is that which is not immediately available, does not relieve symptoms, and sets unrealistic goals.

The low socio-economic class, desocialised patient is at a great disadvantage in obtaining adequate therapy for his alcoholism. Patients do best when they are treated by therapists of similar social background, which means that therapists from classes IV and V should be trained and could probably be very useful in extending the scope of alcoholism treatment. The treatment programme has to take into account the immediate needs of the patient, and it should therefore be easily available in the community. It should offer a comprehensive plan of treatment that does not rely on the methods of any single theoretical school or approach. The treatment should have definite aims that are explained to, and understood by, the patient. It should involve the patient's family and be supported by agencies in society in general. Treatment should also continue for at least a year and preferably two years. This approach will not produce sobriety in all alcoholics but it will help many of them. It also indicates a hopeful attitude, which is important for the patient and for cultivating a favourable atmosphere for future research and development.

PREVENTION

Medicine has moved over the years from concentrating on treatment to being, increasingly, more concerned with prevention.

Psychiatry has not yet developed so far, although attempts are being made to improve the mental health of specific groups and thereby to reduce the incidence of psychiatric illness. There is no evidence yet that these attempts work to a significant degree. Prevention in the field of alcoholism as the result of social and legal measures has already been shown to be effective if one compares drinking habits now with those of two centuries ago but further, more effective, prevention is likely to be difficult to introduce. Wilkinson (1970) has proposed a programme for prevention in which changes in the law to make alcohol *more* available to adolescents, with emphasis on teaching them controlled drinking, would be a prime step. Advertising and promotion of alcohol would be controlled to remove the air of excessive masculinity from drinking practices and moderation would again be stressed. Places that at present are devoted solely to drinking would change their function and become principally eating or entertainment places. Wilkinson's rather Utopian proposals were set against an American background, which is very different from the British as regards the use of alcohol. Many of his ideas are already widespread throughout Britain and the changes he suggests would probably have a minimal effect on the prevalance of alcoholism in the U.K.

In the prevention of alcoholism, the main aims should be to reduce the total amount drunk at any time and to have strict controls on drunkenness. The ways in which these aims might be achieved include the use of legislation, education, taxation and advertising. In other words, quite apart from any directly therapeutic approach, a massive "social-engineering" campaign would be required and at present society is only beginning to accept that there is any need for this.

Drug Dependence

A review of the available literature on the response to treatment of drug abusers is more likely to confuse than enlighten. As with alcoholism, research on treatment outcome is beset with difficulties, and it will be seen that many studies are so grossly deficient in methodology that the amount of useful information they contain is virtually nil. A great number of papers have been written on treatment response, but because so very few conclusions can be made from them it may be worth considering the general format of research design. Clinical psychiatrists and social workers are notoriously badly-trained in scientific methodology, yet the basic principles are relatively easy to apply.

The objectives of research should be precisely defined, otherwise they cannot be measured. The targets of research and observation can be differentiated, usually, into primary and ancillary targets. The existing situation should be recorded, including base-line data, the details depending on the specific requirements of the study. It is usual to describe the treatment population by age, sex, marital and occupational status, psychiatric and criminal record, results of psychological tests, details of how the treatment population was derived, from which source they were referred and what exclusions were made before treatment began. Details of drug-taking histories are vital, together with reliability studies on the information content, and if possible validity checks on the histories (for example, by urine tests to see if drug abusers really are taking the drugs they claim to be taking).

Then there should be a precise description of the treatment manoeuvres. If new, unproven techniques are being used there should normally be careful controls, perhaps with "no-treatment" or "placebo" groups. Following the treatment, there must be precise recording of behaviour change, comparison with the base-line data, and then an evaluation of whether change, if any, has been brought about by the treatment, or possibly by extraneous factors. Are the occurrence rates of the target behaviours true occurrence rates, or as is so often the case, do they merely reflect the intensity of the research effort? Statistical tests should be used whenever possible, but they can be difficult to interpret if multiple parameters of outcome are being measured, and statistically significant treatment outcomes may actually be of very limited clinical significance.

UNITED KINGDOM STUDIES

The patterns of drug dependency have changed so much in recent years that reviews of treatment more than ten years old, which are sparse anyway, are of little more than historical significance. Prior to the 1960s, drug dependency in Britain was a minor problem, confined to "therapeutic" addicts, many of whom were members of the medical, nursing, or allied professions.

Clark (1962) assessed the outcome of a group of medical personnel treated at Crichton Royal Hospital, Dumfries, Scotland, between 1949 and 1960. Fifty patients, out of a total group of 65, were followed up for a period of two to twelve years; they were predominantly general practitioners, males outnumbering females by two to one. Very few details were given about the patients, other than that the majority were addicted to drugs listed in the Dangerous Drug Acts 1965 and 1967 (Dangerous Drug Acts—these Acts have now been replaced by the Misuse of Drugs Act 1971), that the mean number of drug-taking years was four, and that a quarter gave physical pain as the reason for their addiction. No details were given of the treatment methods, but at follow-up, only 28 per cent had overcome their addiction. The criteria for recovery were whether the patients continued to take drugs, whether they required further hospitalisation, and continuance at work. Of the total group, 52 per cent needed further treatment, 26 per cent had no subsequent gainful employment, and only 30 per cent continued at work without interruption. The outlook for patients on D.D.A. drugs (a 14 per cent recovery rate) was very much worse than that for the whole group. Obviously, the overall outlook was very poor for this group, even though it is generally conceded that therapeutic addicts, and those from the professions, respond more favourably than the non-therapeutic addicts who now comprise the great majority of the current addict population.

The care of addicts until recently was undertaken by general practitioners, so that many of the earlier studies are from family physicians. A paper from Hewetson (1967) describes his experiences in anecdotal fashion. Although he reviewed 213 patients whom he had seen in his practice, in 144 of these cases he had merely a passing contact, so that he only treated 69 for periods of up to five years. In 56 cases he withdrew them from their drug of addiction (narcotics), some at home and some in hospital, but then prescribed amidone or methylamphetamine. He quoted these as successes, although they were still taking exceedingly toxic drugs, and he reported abstinence from narcotics for only twenty, and even here this was for periods of less than one year. Of the 144 patients he did not personally treat, only 29 were stated by the Home Office to be off narcotics. Hewetson suggested therefore that the overall success rate for the addicts was 40 per cent (85 out of 213 cases), and considered it to be higher than generally accepted, but his figures are not very credible.

Until the establishment of treatment centres, the management of drug abusers was poorly organised, apparently ineffective, and dependent entirely on the enthusiasm of a few family doctors operating within the Metropolitan area. Connell (1967) echoed the second Brain committee plea for research, and Chapple (1967) suggested that new treatment programmes should be experimental. In spite of this laudable aim, reports from the experimental methods of the Chelsea Addiction and Research Centre (Chapple and Gray 1968, Chapple, Somekh and Taylor 1972) have left much to be desired. The earlier report described 225 patients treated at clinics or at day hospitals. Almost half the patients left the treatment programmes without consent, or were transient. Patients were allocated in an unexplained way to one of three treatment programmes: heroin maintenance, methadone maintenance, or "off narcotics". The absence of random allocation to the various treatments, and the fact that, for some reason, a quarter of the heroin maintenance group were "promoted" to methadone maintenance, invalidates what would otherwise have been a very interesting study. A higher proportion of the methadone group was working, but this could be due to biased selection, as no work data prior to treatment was given.

These workers' tentative conclusions were re-evaluated, after a five-year study of 108 cases of opiate addiction. Of these, 25 were said to be "off opiates", that is, they were not being prescribed opiates by the clinic, although several might have been obtaining black-market drugs; 25 were not adequately followed-up, and the alarming number of 17 had died. As no descriptions were given of either the successful or unsuccessful patients, it is not possible to derive any prognostic variables. However, addicts were divided into three categories, according to the length of time they had been prescribed drugs (no matter how long they might have been obtaining drugs from other sources!), of "early", "pre-chronic", and "chronic" addicts. Their conclusions were that the early addicts did better than the other categories. Another interpretation could be that the less contact with prescribing agencies, the better the outlook, although to be fair, as they were offered quite intensive support, therapy might actually have helped them.

Prior to the widespread establishment of treatment centres, Owens (1967) had developed the integrated Birmingham approach to drug control. His contention was that narcotic addiction is a community problem, not merely a medical matter, and that a local register of addicts and close co-operation with pharmacists and police was essential to contain the number of addicts. Certainly, after his programme was established in Birmingham, a previously steep rise in the numbers of addicts levelled off, although this could have been at the expense of a rise in other towns as addicts migrated elsewhere. Owens's use of continuous narcosis for withdrawal, using a mixture of barbiturates, paraldehyde and chlordiazepoxide compares unfavourably with other regimes. In Brixton prison, methadone substitution and withdrawal over a 5 to 10 day period caused fewer side-effects than the Birmingham series, where there was even a slight mortality rate. I. P. James (1965) rightly views the withdrawal experience more as a product of junkie folklore than a medical problem and we feel that it should not be complicated by excessive medical enthusiasm.

Hicks (1969) has given a valuable description of the organisation of a treatment centre in London prior to the 1968 regulations; 57 patients were assessed as being dependent on heroin, and were offered withdrawal on an out-patient basis, prescriptions being drawn daily from the pharmacy. In an admittedly short follow-up, only 10 per cent of the patients ceased taking heroin, although there was a reduction in the group mean dosage from 216 mg to 132 mg. Hicks graphically illustrated the battles during interviews between doctor and patient over dosage reductions, so that there was little opportunity to develop true rapport with the addicts. He considered separate facilities for addicts to be mandatory, and concluded that graduated withdrawal is a very unsatisfactory treatment mode. He compared the English clinics with those established in the U.S.A. between the years 1919 and 1925, which proved unworkable, and raised the question of compulsory treatment.

Bewley's series of research (1968) of a hundred patients treated in Tooting Bec Hospital, London, was equally discouraging. At follow-up, of at least one year's duration, the majority had relapsed, according to current status figures provided by the Home Office; only 15 were not known to be taking opiates (even this figure might be misleading) and an incredible 13 patients were dead. Even more alarming was the figure of 67 known to have acquired drugs whilst in hospital for treatment, and 27 of these actually managed to obtain drugs from their general practitioners. Bewley considered his patients to be atypical, in that a high proportion had been referred from Brixton prison on court orders, and they possibly represented the most disturbed section, criminally and mentally, of all young British addicts. He suggested, quoting Californian experience, that it might be better to detain addicts for enforced treatment for a year. However, he did have many patients in his series detained under Sections 26 and 60 of the Mental Health Act 1959, and could have hospitalised them for long periods, yet on average they remained in hospital for only three months. He did not give any evidence at all to suggest that patients staying for long periods for rehabilitation fared any better than addicts staying only for physical withdrawal from drugs.

Gardner and Connell (1970) described the first year's operation of a London clinic established after the implementation of the Dangerous Drugs (Supply to Addicts) Regulations 1968. Whilst not in any way a treatment outcome study, there were many pertinent comments on the difficulties and dangers of diagnosing addiction, and the dangers of well-intentioned but unwarranted clinic prescribing. Of 107 patients who claimed to be addicted, 27 were found to have negative urine tests, yet nearly half of these were prescribed opiates blindly, and as subsequently revealed, quite wrongly. The discovery of their inadvertent blunders, which have probably been repeated many times in less well-staffed clinics, led to a change of policy, and gave rise to misgivings about maintenance policies.

Woodside (1973) drew attention to yet another difficulty of follow-up studies, that of obtaining adequate information. At a follow-up of one year of 100 patients treated in Scotland, 56 could not be traced, and only two were known definitely to be out of contact with drug-taking. The patients seen were possibly more typical of drug abusers than those in the London studies. Seventeen were non-opiate users, and the majority (78) used multiple drugs including opiates. Only 64 patients agreed to enter hospital for treatment, and of these, 30 took their discharge against medical advice, two absconded, two were discharged as uncooperative, and two were discharged to police custody. No observable advantages seemed to accrue from hospitalisation, as few were helped towards rehabilitation or gainful employment. Again, serious questions were raised about the efficacy of centres that lacked adequate external controls on the patients.

A review of the experiences of three London units with maintenance treatment is highly recommended as an archetypal example of perplexing and indigestible information. Entitled "Maintenance Treatment of Narcotic Addicts (not British nor a System, but working now)" (Bewley, James and LaFerne, 1972), it presents persuasive evidence of an apparently successful system. The histories of 491 addicts from St. George's, St. Thomas's and Tooting Bec Hospitals are reviewed, although only 397 were followed up. It is stated that 78 per cent were unemployed at entry into clinic or hospital, but this percentage is unaccountably taken, not from a sample of 491 patients or even 397 patients, but from only 125 patients. The summary claims that, of patients who continued attendance at clinic at the time of follow-up, 40 per cent were in employment, suggesting a significant increase in the numbers employed. There is no comment as to the overall employment of the whole follow-up group, or indeed reference to what sample of patients the percentage was based on. An examination of the St. George's sub-sample implies that considerably fewer patients were in work after treatment than before, and casts doubt on the validity of statements that treatment leads to greater stability as measured by work status. Certainly lower arrest rates in one of the sub-samples were shown, but even that may not reflect accurately a diminution in criminal activity, since similar numbers of addicts reported that their sources of income were derived from illicit sources before treatment and at follow-up. The most convincing evidence for the success the authors produce is based on the most dubious index of all, the black-market price of heroin, which was stated to rise from £1 to £6 for each sixty milligrams. For those who have difficulty following the mass of statistics, they supply a graph of the number of these physically dependent on narcotics in Brixton prison. It has nothing whatsoever to do with the main content of the article, and refers to a totally different and unreferenced study, but it does give some indirect evidence that the clinics have met with some success in restraining the numbers of addicts at large.

To conclude, it is difficult, if not impossible, to derive valuable information from the British studies hitherto. The literature from the U.S.A. is generally of a higher quality, although in many ways just as mystifying, and its relevance to the British situation not very clear. Griffith Edwards (1967) gave a concise explanation of the limits of direct and unqualified comparisons between work from the two countries. He stressed the poverty, urban disorganisation and racial disharmony that occur in the U.S.A to a greater degree than Britain, and quoted figures of infant mortality, murder, robbery and divorce as indices of higher social disturbance. However, in spite of these factors and the entrenched black-market trading of drugs in the U.S.A., many interesting features do emerge from those authoritative studies that have been made, largely as in Britain, on narcotic addicts.

AMERICAN STUDIES

In the U.K., only a fraction of the total population of heroin abusers seeks registration or help, and it is likely that in the U.S.A. the numbers of treated patients or known addicts represent only a small proportion of drug abusers. It would again seem that those who come to light are the most psychiatrically disturbed and the most criminally involved, so that the outlook for heroin-takers given in various papers need not be quite so bleak for all. The depressing American figures are based mostly on series of inmates of penal institutions, or those treated at the prison hospitals of Lexington, Kentucky, and Fort Worth, Texas, while many patients have been followed up in New York where the relapse rate may be higher than other parts of the country. John O'Donnell (1964) made the valuable observation that it is difficult to assess abstinence and relapse rates accurately, and the wide variation in outcome could be attributed not to real differences but to errors in assessment based on inadequate evidence. "Abstinence" and "relapse" are clinical judgments made with what evidence may be available, and clinical judgments are often highly unreliable. Little reliance can be placed even on urine tests, which only reflect an addict's present state, and give few clues to his longer-range history.

As in England, the patterns of drug-taking in the U.S.A. have changed, drug addiction in both countries now being a phenomenon predominantly beginning in adolescence. Pescor (1943 *a, b*) found that before 1940 the average age of coming into contact with community agencies lay between thirty and forty, his group of Lexington addicts being of mean age 39·1. In a review of over four thousand patients he found that only 13·5 per cent remained abstinent at a follow-up, ranging from six months to three-and-a-half years; in a high proportion no follow-up data was available, but no less than 7 per cent were known to have died in that short interval.

Lexington Hospital was opened in 1935 as a federal institution dealing solely with narcotic addicts, including both voluntary and involuntary patients, but excluding many considered to be security risks. It has already been described in Chapter 9. The regime is essentially directive and authoritarian, depending on external controls, but does allow patients responsibility for their own actions, giving graduated freedom to individuals according to their progress. It would be difficult to elicit which aspects of treatment were responsible for eventual recovery, and which were irrelevant, if treatment did prove successful, but in fact recovery rates appear poor. Hunt and Ordoroff (1962) reviewed nearly two thousand patients discharged from Lexington and followed up for one to four years. Not only did 90 per cent relapse within that period, but 90 per cent of these relapsed within a very short time of leaving hospital. Duvall and his colleagues (1963), in a five-year study, gave 87 per cent as the total relapse rate, but encouragingly he did find that at the end of the period of study 25 per cent were then abstinent. The comparative figures from Fort Worth and Lexington are similar, and female addicts admitted to Lexington fare no better than the men.

These sad figures were not confirmed by O'Donnell (1964), who found that 44 per cent of a group discharged from Lexington remained abstinent at follow-up. His small group consisted of white patients from Kentucky, so that his findings might reflect only that white addicts from rural areas do better than groups of mixed race from the metropolitan areas of the East coast. However, George Vaillant's long-term study in New York (1965–6 *a, b, c*), of discharged Lexington addicts confirmed that earlier studies had not presented a fair picture of recidivism rates. Stressing that relapse rates should embrace more than one point in time, his survey was of 100 first admissions to Lexington, 50 of Caucasian origin and 50 black Americans (he excluded Chinese addicts and those whose stay did not allow adequate collection of information). A very high proportion were successfully identified after twelve years, and 30 were considered to have had a good outcome. Whilst 90 per cent became re-addicted within two years, for many this proved to be a temporary phase, so that after ten further years only 47 per cent were classified as addicted or institutionalised. Unfortunately, 13 patients had died, all except one in situations implicating drugs or alcohol.

The length of stay in hospital was correlated with short-term abstinence, so that those with detention terms of greater than nine months were three times more likely to be abstinent than those who had served shorter terms. Prison sentences of more than nine months produced a full year's abstinence in 20 out of 30 terms of detention when followed by a year of parole supervision, so that the likelihood of abstinence was fifteen times higher than after voluntary hospitalisation. There was nothing to suggest that those receiving short sentences differed in any material ways, by delinquency histories or severity of addiction, from those receiving longer periods of incarceration. Vaillant found that the most important, single prognostic variable was the addict's ability prior to imprisonment to find and keep employment.

In 1966 the Narcotic Addict Rehabilitation Act (NARA) legislation led to several changes in the running of the Lexington and Fort Worth Hospitals. They became more like hospitals in the true sense; there were fewer restrictions, less security and an encouragement of social interaction, but there were no dramatic changes in the therapeutic methods. Civil commitment of addicts charged with certain offences, and for many who did not face charges, became the law. Addicts could opt for treatment of up to 36 months instead of imprisonment, yet although they "volunteered", not all proved to be co-operative with therapy. Langenauer and Bowden (1971) have reviewed the results of hospital treatment of the first 252 patients discharged from Lexington under the new Act. In the first month, 50 per cent used drugs, including 45 per cent who used opioids exclusively. After six months, only 14 per cent of the patients had not used opioids. After eight months of follow-up 42 per cent had been recommended for re-commitment. Some were detoxified in the community, but neither these nor the ones recommitted were helped by either procedure. Of 16 patients recommitted and re-discharged, 13 used opioids again within the first month. The average time of in-patient care was 5·5 months and from the data given the treatment could be described as either a limited failure or a modest success. Poor selection of candidates for treatment, inexperienced aftercare counsellors and a stringent definition of relapse (opioid use once or more in any given month) may have accounted in part for the indeterminate results.

Stephens and Cottrell (1972) reviewed a further cohort of Lexington and Fort Worth addicts treated under NARA, in which the relapse rate was 87 per cent. Only those addicts over the age of thirty did well, a finding tending to confirm Winick's hypothesis. Civil commitment began in 1963 in New York where experience of voluntary commitment had proved disastrous. In Manhattan State Hospital (before civil commitment legislation), out of one thousand voluntary admissions, 41 per cent had left hospital against advice after eight days, 74 per cent after fifteen days, and 80 per cent after twenty-four days. Only 15 per cent were considered to be candidates for serious rehabilitation—the others were merely using hospitalisation to obtain welfare or assistance with accommodation. In view of these figures, the civil commitment programmes need not be judged too harshly. In the California programme (Kramer *et al.,* 1968) one-third of treated addicts were in good standing one year after discharge, although this figure had dropped to one in six after three years. Strangely the California system endorsed a "treatment" approach although psychiatrists and psychologists were deliberately excluded from direct participation. Had they been integrally involved the correctional personnel might well have improved their figures.

RESULTS OF METHADONE MAINTENANCE TREATMENT

In 1962, Vincent Dole, a research worker in metabolic aspects of medicine who had been until then working on the causes of obesity, turned to the study of the metabolic effects of heroin addiction, and in so doing came to work closely with a clinical psychiatrist, Marie Nyswander. Their introduction of methadone maintenance treatment in the control of opiate abuse is perhaps the most significant and revolutionarily innovative approach in the whole history of addiction although, as we shall point out, a lot of the original enthusiasm has given way to a more tempered view. In 1965 they presented their initial findings from a clinical trial. A group of failed addicts of long-standing showed dramatic disappearance of their narcotic hunger, an improvement in their response to stress, and an interest in obtaining and keeping a job. In 1966 they reported on 128 patients allocated to a maintenance programme, of whom 114 continued in regular treatment, whilst 14 were dropped because of behaviour problems. Before treatment, only 17 per cent had been gainfully employed, but after two years of treatment, 87 per cent were in regular employment.

Following this there was an explosion of methadone maintenance centres across the U.S.A. and an independent committee operating from Columbia University was established to check the results of Dole and Nyswander's work with New York addicts. By 31st March 1968, no less than 871 patients had been admitted to treatment, and only 14 per cent had left (10 per cent discharged, 3 per cent left voluntarily, 1 per cent had died). All were long-standing addicts, but this group was not really representative of New York addicts. On average they were older, 68 per cent being over the age of thirty (compared with 34 per cent on the New York City Narcotics Register), and 48 per cent were white (compared with 25 per cent). Assessment of outcome should therefore be with the qualification that there may have been a pre-selection of a good-outcome population, in spite of the long addictive history, and it should be noted that treatment involved also vocational guidance, medical, social and legal aid as well as the methadone. The employment rate rose from 28 per cent before admission to 85 per cent after two years of treatment. The reconviction rate in the first year was only 11 per cent, compared with 37 per cent of a group of detoxified patients treated elsewhere in New York.

By 1971, the number of addicts in maintenance programmes in New York had risen to 9,000, and Dole (1971) was considering the administrative problems of introducing a total of 25,000 addicts to chemical maintenance. At first sight, the results of his work were tremendously successful and his methods were taken up enthusiastically in the U.S.A., Canada and later in England. It is an unfortunate fact that clinical enthusiasm often overrides objective judgment, so perhaps it is advantageous to re-interpret the plethora of published work on the outcome of this form of treatment. The criteria for success are generally accepted to be as follows:

1. A reduction in the use of heroin.
2. A reduction in the use of other drugs.
3. Continuing involvement in a methadone programme.
4. Reduced craving for heroin.
5. Resistance to heroin-induced euphoria.
6. Improved work record.
7. Decreased criminal activity.
8. Improved mental state.
9. Lowered mortality rates.

Considerable variations in desired goals occur in different programmes, but the criterion most uniformly used is continuance in the programme. This indeed is important, but it would indicate little if the participants continued to use heroin as frequently as before, or showed no decrease in criminal activity. The criteria for discharge vary, and may include voluntary withdrawals and enforced withdrawals due to disruptive behaviour, criminal behaviour and so on. If these last were to be included, then results of treatment based on the residual sample would give an inflated estimate of the efficacy of the programme. Sadly, very few studies have based their success rates on the original patients accepted for treatment, having preferred to report on series excluding "drop-outs".

Dole argued that methadone needs to be administered in the dosage range of 80–120 mg per day for there to be a "blockade" effect against heroin. It was suggested that this high dosage would promote social stability, but an experimental study by Bowling, Moffett and Taylor (1973) does not support this idea. Using employment rate as the index of success, they found no difference between a high dose (over 140 mg over daily) and a low dose (less than 80 mg) group. Not only this, but over half of each group continued to use heroin after stabilisation. Chambers and Bergen (1973) recorded that 10 per cent of stabilised addicts obtained supplements of methadone illegally, and the supplementers were neither initiates into programmes, nor were they from the ranks of those receiving low doses of methadone. Even more alarming is a report from Lexington (Weppner, 1972), that no less than 43 per cent of patients admitted there had used methadone illegally, and that a high proportion of their admissions represented failures of methadone maintenance. One-third of those abusing methadone did so because of its positive qualities, such as the nature of the "kick" and the length of euphoria afforded. It would seem that an increasing number of addicts now regard methadone as their drug of choice, and illicit diversion is becoming a booming industry.

The early methadone treatment programmes excluded patients under twenty or over forty, those with serious medical and psychiatric problems, and alcoholics. Although many programmes now accept patients who would previously have been excluded, almost all employ some screening procedures, which therefore cast doubts on the validity of the results. A prospective study on adolescents demonstrated that it was practicable to allow younger people methadone treatment in that, after a short follow-up period, a group of predominantly black addicts in Boston showed improved work records and some reduction in heroin abuse. This was not related to the amount of methadone they were receiving, and many did continue to use heroin regularly. In the Beth Israel programme, patients selected for treatment (Perkins and Bloch, 1970) included more whites, who were more often employed, less criminal, had fewer psychiatric problems, and abused fewer barbiturates and less alcohol than those not selected. Addicts tended to drop out of treatment in the early part of stabilisation, or in the first year if they received less than 80 mg of methadone a day.

Dole's original programme involved an initiation phase of six weeks' hospitalisation. Obviously this was a time-consuming and very expensive procedure, and later he abandoned it in favour of ambulatory stabilisation. In Philadelphia a careful study was made to ascertain if the intensive in-patient phase, which can include psychological and social support before rehabilitation, was helpful (Wieland and Chambers, 1970). They demonstrated that response to treatment, using four measures of personal and social rehabilitation, was similar in two groups of patients stabilised as out- or in-patients. Both groups showed improvement in clinical state, employment, incidence of heroin abuse, and decrease in criminal activity to a similar level. However, they did not say whether they distributed their patients randomly to either treatment situation, and the addicts treated as in-patients appeared to be more unstable. They were younger and more were single, with lower employment rates and more who were involved in criminal activities. A re-analysis of improvement change might show that the in-patients had changed in greater degree than the out-patients, but the difference is hardly likely to be of any clinical significance.

There is little justification, therefore, for admitting a patient selected to enter a methadone maintenance programme to hospital. If he is treated as an out-patient in America, the cost is unlikely to be more than $2,000 per year, and drops with each succeeding year. The cost of keeping an addict in prison or prison hospital can range up to $20,000 per year. If one assumed that the doling out of cheap or free methadone by clinics reduced the addicts' stealing by half, then this would save the community anything up to $25,000 worth of stolen goods per addict each year. In Washington D.C. the number of addicts sent to jail rose from a 1958 figure of 50 to a 1969 figure of 1,400, and the crime rate rose drastically until 1969. In 1969 there were 10 addicts in methadone maintenance programmes, and this had risen to 2,300 in 1970. Treatment also involved counselling, the use of hospital facilities and halfway houses (DuPont and Katon, 1971), and its effectiveness was measured by reduction in the crime rate. There was an 83 per cent reduction in the crime rate in those who stayed in the programme, and in spite of the one-third of patients who dropped out, the overall crime rate in Washington began to drop. On the other hand, the conclusion that the crime-rate decrease could be attributed to the clinics has been contested by Dobbs (1971), who found that the majority of patients continued to obtain heroin illegally, and the longer they remained in treatment the more likely were they to abuse heroin.

Very high success rates have been claimed for methadone maintenance treatment. Using employment as the index, it could be quoted that the incidence of employment is as high as 71 per cent after methadone treatment (Dole and Nyswander, 1966) and as low as 30 per cent after "drug-free" treatment (Duvall *et al.*, 1963).

The mean employment rate after methadone treatment in all the reported studies is of the order of 52 per cent, compared with 42 per cent for drug-free treatments, and a 30 per cent employment rate prior to treatment. These figures are "true" figures, including drop-outs from treatment, because if they are not included, misleadingly good results can be obtained. The results of methadone treatment looked at in this way are not too good, and only modestly better than drug-free treatments, which currently include many drop-outs from methadone programmes anyway.

Maddux and Bowden (1972) have reviewed many of the methadone programmes, and conclude that the published success rates are ambiguous and exaggerated. Reduced criminal activity is more apparent than real, in that estimates are based not only on shrinking samples but also on unequal time periods. A comparison of total lifetime frequency of crime before methadone treatment can only be compared imperfectly against the crime rate during a relatively short follow-up period. To compensate for unequal time-periods is a matter of simple arithmetic, changing the figures into convictions or arrests per year, but the few studies that have done this have not included drop-outs in their analysis, so that it is impossible to derive reliable figures for a reduction in crime.

Methadone maintenance therapy has clearly not been an unqualified success and it may even have such built-in disadvantages that it will have to be replaced by alternative forms of treatment. However, it has provided a much-needed stimulus and a good deal of therapeutic optimism to workers in the field of heroin addiction. It has also acted as a spur to research and while we are critical of the quality of many of the investigations, they do point the way to more scientific and more clinically-productive work for the future.

REFERENCES

Bergin, A. E., "The Evaluation of Therapeutic Outcomes", in Bergin, A. E. and Garfield, S. L. (eds.), op. cit.

Bergin, A. E. and Garfield, S. L., (eds.), *Handbook of Psychotherapy and Behaviour Change—An Empirical Analysis,* John Wiley, New York, 1971.

Bewley, T. H. and Ben-Arie, O., "Morbidity and Mortality from Heroin Dependence: Study of 100 Consecutive In-Patients", *British Medical Journal,* i: 727–30, 1968.

Bewley, T. H., James, I. P. and LaFerne, C., "Maintenance Treatment of Narcotic Addicts (not British nor a System but Working Now)", *International Journal of Addiction*, 7: 597–611, 1972.

Bowling, C. E., Moffett, A. D. and Taylor, W. J. R., "High Versus Low Dose Maintenance Therapy: An Empirical Test", in Chambers, C. D. and Brill, M. S. S., (eds.), op. cit.

Brain Committee, Interdepartmental committee on Drug Addiction, *Drug Addiction,* H.M.S.O., London, 1961.

Chambers, C. D. and Bergen, J. J., "Self-Administered Methadone Supplementation", in Chambers, C. D. and Brill, M. S. S., (eds.), op. cit.

Chambers, C. D. and Brill, M. S. S., (eds.), *Methadone, Experiences and Issues,* Behavioural Publications, New York, 1973.

Chapple, P. A. L, "Treatment in the Community", *Br. Med. J.,* ii: 500–1, 1967.

Chapple, P. A. L. and Gray, G., "One Year's Work at a Centre for the Treatment of Addicted Patients", *Lancet,* i: 908–11, 1968.

Chapple, P. A. L., Somekh, D. E. and Taylor, M. E., "A 5-Year Follow-Up of 108 Cases of Opiate Addiction", *British Journal of Addiction*, 67: 33–8, 1972.

Clark, J. A., "The Prognosis in Drug Addiction", *Journal of Nervous and Mental Disease,* 108: 411–18, 1962.

Connell, P. H., "Importance of Research", *Brit. Med. J.*, ii: 499–500, 1967.

Davies, D. L., "Alcoholism, Managing the Problem, Treatment Goals", a Paper presented at the Second International Conference on Alcoholism and Drug Dependence, Liverpool, April, 1973.

Davies, D. L., "Normal Drinking in Recovered Alcohol Addicts", *Quarterly Journal of Studies on Alcohol,* 23: 94–104, 1962.

Davies, D. L., Shepherd, M. and Myers, E. "The Two Year Prognosis of 50 Alcohol Addicts After Treatment in Hospital", *Quart. J. Stud. Alcohol,* 1: 485–502, 1956.

Dobbs, W. H., "Methadone Treatment of Heroin Addicts", *Journal of the American Medical Association,* 218: 1536–41, 1971.

Dole, V. P., "Methadone Maintenance for 25,000 Heroin Addicts", *JAMA,* 215: 1131–4, 1971.

Dole, V. P. and Nyswander, M. E., "A Medical Treatment for Diacetyl Morphine (Heroin) Addiction: A Clinical Trial with Methadone Hydrochloride", *JAMA:* 193: 80–4, 1965.

Dole, V. P. and Nyswander, M. E., "Rehabilitation of Heroin Addicts after Blockade with Methadone", *New York State Journal of Medicine,* 66: 2011–17, 1966.

Dole, V. P., Nyswander, M. E. and Kneek, M. J., "Narcotic Blockade", *Archives of Internal Medicine,* 118: 304–9, 1966.

Dupont, R. L. and Katon, R. N., "Development of a Heroin Addiction Treatment Program", *JAMA,* 216: 1320–4, 1971.

Duvall, H. J., Locke, B. Z. and Brill, L. "Follow-Up Study of Narcotic Addicts Five Years After Hospitalization", *U.S. Public Health Report,* 78: 185–93, 1963.

Edwards, G., "Relevance of American Experience of Narcotic Addiction to the British Scene", *Br. Med. J.,* iii: 425–8, 1967.

Edwards, G. and Guthrie, S., "A Controlled Trial of In-Patient and Out-Patient Treatment of Alcohol Dependence", *Lancet,* i: 555–9, 1967.

Efron, D. H., (ed.), *Psycopharmacology: A Review of Progress 1957–1967,* U.S. Public Health Service, Pub. No. 9836, Washington, 1970.

Evans, M., "The Cardiff Plan and the Welsh Unit", *Br. J. Addict.,* 62: 29–34, 1967.

Eysenck, H. J., "The Effects of Psychotherapy: An Evaluation", *Journal of Consulting and Clinical Psychology,* 16: 319–24, 1952.

Gardner, R. and Connell, P. H., "One Year's Experience in a Drug-Dependence Clinic", *Lancet,* ii: 455–8, 1970.

Gerard, D. L. and Saenger, G., "Out-Patient Treatment of Alcoholism", *Brookside Monograph,* No. 4., University of Toronto, Toronto, 1966.

Glatt, M. M., "An Alcoholic Unit in a Mental Hospital", *Lancet,* ii: 397, 1959.

Hewetson, J., "Treatment of Drug Addiction", *Br. Med. J.,* i: 425–6, 1967.

Hicks, R. C., "The Management of Heroin Addiction at a General Hospital Drug Addiction Treatment Centre (In London)", *Br. J. Addict.,* 64: 235–44, 1969.

Hill, M. J. and Blane, H. T., "Evaluation of Psychotherapy with Alcoholics: A Critical Review", *Quart. J. Stud. Alcohol,* 28: 76–104, 1967.

Hunt, G. and Ordoroff, M. E., "Follow-Up Study of Narcotic Drug Addicts After Hospitalization", *U.S. Pub. Hlth. Rep.,* 77: 41, 1962.

James, J. P., "The Addiction Epidemic", *Lancet,* ii: 288, 1965.

Keller, M., "On the Loss of Control Phenomenon in Alcoholism", *Br. J. Addict.,* 67 (3): 153–64, 1972.

Kissin, B. and Platz, A., "The Use of Drugs in Long-Term Rehabilitation of Chronic Alcoholics", in Efron, D. H., (ed.), op. cit.

Kramer, J. C., *et al.,* "Civil Commitment for Addicts: The California Program", *American Journal of Psychiatry,* 125: 816–24, 1968.

Langenauer, B. J. and Bowden, C. L., "A Follow-Up Study of Narcotic Addicts in the NARA Program", *Am. J. Psychiatry,* 128: 41–6, 1971.

Lemere, F., "What Happens to Alcoholics?", *Am. J. Psychiatry,* 109: 674, 1953.

Ley, P., Jain, V. K., Swinson, R. P., Eaves, D., Bradshaw, P. W., Kincey, J. A., Cowan, R. and Abiss, S., "A State-Dependent Learning-Effect Produced in Human Subjects by Amylobarbitone Sodium", *British Journal of Psychiatry,* 120: 511–15, 1972.

Lovibond, S. H. and Caddy, G., "Discriminated Aversive Control in the Moderation of Alcoholics Drinking Behaviour", *Behaviour Research and Therapy,* 1: 437–44, 1970.

MacAndrew, C. and Edgerton, R. B., *Drunken Comportment,* Nelson, London, 1969.

Maddux, J. F. and Bowden, C. L., "Critique of Success with Methadone Maintenance", *Am. J. Psychiatry,* 129: 440–6, 1972.

Madill, M. F., Campbell, S. G., Laverty, S. G., Sanderson, R. E. and Vanderwater, S. L., "Aversion Treatment of Alcoholics by Succinylcholine-Induced Apneic Paralysis: An Analysis of Early Changes in Drinking Behaviour", *Quart. J. Stud. Alcohol,* 27: 483–509, 1966.

McBrearty, J. F., Dichter, M., Garfield, Z. and Heath, G., "A Behaviorally-Oriented Treatment Program for Alcoholism", *Psychological Report,* 22: 287–98, 1968.

Mendelson, J. H., Mello, N. K. and Solomon, P., "Small Group Drinking Behaviour: An Experimental Study of Chronic Alcoholics", in Wikler, A. (ed.) op. cit.

Miller, E. C., Dvorak, B. A. and Turner, D. W., "A Method of Creating Aversion to Alcohol by Reflex Conditioning in a Group Setting", *Qùart. J. Stud. Alcohol,* 21: 424–31, 1960.

O'Donnell, J. A., "A Follow-Up of Narcotic Addicts", *American Journal of Orthopsychiatry,* 34: 948–54, 1964.

Owens, J., "Integrated Approach", *Br. Med. J.* ii: 501–2, 1967.

Pattison, M. E., "A Critique of Alcoholism Treatment Concepts", *Quart. J. Stud. Alcohol,* 27: 49–71, 1966.

Perkins, M. E. and Bloch, H. I., "Survey of a Methadone Maintenance Treatment Program", *Am. J. Psychiatry,* 126: 1389–96, 1970.

Pescor, M. J., "Follow-Up Study of Treated Narcotic Drug Addicts", *U.S. Publ. Hlth. Rep.*, Supply. No. 170, 1943(*a*).

Pescor, M. J., "A Statistical Analysis of the Clinical Records of Hospitalized Drug Addicts", *U.S. Pub. Hlth. Rep.*, Suppl. No. 143, 1943(*b*).

"Progress Report of Evaluation of Methadone Maintenance Program as of March 31, 1968", *JAMA*, 206: 2712–14, 1968.

Rathod, N. H., Gregory, E., Blows, D. and Thomas, G. H., "A Two Years' Follow-Up Study of Alcoholic Patients", *Br. J. Psychiatry,* 112: 683–92, 1966.

Ritson, B. and Hassall, Christine, *The Management of Alcoholism,* Livingstone, Edinburgh, 1970.

Rosenberg, C. M. and Patch, V. D., "Methadone Use in Adolescent Heroin Addicts", *JAMA,* 220: 991–3, 1972.

Rosenberg, C. M., "Retention and Drop-Out Among Addicts and Alcoholics", a Paper read at the Second International Conference on Alcoholism and Drug Dependence, Liverpool, April, 1973.

Smart, R. G., Storm, T., Baker, E. F. and Solursh, L., "LSD in the Treatment of Alcoholism", *Brookside Monograph No. 6,* University of Toronto, Toronto, 1967.

Storm, T. and Smart, R. G., "Dissociation: A Possible Explanation for Some Features of Alcoholism and Implications for Its Treatment", *Quart. J. Stud. Alcohol,* 26: 111–15, 1965.

Stephens, R. and Cottrell, E., "A Follow-Up Study of 200 Narcotic Addicts Committed for Treatment Under NARA", *Br. J. Addict.,* 67: 45–53, 1972.

Straus, R. and Bacon, S. D., "Alcoholism and Social Stability: Occupational Integration of 2,000 Alcoholism Clinic Patients", *Quart. J. Stud. Alcohol,* 12: 231–60, 1951.

Swinson, R. P., "Long-Term Trial of Metronidazole in Male Alcoholics", *Br. J. Psychiatry,* 119: 85–9, 1971.

Taylor, J. A. T., "Metronizadole, A New Agent for Combined Somatic and Psychic Therapy of Alcoholism", *Bulletin of the Los Angeles Neurological Societies,* 29: 158–62, 1964.

Truax, C. B. and Mitchell, K. M., "Research on Certain Therapist Interpersonal Skills in Relation to Process and Outcome", in Bergin, A. E. and Garfield, S. L., (eds.), op. cit.

Vaillant, G. E., "A Twelve Year Follow-up of New York Narcotic Addicts: I. The Relation of Treatment to Outcome", *Amer. J. Psychiat.*, 122; 727–37, 1965–6.

Vaillant, G. E., "A Twelve Year Follow-up of New York Narcotic Addicts: II. The Natural History of a Chronic Disease", *New England Journal of Medicine*, 275; 1,282–8, 1966*a*.

Vaillant, G. E., "A Twelve Year Follow-up of New York Narcotic Addicts: III. Some Social and Psychological Characteristics", *Archives of General Psychiatry*, 15; 599–609, 1966*b*.

Vaillant, G. E., "A Twelve Year Follow-up of New York Narcotic Addicts: IV. Some Characteristics and Determinants of Abstinence", *Amer. J. Psychiat.*, 123; 573–84, 1966*c*.

Voegtlin, W. L., "The Treatment of Alcoholism by Establishing a Conditioned Reflex", *American Journal of Medical Science,* 199: 802–10, 1940.

Walton, H. (ed.), *Small Group Psychotherapy,* Penguin, Harmondsworth, 1971.

Weppner, R. S., "Matrix House. It's First Year at Lexington, Ky.", *HSMHA Health Report 86,* 761–8, 1972.

Wieland, W. F. and Chambers, C. D., "Methadone Maintenance—A Comparison of Two Stabilization Techniques", *International Journal of Addictions* 5: 645–59, 1970.

Wikler, A. (ed.), *The Addictive States, Research Publications of the Association for Research in Nervous and Mental Diseases,* Vol. XLVI, Wilkins and Wilkins, Baltimore, 1968.

Wilkinson, R., *The Prevention of Drinking Problems,* Oxford University Press, New York, 1970.

Woodside, M., "The First 100 Referrals to a Scottish Drug Addiction Treatment Centre", *Br. J. Addict.,* 68: 231–42, 1973.

11 Prevention, legislation and education

PREVENTION

International control

There has been much international activity in drug control throughout the twentieth century. An early milestone was the 1912 Hague Convention that attempted to restrict opiates for medical purposes only. There has been a general failure to introduce international restraints on opium production and to restrict production to medicinal uses because of the economic and, ultimately, political implications. International legislation has ignored alcohol, and concentrated on opium, cocaine and cannabis. In recent years, the United Nations has exerted influence by a series of international conferences, culminating in the 1961 Single Convention on Narcotic Drugs. The United Nations has a Commission on Narcotic Drugs that reports directly to the Economic and Social Council. The Single Convention codified several international treaties controlling the distribution, export, import, cultivation and recording of trading of opiates and other narcotic drugs, cocaine and cannabis.

About half the world's production of opiates is diverted to non-medical use, so that international legislation is a long-term project with much progress yet to be made. The World Health Organisation in Geneva has no legislative function, but gathers information and acts in an advisory role, disseminating data in many directions.

Its expert committees on drugs and alcohol have had a far-reaching effect on the recognition of drug addiction and alcoholism as illnesses, and have stimulated the development of educational and treatment programmes in all countries represented in the United Nations Assembly.

Drug control in the U.S.A.

The U.S.A. was a signatory to the Hague Opium Convention, and introduced legislation to control opiate production and distribution. In 1914, Congress passed the Harrison Acts, which were ostensibly tax acts, but designed to suppress drug-trafficking rather than to generate revenue. The laws, which have since been amended and incorporated into the Internal Revenue Code, exempted doctors from many controls, allowing opiate use in professional practice. It was not apparent how the legislation applied to prescribing for addicts, so that in the period 1919–23 several narcotic dispensaries sprang up under state and municipal control, prescribing opiates to addicts in a very similar way to the current British clinics. These dispensaries were severely censured by the medical profession, and all closed as a result of a Supreme Court ruling that prescribing to addicts was illegal under the Harrison Acts. Marijuana came under similar controls with the Marijuana Tax Act 1937, which has also been incorporated into the Internal Revenue Code.

In 1932 the Uniform Narcotics Act, dealing with "small-time" traffic in drugs, was adopted in some form by most of the states of the Union. This allowed doctors to prescribe opiates if acting in good faith, but introduced enormous penalties for illegal possession and distribution of drugs, in some states amounting to the death sentence. In recent years, penalties have become generally more severe and mandatory minimum sentences have deprived the courts of the ability to use realistic enforcement techniques such as probation. Federal laws have ignored the distinction between addicted people possessing drugs for their own use, and others dealing for profit. Addiction was almost regarded as a criminal offence in itself, but fortunately a Supreme Court ruling in California defined addiction as an illness, and ruled that punishment was unconstitutional.

As early as 1959, the Californian Legislature introduced progressive laws which led to the development of pilot programmes for the treatment and parole of narcotic offenders. In 1962 the

Metcalf-Volker Act in New York called for the development of comprehensive plans for "civil commitment", allowing voluntary admission to hospital as a condition of probation, and also admission on court certification. The Arrested Narcotic Addict Commitment Act came into force in 1963, allowing civil commitment for a maximum period of 36 months, with initial in-patient care followed by supervision by the Department of Mental Hygiene. Civil commitment became the priority for addicts, unless they were involved in multiple felonies or the interests of justice dictated otherwise, but criminal proceedings lying dormant could be revived if co-operation with civil management proved poor.

In 1966, the Narcotic Addict Rehabilitation Act (NARA) gave a sweeping federal mandate for civil commitment, and provided a complete change of official attitude towards addiction. It allowed for treatment to include innovative methods and research as a major component, made prevention the ultimate objective, and recognised after-care for the first time. Now, not only can addicts be committed before or after conviction, but even if they are not facing criminal charges. (This is quite different from British law, under which addicts cannot be compulsorily detained by virtue of addiction alone.) The National Institute of Mental Health (N.I.M.H.) is responsible for planning and administration, but the Surgeon General can delegate his functions for treatment to private and public agencies. This has led to the great boom of community-based treatment programmes on a contractual basis, many of which are being carefully assessed by N.I.M.H. This branch of the Health Service has also taken over the running of the massive Lexington and Fort Worth centres, which have been re-designated as model research units.

NARA came at a time when the credibility of earlier approaches to drug addiction was low. Greater pressures for rehabilitation of addicts increased when it was discovered that many soldiers returning from Vietnam were addicted to opiates. President Nixon appealed for great increases in federal funds and the establishment of a new supervising group, the Special Action Office for Drug Abuse Control. Emphasis on rehabilitation meant an emphasis on cure, so that a split has occurred between advocates of commitment and abstention, and advocates of maintenance programmes. Proponents of "law and order" policies have made successful stands on drug matters, so that demands have been made for swingeing increases in statutory minimum sentences for heroin dealing.

Drug control in the U.K.

In 1971 the Misuse of Drugs Act completed its passage through Parliament. It superseded the Drugs (Prevention of Misuse) Act 1964, and the Dangerous Drugs Acts of 1965 and 1967, which were repealed. Much of the content of earlier legislation was embodied in the new statutes. The 1964 Act was really emergency legislation, in that it applied to amphetamines and LSD that were not then controlled adequately. Indeed, the whole legislation had proved to be totally inadequate and not adaptable to changing circumstances. The major weakness was an inability to restrict irresponsible prescribing by members of the medical profession. The 1967 legislation, in regulations that took effect in 1968, restricted the right of doctors to prescribe, but only with regard to cocaine and heroin, and this proved insufficient. The General Medical Council could only act after doctors had breached the law, or where serious allegations of professional misconduct had been made, and its machinery was ponderous and dangerously slow.

The major provisions of the 1971 Act were as follows:

1. The setting up of a new Advisory Council on the Misues of Drugs.
2. The restriction of import and export, supply and possession of drugs, except in certain circumstances (e.g. when prescribed by a doctor).
3. Powers to make regulations to prevent misuse:
   (*a*) Control over supply, security and recording of transactions.
   (*b*) Reporting by doctors of cases of addiction.
   (*c*) Prohibition of doctors' supplying and prescribing certain drugs.
4. Sanctions on irresponsible prescribing:
   (*a*) If an individual doctor acts in an irresponsible way, the Home Secretary can withdraw his right to supply specified drugs.
   (*b*) The setting up of tribunals and professional panels to investigate cases of alleged irresponsible prescribing.
   (*c*) Machinery to investigate suspected problems and gather evidence.

5. The introduction of new penalties for possession and supply of controlled drugs. Drugs in the Act are in three cagegories:
   A—heroin, morphia, etc., maximum sentence for supply being 14 years imprisonment;
   B—cannabis, amphetamine, etc., maximum sentence for supply being 14 years;
   C—benzphetamine, methaqualone, etc., maximum sentence for supply being 5 years.

The law allows for lower penalties for possession of drugs, i.e. a legal distinction is made between the "user" and the "pusher", a difference which has been widely recognised informally in legal circles, but poorly understood. However, the law now recognises the offence of "possession with intent to supply", a circumstance difficult to define, but undoubtedly not meant for small-time dealers of cannabis. Sentences have certainly increased since 1972, when the Act took effect, but not always in proportion to the scale of the illegal activity. There have been severe criticisms of its working, in that the punishments are severe and the powers given to law enforcement too sweeping, but surprisingly the medical profession has accepted the invasion of its disciplinary function without audible protest.

LEGISLATION

The law and cannabis

The Wootton report (1968) felt that the possession of a small amount of cannabis should not, normally, be regarded as a serious crime punishable by imprisonment. The committee recommended that, in the interests of public safety, it was necessary to maintain restrictions but unlawful sale or supply should be punishable, at most, by a prison term not exceeding two years. The 1971 Act introduced maximum sentences of seven years for possession and fourteen years for supply, and in so doing, completely disregarded the eminently reasonable Wootton report. The Presidential Commission on Marijuana and Drug Abuse in the U.S.A. under Raymond Shafer, and the Le Dain report from Canada, agreed that criminal penalties were too harsh, and even felt that the private use of cannabis should not be treated as are other criminal offences. It is an odd situation that the more committees pronouncing cannabis to be less toxic than hitherto believed, the fewer politicians there are willing to accept their views. However, the Le Dain report, which did not recommend that cannabis be legalised but suggested that it be switched from the Narcotic Control Act to the Food and Drugs Act, has been incorporated into government policy in Canada. A remarkable and very enlightened view was that criminal records involving drugs should be automatically annulled after a crime-free period of two years. The Le Dain Commission was greatly concerned about the effects of cannabis and other drug offences marring the professional and vocational opportunities of the young, and subsequently interfering with their free movement and enjoyment of public rights. To its great credit, this committee felt that all previous convictions, of whatever nature, should be dealt with in the same way, given evidence of maturity and social responsibility. British politicians could read the report with some benefit and might consider amending the 1971 Act, to remove cannabis from the list of class B drugs, and to make separate provisions regarding it. There is not the slightest possibility that cannabis smoking will be eradicated by positive legislation, and the manifest unfairness of the Act elicits bitterness, even from those who have never taken drugs. Only a fraction of the population favours legalisation of cannabis, but that minority is growing. Whilst we have reservations about the legalisation of any further drugs, we feel that inevitably, in the not-too-distant future, cannabis will cease to be penalised and it will pass into the realm of private morality and self-determination. Legalisation is quite impossible at present, because laws controlling it, in the same way as alcohol, could not be enforced, since, for example, there is no way of estimating how much a person has consumed. Ultimately, legalisation might bestow the benefit that police activity could be diverted to more serious matters, manufacture could be controlled to introduce quality checks, and considerable revenue could be levied by taxation.

Strict legislation with drugs other than cannabis has proved that it can be effective. In Ireland, where there are restrictions of import, distribution and sale of amphetamines, a remand-home study showed a great decrease in usage, as measured by urine tests. A fall occurred in delinquent boys from 11·4 per cent positive for amphetamines to 0·6 per cent, from the last quarter of 1969, prior to legislation, to the first quarter of 1970, after legislation (Wilson, 1972).

Compulsory treatment

The second Brain Committee (1965) was mindful of the likelihood that many addicts would not attend treatment centres, and that others who had embarked on treatment would wish to break it off. It was thought by the committee that the staff of the treatment centres should have the power to enable them to detain patients compulsorily during crises occurring in treatment, and it was recommended that legislation be enacted to this end. The Government rejected the advice, but there is still an influential group of professional workers who feel that compulsory admission to, and detention in, hospital is reasonable when all else has failed. It is possible under carefully defined circumstances, to admit addicts under Sections 25, 26, 29, 60 and 65 of the Mental Health Act 1959 and to restrain them under Section 30, but mental illness other than addiction, or psychopathy or subnormality, must also be present or suspected. None of these allow for mandatory after-care, which is so necessary in preventing relapse. Section 4 of the Criminal Justice Act 1948 allows for admission to hospital for up to twelve months in cases of mental disorder, together with outpatient care and probation after-care of varied length. Admission is voluntary in the sense that hospital authorities cannot detain patients as under the Mental Health sections, but patients who take their discharge do so at the risk of being returned to court as being in breach of their probation order. This Section has proved a valuable one, more valuable for treating addicts who have offended than Section 60 of the Mental Health Act 1959, in our experience.

Alcohol and the law

Laws concerning alcohol in the U.K. are quite different in character from those concerning drugs, being less stringent but more complex. Alcohol consumption is a perfectly legal activity; there are no limits on domestic consumption, and no quantity restrictions on public consumption unless it gives rise to inappropriate behaviour, or poses a risk to others. Complex licensing laws govern the public availability of alcohol beverages, and restrict supply to a limited number of premises. Tax laws yield enormous funds to the Exchequer, whilst the criminal law censures excessive consumption in several ways. The tax laws are of indirect interest, in that they contribute to the prices of beer, wines and spirits and, therefore, to some degree regulate consumption. Indeed, economic factors are perhaps more important than any others in limiting consumption, and are followed in importance by the licensing laws. Domestic production of beer and wine has recently accelerated, but home-distillation of spirits is severely curbed.

The present licensing system depends on the proposition that alcoholic beverages cannot be supplied at all without prior permission and various licences govern sales both in and outside licensed premises. "On-licensed" premises include public houses (which can open for no more than nine-and-a-half hours each weekday, with a compulsory two-hour break) and restaurants and clubs, which are given more liberal hours. Licenses are issued by committees of magistrates, who can transfer and remove licences and have limited discretionary powers. "Off-licensed" premises are allowed to open from 8.30 a.m. to 10.30 p.m., with shortened hours on Sundays. Children under the age of eighteen cannot buy drinks in licensed premises, nor can they drink them in bars, whilst children under fourteen years of age are not allowed into licensed premises. (There are some exceptions to these general rules.) The current law on drinking is reasonable, allowing several hours of drinking each day and imposing only moderate restrictions in the public interest. The Errol report (Report of the Departmental Committee on Liquor Licensing, 1972) has reviewed the evidence for changes in availability of intoxicating liquor and has debated whether increased opening hours might increase the incidence of abnormal drinking. It accepted the view that increasing consumption of alcohol is likely to be spread amongst normal and heavy drinkers, but felt that very considerable relaxations in licensing legislation would be required to produce a significant increase in drinking habits when compared with all the other environmental and personal factors that determine consumption. The members felt the changes that they had recommended were reasonable in the context of current opinion and future expectation of social change.

Recently, leisure and drinking habits in Britain have changed. Public houses provide a wider range of services but are, nevertheless, reducing in numbers, as demands are being made for more flexibility in hours and for more family facilities. Working hours in factories and offices are reducing, and a system of more flexible working hours is slowly being introduced, a phenomenon that may accelerate rapidly. The Errol Report concluded that legislation ought to be adaptable and not based on the assumption that there is a static social situation, and that it ought to be acceptable to general public opinion but still allow for as yet unforeseen future trends. In particular, they felt that there was public support for greater relaxation of the law, particularly among the young. If the law were to ignore consumer expectation, it would fall into disrepute, but it should also contain safeguards in the public good, whilst not being determined by attitudes based on social conditions prevailing at the turn of the century.

The proposals contained in the Errol Report have wide-reaching implications that do not all concern us here. Its major relevant recommendations are as follows:

1. Licences should not be refused merely on the grounds that there is no market demand for new facilities, or to protect existing licence-holders.
2. Public houses may remain open from 10.00 a.m. to 12.00 midnight, but there is no obligation for them to be open for all these hours. The Licencee can open or close as he sees fit within these hours, and licensing authorities can also modify opening hours in several ways.
3. Off-sales may be available from 8.30 a.m. to 12.00 midnight, with similar regulations to the supply of on-sales.
4. The minimum age for the purchase and consumption of drinks should be reduced from eighteen to seventeen, and those under the age of fourteen can enter bars under specified conditions, although the general rule that it is an offence to be in a bar under the age of fourteen should remain.
5. The social effects of any future legislation should be monitored by measuring changes in consumption, drinking habits and the incidence of alcohol abuse, this research being carried out under the supervision of an interdepartmental working party.

If these recommendations are implemented there will be an expansion in the number of retail outlets for alcohol, with the prospect of a certain but as yet undeterminable increase in the amount of alcohol beverages sold. The committee accepted that the age-limit of eighteen years is widely abused already and lowering the limit merely gives official approval to an existing situation. The onus is on the licensee to recognise under-age drinkers and if they find it difficult now to differentiate 17- from 18-year-olds, it is unlikely that shifting the age-limit downward will improve their powers to discriminate between 17- and 16-year-olds. It is possible that the number of under 17-year-olds who drink in bars will increase substantially, but, interestingly, the number of people under-age found buying or drinking since 1964 has not substantially altered, as can be seen from Table XI.

TABLE XI
Incidence of under-aged drinking or buying of alcohol, 1964–70

Year	*Number prosecuted*
1964	4,207
1966	3,626
1968	3,808
1970	4,548

It hardly needs stating that these figures represent probably only a tiny minority of under-age people who drink, not only each year but each *day* in bars, and that the police are not unduly concerned about this facet of their supervisory role. Drunkenness is a more noticeable consequence of drinking and the incidence has increased amongst young people in the past ten years, in both the under eighteen and the eighteen to twenty-one age groups.

TABLE XII
Drunkenness convictions in the U.K., 1964 and 1974

	Male	*Female*
1964		
Under 18	1,775	77
18–21	7,262	210
1974		
Under 18	4,644	374
18–21	14,293	839

Being found drunk on a highway or other public place is an offence against the law, under the Licensing Act 1972. This is termed "simple drunkenness" as opposed to "drunkenness with aggravations" in which the act is compounded by other forms of antisocial behaviour, or a serious risk is present, as when the individual is drunk in charge of a herd of cows, a horse or a steam engine! The number of drunkenness offences has risen as follows:

TABLE XIII
Drunkenness convictions in the U.K., all ages

Year	*Number prosecuted*
1959	65,187
1964	76,842
1969	80,502
1972	103,203

These figures do not show the total number of individual offenders (which is perhaps half of the number of offences) as many offenders appear several times before the court in the course of a year. Indeed, it is easy to find many inhabitants of hostels and "doss-houses" who have appeared before the courts more than a hundred times each! Minor single offences are usually settled by fines or short-term imprisonment but with repetitive offences, the courts may be at a loss to know what to do. Many cases of simple drunkenness are brought to casualty departments of hospitals and are then removed by the police, when medical complications have been excluded or treated. When detoxification centres become operational this unsatisfactory state of affairs may be ended, but until then, an endless number of drunks will be brought before the courts and dealt with by futile measures. Habitual offenders go from prison to prison, fail to pay fine after fine, and are referred to treatment agencies by a haphazard and illogical process. Those who are referred for help often receive an unsympathetic hearing and arrive in prison notwithstanding. Courts can treat alcoholism as a mental disorder under the Mental Health Act 1959, and can refer alcoholics under Sections 60 and 65 of the 1959 Act or Section 4 of the Criminal Justices Act 1948. Alcoholics can also be dealt with compulsorily by the civil sanctions of Sections 25, 26 and 29 of the Mental Health Act 1959. Section 29 allows for observation for a three-day period on the recommendation of only one doctor, whilst Section 25 is a twenty-eight-day observation order requiring the signatures of two doctors. Few alcoholics derive lasting benefit from short-term admission, but many are willing to remain in hospital as voluntary patients. For those for whom treatment is imperative despite lack of co-operation, Section 26 allows up to one year of enforced medical care, and Section 30 allows voluntary patients to be restrained if the medical officer responsible for the patient considers that his or her health is at risk.

EDUCATION

It is hardly surprising that more attention is being paid to education now that the deficiencies of treatment, legislation, and law enforcement have been realised. Unfortunately, there is as yet very little agreement about the aims and purposes of education, and even less about the methods that should be used. Adults often seem unable to understand their own drug use or appreciate the different preferences of the younger generation. We should make no distinction between alcohol, tobacco, illegal drugs, or proprietary medicines in the context of education, and they should be dealt with together. To make them separate issues is to accept a logical fallacy that has been so vigorously exploited by younger people, who delight in illustrating the inconsistencies of their elders.

As it is nearly impossible to avoid statements that contain elements of value judgment, it may be worth while to outline our personal views about drug-taking and the aims of education relevant to this. We would not presume to condemn any form of drug-taking as intrinsically "bad". The benefits of consuming alcohol probably outweigh the disadvantages, and tobacco smoking is so commonplace that it would be unrealistic, in the short term, to expect the majority of the population to stop smoking. If a "safe" cigarette could be introduced, which did not contribute to chronic bronchitis, lung cancer, or coronary thrombosis, amongst other serious diseases, then the major reason for discussing its disadvantages would disappear. But, as doctors, we have been in daily contact with the disastrous consequences of cigarette smoking, seen many men die needlessly at premature ages, and seen the havoc wreaked in the bereaved families. There are few ways of dying that are so prolonged, painful, and distressful for all concerned as the death from lung cancer.

As doctors it is our duty to alleviate suffering, and ultimately our most important function must be to prevent, rather than cure, disease. Almost every heroin addict we have seen has at some time expressed regret about his state, and few established heroin addicts (as opposed to beginners) encourage others to follow their lead. Many feel deeply about their situation but are unable to alter it, whilst others feel very bitter about the treatment they have received from society, and the few opportunities they feel they have been given. However, not all drug-takers are "junkies" and it would be unwise to design an educational programme just to protect the interests of the minority. More damage is caused by misunderstandings, cultural disparities, poor parent-child communication and certain vested interests of the Establishment than by drugs. Education designed to affect the behaviour of one segment of the population by biased propaganda is, in our minds, unjustifiable. Nevertheless, we would accept that youth-orientated programmes of the proper sort are important, although adult programmes should run a close second.

It is undeniable that drug-taking is increasing, yet, oddly, statements about children taking drugs at school often elicit very hostile responses by parents and teachers, as though denial can make the phenomenon disappear. A primary aim of education should be to gain knowledge of the present situation without resorting to emotional utterances about "drug scares" or "the drug menace". A memorable sight was that of a senior policeman, at a conference of sixth-formers, waving a huge chunk of compressed cannabis resin at his audience and crying to them "to turn back the tide of this evil menace". His metaphor was an apt one, since one suspects that his appeal was as effective as King Canute's and it has to be said that emotional appeals of this kind will not stop children experimenting with drugs and will very likely be greeted with derision.

An aim of education is to help people make mature judgments about situations. Drug education should be factual and earnest, but rarely is. There is an unfounded suspicion that factual information does not discourage, but encourages, experimentation with drugs, and this has given rise to an attitude that is ambivalent at best and antagonistic at worst towards the presentation of honest accounts. What needs to be said straightaway is that, if people wish to dissuade youngsters from taking drugs, the techniques they have used hitherto show a lamentable ignorance of the effective methods of influencing human behaviour.

An impartial approach to drug education really involves a fundamental change in the teaching of human biology as a whole. It must, for example, enable people to understand the effects of drugs on the human organism, and to make them more responsible in the use of all chemical substances, including food. Over-eating and obesity are greater contributory factors to premature mortality than drinking, drug-taking, or smoking combined! In a sense, it is impossible to reach scientific and impartial decisions about anything as complex as drug-taking, because the information is so vast that it could never be fully presented. So, we would accept that "factual" cannot be interpreted literally here, but has to be an approximation or condensation of the truth. Even if it were possible to present all the factual material available, it would be impossible to predict that rational decisions would be made as a consequence, as this would depend on the previous experience of the recipient. "Impartial" presentations about drugs usually imply that rational decisions will lead to the rejection of drug-taking, a premise that in itself must bring the "impartiality" into doubt!

A lesson in failure: the control of smoking by education campaigns

An excellent critical review of the ineffectiveness of cigarette-smoking control procedures has been compiled by a former colleague of ours, Peter Bradshaw (1973). His contention is that projects have been misconceived both in content and in form, and that their only merit has been the enthusiasm shown by the health campaign organisers. The extraordinary confidence in their audience's rationality displayed by anti-smoking propagandists is not adequately supported by results. The dissemination of information about health hazards in the 1960s, on a national scale, had a negligible long-term effect on consumption figures.

Health education dispensed at a local level in more concentrated and organised ways has proved equally disappointing. None of the fourteen American and British surveys that Bradshaw reviewed had any more than a minor effect, and some had no effect at all. The campaigns drew upon arbitrarily-selected propaganda techniques, haphazardly grouped together. Often they involved publicity drives using television and radio, newspaper advertisements, articles, leaflets, posters, films, talks, exhibitions, banners and even loud-speaker vans, but there was no appreciable change in the numbers smoking. The construction of the campaigns was largely rational but Bradshaw felt that research from social psychology, of the independent variables affecting the successful use of persuasive communication, had been ignored by the campaign organisers. Vital areas, such as the reasons given by smokers for not heeding publicised health hazards, have not been explored. Very few studies have employed adequate control groups, so that firm conclusions could rarely be reached about even the few well-conceived campaigns.

Bradshaw also reviewed the results of treatment in anti-smoking clinics, which incidentally provides us with some pertinent information about the whole of the addiction-treatment scene. The design of the numerous studies in this field has been much better and there has been more effective use of controls than in work on other areas of drug addiction. The overall median success rate for four different clinical approaches comprising 34 groups was 37 per cent, with a range from 8 to 84 per cent. The treatment groups were: medication procedures (using the drug Lobeline mostly); a variety of individual and group counselling measures; combined medication-counselling methods; and behaviour therapy techniques, including stimulus satiation and aversion relief. All of the groups except counselling procedures proved superior to no-treatment controls, but four to six months after treatment only 16 per cent remained abstinent in those few groups that included long-term follow up; these are figures reminiscent of the relapse rates for alcoholism and drug addiction.

Gloomy response rates such as these might suggest that there may be no answer to the cigarette-smoking problem, but Russell (1973) feels that the answer may lie in price control. Comparison of the price of manufactured cigarettes and the rate of consumption by British males during the period 1946–71 revealed a strong inverse relationship. For each old-penny rise in the cost (i.e. after correcting for overall price rises) a fall occurred of 40 cigarettes per person per year. Russell feels that the elimination of smoking is an extreme goal, and acceptable, controlled smoking of cigars rather than cigarettes should be the aim, since cigars and pipes lower the absorption of toxic substances from the combustion of tobacco, and are smoked less frequently than cigarettes. Successive annual "true" price rises of 5 per cent would probably be highly effective in depressing consumption. If cigarette advertising were barred and cigar advertising intensified, and prices raised by 10 per cent each year, cigarette smoking could be eliminated in ten years, in Russell's view.

It would be interesting to know whether price rises affect heavy or light smokers proportionately more. If licensing hours and prices have a much smaller effect on alcoholics than environmental factors, it might be suspected that, in parallel, heavy smokers (i.e. those more truly addicted) would not smoke much less with price rises alone. Russell criticises the "safe" low-nicotine cigarette. Smokers who switch to low-nicotine cigarettes unknowingly puff more to increase the nicotine intake, and in so doing inhale more carcinogenic tar-substances. Recent advertisements, showing tables of nicotine content of cigarettes, are based on misguided reasoning and may increase the dangers, especially the danger of lung cancer.

Persuasive techniques in education

Educationalists generally agree that the aims of drug education programmes in schools are to reduce the incidence of drug-taking and to identify early drug users. Some feel that if drug-taking is low in incidence, then education should be minimal, in the interests of the majority who have not taken drugs. Most feel that it is imperative not to glamourise drug-taking and some prefer not to give sets of factual instruction lest they invite experimentation. Authoritarian injunctions on drinking, smoking or drug-taking are likely to be ignored. Davies and Stacey (1972) have shown that adolescent drinking is controlled by teenagers themselves, and that sanctions influence *where* young people consume alcohol rather than whether or not they consume it. Some young people resort to early alcohol use or drug use as an expression of their rejection of adult norms and values, the more so if their parents are actively disapproving. If children were introduced to the controlled use of alcohol in social settings as an acceptable mode of behaviour, they might use it less as a means of rejecting authority in disadvantageous situations outside the home.

George Birdwood writes with more good sense than most about drug education, but even he falls into many traps. He decries the use of TV or films because they are emotive media, liable to play on teenagers' emotional instability, as well as talks by experts because they generate excessive interest, and factual instructions because they invite experimentation (he quotes sex education as leading to experimentation, as though not to experiment sexually would be the desired norm in adolescence!). According to him, the dangers of drug-taking should not be stressed; authoritarian proscriptions should be forbidden, and ex-addicts should not be allowed to relate their experiences, lest the message that addiction can be cured may become misleadingly communicated. It seems unfortunate that so many remedies should be condemned out of hand. Television is not inherently emotive, and even if it were, appeals can be potent manipulators of opinion. It would be very sad if all experts were cast into limbo and their expertise wasted, or if ex-addicts could not help others to avoid the mistakes they themselves had made.

Birdwood himself believes that the only answer lies in the use of small-group discussion and discussion groups do have many advantages. He thinks that they are lively, interesting and relevant for all concerned, but not all teachers are as interesting and articulate as Birdwood, nor can they all stimulate their audiences to the same useful extent. We suggest that there should be no dogmatic pronouncements about whether films, television, lectures or discussion groups are the most appropriate educational tools. There should be an understanding of the fundamental influences in communication, and the use of these in optimal ways in whatever media are chosen.

Audiences do respond favourably to persuaders who have expertise. The greater the expert's knowledge, the greater his credibility and the greater his ability to influence, especially if his knowledge is imparted without bias. Credibility is not a constant state; it is continuously being questioned and influenced by the nature of the communication itself, and by the audience's perception of the trustworthiness of the communicator. If a communicator initially expresses views held by his audience, the greater will be his subsequent effectiveness. It would be sensible therefore for any lecturer to have some prior knowledge of each audience's background, intelligence and attitudes to drugs, so that he does not alienate its members with his opening remarks. Thereafter, he can ask for, and achieve (unless he has low credibility for some other reason), an attitude change that will depend upon the discrepancy between his own and his audience's initial position.

Drug and alcohol education in schools is characteristically dispensed to groups, each with their unique structure and affiliations. The more voluble a group is in expressing its opinions, the more difficult it is to change it. But opinions derived from active participation are known to be more persistent over time. Group discussions are, therefore, useful if the group leader can elicit democratic opinion, yet control individual deviation. People who closely identify with the group's norms will welcome material acceptable to that group and will reject conflicting ideas, but the persistent disagreement of a tiny minority can prove disruptive and may profoundly alter the acceptability of a message. If means can be found to reduce the status of persistent minority opinion, then a balance can be restored.

So often in teaching we find that a lecturer successful in one situation fails miserably in another, because adequate thought has not been given to the individual tailoring of the message, or to the form of delivery to the audience. Even in the best lecture, attention wanders for as much as 60 per cent of the time. The topics of daydreaming concern the priorities we have in life, so that sex, food and leisure figure importantly. The astute communicator can take advantage of this by structuring irrelevancies to his advantage, cracking jokes, making witty comments that may have little to do with the core message but make him appear more favourable and therefore improve the credibility of his message. Surprisingly, astutely-used distractors can actually increase attitude change, even if there is reduced recall of the proceedings.

Elms (1966) described an interesting experiment in which active smokers were asked to act to dissuade others from smoking and not unpredictably the behaviour they showed was discordant with their normal smoking behaviour. Such inconsistency creates an internal disharmony of thinking—a situation referred to as "cognitive dissonance". This particular situation was resolved by the role-playing dissuaders actually shifting their own situation and becoming less favourable to smoking, an attitude change that produced a correspondingly-reduced smoking behaviour. Such an experiment suggests many exciting possibilities for health education, for example, games in which children take on the policeman's role, the doctor's role, social worker's role, and so on, thus exploring and gaining insight into different viewpoints. In the Elms's study, the audience also showed a hardening of attitudes towards smoking, but their views proved more fickle than those of the active participants, of whom 46 per cent smoked less (as against 27 per cent for the listeners) at follow-up. We would suggest that active role-playing is perhaps the most effective way to date of changing previously "unaccepting" positions towards a more favourable view.

There is a commonly held firm belief that fear arousal has high efficacy as a means of persuasion. There is some substance to this view, although there is much conflicting evidence. For example, smokers exposed to horrific films about lung cancer have become motivated to seek chest X-rays rather than necessarily reducing their smoking. One theory to explain the influence of fear-arousing communications is that only moderate levels of fear are effective, and both high and low anxiety levels interfere with propaganda. Individuals vary in their kind of arousal, so that for some, high-arousal appeals would be more suitable, and for others low-arousal appeals. On the whole, it seems that less intelligent people respond to emotional appeals, and the more intelligent to low-anxiety appeals. Fear-arousal motivates people to action, so that it is important to make explicit and realistic suggestions for appropriate action to an audience.

It would seem that to have a lasting effect, drug education should not be restricted to specific units of teaching time, but instead should be spread over periods, perhaps over years, beginning in junior school. It should be introduced informally, incorporated generally into health education courses, and be concerned more about the emotional needs of the users than with sterile accounts of drug action. There is disagreement about who should teach children, although many feel that counsellors would be the best agents (Dorn, 1972). Unfortunately, there are few such professionals in the U.K., and, rather discouragingly, in the U.S.A. counsellors commonly seem to be no better informed than many teachers about drug knowledge.

Schuman (1971) showed films to groups of counselling teachers and students. The films alluded to drug-taking without being explicit, illustrating adolescent rebellion and anti-authority feelings, loneliness and despair, with peer-pressures to gain status. The counsellors made subtle and sophisticated interpretations of the abnormal behaviour they viewed, but most of them consistently failed to relate it to drugs. Only 12·5 per cent of them correctly identified drug references. Schuman suggested that the innovative films he used might be helpful in stimulating children and in avoiding the frequent resort to cliches and stereotypes that many programmes in this area use. He felt that the situational and motivational aspects of drug-seeking behaviour should be examined more than the pharmacological aspects and that teachers had much to learn from the, often better-informed, children. Munoz and Parada (1970) found that 94 per cent of teachers had little or no information about alcoholism, and that only 28 per cent would be willing to participate in a preventive programme.

Adult education

It is evident from the figures about teachers that many people are relatively uninformed about the actions of drugs, the adverse actions of alcohol, and the abuse of these substances; there are grave deficiencies in the training of professional people as well as in the education of the laity. The World Health Organisation, from the time since Professor Jellinek was its alcoholism consultant, has spent increasing amounts of its resources on combined approaches to education and treatment. The International Council on Alcohol and Addictions in Lausanne also organises international congresses, conferences, seminars and symposia for professional workers and the general public in many countries. In Britain the Health Education Council is associated with an annual summer school on alcoholism, and there have been major interdisciplinary international conferences in London, Liverpool, Cardiff and Dublin in recent years. Professional and voluntary associations are numerous, but notable are the Association for the Prevention of Addiction, the Institute for the Study of Drug Dependence, and the National Council on Alcoholism. At a local level, organisations such as the Merseyside Council on Alcoholism have made pioneer assessments of their role in education, treatment and early recognition of alcoholism. The Merseyside Council is notable for the care with which it monitors its service efficacy. Few others, out of many thousands of local organisations, make any serious attempt to evaluate their impact in the sphere of education. No one *really* knows whether poster-campaigns, leaflets, audio-visual aids, pamphlets, or educational literature of any kind accomplish their goals.

Research by former colleagues in the Department of Psychiatry in the University of Liverpool, on doctor-patient communications, may have important repercussions for health education. Many people fail to understand medical information because it is presented to them in language they do not comprehend (Ley, 1972). Dr. Ley and his co-workers found, on analysing five routine explanatory X-ray leaflets, that as few as 40 per cent of the people reading them could understand them (Ley *et al.*, 1972). These leaflets were meant to provide reassurance through the explanation of several complex investigations such as bronchograms and barium meals, which might be expected to induce anticipatory anxiety. Re-writing of these leaflets with simpler wording and shorter sentences considerably improved their understandability.

Ley (1973) has reviewed a number of measures of comprehensibility, especially the Flesch Reading Ease Score, and has given a practical guide to the use of its formula. He quotes tables giving the numbers of the population who would be expected to understand material with a given Reading Ease (R.E.) score—obviously there is a correlation with intelligence. We would suggest that much educational literature is inappropriate to the audience which receives it, and that the application of comprehensibility tests might help the tailoring of material to the intended audience. This would be highly relevant as applied to educational material related to alcohol and drug abuse.

REFERENCES

Birdwood, G., "A Community Approach", a Paper presented at the 2nd International Conference on Alcoholism and Drug Dependence, Liverpool, 1972.

Bradshaw, P. W., "The Problem of Cigarette Smoking and its Control", *International Journal of Addiction,* 8: 353–71, 1973.

Brain Committee, *Drug Addiction: The Second Report of the Interdepartmental Committee,* H.M.S.O., London, 1965.

Davies, J. and Stacey, B., *Teenagers and Drinking: A Developmental Study in Glasgow*, H.M.S.O., London, 1972.

Dorn, N., "Drug Education—is it Effective?", *Drugs and Society,* 1 (9): 21–4, 1972.

Elms, A. C., "Influence of Fantasy Ability on Attitude Change Through Role Playing", *J. Rep. Soc. Psychol.,* 4: 175–80, 1966.

Erroll Report, *Report of the Departmental Committee on Liquor Licensing,* H.M.S.O., London, 1972.

Le Dain Commission, *Cannabis: A Report of the Commission of Inquiry into the Non-medical Use of Drugs,* Information Canada, Ottawa, 1972.

Ley, P., "Comprehension, Memory, and the Success of Communication with the Patient", *Journal of the Institute of Health Education,* 10: 23–9, 1972.

Ley, P., "The Measurement of Comprehensibility", *J. Instit. Health Educ.,* 11: 17–20, 1973.

Ley, P. *et al.,* "The Comprehensibility of some X-ray leaflets", *J. Instit. Health Educ.,* 10: 47–54, 1972.

Munoz, L. C. and Parada, A., "Teaching about Alcoholism in Schools", in Popham, R. E., (ed.), op. cit.

Popham, R. E., (ed.), *Alcohol and Alcoholism, University of Toronto,* Toronto, 1970.

Russell, M. A. H., "Analysis of Prices and Consumption of Cigarettes", *British Journal of Preventive and Social Medicine,* 27: 1–7, 1973.

Schuman, S. H., "Drug Perception and the Student-Teacher Gap", *Journal of the American Medical Association,* 659–63, 1971.

Wilson, C. W. M., "Amphetamine Abuse and Government Legislation", *British Journal of Addictions,* 67: 107–12, 1972.

Wootton Report: *Report by the Advisory Committee on Drug Dependence: Cannabis,* H.M.S.O., London, 1968.

12 Current problems—future developments

In the previous chapters we have attempted to present an overview of the effects of the main dependency-producing drugs (apart from tobacco), the extent to which people are at risk of developing dependency and the subsequent effects if they do become dependent.

It is now possible to draw certain conclusions about the actions of the various drugs, about the people who are liable to be affected and about some of the ways in which they can be helped. As in any other field, the presence of well-established facts permits the development of attitudes that can be defended on logical, rather than emotional, grounds. Reliable data also allow us to produce testable hypotheses, with subsequent further refinement of knowledge, which can lead to progressively more constructive changes in attitudes.

We feel that it is important to stress once more this matter of the attitudes that are generally held about drug-dependents. It has to be accepted that most people still have negative feelings towards drug-dependents and this is understandable, and even reasonable, to a certain degree. Drunken alcoholics or people high on "speed" or LSD are unpredictable and are often frightening for that reason. If they happen to be in charge of a vehicle they are capable of harming innocent people. At other times they may act out aggressive urges when they are disinhibited, urges that would and should ordinarily be controlled. There is nothing attractive about the heroin addict suffering torments in a withdrawal state, nor about the alcoholic who is so drunk that he cannot control the functioning of his legs, bladder or bowels. However, we hope that we have been able to make it clear that such consequences are not inevitable and that dependency on a drug does not inevitably turn someone into a monster. The majority of drug-dependents are at least as miserable with their condition as are the onlookers who condemn them.

It is important to be clear about the target of an attitudinal statement. If a child does something of which one disapproves, there is a choice of saying: "You are a bad boy and you keep doing things to annoy me", or else: "That was a bad thing to do, don't do it again". In the first statement, the child is labelled as being "bad" and he receives no information as to how he can prevent the label from being applied again. In fact he has every expectation that it *will* be reapplied. In the second statement, the action is identified, labelled and proscribed, and, one hopes, the self-esteem of the child is left relatively unharmed. Similarly, the attitudes that "alcoholics are drunken menaces" or that "anyone who smokes 'grass' is mentally ill", indicate that the person holding these opinions is most unlikely to offer any help to the people so described. We would agree with anyone that alcoholism and drug dependence are terrible conditions from which to suffer. On the other hand, alcoholics and drug-dependents are frequently *not* terrible people and given the chance (or sometimes it has to be many chances) a good proportion of them will be able to overcome their dependencies. It has to be stressed again and again, particularly to those in the health-care agencies, that attitudes to treatment outcome have a tremendous influence on the *actual* outcome for any group of patients so that, short of fatuous optimism, there is every reason for taking a positive therapeutic approach. At the same time, it has to be admitted that changing everyone's attitudes to drug dependency would not by itself solve the many problems we have discussed earlier. Nevertheless, it makes a constructive start.

To turn to the consideration of alcoholism specifically, we will examine possibilities for further work in the areas of the definition of normal drinking, the extent of alcoholism and also the causes, effects, treatment and prevention of the disorder. Thereafter, we shall consider the same topics in relation to drug dependency.

Alcoholism

NORMAL DRINKING

The studies of the variations in national, cultural, class, age and sex differences in drinking habits quoted earlier allow us to understand the range of normal drinking under various influences. Where normal drinking for any society borders on the excessive, as for example in France, there is a lot of work to be done in finding ways in which the population can persuaded, or maybe coerced, into drinking less.

EXTENT OF ALCOHOLISM

As already stated, alcoholism is not a separate, specific disease entity that can be identified as different from the state of normal drinking. The fully-blown case of alcoholism with withdrawal symptoms, morning drinking and gastritis is easily identifiable, but the point at which drinking crosses the limit of normality is much more difficult to determine.

Alcoholism surveys have tended to diagnose the condition in terms of the symptoms presented by alcoholics who come for treatment. Conducting a survey using a questionnaire based on these symptoms may well identify a population consisting mainly of people who would eventually seek treatment for alcoholism. In fact, the majority of alcoholics never seek treatment at all, and it is probable that many of them improve spontaneously.

At present we have no way of knowing for certain how many alcoholics there are in a particular population. If it were possible to carry out a survey of the population, using a reliable drinking-history questionnaire combined with direct observation of drinking habits and random blood samples for alcohol levels, this would increase the accuracy of our knowledge; but unfortunately this is not possible. It would represent an enormous intrusion into peoples' privacy and is neither justifiable nor practical.

The task of estimating the prevalence of alcoholism would be made easier if medical records were consistently accurate and were available for perusal by investigators. But so long as there is a stigma attached to alcoholism and an inquest is necessary in alcoholism deaths, then doctors will under-report alcohol-related deaths.

Wilkins (1972) has reported on a method for identifying people at risk of developing alcoholism and this method could probably be used by helping agencies. His suggestion of a central "at-risk" or "definite alcoholism" register would undoubtedly provide more accurate data than we have at present but one has to acknowledge the dangers inherent in any large data bank containing detailed personal information.

Surveys such as that carried out by Moss and Beresford Davies (1968) in Cambridgeshire represent the most accurate method so far devised for identifying and counting alcoholics in the general community. The main difficulty with this type of survey lies in defining the signs and symptoms that are absolutely indicative of alcoholism, to prevent some alcoholics from being excluded and non-alcoholics from being included. Also, the dangers of the investigator building in his own biases are very great where the object of the study is ill-defined and where observations are open to arbitrary decision.

THE CAUSES OF ALCOHOLISM

As already indicated, simplistic statements like "alcoholism is caused by factor X" have not been shown to stand up to investigation. The causes of alcoholism are multifactorial and even the relative influences of personality structure, early upbringing and genetic influences have not yet been determined, although each may have significance.

The differing sub-types of alcoholism may turn out to have relatively different causes. The recent genetic study of Goodwin and his colleagues (1973), and the frequent association of alcoholism with manic-depressive psychosis, which is itself genetically influenced, raise once more the question of inborn susceptibility to alcoholism. The study of the relative risk of development of alcoholism within the families of alcoholics and of non-alcoholics needs a great deal more clarification. The association of alcoholism with manic-depressive psychoses also raises the possibility that it might be possible to prevent alcoholism developing in *some* people by the use of lithium, which has been shown to be prophylactic in these affective psychoses.

THE EFFECTS OF ALCOHOL ABUSE

Alcoholism, as it is seen in hospital, is frequently complicated by concomitant physical illness. The reason for believing that the prolonged intake of alcohol causes physical illness may partly be due to the observation of those people with illnesses like peptic ulcer who have to seek medical treatment. The unidentified alcoholic often remains hidden because he fails to develop such ailments. Are there, therefore, genetic influences in the appearance of secondary illnesses? Females appear to develop conditions such as alcoholic dementia relatively more frequently than male alcoholics and they often do so earlier in their drinking career, suggesting an inherent protective factor in the case of the men.

The social effects of alcoholism such as job loss, marital breakdown and drunkenness arrests could probably be altered by the introduction of educational and treatment programmes. It can be shown that, for the alcoholic who is not grossly personality-disordered or psychotic, it is possible to avoid finishing up homeless, alone and disowned by society. These features of alcoholism are not primary symptoms, but are secondary effects, to a considerable extent determined by society's inability to deal constructively with the problem.

TREATMENT

The necessity for treatment should be underlined. Some psychiatrists (for example Szasz), are of the opinion that psychiatric treatment should never be forced on patients and that they should be left to arrive at their own solution even if, in some cases, this means committing suicide. It appears to the present authors that in established alcoholism, the freedom of choice to continue drinking or to stop has been lost by the patient and he can no longer make for himself a rational decision between abstinence and further drinking. The humane approach is to offer therapy but the use of compulsory treatment raises difficult ethical problems. It is justifiable if the patient is suicidal, acutely psychotic or so brain-damaged as to be unaware of his actions, but compulsory treatment of an alcoholic merely because he relapses frequently is probably not justified in most instances.

The aims of treatment have been discussed earlier. If social drinking is to become the aim for some alcoholics, it is going to be necessary to identify accurately those who stand a good chance of controlling their future alcohol intake and those who do not. At present, a trial of "good prognosis" alcoholics (in terms of the factors found by Davies (1962), and by Gerard and Saenger (1966), appears to offer a partial solution to this problem. Those people showing the characteristics that appear to correlate with the ability to drink in a controlled manner could justifiably be randomly allocated to an abstinence treatment regime, or a controlled drinking regime. For worthwhile results, it would be necessary to have close follow-up of the subjects for a number of years at least, and preferably for a lifetime, to determine which drinking, or non-drinking, pattern best suited which individuals.

The techniques for encouraging abstinence appear most useful for middle- or upper-class, socially stable, non-psychopathic alcoholics. For the rest of the alcoholic population, the results have been largely disappointing, with occasional exceptions such as the effectiveness of hostel care. Sure techniques for producing prolonged controlled drinking are as yet unknown, but the possibilities offered by blood alcohol concentration discrimination-training and systematic social conditioning have yet to be investigated.

The questions to be answered as regards treatment are still those raised by Pattison in 1966; namely, which treatment, by whom, under which circumstances, for which alcoholic, and in what stage of development of the condition, will produce the best results? Although it has been shown that some forms of treatment are better than others for up to two years, in certain groups of patients it has not yet been shown that over a lifetime a treated alcoholic does consistently better than an untreated one. The decision to offer no treatment to someone who presents at a treatment facility undoubtedly raises ethical difficulties. It is easy to be scientific and to say that, if you cannot show that your treatment helps, you are not in fact withholding anything of value. However, there is always a great pressure to do something for a sufferer who asks for help, and, until it is possible to discover whether or not treatment is actually harmful, one feels morally obliged to do something positive. Nevertheless, there is some possibility that the insistence on abstinence may prevent alcoholics from undergoing natural remission to a state in which they could drink socially again. Repeated failure to achieve the impractical goal, total abstinence, may assert to himself and to others the worthlessness of the alcoholic and may impart to both parties a complete loss of hope of recovery.

GENERAL RESEARCH STRATEGY

In all research, it is essential that the measures used for any parameter (for example, assessment of recovery) should be clearly defined, be capable of application by another independent researcher and be relevant to the study. Let us hope that, in the future, researchers will not describe studies on a group of "alcoholics", but will instead define the diagnosis of alcoholism in strict, reproducible terms. Diagnoses based simply on the findings of one clinician are no longer acceptable, but should always be open to confirmation or refutation by an independent diagnostician.

A great deal of energy has been wasted by the use of treatments in groups of patients without the use of control groups receiving either no treatment, a placebo treatment or a standard, accepted treatment. Without a doubt the single case report of a marked response to therapy by a particular patient is always of interest in that it may lead on to a new advance, but the repetition of uncontrolled applications of treatment is wasteful and frequently misleading.

In assessing the effects of treatment, single measures such as the achievement of sobriety, should be avoided, and instead ratings applying to several areas of functioning should be devised before the outset of the trial. In a therapeutic trial the person assessing the change brought about by intervention should, ideally, be able to rely on measures such as psychological or biochemical tests, which are independent of observer error. He himself should not have been involved in the therapy and he has to be unaware which specific treatment has been administered. More than one observer should be involved, there should be no collusion in their ratings, and information should be gathered from other sources as well as from the patient in any trial concerned with behavioural change. The particular population to be studied should be rigorously defined at the outset and the hypotheses to be tested clearly formulated. Having decided on the population and the "treatment" or "no-treatment" conditions, all clients matching the selection criteria should be allocated randomly to the investigative programme and followed up for the period of the trial, whether or not they complete the treatment.

At the end of such a trial, it is then possible to report specific findings relating to the group and to the treatment studied, and all that is left is to resist the temptation to generalise too widely to other groups of patients. It is only by the application of such rigorously-structured methods to our research methodology that precise conclusions can be reached. There is no reason to think that alcoholism (or drug dependence) is any less susceptible to such an approach than any other subject worthy of study. Until lately, it happens that careful investigative methods and closely-defined criteria were not commonly employed. Nowadays, this situation is changing and worthwhile results are beginning to emerge. We, therefore, make no apologies for dwelling on the necessity for discipline in the approach to research in this field. Sloppy thinking and soft-centred attitudes towards treatment do little to ameliorate a problem that, in our civilisation, is rapidly advancing to a state of widespread tragedy.

Drug dependence

Western government studies on drug abuse stand, row after row, on bookshelves—the Le Dain report, the Wootton report, presidential advisory committee reports, congressional commission reports—and almost without exception they complain bitterly about the lack of information and the paucity of research. In fact, although research may still be in its infancy, there is a huge output of printed material each year in many important journals, so much so that it is difficult to keep abreast of it all. As with alcoholism, the major faults of research are that it tends to be done in piecemeal fashion, lacking co-ordination, especially between the basic and applied fields, and that field research only occasionally pays heed at all to the methodological procedures of scientific enquiry.

Some of the best research emanates from basic life-science

laboratories, where various levels of brain activity and drug effects are nowadays being evaluated. The brain is an incredibly complex communications system, with millions of nervous impulses passing in all directions, transmitted from one cell to another though the actions of transmitter substances. Abuse of various drugs can alter the uptake of transmitter substances at the active sites. Amphetamine blocks the uptake of catecholamines at the base of the brain, as do cocaine, LSD and opiates. Altered levels of catecholamines or indoleamines, both groups of transmitter substances, undoubtedly affect mood and learning processes, but there has been little work on the correlation of cellular sites of action with the grosser effects of drugs, and even less with the molecular sites of action of drugs.

The amounts of transmitters produced depend on enzymes and these can be stimulated by continued drug administration. It is known, for example, that tyrosine hydroxylase activity can be increased by several drugs, as may possibly tryptophane hydroxylase, and thereby the chemical equilibrium of the structures at the base of the brain is profoundly altered. But drugs can also affect protein synthesis in the brain, especially of ribonucleic acid, and it is known that those which impair protein synthesis can impair the development of tolerance towards morphine, at least in rats. It has been suggested that the formation of certain types of protein is associated with physiological addiction. It is even possible that tolerance is due to antibody production after chronic opiate or cannabis administration, yet no antibodies have so far been demonstrated, although immunological mechanisms in the body are certainly altered.

Neural transmission can be altered by transmitter substance release, but equally, it can be affected by the amount of fats in the nerve-cell sheaths, yet whilst the nerve-fibre phospholipid is changed by certain drugs it is uncertain whether this has a direct relationship to the development of addiction. The elucidation of such problems will be sought in the coming years. We already know that morphine depresses the function of the pituitary gland, the master-gland directing the sex, thyroid and adrenal glands. The pituitary, in turn, responds to the influence of the hypothalamus, where opioids can act either through the release of transmitter substances, or directly on the neuro-secretory cells. Morphine, like many centrally-acting substances, also has a peripheral action, so that future studies will have to distinguish the relative importance of the different sites of action as the primary determinants of the addicting process.

Research on the pharmacological action of opiates and barbiturates has taken place over many years, but as the active constituents of cannabis have only recently been isolated and synthesised, studies of tetrahydrocannabinols (THC) at the enzyme level are still few, though increasing. Indeed, we can still say little with certainty about the actions of cannabis, not only as regards its pharmacological effect, but also in the psychological and clinical spheres. There are as many reports saying cannabis is harmful as there are saying it is harmless, and the suspicion is that the answer must lie between these opinions. Recently, examination of lung biopsies from American soldiers who have smoked marijuana have revealed pre-cancerous changes, and hashish smokers are known to have lowered resistance to diseases such as virus infections. If confirmation occurs that cannabis has a long-lasting effect on DNA production by animal cells, this might change opinions that cannabis is no more than mildly intoxicating and generally harmless.

Many pharmacologists still believe that cannabis produces neither tolerance nor physical dependence, but a number of laboratories have shown that tolerance can develop in experimental animals, and even physical dependence has occurred in monkeys. Reports from Greece and Turkey in which high doses of THC were given to rhesus monkeys state that the animals would initiate and maintain self-administration of the drug to prevent an abstinence syndrome. Withdrawal effects included aggression, yawning, muscular twitching, light sensitivity, autonomic dysfunction, and strange behaviours such as eating faeces and hair-pulling. It is possible that human marijuana smokers may not suffer such consequences of withdrawal, but Eastern reports of withdrawal syndromes including bizarre, psychotic-like behaviour in ganja smokers may have to be given credence. There are suggestions too that cannabis can even induce a cross-tolerance to alcohol and to narcotic analgesics.

It is widely accepted that drug addiction is not only a physiologically altered state, but also a conditioned psychological response, This has been demonstrated in animals but not convincingly in humans. John Teasdale (1973) showed photographs of syringes and the injection sequence to heroin addicts, and found subsequent changes in psychological tests suggestive of abstinence symptomatology. Unfortunately, he was unable to present physiological data because his equipment proved unreliable, but his experiments will certainly be repeated. It is possible that return to "drug" environments precipitates a conditioned response, but would this be sufficient to account for relapse? Trest (1973) showed that classically-conditioned responses in rats, in which stimuli were paired with the reduction of morphine abstinence, are more difficult to extinguish than those in which stimuli were paired with abstinence onset. Just what importance conditioning during withdrawal has in affecting the likelihood of re-addiction in humans is not clear, but Trest's experiment is a good example of how animal learning experiments may lead eventually to therapeutic advances. Already a few treatment methods have used classical conditioning paradigms, albeit with limited success.

A continuing cause for concern is the need for identification of drugs ingested by persons suspected of taking them, a vital issue in treatment centres. Established techniques of thin-layer chromatography or gas chromatography are not available to all treatment centres, and are not always reliable. There are still no clinically useful tests to identify LSD or cannabis derivatives in human blood or urine samples, and clinicians may have to wait long periods before analyses for morphia, barbiturates or morphia give positive results. The need for quick and reliable identification of unknown substances has given rise to new technologies. Recently, gas chromatography and mass spectometry have been combined, with the use of computers to match spectra instantly with the spectra of known drugs filed in the computer. Such advances have helped in identifying drugs for law-enforcement and medico-legal purposes, but other potential applications are legion. In the U.S.A., new methods of immuno-assay involve the mixing of morphine with morphine-binding antibodies, and measuring the bound antibodies by spectrometry. Other systems identify morphia indirectly, for when morphia is added to an enzyme-antibody solution, it displaces the enzyme, and measurement of the enzyme activity reflects the amount of morphia present. Such systems are being developed commercially and relatively inexpensively, and have the advantage that they are portable and simple to operate They can be used to identify not only drugs of abuse but also to measure blood levels of therapeutic substances. Currently in clinical psychiatry, only one drug, lithium, used in the treatment of mania and depression, is routinely monitored. Doctors are becoming increasingly aware that it is important to measure other drugs too, and for example, an adequate tricyclic antidepressant serum level may be a critical factor in determining a positive response in the drug treatment of endogenous depression. Whereas today, a clinician has only intuition and experience to guide him, and has no accurate way of knowing whether he has prescribed the right amount of medication, advanced drug-detection systems derived for use in forensic medicine may yield the answer to clinical dose-monitoring in non-addicted patients.

An outstanding problem is the lack of knowledge of the natural history of drug-taking. A working party of the Medical Research Council, which is becoming very interested in drug-abuse research, pointed to the need for prospective studies to assess the process whereby drug-takers are initiated into drug-taking, and escalate or relinquish drug use; the differences between "experimenters" and habitual users; and factors that seem to be related to drug use such as parental attitudes, sexual adequacy, school achievement, and peer-group influence. The longest prospective study, still on-going, is that of George Vaillant in New York, which has now been in existence for twenty years. His follow-up study of 100 addicts discharged from Lexington has revealed a mass of details about the life history of narcotic addicts in urban America, and is an outstanding example of how painstaking and relentless enquiry through numerous sources can pay off handsomely (Vaillant, 1973). As an example of the type of information such an investigation can yield, it has shown that, even after this time, a significant number remained addicted and in trouble well past the age of forty, and although 35 per cent were stable and abstinent, 23 per cent had died, most in unnatural circumstances.

In England, a prospective study of people approaching drug-treatment centres for the first time began late in 1970, and was planned to run for five years. Already the demographic characteristics of the subjects have been described (Blumberg *et al.*, 1973). Most were in their early twenties, and had been using opiates from black-market sources regularly before coming to the notice of London clinics. Almost all had previous convictions for drug offences or other illegal activities, and most were well-entrenched in the drug underworld. Most were regular "fixers", with few or no abstentions of more than a fortnight, and those who did abstain for long periods often had little choice in the matter (for example, many of them were in prison). The main value of this study will come when the base-line data are correlated with outcome measures of continued or discontinued drug usage, so determining those variables related to treatment success or failure and hence identifying the "at-risk" groups.

Another study, this time from the Institute of Psychiatry, is a longitudinal investigation of cannabis smokers in three London areas (Crow, 1973). Crow and his colleague David Triesman recognised that a representative sample of users was impossible to obtain, but they did gather information on a heterogeneous population from different social backgrounds. The two major groups followed up were persons appearing before the court for the first time on cannabis offences, and persons with no official cannabis offences. At the first stage of follow-up, after twelve to eighteen months, 9·5 per cent of the court group and only 3·5 per cent of the non-court group had subsequent drug-offence convictions, and only one person out of a total number of 339 became a registered heroin addict. A surprisingly large number (61 per cent) of the court group had other convictions antedating their cannabis offences, and had substantial drug-abuse histories, so they seemed to be an arrest-prone and delinquency-prone group. The early follow-up did not give any clues that conviction might reduce the drug consumption of the cannabis users. What role the law plays, if any, as a deterrent is not at all clear. Only a tiny proportion of cannabis smokers are ever brought to account, and they probably because they are already known to the authorities through previous convictions. There must, inevitably, be further prospective studies of selected populations, which will throw much-needed light on the natural history of drug abuse.

TREATMENT

In a previous chapter (Chapter 9) covering treatment response, mention was made of a prominent treatment mode, the therapeutic community. Of all the communities such as Daytop, Synanon, Phoenix House, X-Kalay, the best descriptions have been given by Yablonsky of Synanon (1963), which was also the earliest. Unfortunately, he has presented little convincing evidence that therapeutic communities are effective in treating drug abuse, despite claims of considerable success. In 1968 an exciting pilot scheme began in the U.K. in the Wessex Region, based on a Phoenix House model, named Alpha House (Greden, et al. 1973). Housing up to twenty-five residents at any one time, the centre has treated poly-drug rather than purely narcotic addicts. Costing £46 per person per week in 1973, it still remains to be seen whether results are proportionate to expenditure, since alternatives such as borstals and prison cost much less. A large number of residents stayed less than six weeks, but of those who remained for more than sixteen weeks, 50 per cent were either abstinent or had reduced considerably their drug consumption, which, on the face of it, appears encouraging.

The Wayne committee report (1968) suggested the establishment of several specialised hostels, but with few exceptions the ones set up have paid little attention to programme evaluation. Although Yablonsky claimed that a high proportion of Synanon residents who stayed for more than six months remained abstinent, he did not say how many dropped out early, and the selection process initially may have been biased. Weppner (1973) found that Matrix House, a community related to Lexington Hospital in the U.S.A., catered for a group of ex-addicts who differed greatly from street addicts generally, being of better socio-economic background, younger age group, and different ethnic and marital status. They had not been involved in such serious crimes, had fewer arrests, less time in prison, and shorter addiction histories. However, addicts who left the community prematurely tended to resemble street addicts. It will be vital to discover whether therapeutic communities can cure established addicts, or are effective only in dealing with less serious cases. A hostel in California (Berecochea and Sing, 1972) for civilly-committed addicts, providing a bridge between structured institutional life and parole, proved very disappointing. There was no pre-selection of candidates from the correctional institutions, and the residents proved highly uncooperative and prone to absconding. At follow-up of one year, placement in the hostel seemed to show no measurable effect in reducing drug usage or halting return to criminal behaviour. Will English hostels fare any better?

Methadone maintenance programmes have proved more popular than success rates seem to justify. The search goes on for a methadone-like substance that has an effect of greater duration, has a heroin blockade action yet does not give rise to euphoria, and is safe and non-toxic. Levomethadyl (Zaks *et al.*, 1972) is a drug that is similar to methadone, but needs to be given only three times a week. Early clinical trials have shown that 30 to 80 mg thrice weekly gives as much protection as 100 mg daily of methadone, and urine tests on former addicts have shown a very low abuse rate for other drugs up to six months after maintenance has begun. Clearly major trials of this and similar narcotics will soon be under way.

Narcotic antagonists do not yet have an established place in the treatment of opioid addiction. Cyclazocine will block the effects of 25 mg of heroin for a period of up to twenty-four hours, but patients learn to circumvent its action by injecting heroin before a blocking dose is reached, or after peak protection has passed. The latter manoeuvre can be prevented by administering the antagonist in divided dosage, but mandatory clinic attendance several times a day is not a convenient or attractive proposition. Cyclazocine itself causes a physical addiction, yet it only relieves rather than suppresses narcotic hunger. Naloxone is a similar drug, requiring doses of 2,400 mg daily to block 25 mg of injected heroin for twenty-four hours (Zaks *et al.*, 1971). Blockade does not last long with small dosages, and higher dosages give rise to side-effects. A pilot study of 52 parolees given 200–800 mg daily proved disappointing. Only 13 per cent remained in the programme for twelve months, and only 37 per cent remained abstinent from their drugs of addiction.

The optimal antagonist should be orally administrable, should have a duration of at least a week, and should not be itself dependency-producing. Naltrexone is a new drug known to be seventeen times more potent than naloxone, yet with no analgesic activity and little mood-altering action. At a dose level of 50 mg daily it produces an effect similar to 4 mg cyclazocine. It does seem to have advantages over other antagonists, but still requires daily administration, and has not yet been subjected to clinical trials.

The rationale for antagonists (based on learning theory) is that they act as negative reinforcers, that is, they block the incentive value of heroin. Cyclazocine and naloxone can also be viewed as having aversive stimulus characteristics if given after heroin use. Other treatments based on classical conditioning paradigms and using aversion have been described, but are of uncertain value. Reviews of behavioural treatments of drug addiction include those by Droppa (1973) and Miller (1973). Even group-orientated programmes like Synanon can be seen in behavioural rather than dynamic terms, as attempting to change criminal and drug-seeking behaviour by negative reinforcement. Shaping procedures, punishment, reinforcement of assertive behaviours, can all be identified.

Hitherto, there have been few comprehensive models to account for the commencement and maintenance of addiction in behavioural terms, and behavioural treatments offered have been fragmented and narrow in scope. Solomon and Marshall (1973) have outlined a model in which acquisition is facilitated by the pleasurable properties of the drug experience, or conversely, a reduction in environmental aversive stimuli, together with contingent social reinforcement. The processes determining commencement differ from those maintaining drug-taking, which include avoidance of withdrawal, but more importantly, environmental stimuli that have acquired the properties of discriminative stimuli for the rewarding effects of drug usage. Treatment implications are that the patient's environment has to be restructured to provide non-drug reinforcers, alternative mechanisms for coping with stress and enhancing self-regard have to be learned, and efforts should be made to reduce response probability, if the stimuli are kept constant. The suggested treatments allow the isolation of the relevant therapeutic variables, within a comprehensive broad-spectrum behaviour therapy. No patients have yet been treated in the framework these authors have defined, so the proposals, though interesting, remain somewhat academic.

EDUCATION AND LEGISLATION

Drug-abuse treatment evokes extreme opinions, but drug education is an even more hotly debated issue. In 1972, a group of English health educators produced a pop record, critical of drug-taking, aimed at counteracting pro-drug propaganda disseminated by so much popular music. Tactics such as these, with vague and immeasurable goals, are to be condemned as are old-fashioned scare techniques. Information-based programmes are becoming unpopular (because no one can agree what the "facts" really are), and there is a move toward teaching how to live in a drug-taking world (a realistic approach) and to forestall the serious ill-effects of experimentation. Drug education, aimed at preventing or ending drug use, does not appear to succeed. If it is to be successful, education must respond to the interest and motivations of the audience, should reduce blatant hypocrisies, should stimulate involvement in alternatives to drug use, and should expose inconsistencies in attitudes toward drug use, which are present in all of us.

The Le Dain commission reports helped to make Canadians the best informed and most sophisticated of all Western peoples about drug use and abuse, and stimulated open and often heated discussion about legislation and treatment. The final report on treatment split the commissioners into a majority group that recommended compulsory treatment, and a minority group that did not. The controversial suggestion was, that police could bring any person suspected of being an addict before a magistrate, who could refer the matter to a physician, who could in turn advise commitment to a residential centre for up to three months. The intent of the commission was not to enforce treatment without regard to the individual, but to allow him to reflect on his situation, and consider further voluntary treatment. Heroin maintenance treatment was suggested for the total failures, although the only female commissioner promoted the idea of the establishment of widespread clinics offering opiates for sale to addicts.

Publication of the final report was delayed for several months, and there have even been suggestions that it was re-written in sections. It is not known whether any of the recommendations will ever be translated into legislation, as many observers were surprised at the law-enforcement stance of the whole volume. In the U.S.A., there has been a recent change toward more punitive legislation and away from the liberal approaches favoured in other countries, especially Britain. In British Columbia, radical changes are being proposed in the drug laws. Drug abusers would be forcibly detained by court order after a period in a detoxification centre and, if addicted, would have to spend a period in "quarantine". The U.S.A. had been experimenting with voluntary commitment, yet now the usually more liberal Canadians are planning to return to harder-line policies. Civil-rights group will not look favourably upon the limitations on liberties that will occur if the projected laws are implemented, but what happens in Canada may have a profound effect in legislation throughout the whole world.

As with alcoholism, we are in a situation of flux and rapid change, but equally, we can say that drug abuse is a subject eminently worthy of study in order to define its nature, to estimate its extent and to see whether prevention or worthwhile intervention are feasible. The field can be confusing to the onlooker, but this is true where any new endeavour is taking place.

Systematic research on drug abuse *is* a new endeavour, but one highly to be commended. After writing this book, and having reviewed such an enormous mass of data, we are optimistic that real advances are possible. To quote Shakespeare: "Tis a consummation devoutly to be wished".

REFERENCES

Berecochea, J. E. and Sing, G. E., "The Effectiveness of a Half-Way House for Civilly Committed Narcotic Addicts", *International Journal of Addictions,* 7: 123–32, 1972.

Blumberg H. *et al.,* "British Opiate Users: People Approaching Drug Treatment Centres", a Paper presented at the Second International Conference on Alcoholism and Drug Dependence, Liverpool, April, 1973.

Crow, J., "Management by Law: A Study of Two Groups of Cannabis Users", a Paper presented at the Second International Conference on Alcoholism and Drug Dependence, Liverpool, April, 1973.

Davies, D. L., "Normal Drinking in Recovered Alcohol Addicts", *Quarterly Journal of Studies in Alcoholism,* 23: 94–104, 1962.

Droppa, D., "Behavioural Treatment of Drug Addiction: A Review and Analysis", *Int. J. Addict.,* 8: 143–61, 1973.

Gerard, D. L. and Saenger, G., "Outpatient Treatment of Alcoholism", *Brookside Monograph No. 4,* University of Toronto, 1966.

Goodwin, D. W., Schulsinger, F., Hermanson, L., Guze, J. B. and Winokur, C. T., "Alcoholic Problems in Adoptees Raised Apart from Alcoholic Biological Parents", *Archives of General Psychiatry,* 28: 238–43, 1973.

Greden, J. F., Morgan, D. W. and Flenkel, S. I., "Drinking Patterns in an American Military Population", a Paper Presented at the Second International Conference on Alcoholism and Drug Dependence, Liverpool, April, 1973.

Kurland, A. A. and Krantz, J. C., "Naloxone and the Narcotic Abuser: A Low-Dose Maintenance Program", *Int. J. Addict.,* 8: 127–41, 1973.

Le Dain Commission, *Reports of the Commission of Inquiry with the Non-medical Use of Drugs,* Information Canada, Ottawa, 197x–xx.

Miller, P., "Behavioural Treatment of Drug Addiction: A Review", *Int. J. Addict.,* 8: 511–19, 1973.

Moss, M. C. and Beresford Davies, E., *A Survey of Alcoholism in an English County,* Geigy, London, 1968.

Pattison, M. E., "A Critique of Alcoholism Treatment Concepts", *Quart. J. Stud. Alcohol.,* 27: 49–71, 1966.

Report of the Advisory Committee on Drug Dependence, H.M.S.O., London, 1968.

Solomon, E. and Marshall, W. L., "A Comprehensive Model for the Acquisition, Maintenance and Treatment of Drug-Taking Behaviour", *British Journal of Addiction,* 68: 215–20, 1973.

Szasz, T., *The Myth of Mental Illness,* Harper & Row, New York, 1961.

Teasdale, J. D., "Conditioned Abstinence in Narcotic Addicts", *Int. J. Addict.,* 8: 273–92, 1973.

Trest, J., "Differential Classical Conditioning of Abstinence Syndrome in Morphine-Dependent Rats", *Psychopharmacologia,* 30: 153–61, 1973.

Vaillant, G. E., "A 20-Year Follow-Up of New York Narcotic Addicts", *Arch. Gen. Psychiat.* xxx: 237–46, 1973.

Weppner, R. S., "Some Characteristics of an Ex-Addict Self-Help Therapeutic Community and its Members", *Br. J. Addict.,* 68: 73–9, 1973.

Wilkins, R. H., "The Detection of the Abnormal Drinker", Paper read at Symposium on the Alcoholic in General Practice, University of Manchester, 1972.

Wootton Report: *Report by the Advisory Committee on Drug Dependence: Cannabis,* H.M.S.O., London, 1968.

Yablonsky, L., *The Tunnel Back: Synanon,* Macmillan, New York, 1963.

Zaks, A. *et al.,* "Naloxone Treatment of Opiate Dependence", *Journal of the American Medical Association,* 215: 2108–10, 1971.

Zaks, A., Fink, M. and Freedman, A. M., "Levomethadyl in Maintenance Treatment of Opiate Dependence", *JAMA,* 220: 811–13, 1972.

Index